One World Archaeology

Series Editors
Heather Burke
Gustavo Politis
Gabriel Cooney

For further volumes:
http://www.springer.com/series/8606

Sarah Byrne · Anne Clarke · Rodney Harrison ·
Robin Torrence

Editors

Unpacking the Collection

Networks of Material and Social Agency
in the Museum

 Springer

Editors
Sarah Byrne
Centre for Museums, Heritage,
    and Material Culture Studies
Institute of Archaeology
University College, London
London, UK
s.byrne@ucl.ac.uk

Rodney Harrison
Faculty of Arts
The Open University
Milton Keynes, UK
rodney.harrison@gmail.com

Anne Clarke
Department of Archaeology
School of Philosophical and Historical
    Inquiry
University of Sydney
Sydney, NSW, Australia
annie.clarke@sydney.edu.au

Robin Torrence
Australian Museum
Sydney, NSW, Australia

and

School of Philosophical and Historical
    Inquiry
University of Sydney
NSW, Australia
robin.torrence@austmus.gov.au

ISBN 978-1-4419-8221-6   e-ISBN 978-1-4419-8222-3
DOI 10.1007/978-1-4419-8222-3
Springer New York Dordrecht Heidelberg London

Library of Congress Control Number: 2011928911

Springer is part of Springer Science+Business Media (www.springer.com)

Contents

Contributors

Lindy Allen Indigenous Cultures, Museum Victoria, Melbourne, VIC, Australia, lallen@museum.vic.gov.au

Sarah Byrne Centre for Museums, Heritage and Material Culture Studies, Institute of Archaeology, University College, London, London, UK, s.byrne@ucl.ac.uk

Anne Clarke Department of Archaeology, School of Philosophical and Historical Inquiry, University of Sydney, Sydney, NSW, Australia, annie.clarke@sydney.edu.au

Susan M. Davies Independent Scholar, Arundel, QLD, Australia, susiedavies@optusnet.com.au

Louise Hamby Research School of Humanities and the Arts, Australian National University, Canberra, ACT, Australia, lousie.hamby@anu.edu.au

Rodney Harrison Faculty of Arts, The Open University, Milton Keynes, UK, rodney.harrison@gmail.com

Kelley Hays-Gilpin Department of Anthropology, Northern Arizona University, Flagstaff, AZ, USA; Museum of Northern Arizona, Flagstaff, AZ, USA, kelley.hays-gilpin@nau.edu

Chantal Knowles Department of World Cultures, National Museums Scotland, Edinburgh, Scotland, c.knowles@nms.ac.uk

Alexandra Loumpet-Galitzine University of Yaounde, Yaounde, Cameroon; Asia-Pacific Network, CNRS-FMSH, Paris, France, loumpet.galitzine@gmail.com

Colin McEwan Department of Africa, Oceania and the Americas, The British Museum, London, UK, cmcewan@thebritishmuseum.ac.uk

Fiona Parrott Department of Sociology and Anthropology, Faculty of Social and Behavioural Sciences, University of Amsterdam, Amsterdam, The Netherlands, f.r.parrott@uva.nl

Jude Philp Macleay Museum, University of Sydney, NSW, Australia,
jude.philp@sydney.edu.au

Maria-Isabel Silva Museum Centro Civico Ciudad Alfaro, Montecristi, Ecuador,
mi-silva@illinois.edu

Pieter ter Keurs Department of Collections and Research, National Museum
of Antiquities, Leiden, The Netherlands, p.terkeurs@rmo.nl

Robin Torrence Australian Museum, Sydney, NSW, Australia; School of
Philosophical and Historical Inquiry, University of Sydney, Sydney, NSW,
Australia, robin.torrence@austmus.gov.au

Chris Wingfield Pitt Rivers Museum, Oxford University, Oxford, UK,
chris.wingfield@prm.ox.ac.uk

Part I
Introduction

Chapter 1
Networks, Agents and Objects: Frameworks for Unpacking Museum Collections

Sarah Byrne, Anne Clarke, Rodney Harrison, and Robin Torrence

Abstract Although on face value, museum collections are largely perceived as static entities hidden away in storerooms or trapped behind glass cases, new research shows that over time and across space interactions between objects and a wide range of people have generated a complex assemblage of material and social networks. Based on a broad collection of source materials, studies examining the people who made, sold, traded, studied, catalogued, exhibited and connected with objects reveal a dynamic set of material and social agencies that have been instrumental in creating, shaping and reworking museum collections. By integrating and reworking theories about agency and materiality and by drawing on insights from Actor-Network Theory, contributors to this volume have uncovered new ways to think about relationships formed between objects and individuals and among diverse groups spread across the globe. The research also demonstrates that ethnographic collections continue to play important roles in supporting and reworking national identities as well as to challenge these through ongoing negotiations and sharing of ideas among both the guardians of these objects and their creator communities. These insights have important implications for designing curatorial practices in the future.

S. Byrne (✉)
Centre for Museums, Heritage and Material Culture Studies, Institute of Archaeology,
University College, London, London, UK
e-mail: s.byrne@ucl.ac.uk

A. Clarke
Department of Archaeology, School of Philosophical and Historical Inquiry, University of Sydney,
Sydney, NSW, Australia
e-mail: annie.clarke@sydney.edu.au

R. Harrison
Faculty of Arts, The Open University, Milton Keynes, UK
e-mail: rodney.harrison@gmail.com

R. Torrence
Australian Museum, Sydney, NSW, Australia; School of Philosophical and Historical Inquiry,
University of Sydney, Sydney, NSW, Australia
e-mail: robin.torrence@austmus.gov.au

S. Byrne et al. (eds.), *Unpacking the Collection*, One World Archaeology,
DOI 10.1007/978-1-4419-8222-3_1, © Springer Science+Business Media, LLC 2011

Introduction

Behind the scenes at museums the world over are thousands upon thousands of artefacts. These objects, removed from other lives, other places, other times, are neatly labelled, catalogued and packed away out of sight, rarely displayed and infrequently studied. The processes by which these collections are formed remain obscure to many visitors and creator or source communities alike, perhaps because of their ubiquitous presence in the museum environment. The chapters in this book make it clear that the complex processes by which objects were assembled during the late nineteenth and early twentieth centuries to form today's museums were not 'natural' or predetermined developments. Instead, they resulted from diverse and complex cultural practices which integrated wide reaching networks of varied persons, places and things (see also Stocking 1985; Steiner 1994; Phillips 1998; Phillips and Steiner 1999; Thomas 1999). Furthermore, the processes by which museum collections took shape have continued and are still active in the present. The act of 'unpacking' museum collections seeks to problematise collections as material and social assemblages through an interrogation of how they developed, the impacts they have had over time and the roles they continue to play in the contemporary world. The studies show that museum collections have been and are still active in forming social relations between varied persons and groups, including creator communities, collectors, anthropologists, curators, auctioneers and museum administrators, all of whom have also been shaped through interactions with each other and with the material objects. The impact of museum collections as social assemblages travels far beyond the museum walls and influences many aspects of past and contemporary life, including processes of colonial and postcolonial governance (e.g. Bennett 2010), the way we understand ethnic and cultural diversity (e.g. Griffiths 2002; Edwards and Hart 2004) and our relationship with time, objects and place (e.g. MacDougall 2006; Pinney 1997).

As we have pre-empted in the statements above, one of the important conceptual contributions this book makes is its treatment of museums not merely as *material* assemblages but also as *social* collections (see also Gosden et al. 2007). By saying this, we mean that museums, the people who staff and run them, the objects and the various individuals and processes which led to them being there, those who visit them and those who encounter the objects within them in various media are all part of complex networks of agency. This agency does not cease with the acquisition of objects from their creator communities, but is ongoing in the material processes of curation and display and in the social processes of visiting, researching, learning and 'knowing' things (after Gosden et al. 2007; see also Bennett 2010) which arise from them. As Lindy Allen and Louise Hamby (Chapter 9) note, the contemporary processes of negotiating with creator communities about how they engage with collections has turned the museum itself into an active field site where existing knowledge structures are contested and regenerated. Indeed, to distinguish between the social and material aspects of these processes is impossible, as museums are simultaneously social *and* material. Unpacking museum collections involves acknowledgement of the fundamental entanglement of the material and the social. Indeed, the social is inseparable from the material (Latour 2005, see further discussion below).

The book has a wide global coverage, featuring case studies from North and South America, the United Kingdom, Europe, Africa, the Mediterranean, Southeast Asia, the Pacific region and Australia. Its chronological spread is equally broad, drawing on studies of collections that were formed throughout the eighteenth, nineteenth and twentieth centuries as well as their ongoing relevance to contemporary debates regarding national and community identity. Another important aspect of the book is the wide range of methodologies and approaches used to analyse the complex networks that create collections. Databases, auction catalogues, museum accession and registration records, diaries, journals, letters, images, memory work and personal testimonies, as well as the material characteristics of objects all comprise data in the case studies. The use of such disparate research materials underscores the richness of sources available to the broad project of unpacking the collection. In drawing together a range of contributors from both within and outside of the museum profession, this book seeks not only to draw out the particulars of individual case studies but also to look across them to develop a set of broad themes which help us to understand the processes and networks of agency which sit behind the material and social assemblages under discussion. These themes are not only of relevance to understanding the formation of museum collections in the past but, because they are ongoing, are also of relevance to contemporary museum practices and the engagement of the public with museums today. A better understanding of these issues will allow collections to be more widely appreciated and better used, both as institutions and as material and social assemblages in the present. It will also allow the sort of material and social agency which is present within museums to be understood and utilised more effectively as we move forward into the future.

The book focuses on the twin themes of *materiality* and *agency* and the ways in which these manifest as a product of the distinct social and material networks associated with museum collections. By looking at the social relations in which collections have been embedded and continue to function, the chapters also contribute to a better understanding of the meaning of human/object relations. The materiality and longevity of collections themselves mean that they create relations that are not just a phenomenon of the past but continue to be re-negotiated in the unfolding present.

It is now considered axiomatic that museums, as artefacts of colonial governmentality and the regulation of metropolitan cultural practices, are both products and producers of modernity (Bennett 1995, 2004, 2010). While museums have been studied in relation to the processes involved in collecting (e.g. Schildkrout and Keim 1998; Thomas 1991, 1994; O'Hanlon and Welsch 2000; Gosden and Knowles 2001; Henare 2005) and in discussions surrounding the agency of objects (e.g. Gell 1998; Herle 1998, 2005; Gosden 2005; Harrison 2006), exploration of the forms of agency embodied through processes of collection, assemblage and display of objects in museums has only just begun. The studies in the book demonstrate that the exploration of such agency involves a two-way process. On the one hand, unpacking collections can contribute to how theoretical concepts of agency and materiality are developed. On the other hand, once established, these can also help unpack the meaning of collections and thereby contribute to how the material is interpreted and presented.

Approaching Agency

A significant literature has grown up around the idea of agency in archaeology and anthropology. Of note here are theoretical developments in archaeology that have focussed on the social agency involved in the production of artefacts (see further discussion in Harrison 2010). For example, Marcia-Anne Dobres (2000; see also Dobres and Robb 2000) suggests that people experience technology and material culture in an embodied way. Technologies involve a series of interactions, both material and social, which occur as people undertake practical or material action in the world. Hence, both people and technology simultaneously constitute, shape and become shaped by one another (Dobres 2000: 127; see also Gell 1998). Dobres characterises technologies as socially constructed undertakings in which material objects develop their own life histories, taking on a multiplicity of meanings. A recursive process binds together human actors, products, artefacts, landscapes, materials and meaning: 'agency and practice are no less the heart and soul of human technology' (Dobres 2000: 128). Thus, artefacts are involved in a complex web of agency, as they produce and are produced by their interactions with other agents and the world. Tim Ingold's (2000) work on the agency involved in processes of artefact production has been equally important in this regard. He suggests, for example, that artefact forms 'grow' like organisms, and are generated from complex interactions among the artefact-makers, their social and natural environment and the particular material qualities of the raw materials which are used in their manufacture.

While archaeology has largely focussed on the agency involved in artefact *production*, within the fields of anthropology, sociology and museum studies, the emphasis has tended to fall on the agency involved in processes of *display* and *reception*. For example, Tony Bennett (1995) has highlighted the 'exhibitory complex' of museums and the ways in which they regulate social practices and act as educational and reformatory institutions. Barbara Kirshenblatt-Gimblett (1998) has focussed attention on the agency of display and how specific techniques of display, as much as the things which are displayed, are integral to the way in which messages are received by museum goers. James Clifford (1988) has similarly probed the categories of art and artefact and the ways in which they structure people's encounters with museum objects. He emphasises museums as 'contact zones', that is spaces in which cultures are actively created and contested (Clifford 1997). Following on from this work, the issue of agency in relation to power and control has formed a major preoccupation for a number of authors within the context of the repatriation debate and a broader consideration of the politics of the ownership of museum objects. A consideration of the politics and ethics of ownership and display in a postcolonial context has been implicit in many considerations of contemporary agency within the museum (e.g. Greenfield 1996; Barringer and Flynn 1998; Fforde et al. 2004; Kramer 2006; Cuno 2008).

Although the case studies in this book build on these previous concepts of agency, they go further by showing that there are multiple kinds of agency expressed within the complex long-term processes that contribute to museum collections. The major forms of agency discussed in the chapters are listed in Fig. 1.1. Although some chapters focus primarily on one type of agent, for example Robin Torrence and Anne Clarke (Chapter 2) on creator communities, Rodney Harrison (Chapter 3) on auction houses, and Sarah Byrne (Chapter 14) on museum curators, many of the studies expose the wide range of agents who have and continue to form (and transform)

CREATOR COMMUNITY
- production
- use/display
- gifting/selling
- withholding/hiding

FIELD AGENT/COLLECTOR
- collecting
- stealing/taking
- selecting/disposing
- classifying, recording, storing, publishing
- exhibiting
- gifting/selling/exchanging

COLLECTOR/MIDDLEPERSON/BROKER/AUCTION HOUSE
- selecting/disposing/selling
- exchanging/selling
- classifying, recording, storing, publishing
- exhibiting
- gifting/selling/exchanging

MUSEUM/CURATOR
- selecting/disposing
- exchanging/selling
- classifying, recording, storing, publishing
- exhibiting
- re-engaging with creator communities
  (repatriating/acquiring things and knowledges)

PUBLIC
- visiting/not visiting
- viewing
- learning
- passing on knowledge/contesting
- circulating references/images

Fig. 1.1 Examples of the multiple kinds of agency expressed within the complex long-term historical processes that contribute to museum collections

collections. In several studies, the ongoing interaction between the agencies of creator communities and museums is highlighted (Chantal Knowles Chapter 10; Allen and Hamby Chapter 9; Kelley Hays-Gilpin Chapter 8; Colin McEwan and Maria-Isabel Silva Chapter 11), whereas Jude Philp (Chapter 12) and Chris Wingfield (Chapter 5) describe the complex web of relationships formed through the actions of collectors and museums as well as interactions between museums. Pieter ter Keurs' (Chapter 7) study of early nineteenth century Dutch collecting is notable for revealing the broad ranging links among the creator community and 'scholars, agents, local politicians, and middlemen'.

Conceptualising collections in relation to Actor-Network Theory (ANT, see further discussion below) comfortably accommodates this multiplicity of agents. As each agent is effectively a single node within the network, no hierarchies, natural starting points or priorities are assumed. This is what Latour recognises when he suggests that the social (and in particular social practice) is 'flat'. Reckwitz's summation is that 'what we can find is nothing more than the "flat" level of social practices. Yet, in these practices, material things are routinely drawn upon and applied by different agents in different situations' (Reckwitz 2002: 209–210) is particularly relevant here. This volume investigates a wide range of practices involved in assembling museum collections. Flattening these practices out so that no hierarchies exist means that all actions are seen as equally important. This in turn provides a variety of routes into studying museum collections.

One of the outcomes of approaching social practice in a non-hierarchical manner is that forms of agency that had not been given a great deal of attention previously are now explicitly recognised. We particularly highlight the actors frequently referred to as 'source communities', although we prefer the designation 'creator communities'. We have chosen this term to recognize them as active and participatory in the same way that the terms 'collector', 'curator', 'trader', 'visitor/consumer' and 'researcher' imply. Clearly, all agents involved in the formation of collections are part of the process of transforming and co-creating objects through their engagement with them, be it the transformation of 'tools' into 'commodities' through trade, or 'commodities' into 'artefacts' through curation. However, we think it is important to recognise the particular creative engagements of those who initiated the objects. The agency of these creator communities has often remained hidden in historical accounts of ethnographic collecting (but see O'Hanlon and Welsch 2000; Gosden and Knowles 2001; Torrence 2000) as it is considered difficult to 'observe' in the historical record (e.g. Dening 2004). Importantly, several chapters point out that creator communities have taken a positive action to 'withhold' objects rather than offer them for sale or exchange. This form of agency can be 'read' from the absences or gaps in museum collections (see also Küchler 2002: 167). While such absences might previously have been interpreted as intentioned acts of forgetting by the agents of power within museums, authors have recently begun to re-examine gaps within representations in contemporary museum collections as active processes of withholding and part of an effective strategy by creator communities for managing public and private memory (see Peralta 2009). For example, Susan Davies' (Chapter 4) exploration of documented trading encounters between westerners and peoples of the southwest coast and Fly River estuary in Southwest New Guinea during the second half of the nineteenth century reveals an under-representation, or complete absence, of valued articles such as dogs' teeth necklaces and shell ornaments which Papuans received through trade with Torres Strait peoples. Indeed, Davies demonstrates that sometimes information about the producers can indeed be ferreted out of such journals and diaries. Similarly, Torrence and Clarke (Chapter 2) point to the near absence of *toea* in late nineteenth and early twentieth century auction and sale catalogues as evidence to suggest that westerners were deliberately excluded from traditional systems of exchange in British New Guinea. Ter Keurs (Chapter 7) also notes that the early ethnographic collections made in the Dutch East Indies largely comprise 'easily replaceable' objects and material that might have had 'great ritual importance' was excluded.

These analyses of collections also reveal how agency works on different scales. Some collections and forms of agency are intensely private and local, whereas others operate at a national or international scale. For example, on a global scale Knowles (Chapter 10) explores the *shared* agencies of Scottish and Canadian Tlicho Nations embodied in an exhibition of a series of artefacts which both nations consider to be part of their cultural patrimony and heritage. While questions of ownership and the legacy of colonial power relations emerge here, Knowles focuses our attention on the processes of collection which bound these two nations together and the display of a collection which both reinvigorated old networks of association and created new ones. A similar scale of interaction is demonstrated by ter Keurs (Chapter 7) in his exploration of the economic and political networks that shaped early nineteenth century Dutch collecting practices in the Dutch East Indies and the Mediterranean. A sense of how forms of political agency and symbolic power embodied within objects from the deep past can continue to have efficacy in the present is demonstrated by McEwan and Silva (Chapter 11), who show how late pre-contact Manteño stone seats have continued to play a key role in Ecuadorian iconographies of national identity. By contrast, Fiona Parrott (Chapter 13) unveils the private collecting practices connected with episodes of loss and bereavement in contemporary South London households. Yet such private, individual practices are no less connected with broader networks of agency, as demonstrated by Wingfield (Chapter 5). His study of the Pitt Rivers Museum's databases reveals traces of the 'donors, loaners, dealers and swappers' who have been involved in the wider networks out of which the museum has formed. Their actions are simultaneously private and collective as a part of this broader network.

A different form of *material* agency is explored by several authors. Building on the work of Alfred Gell (1998), Harrison (Chapter 3; also see Harrison 2006, 2010) draws attention to the ways in which objects themselves can exert agency in interactions between humans and non-humans. Harrison observes that northern Australian Kimberley points have exerted ongoing agency in captivating and enchanting collectors and the museum-going public, long after they might be assumed to have ceased to have efficacy as collected objects. Similarly, in her exploration of how collected objects operated as 'ambassadors', Knowles (Chapter 10) argues that the museum objects were agents of representation for both individuals and nations. For instance, she describes how a stone pipe expresses what it means to be Tlicho, while at the same time stands for aspects of Scotland's past. The way that objects play an active role in creating and supporting personal, tribal and national identity is also highlighted in a number of chapters. For instance, Hays-Gilpin (Chapter 8) discusses the many types of identity (individual, gender, clan, village, etc.) that are expressed and reinforced in the objects commissioned by the Museum of Northern Arizona, whereas ter Keurs (Chapter 7 and also ter Keurs 2007) argues that objects collected from distant lands played an important role in imperial and colonial nation building. Finally, Alexandra Loumpet-Galitzine's study (Chapter 6) describes a case in which objects that have 'escaped' from the museum by way of contemporary mass media exert agency within the context of modern advertising. Her description of how a range of ethnographic objects, and in particular a mask from Cameroon, are transformed and reinterpreted within billboards in Paris illustrates the agency of decontextualised objects. What is particularly intriguing is that although the objects are intended to re-enforce French identity and support the new Musée du Quai Branly, their agency in fact serves to transform the aura of the supposedly postmodern museum into an old-fashioned colonial enterprise.

Actor-Networks

Several of the chapters in the collection draw on Actor-Network Theory (ANT) in an attempt to reconceptualise the agency of objects contained within museum collections. Like others working in this field (e.g. Larson et al. 2007; Gosden et al. 2007; Cameron and Mengler 2009), some contributors have found the network metaphor a useful way of conceptualising the complex series of relationships between humans and objects which constitute the museum as an institution. ANT was developed by sociologists and scholars working in the field of Science and Technology Studies as a critique of conventional social theory (e.g. Latour and Woolgar 1979; Latour 1987, 1993, 1996, 1999, 2005; Callon 1986; Law and Hassard 1999). It has been described as a material-semiotic method (Law 2008) which simultaneously maps the relationships between 'things' and 'concepts', using the network as a metaphor for understanding the ways in which these things are interconnected. Importantly, ANT emphasises that these networks are composed of a mixture of humans and 'non-humans' or things (see Law [1992] 2003). In the case of museum collections, these networks are composed of not only museum curators, collectors, creator communities and the museum-going publics but also of the collected objects themselves, their technologies of display, the laboratory spaces in which they are stored and the tools which are used for their research, alongside the buildings in which they reside, the images that represent them and the texts which are written about them. Indeed, ANT emphasises the extent to which almost all social relations are mediated by way of material things, and that all actions are simultaneously material *and* conceptual, physical *and* symbolic. This point is developed particularly by Wingfield (Chapter 5) in his exploration of the social and material relationships between objects and people embodied in the English Collections at the Pitt Rivers Museum.

In addition, ANT suggests that networks are not fixed constructions, not 'things', but metaphors or frameworks to help us describe flows or 'translations' (Latour 2005: 132) of one form or another. It does this through an acknowledgement of the distributed nature of agency. By distributed agency we mean that people cannot enact agency on their own. They require the scaffolding of other people and things to make actions happen in the world. In the case of nineteenth century museum collectors, for example, it is impossible to think of them as working in isolation. They rely not only on the technologies which enable travel and the objects with which they trade, the creator communities who produce the items and indeed the items themselves but also on the museum itself as a storage facility and the series of ideas that underpin the need to develop such collections (see also Gosden 2000). All of these different objects and people work together to define the museum collector as such. ANT helps us to see networks in operation at a range of different spatial and chronological scales and to consider the ways in which networks enable agency of different kinds. This point is explored by Byrne (Chapter 14), who follows A.C. Haddon from the field to the museum and traces his relationship with creator communities, professional colleagues, auction houses, dealers, missionaries and museum staff, revealing how the objects in the Horniman Museum make durable both his own and the agency of these various actors.

ANT also emphasises the material basis of knowledge construction. The roots of ANT in Science and Technology Studies established an early interest in the ways in which knowledge was tangibly produced. In *Laboratory Life: The Social Construction of Scientific Facts* (Latour and Woolgar 1979) and *Science in Action: How to Follow Scientists and Engineers Through Society* (Latour 1987), the authors argue that the social construction of scientific facts can be studied ethnographically in the laboratory, where knowledge is produced both in the action of routine laboratory practices and in a range of associated actions, including the publication of scientific chapters and the financing of research. Latour and Woolgar (1979) draw attention to the way in which a scientist's credibility is indistinguishable from their results, and the ways in which their credibility is actively constructed by way of the 'technology' of their CV. This is relevant to the study of museums, as material objects form the basis for the construction of various 'social facts' which influence not only the ways in which people related to one another in the past and present but also, for example, the ways in which colonial subjects are governed (e.g. Bennett 2009, 2010). This point is explored by Harrison (Chapter 3) in relation to the production of ideas about Empire through the process of souveniring.

Materiality

One of the distinguishing features of many chapters in this book is the way in which they apply what might be termed a broadly 'archaeological' approach to a range of source materials, in the sense in which they recognise the fundamental 'materiality' of museum collections (see also chapters in Gosden et al. 2006). Although saying that collections are 'material' in nature might seem to be an obvious point, many analyses of museum collections have ignored the distinctive sensual and corporeal qualities of the actual objects, in favour of research which explores them as symbols or 'texts'. While 'taking things seriously' (c.f. Webmoor 2007) is one of the outcomes of engaging with the concepts of Actor-Network Theory, the contributors to this book seek to read a wide range of different sources 'against the grain' to explore the question of agency in relation to museum collections. In addition, a diversity of locations form the research sites for the chapters, ranging from private households and creator communities to auction houses, archives and museums. Yet, even when exploring the most 'documentary' of these sources, such as auction catalogues (Chapters 2 and 3), the contributors treat them not only as texts but also as material things in their own right: that is as artefacts whose distinctive material qualities also have agency in social relations.

A wide range of archaeologists have noted how the intrinsic physical properties of some materials have long been used by people to enrich sensual experience, create social links and support concepts of valuation (e.g. Demarrais et al. 2004; Tilley 2004; Torrence 2005). Through focussing on the material qualities of objects and collections, contributors have explored the concept of agency from innovative angles. The ways in which objects are manufactured to 'captivate' and catch the attention of an audience, be it traders, collectors, antiquarians or a museum-going public, has received the attention of a number of authors here. Drawing on an established interest in these topics within anthropology (e.g. Strathern 1988; Gell 1998; Morphy 1992, 1998, 2001), Harrison explores the captivating qualities of Kimberley Points and the ways in which the presentation of artefact sellers' catalogues themselves tapped into forms of colonial desire for collectors. This is an argument which is echoed by Torrence and Clarke (Chapter 2), who draw attention to a class of objects within the catalogues, including such items as 'man-catchers' and decapitating knives, which are produced to 'dazzle' and enchant collectors. Significantly, they note a changing chronological emphasis from man-catchers to decapitating knives in the auction catalogues, possibly representing a shift in the ability of man-catchers to captivate collectors once they become well known to them (see also Harrison 2006).

The ability of objects to operate as mnemonics, involuntarily triggering significant personal memories, has long been understood. Indeed, we recognise such events in popular parlance as 'Proustian memories' in reference to Marcel Proust's (1913–1927) account of distinct memories evoked by a range of scents in his seven part novel À la recherche du temps perdu. The relationship between objects, materiality and memory is explored by a number of contributors. Harrison (Chapter 3) makes an important distinction between the practices of collecting and souveniring, arguing that souvenirs 'function to address the gap between experience and memory'. Similarly, Parrott (Chapter 13) explores the role collecting plays in peoples' attempts to remember others and be remembered themselves in the face of death and bereavement, seeing acquisition events as important markers in personal histories. Harrison (Chapter 3) goes on to suggest that in aggregate, colonial souvenirs had the potential to act not only within representations of personal histories but also as collective 'splinters of memory' of the colonial world that helped to shape and create a vision of Empire and the fundamentally material basis of colonialism. The relationship between individual objects and collective memory is similarly explored by Allen and Hamby (Chapter 9), who describe the ways in which photographs and artefacts have formed the basis for collective remembering of traditional indigenous technologies and practices, a point which is also drawn out by Knowles (Chapter 10) in relation to the Tlicho Nation in her analysis. In contrast, Loumpet-Galitzine's (Chapter 6) study of the recontextualisation of museum objects into advertising illustrates the power of these images in stimulating memory of previous times, particularly, the glory of the French Empire.

Object Biography

The metaphor of object biography (e.g. Hoskins 1998; Herle 1998, 2005; Gosden and Marshall 1999) derived from concepts proposed by Appadurai (1986) and Kopytoff (1986) provides an excellent framework for visualising the new perspectives that arise when the theoretical concepts of agency and Actor-Network Theory are considered in relation to the materiality of ethnographic collections. Although most of the case studies focus on a limited set of nodes in which the agency of a single set of actors operates in conjunction with objects to create a set of social relations or networks, when they are taken together, one can trace how a wide range of different forms of agency come into play at various stages in an object's life history. This point is especially clear in the studies that track particular collections or social relations over time. For example, Knowles (Chapter 10) describes the history of particular objects from their original manufacture in Canada by Tlicho in the mid-nineteenth century up to a 2008 exhibition of these objects at the National Museum of Scotland. Over this long period, the artefacts passed back and forth through a number of hands and played seminal roles in forging the identities of the two nations. Philp's (Chapter 12) study focuses on the opportunistic ways in which collections are formed, following the path of one individual and two museums. She documents the complex histories that result from the variety of pathways along which objects flow, including their continued movement in museum environments and the way in which this has forged long-lasting links between New Caledonia and Australia.

Pulling together all the case studies, it is useful to make a simplified map of the myriad of trajectories that ethnographic objects and collections have followed and then consider the ways in which networks have been created as various kinds of agency interact with the materiality of the objects to express themselves. The list of actors and actions in Fig. 1.1 can be envisaged as the basic elements of a flow diagram through which ethnographic object pass, resting at times in various collections and then often moving on or re-engaging with creator communities. Obviously this scheme is intended to represent a generic set of relationships and may not reflect the full range of diversity represented in actual museum collections. Similarly, none of the categories should be considered to be fixed, but significant overlaps, translations and flows could be expected between categories. Nonetheless, this generic scheme illustrates the wide range of sites and different forms of agency which were part of the creation and ongoing lives of museum collections.

Rather than tracking individual objects through time, another productive way to employ the biographical approach is illustrated in Hays-Gilpin's (Chapter 8) account of interactions between Hopi artisans and the Museum of Northern Arizona (MNA) over 80 years. In this case, the collections housed in one institution form the setting for a study of changes in the nature of agency of the two classes of actors through time. What is especially striking is that despite variations in the strength and nature of the ways in which MNA sought to influence Hopi crafts, the importance of expressing identity through the objects has been a constant. Wingfield's (Chapter 5) unravelling of historical processes at the Pitt Rivers Museum through tracking networks in the acts of exchange fossilised in the museum accession registers also enables him to identify broad processes that characterise how English producers, collectors, donors and museum curators have interacted over time.

While studying object biographies provides valuable insights into long-term change, tracing human biographies are equally important, precisely because they do the very opposite: that is they provide an appreciation of change in the short term. Unpacking the agency involved in assembling museum collections means considering the face-to-face interactions and experiences of the many individuals involved in the production and collection process. In this respect, time and change are measured in relation to human lifetimes and generations rather than historical events or time periods. Museums have undergone continued criticism for presenting indigenous material culture ahistorically and for not communicating the nuances of local cultural change. This legacy, inherited from the nineteenth century, whereby ethnographic objects were presented as 'frozen in a historyless stasis' (Pietz 1996) has not, as yet, fully abated. Dauber (2005: 122) suggests that this lack of attention on the subtle aspects of change represents a continued form of paternalism because 'there is no clear resolution of how, and indeed if, these people managed the inevitable social ruptures that faced them'.

Parrott (Chapter 13) clearly demonstrates the rapidity with which objects can be ancestralised. In one generation, a collection of miniature cars went from being an active part of a person's contemporary identity to being part of another's 'memory work'. Similarly, Davies (Chapter 4) highlights how trading preferences can alter within a generation. In this case, European trade items were subsumed into indigenous regional trading networks in Southwest New Guinea. Byrne's study (Chapter 14) outlines how Haddon's collecting practices at the Horniman Museum evolved and changed in respect to both emerging ideas about anthropology and his own personal field experiences. Just as artefact collectors can change their relationship with a particular object many times over, creator communities are equally susceptible to changing fads and fashions. Indeed, Hays-Gilpin (Chapter 8) stresses this by acknowledging how Hopi pottery has had 'a long history of flexibility and change' and 'archaeologists can look at a fragment of painted pottery from anywhere in Arizona or New Mexico and infer a date within a 50-year interval'.

Torrence and Clarke (Chapter 2) reveal the agency of creator communities and collectors alike by analysing the fluctuations in the artefact market. In a bid to facilitate engagement, it is not surprising that museums like to trace the long-term relationships that communities have with particular objects. While this approach is empowering and suggests a strong sense of cultural identity, attention to the more sudden shifts, disjunctures and departures that communities undergo in their attitude to material culture is also important because it shows how groups changed their practices and beliefs in relation to each other and not apart from each other. Here again, the benefit of unpacking the collections in terms of tracing networks of interaction comes to the fore, because networks allow both the implications and material traces of short-term shifts and long-term patterns to be explored.

Uncovering Social Connections

One of most important insights of this book is that when you open the museum cabinets and unpack their collections, you find all sorts of links and connections that spread across time and space. We suggest that it is important to begin to think of museums and other forms of collection as 'processes' (rather than 'things') that create and transform vast social and material assemblages. Museums, collections and their objects are alive, have their own histories and continue to have agency in the present. Taken together, the chapters illustrate the complexity of the social connections that lie behind all collections. While some contributors focus on the characteristics of particular nodes within these networks, the book as a whole points to the complexities and interconnections that mesh and bind museum collections together in time and space.

In characterising collections as 'networks' or social and material 'assemblages', we think it helpful to consider the range of human and non-human agents involved, many of whom are represented in Fig. 1.1. The contributors to this volume reveal and analyse the wide array of social networks created through the interactions between objects and agents, similar to the 'meshworks' described by Ingold (2007: 35; Knappett 2007). Creator communities, collectors, museum personnel, and even museums themselves all participate in the generation of these social and material networks. Another important point that emerges from these chapters is that field collection is only one of a wide range of mechanisms by which collections are formed. What the chapters show is that at every stage of creating a collection, from the field to the storeroom, from display to repatriation, another suite of links and interconnections are created.

Creator Communities in the Past, Present and Future

Many of the contributors to this volume are interested in trying to focus attention on the agency of individuals and collectives in creator communities who produced the materials which were later collected and assembled together for display. Torrence

and Clarke (Chapter 2) draw attention to the ways in which auction and sale catalogues of ethnographic artefacts dating to the late nineteenth and early twentieth
centuries identify changing patterns of negotiation between indigenous makers and
western consumers. In their case study of artefacts from British New Guinea, they
show how Papuans had an active role in determining the kinds of goods that later
formed the core of private collections and public institutions. Similarly, Harrison
(Chapter 3) also turns his attention to auction catalogues, suggesting that particular
objects which were manufactured explicitly with trade and display in mind might
be explored as indicators of indigenous agency, and the ways in which the agency
of objects might be investigated in a museum context. This is a theme which also
emerges from Hays-Gilpin's (Chapter 8) study of the relationships between Hopi
artists and the MNA, who can be seen as co-creators of the museum's Hopi art collections through the MNA's history of suggesting particular designs and artefact
types to the Hopi to produce, and the Hopi's acceptance and resistance of different suggestions. Knowles' chapter (Chapter 10) provides an interesting indigenous
perspective on creator community agency. Based on the poor quality of some of
the artefacts, the Tlicho informants suggested that objects were made especially for
sale to Scottish traders, perhaps even on commission. Following from that conclusion, they also felt that the producers achieved 'a fair deal' in their trade; in other
words, they acknowledged the agency of the indigenous makers to decide what and
to whom to sell objects.

Each transaction between creator communities and collectors has its own pecu-
liar and distinct history and historicity; each is fixed in a particular moment in time.
This is a point explored by Davies (Chapter 4), who shows that it is sometimes difficult to distinguish between traders and collectors and that both are bound in time
by the event or process of trade. She suggests that the definition of 'trader' and
'collector' is only one way of dividing these agents, who are all equally implicated
in the material processes which bring them together. The ways in which creator
communities and the museum are bound together is also explored in Allen and
Hamby's (Chapter 9) discussion of collaborative projects between Museum Victoria
and Indigenous Yolngu (Arnhem Land) and Pama (Cape York) communities. They
reveal the contemporary museum environment to be both a *contested site* where
knowledge is negotiated and a *field site* where contemporary and historical indigenous agency emerges. McEwan and Silva's (Chapter 11) chapter demonstrates how
particular museum objects, in their case, the Manteño stone seats from Ecuador,
have the potential to simultaneously bind creator communities to ancestral sites in
their landscapes while actively forging relationships between them and museum
personnel which in turn can stimulate local cultural heritage initiatives.

Collectors

Field collectors represent another agent in the museum network. Several contributors take a biographical approach to explore the ways in which individuals'
life histories are implicated in museum collections. This is evident in Philp's

(Chapter 12) study of objects from New Caledonia in the Australian Museum collected by Charles Hedley, who visited La Grande Terre on his holidays late in
1897, when he collected ethnographic and zoological specimens and organized
an exchange of objects with the then Colonial Museum of Noumea. The chapter
investigates the historical background to this exchange and the circumstances under
which cultural objects and zoological specimens were given equivalent values and
the objects and specimens literally 'swapped'. Similarly, Parrott's (Chapter 13) work
on private collecting in South London households draws out the life biographies of
individuals, and the ways in which their own personal histories influence their collecting practices. ter Keurs (Chapter 7) shows clearly that in addition to the personal
histories of individuals in understanding their collecting practices, we must also
consider the political context and the personal networks in which individuals were
involved as part of their collecting practices.

Museum Personnel

The agency of museum staff has often been marginalised in favour of that of field
collectors. The events and actions within the museum are often not seen as interesting in their own right. But museum personnel had an integral role to play in
the formation and display of museum collections, as well as in the dissemination
of information which played a role in broader processes such as colonial governance. This point is made clear by Philp's (Chapter 12) study of Hedley's collecting
in New Caledonia and Byrne's (Chapter 14) analysis of A. C. Haddon's role at the
Horniman Museum over the period 1902–1915 that show both curators to have been
pivotal agents, whose actions were influenced by a range of other agents, both material and social. Similarly, Wingfield (Chapter 5) identifies the way in which a series
of museum personnel, as well as donors and collectors, had a central role in the
formation of English Collections at the Pitt Rivers Museum. For some museums,
for example the MNA discussed by Hays-Gilpin (Chapter 8), there has been sustained and direct engagement between artefact-makers and museum staff. In many
other instances, the influence is less purposeful, but nonetheless important, as in
the case of the role of museums in selecting for particular Kimberley Point forms
discussed by Harrison (Chapter 3). Allen and Hamby (Chapter 9) highlight how
negotiations with creator communities are having a significant ongoing influence on
both the display and knowledge about particular artefacts and collections at Museum
Victoria.

Museums as Institutions

A premise that many of the contributors deconstruct is that museums should be
defined in opposition to the 'field' of collection in traditional anthropological
thought. Indeed, Allen and Hamby (Chapter 9) show that the contemporary museum
environment is itself a field site where knowledge is negotiated and created (see also

Bennett 2009, 2010), and a place where people might engage in the regeneration and maintenance of knowledge and the construction of group identity. The ways in which museums have been both a positive and oppositional force in the negotiation of identity are explored by several contributors, including Harrison (Chapter 3) and Hays-Gilpin (Chapter 8). Wingfield's (Chapter 5) exploration of the networks involved in the formation of the English Collections at the Pitt Rivers Museum similarly foregrounds the agency of the museum as an institution by placing the museum at the centre of his analysis. Another important observation concerns the way in which museums transform 'everyday objects' into new things through processes of selection, reassembly and display. These points are also explored by both Parrott (Chapter 13) and Harrison (Chapter 3). Similarly, the agency of museums in helping to create new markets for particular forms of objects is highlighted by a number of contributors, including Hays-Gilpin (Chapter 8), Harrison (Chapter 3) and Torrence and Clarke (Chapter 2), while others, such as Philp (Chapter 12) and Wingfield (Chapter 5) emphasise the social relations that underlie exchanges of ethnographic objects and natural history specimens among museums.

The Ongoing Agency of Contemporary Museum Collections

Another important focus for contributors to the volume is the ongoing agency and relevance of museum collections in the contemporary world. The chapters posit a range of strategies for both bringing and keeping museum collections alive. Allen and Hamby's (Chapter 9) suggestion that *collections* research should become more akin to *field* research extends the potential for creative collaboration, much like Clifford's (1997) notion of museums as 'contact zones'. While some museums have experienced a long history of collaboration, such as the Hopi tribe and the Museum of Northern Arizona (Hays-Gilpin Chapter 8), there has been a marked escalation in recent years in the number of museums endeavouring to engage communities in their research (Peers and Brown 2003). Such collaboration creates new social networks, instils museum objects with new lifeblood and challenges museums to assess their contemporary relevance. While Wingfield (Chapter 5) makes the point that accessioning museum objects is one of the most significant 'acts of detachment', the potential for these collections to be brought back to life is always present once an agent invests interest in them, be it museum staff or community member. Indeed, Harrison (Chapter 3) argues that museums are in a continual process of being reassembled, thereby creating new networks of action. The extent to which certain objects are alive for creator communities depends significantly on community memory. In some cases, objects can directly embody the ancestors while simultaneously retaining contemporary relevance. For example, *katsina* dolls continue to play a social and economic role for the Hopi as well as being directly associated with their ancestors (Hays-Gilpin Chapter 8). In contrast, objects which appear to have remained dormant can re-emerge as significant symbols of social and political identity, as in the case of late pre-contact

Manteño stone seats used by the newly elected government of President Rafael Correa in Ecuador (McEwan and Silva Chapter 11). The way in which museum objects are conceived as being 'alive', or indeed the trajectories in which they can be brought to life, will naturally vary depending on who is interacting with the object, be it museum staff, visitor or community member. Yet the power of objects as mnemonics to re-connect people to other places and times is something shared by collectors (Parrott Chapter 13; Harrison Chapter 3), communities (Allen and Hamby Chapter 9; Knowles Chapter 10) and the public at large (Loumpet-Galitzine Chapter 6).

An important debate that emerges from the volume is the way in which collaboration should take place. Allen and Hamby (Chapter 9) suggest a more 'organic' process where a range of strategies are needed to facilitate community engagement, given the complex networks of agency surrounding each object. On the other hand, Hays-Gilpin (Chapter 8) highlights the significance of the formal 'Memorandum of Understanding' signed between MNA and the Hopi in moving the relationship from 'one of paternalism to collaboration and reciprocity'. Knowles' chapter (Chapter 10) foregrounds the importance of timing; the fact that the Tlicho first put on an exhibition about themselves before objects were displayed as representing shared Scottish and Tlicho history was important in that case. McEwan and Silva (Chapter 11) reflect on the need to work within a set of values and a framework which is determined within the descent community rather than imposed from outside.

Collaboration brings collections alive in many diverse ways. Hays-Gilpin (Chapter 8) suggests that the way museums group and classify objects can have little to do with their social meaning and use. Therefore, re-situating local agency provides new frameworks in which museums can research, document and display artefacts. Museum collections not only reflect colonial relations but also establish and bind different communities together in a complex series of postcolonial relations in which the items themselves are partially implicated. They can bring members of the same community together by unlocking oral histories and reconnecting people with their landscapes (Knowles Chapter 10). The reproduction of ancestral objects can legitimise, consolidate and transform group identity (Allen and Hamby Chapter 9; McEwan and Silva Chapter 11), creating new networks that extend above and beyond the walls of the museum.

Highly significant is the attention given in this book to the shared and entwined agency at the heart of collections, since this provides depth to what has become the leitmotif of museum and heritage studies: the repatriation debate. The chapters demonstrate the ways in which multiple groups can simultaneously lay claim to collections and objects as significant parts of their cultural heritage and identity (e.g. Knowles Chapter 10), pointing to the more nuanced arrangements that might arise as a result of changing regimes of community identification in an increasingly globalised and transnational world. Discussion of the rubrics of cross-cultural interaction manifested within collections should not be reserved for debate between academics, but rather should be discussed with communities when they encounter museum collections so as to potentially encourage and facilitate construction of a shared narrative. For example, Allen and Hamby (Chapter 9) point out that Aboriginal community members were extremely interested in the history of the objects after they left their ancestors' community.

This volume suggests that museum collections can also be brought alive and contribute to contemporary cosmopolitan identities, not only through community engagement but also through new and creative forms of curatorial practice. Museums have tended to be seen as institutions which are relics that reflect cultural practices from the past, but changes in museum practices clearly impact on the development and maintenance of contemporary identities (Hays-Gilpin Chapter 8). Many of the curatorial practices described in this book directly facilitate collaboration, for example devising exhibitions (Knowles Chapter 10), carrying out collections research (Allen and Hamby Chapter 9), supporting production and sale of traditional artefacts (Hays-Gilpin Chapter 8) and campaigning against the illegal trafficking in looted objects (McEwan and Silva Chapter 11). In addition, the identification of indigenous agency in other chapters (ter Keurs Chapter 7; Torrence and Clarke Chapter 2; Harrison Chapter 3) has the potential to create suitable research frameworks for future collaboration.

Building on New Insights

Although museums are no longer seen as the primary conservers and keepers of collections that represent the materiality of the known world, it is a truism that many institutions still bear the indelible imprint of that original nineteenth century ideal. Ethnographic collections owe their origins and a large proportion of their objects to the intellectual pursuits of collection, description and classification that dominated the human and natural sciences from the eighteenth to early twentieth centuries (alongside the diplomatic and economic use of objects by their indigenous producers and traders). The collecting urge has been more subdued in the past 80 or so years for a range of reasons, including changes in museum practices, the growth of the so-called 'primitive art' market that has moved many ethnographic objects beyond the acquisition budgets of museums, and global indigenous rights movements that have challenged the legitimacy and hegemony of the museum. At the beginning of this chapter, we took the image of dusty museum shelves filled with objects rarely displayed and studied to set the scene for unpacking the collection. What do we think this volume has contributed to this process? In many ways the presence and material properties of collections created predominantly in the late nineteenth and early twentieth century act as a time trap reinforcing public and sometimes professional perceptions of creator communities in the form of the traditional. However, as the chapters in this book clearly show, objects and collections are not and never have been static entities, either from the perspective of the underutilised storerooms or in terms of the biographical trajectories of individual objects and assemblages.

The new research presented here opens up many possibilities for the future exploration of the networks and social relations that both form and are formed by collections. The geographical coverage could be expanded to see how these networks operate in other cultural contexts, particularly in museums outside the western world. Similarly, the types of ethnographic collections could be enlarged to include other types of objects, such as photographs, films and sound recordings. Another productive avenue of future research is to compare and contrast the social processes surrounding the formation of collections held in other cultural institutions, such as archaeology, art, social history and natural history collections, or to expand even further to look at a broader form of collections in bodies such as archives, libraries or zoos (e.g. Holtorf 2008). Would we see similar or different actors, forms of agency, expressions of materiality and networks from such comparative studies? The importance and value of ethnographic collections within the museum environment has undoubtedly diminished in recent times as their relevance and role in contemporary cultural institutions is questioned and challenged. Understanding how these collections embody social relations between cultures, places and individuals, from the present day back into the past, is one way of creating connections with modern visitors and descendant communities alike.

The conclusions that can be drawn from the case studies in this book are that museums and their collections are simultaneously social *and* material. Objects are constituted by and create social relations and networks, firstly at their points and places of origin and then through the various transformations of context, meaning and practice that travel across time and space. Although the base physical properties of objects may retain a certain degree of stability or stasis over time (allowing for processes of decay), the same cannot be said for the ways in which objects are collected, curated, analysed, interpreted, exhibited and repatriated. In considering these interlinked themes of agency, materiality and actor networks, a new framework for viewing collections emerges. This new research positions museum collections as dynamic, interconnected, social and material assemblages, with important implications for contemporary museum practice. A focus on the many kinds of actors whose lives have been, and continue to be intimately entwined with museum objects, gives these historical collections a new life force and relevance in contemporary society.

Acknowledgements Many of the chapters in this book were first presented at the Sixth World Archaeological Congress (WAC-6) in Dublin in July 2008, where we were treated with ample time for extensive discussion that helped clarify ideas and expand our theoretical horizons. We are grateful to participants and all those present at the session who enlivened the debates. We especially want to acknowledge the important contribution of the late Blaze O'Connor, one of the WAC-6 organisers who helped make our session so productive. We also thank Joshua Bell and Chris Gosden for their insightful and helpful comments on the book proposal and manuscript, respectively. Finally, we acknowledge our indigenous and non-indigenous friends, collaborators and informants who have taught us so much about agency and engagements with museum collections.

References

Appadurai, Arjun
    1986 Introduction: Commodities and the Politics of Value. In *The Social Life of Things: Commodities in Cultural Perspective*, edited by Arjun Appadurai, pp. 3–63. Cambridge University Press, Cambridge.

Barringer, Tim J., and Tom Flynn (editors)
   1998 *Colonialism and the Object: Empire, Material Culture, and the Museum.* Routledge, London and New York.

Bennett, Tony
   1995 *The Birth of the Museum: History, Theory, Politics.* Routledge, London.
   2004 *Pasts Beyond Memories: Evolution, Museums, Colonialism.* Routledge, London.
   2009 Museum, Field, Colony: Colonial Governmentality and the Circulation of Reference. *Journal of Cultural Economy* 2(1–2): 99–116.
   2010 Making and Mobilising Worlds: Assembling and Governing the Other. In *Material Powers: Cultural Studies, History and the Material Turn,* edited by Tony Bennett and Patrick Joyce, pp. 188–208. Routledge, London.

Callon, Michel
   1986 Some Elements of a Sociology of Translation: Domestication of the Scallops and the Fishermen of St Brieuc Bay. In *Power, Action and Belief: A New Sociology of Knowledge,* edited by John Law, pp. 196–223. Routledge, London.

Cameron, Fiona, and Sarah Mengler
   2009 Complexity, Transdisciplinarity and Museum Collections Documentation: Emergent Metaphors for a Complex World. *Journal of Material Culture* 14: 189–218.

Clifford, James
   1988 *The Predicament of Culture: Twentieth-Century Ethnography, Literature, and Art.* Harvard University Press, Cambridge.
   1997 *Routes: Travel and Translation in the Late Twentieth Century.* Harvard University Press, Cambridge.

Cuno, James
   2008 *Who Owns Antiquity? Museums and the Battle over Our Ancient Heritage.* Princeton University Press, Princeton.

Dauber, Christine
   2005 Revisionism or Self-Reflexivity at the South Australian Museum: The Museumising Imagination in the Postcolonial Era. *Journal of Australian Studies* 29(85): 113–125.

DeMarrais, Elizabeth, Chris Gosden, and Colin Renfrew (editors)
   2004 *Rethinking Materiality: The Engagement of Mind with the Material World.* Cambridge University Press, Cambridge.

Dening, Greg
   2004 *Beach Crossings: Voyaging Across Times, Cultures and Self.* Melbourne University Press, Melbourne.

Dobres, Marcia-Anne
   2000 *Technology and Social Agency: Outlining a Practice Framework for Archaeology.* Blackwell, Oxford.

Dobres, Marcia-Anne, and John Robb (editors)
   2000 *Agency in Archaeology.* Routledge, London and New York.

Edwards, Elizabeth, and Janice Hart (editors)
   2004 *Photographs Objects Histories: On the Materiality of Images.* Routledge, London.

Fforde, Cressida, Jane Hubert, and Paul Turnbull (editors)
   2004 *The Dead and Their Possessions: Repatriation in Principle, Policy and Practice* (2nd edition). Routledge, London.

Gell, Alfred
   1998 *Art and Agency*. Oxford University Press, Oxford.

Gosden, Chris
   2000 On his Todd: Material Culture and Colonialism. In *Hunting the Gatherers: Ethnographic Collectors, Agents and Agency in Melanesia, 1870s–1930s*, edited by Michael O'Hanlon and Robert L. Welsch, pp. 227–250. Berghahn Books, New York and Oxford.
   2005 What Do Objects Want? *Journal of Archaeological Method and Theory* 12: 193–211.

Gosden, Chris, and Chantal Knowles
   2001 *Collecting Colonialism: Material Culture and Colonial Change*. Berg, Oxford.

Gosden, Chris, Frances Larson with Alison Petch
   2007 *Knowing Things: Exploring the Collections at the Pitt Rivers Museum 1884–1945*. Oxford University Press, Oxford.

Gosden, Chris, and Yvonne Marshall
   1999 The Cultural Biography of Objects. *World Archaeology* 31(2): 169–178.

Gosden, Chris, Ruth Phillips, and Elizabeth Edwards (editors)
   2006 *Sensible Objects: Colonialism, Museums and Material Culture*. Routledge, Abingdon and New York.

Greenfield, Jeanette
   1996 *The Return of Cultural Treasures* 2nd ed. Cambridge University Press, Cambridge.

Griffiths, Alison
   2002 *Wonderous Difference: Cinema, Anthropology, and Turn-of-the-Century Visual Culture*. Columbia University Press, New York.

Harrison, Rodney
   2006 An Artefact of Colonial Desire? Kimberley Points and the Technologies of Enchantment. *Current Anthropology* 47: 63–88.
   2010 Stone Artefacts. In *The Oxford Handbook of Material Culture Studies*, edited by Dan Hicks and Mary C. Beaudry, pp. 515–536. Oxford University Press, Oxford.

Henare, Amiria
   2005 *Museums, Anthropology and Imperial Exchange*. Cambridge University Press, Cambridge.

Herle, Anita
   1998 The Life Histories of Objects: Collections of the Cambridge Anthropological Expedition to the Torres Strait. In *Cambridge and the Torres Strait: Centenary Essays on the 1898 Anthropological Expedition*, edited by Anita Herle and Sandra Rouse, pp. 77–105. Cambridge University Press, Cambridge.
   2005 Whales' Teeth, Turtleshell Masks, and Bits of String: Pacific Collections and Research at Cambridge. *Journal of Museum Ethnography* 17: 32–57.

Holtorf, Cornelius
   2008 Zoos as Heritage: An Archaeological Perspective. *International Journal of Heritage Studies* 14(1): 3–9.

Hoskins, Janet
   1998 *Biographical Objects: How Things Tell the Stories of People's Lives*. Routledge, London.

Ingold, Tim
   2000 *The Perception of the Environment: Essays in Livelihood, Dwelling and Skill*. Routledge, London.
   2007 Materials against Materiality. *Archaeological Dialogues* 14: 1–16.

Kirshenblatt-Gimblett, Barbara
  1998 *Destination Culture: Tourism, Museums, and Heritage*. University of California Press, Los Angeles.

Knappett, Carl
  2007 Materials with Materiality. *Archaeological Dialogues* 14: 20–23.

Kopytoff, Igor
  1986 The Cultural Biography of Things: Commoditization as Process. In *The Social Life of Things: Commodities in Cultural Perspectiv*e, edited by Arjun Appadurai, pp. 64–91. Cambridge University Press, Cambridge.

Kramer, Jennifer
  2006 *Switchbacks: Art, Ownership, and Nuxalk National Identity*. University of British Columbia Press, Vancouver.

Küchler, Susanne
  2002 *Malanggan: Art, Memory and Sacrifice*. Berg, Oxford and New York.

Larson, Frances, Alison Petch, and David Zeitlyn
  2007 Social Networks and the Creation of the Pitt Rivers Museum. *Journal of Material Culture* 12: 211–239.

Latour, Bruno
  1987 *Science in Action: How to Follow Scientists and Engineers Through Society*. Harvard University Press, Cambridge.
  1993 *We Have Never Been Modern*. Harvard University Press, Cambridge.
  1996 *Aramis, or the Love of Technology*. Harvard University Press, Cambridge.
  1999 *Pandora's Hope: Essays on the Reality of Science Studies*. Harvard University Press, Cambridge.
  2005 *Reassembling the Social: An Introduction to Actor-Network Theory*. Oxford University Press, Oxford.

Latour, Bruno, and Steve Woolgar
  1979 *Laboratory Life: The Social Construction of Scientific Facts.* Sage, Beverly Hills.

Law, John
  1992 [2003] Notes on the Theory of the Actor Network: Ordering, Strategy and Heterogeneity. http://www.comp.lancs.ac.uk/sociology/papers/Law-Notes-on-ANT.pdf, accessed 23 March 2010.
  2008 Actor-Network Theory and Material Semiotics. In *The New Blackwell Companion to Social Theory* 3rd ed., edited by Bryan S. Turner, pp. 141–158. Blackwell, Oxford.

Law, John, and John Hassard (editors)
  1999 *Actor-Network Theory and After*. Blackwell, Oxford.

MacDougall, David
  2006 *The Corporeal Image: Film, Ethnography, and the Senses*. Princeton University Press, Princeton.

Morphy, Howard
  1992 From Dull to Brilliant: The Aesthetics of Spiritual Power Among the Yolngu. In *Anthropology, Art and Aesthetics*, edited by Jeremy Coote and Anthony Shelton, pp. 181–208. Clarendon Press, Oxford.

Morphy, Howard
  1998 *Aboriginal Art*. Phaidon, London.
  2001 Seeing Aboriginal Art in the Gallery. *Humanities Research* 8(1): 37–50.

O'Hanlon, Michael, and Robert L. Welsch (editors)
    2000 *Hunting the Gatherers: Ethnographic Collectors, Agents and Agency in Melanesia, 1870s–1930s*. Berghahn Books, New York and Oxford.

Peers, Laura L., and Alison K. Brown
    2003 *Museums and Source Communities*. Routledge, London and New York.

Peralta, Elsa
    2009 Public Silences, Private Voices: Memory Games in a Maritime Heritage Complex. In *Heritage and Identity*, edited by Marta Anico and Elsa Perlata, pp. 105–116. Routledge, London and Abingdon.

Phillips, Ruth B.
    1998 *Trading Identities: The Souvenir in Native North American Art from the Northeast, 1700–1900*. McGill-Queen's University Press, Washington.

Phillips, Ruth B., and Christopher B. Steiner (editors)
    1999 *Unpacking Culture: Art and Commodity in Colonial and Postcolonial Worlds*. University of California Press, Berkeley.

Pietz, William
    1996 Fetish. In *Critical Terms for Art History*, edited by Robert S. Nelson and Richard Shiff, pp. 197–198. University of Chicago Press, Chicago.

Pinney, Christopher
    1997 *Camera Indica: The Social Life of Indian Photographs*. University of Chicago Press, Chicago.

Reckwitz, Andreas
    2002 The Status of the "Material" in Theories of Culture: From "Social Structure" to "Artefacts". *Journal for the Theory of Social Behaviour* 32(2): 195–217.

Schildkrout, Enid, and Curtis A. Keim (editors)
    1998 *The Scramble for Art in Central Africa*. Cambridge University Press, Cambridge.

Steiner, Christopher B.
    1994 *African Art in Transit*. Cambridge University Press, Cambridge.

Stocking, George W. (editor)
    1985 *Objects and Others: Essays on Museums and Material Culture*. Wisconsin University Press, Madison.

Strathern, Marilyn
    1988 *The Gender of the Gift*. University of California Press, Berkeley.

ter Keurs, Pieter (editor)
    2007 *Colonial Collections Revisited*. CNWS Publications, Leiden.

Thomas, Nicholas
    1991 *Entangled Objects: Exchange, Material Culture and Colonialism in the Pacific*. Harvard University Press, Cambridge.
    1994 *Colonialism's Culture: Anthropology, Travel and Government*. Polity Press, Cambridge.
    1999 *Possessions: Indigenous Art/Colonial Culture*. Thames and Hudson, London.

Tilley, Christopher
    2004 *The Materiality of Stone: Explorations in Landscape Phenomenology*. Berg, Oxford.

Torrence, Robin
    2000 Just Another Trader? An Archaeological Perspective on European Barter with Admiralty Islanders, Papua New Guinea. In *The Archaeology of Difference: Negotiating*

Cross-Cultural Engagements in Oceania, edited by Robin Torrence and Anne Clarke, pp. 104–141. Routledge, London.

2005 Valued Stone: How So? In *Many Exchanges: Archaeology, History, Community and the Work of Isabel McBryde*, edited by Ingereth Macfarlane, with Mary-Jane Mountain and Robert Paton, pp. 357–372. Aboriginal History Monograph 11. Aboriginal History, Canberra.

Webmoor, Timothy
2007 What About 'One More Turn After the Social' in Archaeological Reasoning? Taking Things Seriously. *World Archaeology* 39(4): 547–562.

Part II
Processes and Perspectives

Chapter 2
"Suitable for Decoration of Halls and Billiard Rooms": Finding Indigenous Agency in Historic Auction and Sale Catalogues

Robin Torrence and Anne Clarke

Abstract At first glance, auction and sale catalogues of ethnographic artefacts dating to the late nineteenth and early twentieth centuries appear to record merely the desires of colonial collectors. Our detailed study of changes in proveniences, types and prices shows how an archaeological approach to assemblages coupled with appropriate analytical strategies can uncover changing patterns of negotiation between indigenous makers and western consumers. We begin with a broad regional comparison of cross-cultural interaction as witnessed in the catalogues and then turn to a finer scale case study based on catalogue entries relating to the colony of British New Guinea, commonly called Papua. These analyses provide insights into how indigenous artefact producers and traders in the Pacific region made creative responses to market opportunities.

Catalogues of Curios

One consequence of western commercial and colonial expansion into the uncharted lands beyond Europe was the development of a market for ethnographic objects or 'curios' as they were commonly labelled. Beginning in the fifteenth and sixteenth centuries, classical antiquities were a desirable commodity for collection and display, especially amongst the wealthy elites of Europe, but by the end of the nineteenth century literally tens of thousands of objects obtained from indigenous (frequently described as 'tribal') artefact producers in the Americas, Africa, Asia, Australia and the Pacific region were sold to museums and private collectors,

R. Torrence (✉)
Australian Museum, Sydney, NSW, Australia; School of Philosophical and Historical Inquiry, University of Sydney, Sydney, NSW, Australia
e-mail: robin.torrence@austmus.gov.au

A. Clarke
Department of Archaeology, School of Philosophical and Historical Inquiry, University of Sydney, Sydney, NSW, Australia
e-mail: annie.clarke@sydney.edu.au

S. Byrne et al. (eds.), *Unpacking the Collection*, One World Archaeology,
DOI 10.1007/978-1-4419-8222-3_2, © Springer Science+Business Media, LLC 2011

often through the catalogues produced and distributed by auction and sale houses. Well-known examples were produced by the London-based private dealers Webster (1897–1899; 1899; 1900; 1901; 1900–1901) and Oldman (1976) and the Stevens (1885–1939) auction house (Figs. 2.1 and 2.2).

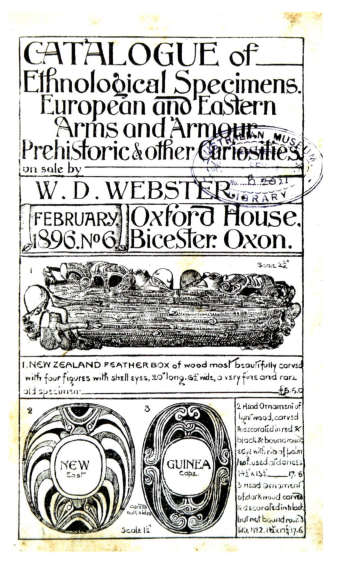

Fig. 2.1 Cover of Webster sale catalogue for February, 1896 illustrates the large contrast in price between a carved wooden box from New Zealand at £5 5s versus two highly decorated head ornaments from New Guinea at around only 17s 6d (Photo by James King, courtesy of the Australian Museum Research Library)

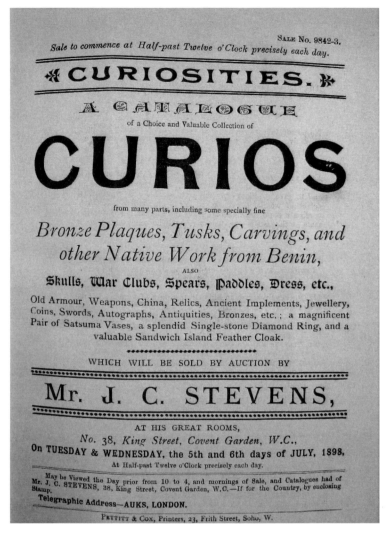

Fig. 2.2 Cover of Stevens catalogue for July 5 and 6, 1898, illustrates the wide range of ethnographic curios, antiquities and antiques available for auction, including looted material from Benin City and a feather clock from Hawai'i (Photo by Robin Torrence, courtesy of the British Museum Anthropology Library)

At first glance the catalogues might seem to be solely the product of a commodity-based market driven by the collecting desires of western society. While these were certainly important stimuli, we argue that they also provide a record of how indigenous artefact makers and traders actively participated in the material transactions that were an integral part of colonial society. These illustrated lists of objects provide tantalising insights about the indigenous artefact producers who were otherwise the silent partners in the documents and records of colonial relationships. Viewed in this way, the catalogues may also provide an as yet untapped source of information about the nature of the interactions between indigenous groups and westerners, what Adams (2009: 17) has termed 'the other side of the collecting encounter'. Based around a case study of auction and sale catalogues, our paper offers preliminary ideas about how an archaeological approach can begin to overcome the seemingly intractable problem of extracting indigenous agency from the material histories of colonialism.

Collections, Catalogues and Colonialism

The Webster, Oldman and Stevens catalogues in our study are situated in the time period of the late nineteenth and early twentieth centuries when the British colonial administration in New Guinea was in a phase of political, commercial and bureaucratic consolidation. The ethnographic objects portrayed in them do not, for the most part, originate from phases of initial exploration or early contact but instead can best be understood as components of the early period of colonial life when systems of interaction and exchange were in the process of being established and understood by both the local populations and the colonial authorities (Anonymous 1969). Gosden and Knowles (2001: xix–xxi) note that in colonial New Guinea, objects and the many ways in which they were traded and exchanged actively mediated and created colonial culture.

> …colonial New Guinea was not made up of two separate societies, New Guineans and colonials in collision and confrontation, but rather came to be a single social and cultural field of mutual influence, in which all people, black and white, were linked through the movement of goods and the definition of roles, statuses and forms of moralities' (Gosden and Knowles 2001: xix).

In this view of colonialism, the agency of artefact producers is a key ingredient in the complex cross-cultural engagements and the resultant material outcomes such as museum or private collections or, indeed, the auction and sales catalogues themselves. At the simplest level, engagement and exchange centred around material culture created a set of relationships between makers, receivers and the objects. However, if we focus only on a single element, for example one or more collectors to the exclusion of the others, then not only do we risk losing sight of how all three are intimately entwined but the process of how colonial culture was produced and reproduced through these exchanges also becomes obscured. It is therefore somewhat ironic that within much contemporary museology ethnographic collections have provided richer information about the collecting society, than about the people who made and offered them for trade (e.g. Cochrane and Quanchi 2007; Peterson et al. 2008).

In contrast, recent studies of the cross-cultural relationships that arose from the events and processes of colonialism now encompass, almost as a given, the recognition that indigenous people were rarely passive actors in the myriad of exchanges and encounters that occurred across the globe, including those that involved objects (e.g. Thomas 1991; Torrence and Clarke 2000; Gosden and Knowles 2001: xix; Adams 2009). For example, a rare insight is provided by an observer on the 1870s *Challenger* expedition, who made the wry comment that people from the island of Manus, 'soon took to making trade goods, shell hatchets and models of canoes, e.g., which were as badly made as the trade gear which we gave in exchange' (Moseley 1892: 390). Recent attempts have initiated the reinterpretation of museum collections as the product of complex interactions between coloniser and colonised (e.g. Thomas 1991, 1994; Schildkrout and Keim 1998; Phillips and Steiner 1999; Gosden and Knowles 2001; O'Hanlon and Welsch 2000; Harrison 2006; Adams 2009), but these studies have shown that detecting the concrete effects of indigenous agency is surprisingly problematic.

Despite the wide recognition that indigenous agency existed, Thomas (2000: 274) has noted that 'it is striking just how difficult it is to recover and characterise indigenous agency in any specificity, from the historical record'. One obvious problem is that the documentation associated with objects, whether museum registration entries or catalogue descriptions, rarely provides information about the motivations and choices of collectors and vendors, let alone those of the indigenous producers and traders of the objects. It is possible to trace the movement of objects through the colonies to a certain degree, for example, through diary entries of early missionaries, traders, explorers and the official British colonial records, but again this evidence usually only provides tentative clues about the active roles of indigenous participants.

Since conventional archival approaches to the analysis of collections are limited in the extent to which they will be able to disentangle and draw out the material signature of indigenous agency, additional conceptual frameworks and methodologies should be sought. One way of moving beyond the methodological impasse is to re-interpret ethnographic objects, whether as stored in museum collections or as presented in sale and auction catalogues, as the tangible, material manifestations of how indigenous producers negotiated their social relationships in colonial contexts. If historical records and ethnographic accounts have proved somewhat opaque in terms of unpicking the complex social relations and interactions mediated through the collection of objects, could analytical approaches adopted from archaeology provide a different perspective on the role of indigenous agency in these exchanges? It could be argued that previous attempts to uncover agency from the study of objects have been sidetracked from the more mundane characteristics of materiality by the rich texture and fine-grained nuances offered by documentary evidence and oral testimony.

To readdress this balance, we have returned to an object-centred, assemblage-based approach common to archaeological research. Assemblages in this type of analysis consist of artefacts where the relationships between them are regarded as the consequence of deliberate human action. We begin with the assumption that auction and sale catalogues can be treated as a form of ethnographic assemblage. In this sense they have been formed in a similar way to collections held in museums.

Given this similarity, auction and sale catalogues provide an additional set of data with which to examine indigenous agency.

There is a close relationship between the objects offered for sale in the auction catalogues and the ethnographic collections of colonial period museums which acquired many objects from them. For example, handwritten notes in the margins of the British Museum's copies of some Stevens catalogues indicate which objects were of interest to the Museum and what prices were paid for them. The British Museum purchased a number of items from the Goodwin collection advertised in Stevens Sale (No. 6930) on 23 June 1885 (Hassell, personal communication). In addition, the objects displayed in the catalogues, brought together by the activities of collectors and traders, contain objects organised and classified in a manner similar to formal museum collections. Objects tend to be grouped in the first instance by geography, for example as originating from Asia, British New Guinea or Oceania, then according to types, such as paddles, masks or axes and, occasionally, by event or collector, as, for example *A Catalogue of the Well-Known Ethnographical Collection Formed by Mr Frank Hyams, During His Sojourn in the South Seas, which include the Fine Old Collection Originally Formed by Mr W. T. Sturt, of Suva, Fiji* (Stevens 1907).

One of the potential difficulties in extracting the role of indigenous producers from ethnographic collections is the problem of moving between different scales of evidence; that is between individual events and resulting process. Object-centred analyses have tended to focus on artefact biographies, distinctive artefacts or specific artefact types; for example clubs (Thomas 1991), man-catchers (O'Hanlon 1999) and masks (Adams 2009). This, together with the particular and localised nature of much historical and ethnographic evidence has tended to strand object analysis at the level of the event. The archaeological approach offered by this study has focused on assemblages as well as specific classes of objects and therefore allows us to draw out some of the broad processes of cross-cultural interaction between indigenous artefact producers and the many collectors and traders who operated in European colonies in the late nineteenth and early twentieth centuries.

Before Ebay™

Ethnographic or tribal art did not become a major sale item until the late nineteenth century, although many of today's famous auction houses had begun trading in the eighteenth century. Cheaper printing based on the invention of lithography in Germany (King 2006a: 14), the use of photography as a medium of visual representation and the development of a reliable international mail system were arguably all elements in the rapid transformation of the international market in ethnographic objects. The Australian Museum in Sydney, for example, received a catalogue from either Webster or Oldman every couple of months, with only a month or two between publication in Britain and accessioning by the Museum as evidenced by date stamps on the catalogue covers (Fig. 2.1).

The addition of ethnographic artefacts, including a wide range of much cheaper but still exotic items, considerably expanded the previous antiquities-dominated markets beyond relatively expensive elite objects: for example, arrows, clay pots and some body adornments. It is arguable that the cheap prices of only a few pence for many artefacts made them available for purchase by people other than the wealthy upper classes who had been the major consumers of antiquities. This broadening of the potential pool of consumers is most likely due to a number of factors including the expansion of the middle class in the colonies (e.g. administrators, clerks, plantation managers, trade store owners, missionaries and policemen), the beginnings of the international tourism industry and the public displays of ethnographica in the international exhibition halls of the late nineteenth century. Indeed, King (2006b: 57) suggests that the British artefact dealer W.D. Webster, participated in international exhibitions at Earls Court, to take advantage of the great public interest in ethnographic objects.

Our dataset, summarised in Table 2.1, is based on analyses of three sets of auction and sale catalogues from London-based firms. Both Webster and Oldman were specialist retailers of ethnographica, whereas Stevens sold all manner of collectables including natural history specimens, fossils, antiquities, ethnographica and other curiosities, as illustrated in Fig. 2.2. The oldest firm was a wholesale auction house run by Henry Stevens, where ethnographic objects made up only a small proportion of the stock. Museum registration data and the handwritten notes in the margins of catalogues in the British Museum show that he sold to both Webster and Oldman as well as to the Museum.

Table 2.1 The number of auction catalogues and objects in catalogues included in the study

Catalogue	Dates	Years	Volumes	Total objects	Papuan objects
Webster	1895–1901	7	31	5323	940
Oldman	1901–1913	14	115	6637	361
Stevens	1885–1939	47	63	59101	977
Totals			209	71061	2278

W.D. Webster is thought to have been the first dealer to use illustrated catalogues (King 2006b: 55), five volumes of which were produced between 1895 and 1901. The first 4 years include beautiful black-and-white, hand-drawn illustrations (Fig. 2.3), but these were replaced by photographs in 1898. It is from Webster's catalogue for February 1896 that the widely used descriptor, '... suitable for decoration of Halls & Billiard Rooms' first occurs (Fig. 2.4). According to King (2006b: 59), Webster was the last of the dealers not reliant on the dispersal of museum collections for his stock and instead sourced his sale material directly from traders.

The final component of the sample is a series of auction catalogues from the collector W.O. Oldman, produced between 1901 and 1913, much in the style of W.D Webster. According to the useful history in Waterfield (2006), Oldman continued dealing in artefacts after 1913, but sent out artefact lists with photographs attached only to contacts made from the period of catalogue production. Oldman built up

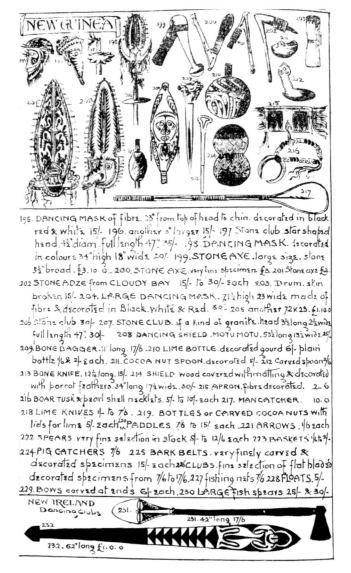

Fig. 2.3 A typical page from the Webster catalogue illustrates the detailed drawings and the types of information found in the entries. It is notable that stone objects attracted relatively higher prices than highly decorated dancing masks. Multiples of items such as lime knives, spears and bark belts are listed but not illustrated (Photo by James King, courtesy of the Australian Museum Research Library)

his own private collection of Polynesian artefacts as an insurance policy for his retirement in 1927 and created a private museum in his house in Clapham, London (Waterfield 2006). In 1948 his private collection was bought by the Government of New Zealand and then distributed amongst a number of regional museums.

From

W. O. Oldman, *Dealer in Weapons & Curiosities,*
77, Brixton Hill, London, S. W.

List No 14.

A Selection of Specimens suitable for Trophies in Halls.
Billiard Rooms, &c.,

XMAS. 1903.

—— **South Sea.** ——

Shield of wood covered back & front with fine cane, horizontal bands painted in black & zig-zag patterns in lines woven in the cane work Size about 30 x 13 in. This is a fine old specimen & very scarce. Used by the *Eoroko Tribe, Oro Bay, N. E. Coast of British New Guinea.* 8/6

Shield, very similar, not so fine, old. 7/6
Do., slightly damaged. 5/6

2 dozen Arrows about 5 ft. 6 in. long from Thursday Island, dark reed shafts, fine large heads of black wood carved with crocodile & snake designs and filled in with white, human bone points & barbs. These are very old and rare owing to the natives having given up making them some years ago. 1/6 each, 14/6 per dozen.

3 dozen Arrows same as above only heads plain. - /9 ea. 7/6 per doz.

4 dozen New Guinea Arrows, black and brown palm wood heads, reed shafts, many carved, all old, average length 4 ft. 6 in. 3/6 per dozen.

1 dozen Santa Cruz Isl. Arrows, bone tips, carved & painted, different designs, very decorative, scarce. -/9 each or 7/6 the lot.

Bows from New Hebrides, Solomon Isl. and New Guinea. 1/- to 5/6 each.

Spears, Australian, New Guinea and Solomon Isl., old specimens, 1/- to 3/6 each. Clubs with Stone Heads, various types, from 3/6 each. A large selection of cheap Clubs, Implements, Paddles, Model Canoes, Food-Bowls, Dresses, Ornaments, &c. in stock, see Monthly Lists.

All the above specimens are guaranteed genuine. Any may be had on Approval.

Fig. 2.4 *Upper:* A banner inserted at the base of a Webster catalogue (February 1896: 19) illustrates the popularity of items for decorating walls. *Lower:* A special Christmas list of items from the South Seas offered by Oldman in 1903 echoes the same function for ethnographic items (Photo by James King, courtesy of the Australian Museum Research Library)

Our study used the complete set of W.D. Webster catalogues held in the library of the Australian Museum together with a large number of early W.O. Oldman catalogues. We were able to complete the set of Oldman catalogues by consulting the facsimile edition (Oldman 1976). Our sample of Stevens catalogues is held in the Anthropology Library of the British Museum. Since this set was incomplete, we were unable to ascertain how representative it is, although we suspect it is biased towards those retained by curators because they advertise large collections of ethnographic material. Despite these limitations, the J.C. Stevens catalogues are especially important for extending the time range of our dataset beyond World War 1 and providing valuable information about broad scale changes in the artefact market.

Each of the three catalogue sets contains a slightly different range of data. Of the three, the Stevens lists contain the least information, although occasionally detailed histories of objects are provided: for example, for a Hawai'ian feather cloak and a lock of hair from King Edward IV (Stevens 1898: July 5 and 6, p. 11). With exception of several objects, price information is not published and the descriptions of the ethnographic objects are generally basic and short. Through time, the specificity of the locations of items in the Stevens catalogues tend to shift from a particular country to the more general and ambiguous category of 'South Seas'. Illustrations in our Stevens sample is limited to the July 5 and 6, 1898, catalogue that has two pages of illustrations of exquisite *malangan* masks from New Ireland and two photographs of carved wooden Maori objects (Stevens 16 April 1912) and Peruvian pottery (Stevens 10 October 1901). In contrast, both Webster and Oldman published sale prices for the artefacts and their catalogues also contained descriptions of individual artefacts that range from the basic to the relatively detailed, together with either Webster's excellent scale drawings (Fig. 2.3) or photographs (Fig. 2.5).

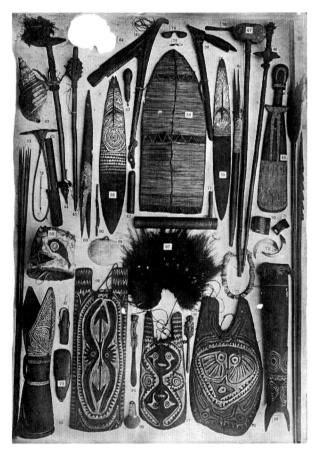

Fig. 2.5 A representative selection of items from Papua. The area blocked off represents a human skull, a common object on Oldman's plates of objects from this region (Oldman 1976: January, 1905, vol. 22 plate 2) (Photo by James King, courtesy of the Australian Museum Research Library)

Our sample shows that between 1895 and 1939 over 71,000 artefacts were offered for sale via the catalogues (Table 2.1). An exact figure is impossible to calculate because many entries describe multiples of objects such as arrows, spears and body ornaments. The time period over which the catalogues range has been identified by King (2006a: 13) as representing the most intense activity in terms of the trade in ethnographic objects in Europe and is also the major period of ethnographic collecting by European and colonial museums. As Fig. 2.6 shows, the number of objects for sale peaked between 1895 and 1903, the time during which Webster obtained objects from a range of traders and collectors, whereas in the following period Oldman predominantly sold objects recycled for sale from existing collections (King 2006b). The later peak in 1926–1930 is more difficult to interpret because of the non-random sample of Stevens catalogues. It is not clear whether this peak represents a change in artefact production and sale in British New Guinea or an increase in the recycling of existing objects. Also in this later period, ethnographica formed a much smaller sample of the total assemblage in the catalogues than before World War I and most of the objects were originally obtained much earlier.

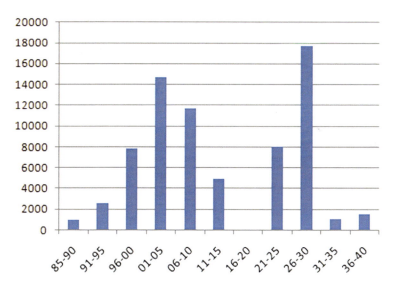

Fig. 2.6 Changes through time in the total number of items listed in the catalogues (dates are listed on the horizontal axis and quantities are shown on the vertical axis)

Western Desires

Not surprisingly, western values and desires are well expressed in the catalogues, particularly in the high demand for weapons, antiquities and elaborate carvings, but, as we argue below, these same patterns also record a range of cross-cultural interactions that occurred during their initial acquisitions. Some catalogues record the impact of a particular historical event: for example, Webster's catalogue no. 24 from 1900 in which the contents are labelled as, 'Taken at Benin City February 1897 by the British Punitive Expedition under the Command of Admiral Rawson' (cf. Fig. 2.2). In this example, the catalogues record the beginning of the market for West African bronzes, which was an important event for kicking off the Primitive arts movement.

'Suitable for the decoration of halls and billiard rooms' (Fig. 2.4) does appear to be an important element of the attractiveness of objects as reflected by the large numbers and high prices for many forms of weaponry and armour, including guns, swords and pieces of armour from Europe and Asia and the many clubs, spears and shields from all around the world. Certain raw materials such as dark wood and green stone (e.g. jade) were highly prized and priced accordingly. Items like shrunken heads, decorated skulls and a Tibetan apron made from human bones all have the desirable qualities of the rare curio and fetish object, which have been well documented as attractors for private collectors (Pearce 1995). Highly decorated, that is, attractive objects, especially where both the function of the object and the decoration are comprehensible to western collectors may indicate the pull of western tastes in the market. The fledgling western aesthetic for Asian, Oceanic and African objects as art forms can also be detected in the types and forms of artefacts for sale and the associated prices.

The range and types of artefacts for sale also reflect late nineteenth and early twentieth century attitudes to other races and ethnicities. Many of the so-called primitive artefacts, such as stone axes, wooden clubs, shields and body ornaments and so on, together with the gruesome decorated human skulls would have re-enforced prevailing racial stereotypes and notions of the primitive and provided the material proof to confirm the theories of cultural evolution current at the time (Stocking 1968; Trigger 1989).

It is also worth considering briefly what the catalogues reflect in terms of gender roles and the organisation of public and private spaces in Victorian and Edwardian houses. The differences in prices between domestic objects and weaponry are most likely related to who had control of family income. There is a predominance of higher-priced objects deemed suitable for the decoration of masculine spaces such as halls, billiard rooms, smoking rooms, libraries and studies (Fig. 2.4). In contrast, the more domestic objects such as body ornaments, combs, cooking pots and baskets suitable for the decoration of drawing rooms, sewing rooms and other feminine spaces fetch much lower prices and are for sale in much lower numbers.

Negotiating the Marketplace

Although the structure and content of the auction catalogues certainly paint interesting pictures about contemporary society and ideology in Britain, the types of items for sale and their prices also reveal important aspects of social relations played out at distance in the colonies. For example, a comparative analysis of prices across the globe reveals variation in how local social interactions were formed in different settings. An analysis of assemblage composition in terms of what objects are represented and what objects are missing is another powerful way to monitor some of the choices made by local communities concerning when and how to interact with the myriad of westerners they encountered. The catalogues also offer ways to trace the beginnings and development of commercial production in terms of Graburn's (1976: 5) 'arts of acculturation'. These include objects aimed at the high-end 'primitive art' market as well as those for wider distribution as souvenirs. To illustrate these points, we present several case studies using the Webster, Oldman and Stevens catalogues. They highlight the productive ways that these fascinating historical documents can yield data about the previously silent indigenous makers and owners of the artefacts that ended up in museums or private collections. We begin by examining the broad social context of exchange and then turn to localised examples of indigenous agency.

The catalogues contain quite substantial amounts of hard data that can be gleaned from the text and the photos or drawings (e.g. Fig. 2.3). These include the source country or region for the item, its type (mask, axe, etc.), function (ceremony, body adornment, weapon, etc.), size, raw materials, nature and amount of decoration, and, very importantly, the asking price. For this study we characterised every catalogue in terms of the number of items represented for each continent and noted the highest and lowest priced item. Then we made a more detailed study of the individual entries from the region consisting of the modern day Papua New Guinea provinces of Western, Gulf, Central, Oro and Milne Bay. To keep our sample to a manageable size, however, we omitted cases that were stated as from the island groups in Milne Bay. These regions are mainly referred in the catalogues as British New Guinea or New Guinea, but we refer to them here by their other commonly used name, 'Papua'.

The Global Market

Our study begins with an analysis of variability at the level of continents. A breakdown of the total objects into regions of origin shows most objects for sale came from Europe (34%) and Asia (28%) followed by Oceania (16%), Africa (14%) and many fewer from the Americas (7%). The relative number of items from Oceania is very high given the very small portion of the globe made up by the Pacific islands. Within this group, Melanesia is the most popular, representing 10% of total objects in the catalogues, but this is not surprising given that our time slice represents the early days of these colonies. In contrast, the smaller amount from Polynesia (3%) is both due to the size of the islands in comparison to other areas and the longer history of contact, beginning with the Cook voyages in the late eighteenth century. It is an interesting exercise to use the catalogue data to compare the processes of interaction that were taking place in Polynesia and Melanesia at the turn of the nineteenth century.

The kinds of items that make up the maximum and minimum priced objects from each catalogue provide a window into the range of interactions that were occurring globally. Of the ten most expensive items, four are from New Zealand, four from Benin City in Africa and two from Asia (Table 2.2). Moving down the list of the most expensive items in each catalogue, Melanesia is not recorded until places 63 (New Britain) and 64 (Solomons) out of 145. The first occurrence of a Papuan artefact is not until place 92, nearly at the bottom. Similarly, of the ten minimum priced objects, five are from Papua with the remainder from Australia, South America and Europe (Table 2.3).

Table 2.2 Summary of the ten most expensive artefacts within the group of objects that represent the maximum priced item per catalogue (price in British pounds and shillings)

Catalogue	Volume	Date[a]	Price	Country	Region	Object name
Webster	27	September 1900	£120	Benin City	Africa	Carved elephant tusk
Webster	2	October 1895	£85	Thailand	Asia	Collection of Siamese instruments
Webster	15	November 1897	£80	Benin City	Africa	Carved elephant tusk
Webster	7	April 1896	£75	New Zealand	Polynesia	Paddle or club
Oldman	130	1913	£52 10s	Tibet	Asia	Apron of human bones
Webster	24	February 1900	£50	Benin City	Africa	Bronze figure
Oldman	81	1911	£46 10s	New Zealand	Polynesia	War canoe prow
Oldman	78	1911	£42 10s	New Zealand	Polynesia	Gateway to a Maori *pa*
Webster	25	April 1900	£40	New Zealand	Polynesia	Adze, club
Webster	19	April 1899	£40	Benin City	Africa	Bronze vase

[a]The precise date is not always provided on Oldman catalogues

We can further interrogate these data by looking at the proportion of the total number of entries from each region that occur as a maximum or minimum priced object. The results depicted in Fig. 2.7 show that despite its small overall contribution to the catalogues, a very large percentage of the Polynesian material, followed by the Americas, is in the highest priced bracket. In contrast, artefacts from Africa, Asia, Australia and Melanesia are notable by their significant contributions to the minimum price category. The comparison of prices on the cover of the Webster catalogue in Fig. 2.1 illustrates this difference. In this case a carved wooden box from New Zealand is advertised at a significantly higher price (£5 5s) than elaborately decorated head ornaments from British New Guinea (17s 6d).

Social factors account for this particularly striking comparison between Pacific neighbours, Polynesia and Melanesia. In the highly stratified societies of Polynesia, many interactions with foreigners were likely to have been brokered by high-ranking individuals, some of whom where just as interested in exotic objects as the British collectors (Newell 2006). The result was limited exchange, contexts leading to a small range of items that reached Europe for sale. The precious greenstone axes and elaborately carved wooden objects obtained from the elites were appropriate

Table 2.3 Summary of the ten least expensive objects within the group of minimum priced items per catalogue (d is British pence)

Catalogue	Volume	Date[a]	Price (d)	Country	Region	Object name
Oldman	57	1907	3	New Guinea	Melanesia	Arrow
Oldman	1	1903	3	Europe	Europe	Copper coins
Webster	8	May 1896	5	New Guinea	Melanesia	Arrow
Webster	6	February 1896	5	New Guinea	Melanesia	Arrows
Oldman	62	May 1908	6	Peru	South America	Spindle whorl
Oldman	1	1903	6	New Guinea	Melanesia	Armlet
Oldman	23	February 1905	6	Paraguay	South America	Arrow or gourd
Oldman	50	May 1907	6	Costa Rica and South Africa	South America and Africa	South American bottle or African rattle
Webster	11	January 1897	9	New Guinea	Melanesia	Arrow
Webster	3	October 1895	9	Australia	Australia	Arrow

[a]The precise date is not always provided on Oldman catalogues

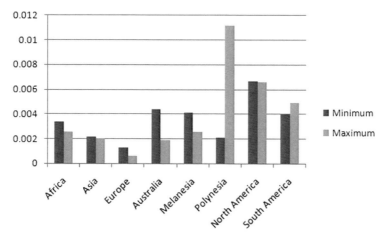

Fig. 2.7 Comparison of the percentage of the total assemblage that is represented by a minimum or maximum priced object among different regions shows that Polynesia is unusual in the large number of high-priced objects, whereas Melanesia and Australia are over represented in the group of artefacts that have the minimum price in a catalogue

objects for creating and cementing social relations (e.g. Fig. 2.1). Social relations between low-status individuals must also have involved exchange, but with much less emphasis on durable objects and perhaps more on foodstuffs or services. Another possibility is that after over a 100 years of contact, the Polynesians, and especially the New Zealanders, had developed their artefact trade to focus on profits achieved from making and marketing elaborately carved status items.

In contrast, the combination of a sizeable quantity of artefacts for sale plus the highest percentage of minimum prices for objects per catalogue implies that the Melanesian traders who were supplying large numbers of cheap or low-prestige objects were accessing a quite different market demographic to that of their Polynesian counterparts. In the more egalitarian Melanesian societies, where the acquisition of status (partly derived through exchange with people outside the immediate clan group, including foreigners) was fiercely competitive, a much wider range of people participated in the production and exchange of goods with westerners. In their eagerness to establish social relations, they offered a very broad range of everyday objects for exchange. So, whereas the Polynesian social interaction sphere in which artefacts circulated was comprised of controlled interactions among elites and/or sale of high-priced objects, the Melanesian artefact trade more closely resembled a free market. Although in both contexts the nature of the goods offered for trade with westerners reflects indigenous agency, it was just the social contexts that differed.

Papuan Traders

The large quantity of artefacts from Papua offered for sale in the catalogues (Table 2.1) is the outcome of social transactions between the local community and the wide range of outsiders (traders, missionaries, explorers, government officials) whom they encountered. As we have seen, in comparison to Polynesia, the assemblage generated from these interactions implies informal, egalitarian transactions through bartering rather than formal gift giving. A more detailed analysis of individual entries in the catalogues helps enrich this picture of cross-cultural relations even further.

Although traders and missionaries had been permanently resident in the region for over 10 years, Britain formally annexed the southeastern part of New Guinea as a Protectorate in 1884, just a year before the first catalogue in our sample, and then repackaged it as a colony in 1888. Its rights over the area were transferred to the newly independent Australia, beginning in 1902 and formalised in 1906, when it was renamed the Territory of Papua (Legge 1972: 115). By far the majority of our data on individual objects from Papua and all our price information are derived from catalogues dated between 1895 and 1913, well after first contact and initial exploration by Europeans. This period, when most ethnographic objects were circulating in Britain, can be described as one of 'settling in' for the colonial and territorial governments. It was a time of considerable expansion for missionaries, traders and miners when the major concern of the colonisers was pacification to assist further exploration and exploitation of resources. The colony was not successful in economic terms, however, as illustrated by the imbalance between imports and exports in the official reports (*Annual Report on British New Guinea* 1886–1902; *The Parliament of the Commonwealth of Australia* 1903–1936). Interestingly, in these documents, natural history specimens and ethnographic curiosities are listed among the colony's exports, although their values were never as high as gold, copper, copra, sandalwood and beche-de-mêr. That goods specifically for trade with local Papuans, such as tobacco, cloth and beads, were regularly recorded as imports also emphasises the importance to the British and Australians of trade with the local community for acquiring necessary supplies of food as well as the highly desired natural resources for export.

Given that ethnographic items are listed as exports in the official records and our sample of catalogues encompasses the time of the massive expansion of ethnographic collections across the world, it is reasonable to question whether and in what ways Papuans capitalised on this expanding market. From case studies of the nearby Admiralty Islands (Torrence 2000), Wuvulu and New Ireland (Buschmann 2009) in Papua New Guinea, as well as Fiji (Thomas 1991), we know that some Melanesian communities did produce goods specifically for trade with foreigners. The lack of similar iconic items together with the abundance of the ordinary objects that dominate the catalogues suggests that Papuans had not developed their market in the same way, possibly because, located near the territorial capital and within the area where most outsiders resided and visited, they had frequent opportunities for bartering and therefore did not need to create special objects to attract commercial activity. Instead, it was the westerners who relied on trade with them to acquire necessary foodstuffs, resources, guides, house staff and local police.

In Papua, it seems that there were related driving forces behind the expansion in the artefact trade. There was a desire on the part of foreign traders to make a healthy profit from sales to collectors back home and this together with the rapid expansion of museums in both Europe and Australia led to the creation of the market for ethnographic objects. Nearly everyone in Papua, including the missionaries, was involved to some extent in the sale of 'curiosities'. Not surprisingly, the artefact producers and hawkers were quick to seize opportunities to obtain desired trade goods through the exchange of their cultural heritage.

By far the most common items that reached the British auction houses from Papua were very ordinary objects used in daily life, rather than in special, spiritual or ceremonial occasions (Fig. 2.3). Weapons and tools for warfare, hunting and fishing (e.g. spears, clubs and axes) make up the largest proportion (35%), but those used as body accessories (26%) are almost as numerous. Admittedly, the category of body accessories represents a mixed bag of everyday and ritual profane items, but most are personal items worn daily (e.g. neck, arm, nose ornaments) and only 10% of these are specifically labelled as masks. Finally, artefacts used in domestic (12%) and leisure activities (10%), such as smoking tobacco and chewing betel nut, make up almost the remainder of the assemblage. Objects that can be classed as 'art' or 'spiritual' are very rare (7%). It is as if people were bartering just what they happened to have on hand or body when they encountered outsiders eager for trade. Although the majority of the items are associated with male activities, a significant amount of female body ornaments shows that women were active in the trading.

The prices of the objects, shown graphically in Fig. 2.8, support the notion that everyday items of low value were mainly offered for trade: 30% of objects were valued at 5 shillings or less, 74% were under 1 pound and 92% under 2 pounds. The

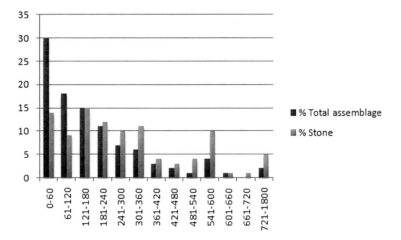

Fig. 2.8 The distribution of prices for stone objects versus prices for the total assemblage. Prices are in British pence; 240 pence is equivalent to one pound

numbers of objects across price categories show a steep decline in abundance as price increases. This evidence suggests that trade in the colonies largely consisted of casual barter involving minimal social interaction of low-value goods typically found within every Papuan household.

A good example of cross-cultural interaction involving western desires and indigenous agency is the trade in stone objects. Stone tools had long been collected by many British amateur naturalists, who were seeking evidence for the evolution of humans (Daniel 1975). These objects also satisfied the desire of a wider section of the community to possess something from a distant 'primitive' culture. Whether still in their wooden hafts or not, stone artefacts were offered for much higher than average prices in the catalogues (e.g. Fig. 2.3). The average price was 26 shillings (median 13 shillings 5 pence) compared to 17 shillings (median 12 shillings 6 pence) for the total Papuan sample. The exchange of stone objects provides an excellent case of how exchange works in cross-cultural situations since both seller and buyer must be satisfied with the outcome. The westerner obtained a valuable artefact and the Papuan received a substantial amount of cash for an object that was rapidly becoming obsolescent because it was much less effective than the new metal tools.

The catalogues also contain a number of items that were possibly designed by Papuans specifically to 'dazzle' or enchant (Gell 1998; Harrison 2006) potential buyers and therefore earn a profit through trade. The most infamous and well known are so-called man-catchers (Fig. 2.3). As analysed in detail by O'Hanlon (1999), man-catchers are flimsy objects whose capacity to restrain and kill a person is highly questionable. Their attraction to buyers was based on how well they fulfilled the British conceptions of 'savage' and 'primitive'. Taking a man-catcher home proved beyond a doubt that the bearer had come into contact with people with a truly primitive culture. Even by the time of the first Webster catalogue, enough man-catchers had been made and successfully sold that they were well known and there was little need to illustrate them individually. Instead, the entries refer to a class of objects in the same way as there are entries for 'spears', 'paddles', 'arrows' and 'clubs' (e.g. Fig. 2.3), rather than providing individualised descriptions as is the case with the majority of objects. Man-catchers are most common in the early Webster catalogues where they were priced up to 17 shillings and 6 pence.

Another candidate for 'dazzlers' are what were generally described as 'decapitating knives'. These are simple pieces of bamboo with a string wrapped around to form a handle. Again they were attractive to British consumers because of the link with cannibalism. Interestingly, decapitating knives are most common in the catalogues between 1903 and 1908, after the man-catchers appear to have gone out of fashion. These may have filled the same role as the man-catchers, but were a cheaper souvenir, although there are also two expensive versions in Oldman (1976) catalogues of 1903 and 1905 in which the decapitating knife is paired with a cane 'head carrier'.

What's Missing?

The absence of particular 'special' kinds of objects in the catalogues is as revealing as the dominance of utilitarian and domestic goods. The withholding of objects not only signals indigenous agency at work but also, more importantly, provides insights into how local communities viewed and interacted with westerners. One of the most striking findings of our study is that items used in traditional forms of exchange are extremely rare among the entries for Papua in our catalogue sample. Their absence is particularly notable because local exchange systems were very active and expanded greatly during the post-contact period of the 1880s through the 1920s due to pacification (Oram 1982: 23).

Within the catalogue entries, there are only five items specifically labelled as 'local currency'. All of these are strings of shells commonly used for exchange in the Milne Bay area, which is given as the provenience for three of the entries. One was collected by Sir William MacGregor, the chief administrator of Papua (1888–1898) (Oldman 1976: Vol. 9, No. 129, item 46 (30840)). Given MacGregor's high status, this item may have originally been a gift presented with the intention to create or cement social ties by incorporating him into the indigenous system of exchange and therefore setting up obligations between this important person and the giver. Interestingly, MacGregor took this item all the way back to England, where, perhaps, outside of its relevant social context, the string of seaweed and shell (on sale for only 6 shillings) held little long-term value for him.

Shell armbands were also central to systems of traditional exchange in many areas of Papua. In particular, one type called a *toea* was incorporated into a long-distance trading system extending between the Motu people in Central Province (near the provincial capital at Port Moresby) and their partners in the Gulf of Papua region (Oram 1982: 16–17). The bonds created through the exchange of shell armbands were likened to kinship ties and were often maintained between families over several generations. The giving of a shell armband, therefore, had important meanings, established obligations and maintained long-term social relationships. Clearly, the presence of only 19 Papuan entries (out of 2278) that mention shell armbands, armlets or bracelets shows that these were offered for exchange only very infrequently. Many of the entries are too general to distinguish whether these are actually indigenous trade items or just body ornaments. Only four specifically mention pairs of armlets or armlets with decorations that match the description of traditional valuables.

In addition to their relative scarcity, the high value given to the armbands by Papuans is reflected in the prices they were prepared to pay to acquire them. Barton (1902, BNGAR: 18–20) reports that the Motu would pay 2 pounds for an armshell. This is an extremely high price given the level of most local salaries and would place the item alongside those at the top end of the sale prices in England for objects from Papua (Fig. 2.8). In contrast, these items were clearly not valued by westerners, as illustrated by their prices in the catalogues of between 6 pence and 7 shillings 6 pence. Reverend Lawes, the first resident English missionary to the south coast of Papua, describes exchanges of armshells between locals in his diary, but he does not appear to have acquired these himself or to have used them in his numerous exchanges to obtain food (Lawes 1876–1884). This is significant because *toea* were used in exchange by Motu with their trading partners to acquire foodstuffs and the majority of Lawes' exchanges were motivated by his need to acquire food. The near absence of *toea* in the catalogues suggests that westerners were deliberately excluded from traditional systems of exchange. In the few cases where someone presented a westerner with a gift, as reflected in the few currency strings and armbands listed in the catalogues, the importance of the social relation signified by the valuable was possibly either not recognised or deliberately ignored. Back in England the item was sold cheaply as a bauble.

Finding Agency in Auction Catalogues

Since the exchange of objects plays a critical role in the mediation and negotiation of cross-cultural interactions, British auction and sale catalogues have proved to be an innovative and fruitful source of information about variations in local social contexts across the Pacific region. Our preliminary case study of Papua in the late nineteenth and early twentieth centuries demonstrates that given an appropriate perspective and methodology, one can investigate indigenous agency from these unusual colonial documents.

Although the catalogues contain a range of useful data about the processes of trade and exchange between indigenous artefact producers and traders, they are not straightforward documents. For example, the lack of price data in the Stevens catalogues restricts sample sizes and time range for certain kinds of analysis. Within the Webster catalogues in particular, some object types such as arrows and spears were difficult to quantify as precisely as more individualised objects because they were often sold in lots of unspecified numbers. The primary limitation of these auction and sale catalogues, however, is that the assemblage composition data are not a direct and straightforward reflection of what was bought and sold in the colonies, particularly in the more recent periods. This property also applies to museum collections. In contrast, some material was passed around various collectors for some years before being listed for sale in these catalogues. As we read through the catalogue sets and became more familiar with both object types and descriptions, it became clear that some unsold objects were recycled over time, sometimes with slightly amended descriptions. These and other observations in themselves provide fascinating insights into British collecting, but that would be the subject of a different study. Despite the filter made up of British preferences, it is worth stressing that the mere existence of material in the catalogues depended on initial choices made by the indigenous owners.

It is clear from this study and from others that have used analytical frameworks common to archaeological research that an assemblage-based approach to museum collections and historical sources has the potential to draw out traces of indigenous agency that more conventional museological and historiographical approaches do not (e.g. Torrence 1993, 2000; Kononenko et al. 2010). While this kind of analysis cannot replicate the fine-grained, nuanced textures of highly situated ethnographic accounts and some historical texts, the broad-scale patterns and trends provide valuable insights into indigenous actions that cannot be accessed in any other way. Even though the object descriptions, classifications and prices in the catalogues come to us via the lens of the western dealer, it is also apparent that other cultural and social factors are at play and these reflect indigenous agency.

The catalogues create a vivid image of cross-cultural exchange in the British territory of Papua at the turn of the nineteenth century. The lack of 'currency', and especially the very important armshells still in use at the time of the catalogues, such as those within the *hiri* trading networks, demonstrates that at this time, indigenous people were neither including westerners within ceremonial trade nor trying to incorporate them into traditional social networks, except in rare cases as with Governor MacGregor. Presumably, the Papuans were not eager to get entangled in reciprocal obligations with the colonisers, a situation that differs considerably with the exchanges between high-status British and indigenous individuals in Polynesia. Instead, the catalogues represent exchange in the early colony as primarily consisting of two spheres: (1) as social relations within Papuan communities or (2) as mainly economic barter with westerners. Over time, the active role of Papuans had a marked impact on the kinds of goods that later formed the core of private collections and public institutions.

Our preliminary analysis of auction catalogues demonstrates the potential of the seemingly prosaic information contained in these unusual historical documents (see also Harrison Chapter 3). By taking an archaeological approach to data on assemblages and individual objects, we can examine trends in the ethnographic artefact market across both space and time. Even the routine elements of a catalogue such as the object descriptions, from the number of words used to the information they contain about the materials, and sizes and decorative elements of objects, provide important data about the relative values of artefact classes, information we hope to analyse in our ongoing study. The analysis and interpretations presented in this chapter show that it is possible to tease out elements of the active participation of indigenous artefact producers in the ethnographic object trade in a quintessential form of western consumerism, namely 'collecting'.

Future studies designed to mine this rich data even further will help increase our understanding of the processes of negotiation and barter that underlie the formation of colonial societies in Papua and elsewhere. It is very clear from this study that different systems of value are operating between the sellers and buyers of objects. One of the important attributes of auction and sale catalogues that deserves further attention is the potential of the price data for teasing out how different systems of value were mediated in colonial societies. Another avenue for future research is the historical dimension of value, tracing how this has changed over time as objects have moved from the status of curios 'suitable for the decoration of halls and billiard rooms' to art pieces destined for gallery spaces.

Acknowledgements Our research and participation at WAC6 was funded by the Australian Research Council, University of Sydney, and Australian Museum. We are very grateful to Leone Lemmer and her staff at the Australian Museum and the Anthropology Library, British Museum, for their support. Special thanks to Rebecca Fisher for historical research and our co-investigators Jude Philp and Erna Lilje for information, encouragement and critique.

References

Adams, Monni
    2009 Both Sides of the Collecting Encounter: The George W. Harley Collection at the Peabody
        Museum of Archaeology and Ethnology, Harvard University. *Museum Anthropology* 32:
        17–32.

Annual Reports on British New Guinea (ARBNG) 1886–1902. British Government, London.

Anonymous (editor)
    1969 *The History of Melanesia: Second Waigani Seminar*. Research School of Pacific Studies
        and the University of Papua New Guinea, Canberra and Port Moresby.

Barton, F. R.
    1902–1903 Addendum to report, C.D. *Annual Report on British New Guinea*, pp. 18–20. British
        Government, London.

Buschmann, Rainer
    2009 *Anthropologies Global Histories: The Ethnographic Frontier in German New Guinea,
        1870–1935*. University of Hawaii Press, Honolulu.

Cochrane, Susan and Max Quanchi (editors)
    2007 *Hunting the Collectors: Pacific Collections in Australian Museums, Art Galleries and
        Archives*. Cambridge Scholars Publishing, Newcastle.

Daniel, Glynn E.
1975 *A Hundred and Fifty Years of Archaeology.* Duckworth, London.

Gell, Alfred
1998 *Art and Agency.* Oxford University Press, Oxford

Gosden, Chris and Chantal Knowles
2001 *Collecting Colonialism: Material Culture and Colonial Change.* Berg, London.

Graburn, Nelson H.
1976 Introduction. In *Ethnic and Tourist Arts: Cultural Expressions from the Fourth World,* edited by Nelson H. Graburn, pp. 1–32. University of California, Berkeley.

Harrison, Rodney
2006 An Artefact of Colonial Desire? Kimberley Points and the Technologies of Enchantment. *Current Anthropology* 47: 63–88.

King, Jonathan C.
2006a Introduction. In *Provenance. Twelve Collectors of Ethnographic Art in England 1760–1990,* edited by Hermione Waterfield and Jonathan C. King, pp. 8–15. Somogy Art Publishers, Barbier-Mueller Museum, Geneva.
2006b W. D. Webster. In *Provenance. Twelve Collectors of Ethnographic Art in England 1760–1990,* edited by Hermione Waterfield and Jonathan C. King, pp. 55–60. Somogy Art Publishers, Barbier-Mueller Museum, Geneva.

Kononenko, Nina, Robin Torrence, Huw Barton, and Ariane Hennell
2010 Cross-Cultural Interaction on Wuvulu Island, Papua New Guinea: The Perspective from Use–Wear and Residue Analyses of Turtle Bone Artefacts. *Journal of Archaeological Science* 37: 2911–2919.

Lawes, Reverend William George
1876–1884 *Journals.* Manuscript on file, Mitchell Library, Sydney.

Legge, J. D.
1972 British New Guinea. In *Encyclopedia of Papua and New Guinea, edited by Peter Allen Ryan,* pp. 115–121. Melbourne University Press in Association with the University of Papua and New Guinea, Carlton.

Moseley, Henry Nottidge
1892 *Notes by a Naturalist: An Account of Observations Made During the Voyages of H.M.S. Challenger.* John Murray, London.

Newell, Jennifer
2006 Collecting from the Collectors: Pacific Islanders and the Spoils of Europe. In *Cook's Pacific Encounters,* pp. 29–48. National Museum of Australia, Canberra.

O'Hanlon, Michael
1999 'Mostly Harmless'? Missionaries, Administrators and Material Culture on the Coast of British New Guinea. *Journal of the Royal Anthropological Institute* 5: 377–397.

O'Hanlon, Michael, and Robert L. Welsch (editors)
2000 *Hunting the Gatherers: Ethnographic Collectors, Agents and Agency in Melanesia, 1870s–1930s.* Berghahn Books, New York, NY.

Oldman, William Ockelford
1976 *Illustrated Catalogue of Ethnographical Specimens from the W. O. Oldman Catalogues (1903–1914).* Hales, Wilberg, London.

Oram, Nigel
  1982 Pots for Sago: The *Hiri* Trading Network. In *The Hiri in History: Further Aspects of Long Distance Motu Trade in Central Papua*, edited by Tom Dutton, pp. 1–35. Pacific Research Monograph 8. The Australian National University, Canberra.

Pearce, Susan
  1995 *On Collecting: An Investigation into Collecting in the European Tradition*. Routledge, London.

Peterson, Nicolas, Lindy Allen, and Louise Hamby (editors)
  2008 *The Makers and Making of Indigenous Australian Museum Collections*. Melbourne University Press, Melbourne.

Phillips, Ruth and Christopher Steiner
  1999 Art, Authenticity, and the Baggage of Cultural Encounters. In *Art and Commodity in Colonial and Postcolonial Worlds*, edited by Ruth Phillips and Christopher Steiner, pp. 3–19. University of California Press, Berkeley.

Schildkrout, Enid and Curtis A. Keim (editors)
  1998 *The Scramble for Art in Central Africa*. Cambridge University Press, Cambridge.

Stevens, J. C.
  1885–1939 *Auction Catalogues with Various Titles*. Privately published, London.
  1885 *A Catalogue of the Goodwin Collection of Curios* (June 23) S6930. Privately published, London.
  1898 *A Catalogue of a Choice and Valuable Collection of Curios, July 5 and 6*. Privately published, London.
  1907 *A Catalogue of the Well-Known Ethnographical Collection Formed by Mr Frank Hyams, During his Sojourn in the South Seas, which include the Fine Old Collection Originally Formed by Mr W. T. Sturt, of Suva, Fiji*. S11285 (May 8). Privately published, London.

Stocking, George W.
  1968 *Race, Culture and Evolution. Essays in the History of Anthropology*. University of Chicago Press, Chicago, IL.

The Parliament of the Commonwealth of Australia
  1903–1936 *British New Guinea. Annual Reports*. Commonwealth of Australia, Brisbane.

Thomas, Nicholas
  1991 *Entangled Objects: Exchange, Material Culture, and Colonialism in the Pacific*. Cambridge University Press, Cambridge.
  1994 *Colonialism's Culture: Anthropology, Travel and Government*. Polity Press, Cambridge.
  2000 Epilogue. In *Hunting the Gatherers: Ethnographic Collectors, Agents and Agency in Melanesia, 1870s–1930s*, edited by Michael O'Hanlon and Robert L. Welsch, pp. 273–277. Berghahn Books, New York, NY.

Torrence, Robin
  1993 Ethnoarchaeology, Museum Collections and Prehistoric Exchange: Obsidian-tipped Artefacts from the Admiralty Islands. *World Archaeology* 24: 468–481.
  2000 Just Another Trader? An Archaeological Perspective on European Barter with Admiralty Islanders, Papua New Guinea. In *The Archaeology of Difference: Negotiating Cross-Cultural Engagements in Oceania*, edited by Robin Torrence and Anne Clarke, pp. 104–141. Routledge, London.

Torrence, Robin and Anne Clarke
  2000 Negotiating Difference: Practice Makes Theory for Contemporary Archaeology in Oceania. In *The Archaeology of Difference: Negotiating Cross-Cultural Engagements in Oceania*, edited by Robin Torrence and Anne Clarke, pp. 1–31. Routledge, London.

Trigger, Bruce
   1989 *A History of Archaeological Thought*. Cambridge University Press, Cambridge.

Waterfield, Hermione
   2006 William Ockelford Oldman. In *Provenance. Twelve Collectors of Ethnographic Art in England 1760–1990*, edited by Hermione Waterfield and Jonathan C. King, pp. 65–77. Somogy Art Publishers, Barbier-Mueller Museum, Geneva.

Webster, W. D.
   1895 *Catalogue of Ethnological Specimens, Arms and Armour, Prehistoric and Other Curiosities*. Volume 1. Privately published, Oxford.
   1895–1896 *Catalogue of Ethnological Specimens, Western and Eastern Arms and Armour, Prehistoric and Other Curiosities on Sale by W. D. Webster*. Volumes 2–10. Privately published, Oxford.
   1897–1899 *Illustrated Catalogue of Ethnographic Specimens, Western and Eastern Arms and Armour, Prehistoric and Other Curiosities on Sale by W. D. Webster*. Volumes 11–20; 23. Privately published, Oxford.
   1899, 1900, 1901 *Illustrated Catalogue of Ethnographical Specimens in Bronze, Wrought Iron, Ivory and Wood from Benin City, West Africa Taken at the Fall of the City in February 1897 by the British Punitive Expedition under the Command of Admiral Rawson*. Volumes 21, 24, 29. Privately published, Oxford and London.
   1900–1901 *Illustrated Catalogue of Ethnographical Specimens from* [a wide range of places] *and Other Localities on Sale by W. D. Webster*. Volumes 25–28, 30–31. Privately published, Oxford and London.

Chapter 3
Consuming Colonialism: Curio Dealers' Catalogues, Souvenir Objects and Indigenous Agency in Oceania

Rodney Harrison

Abstract This chapter explores the potential for a study of colonial curio dealers' catalogues in producing particular forms of colonial desire that contributed to the production of a market in ethnographic souvenirs in Britain and its colonies in the late nineteenth and early twentieth centuries. Curio dealers occupied an integral space in a network which connected museums, tourists and indigenous artisans, but have been largely ignored in studies of colonial relations and material culture. Previous work on Kimberley Points has suggested Indigenous Australians produced markets for the sale of certain curios to colonial collectors which fulfilled complex roles within the groups who manufactured them, as well as those who received them through purchase, trade or exchange. Focussing on the 1929 catalogue of a Sydney-based curio dealer, Tyrells Museum (formerly Tost and Rohu Taxidermists, Tanners, Furriers and Island Curio Dealers), this chapter demonstrates that such catalogues not only have the potential to reveal changes in market demand, price and desirability of ethnographic objects, but also how artefacts were transformed from functional objects into ornaments, changes in their method and context of manufacture, as well as changing colonial relations between indigenous and non-indigenous people.

> *Colonialism is a process by which things shape people, rather than the reverse. Colonialism exists where material culture moves people, both culturally and physically, leading them to expand geographically, to accept new material forms and to set up power structures around a desire for material culture*
>
> *(Gosden 2004: 153).*

Introduction

While much of the literature on collecting and colonialism presently focuses on the role of public museums in relation to the colonial project, this chapter is concerned with the dialogics of production, consumption and value as expressed through the co-production of colonial objects of desire by indigenous people and colonial souvenir and collectors' markets. My interest is the relationship between collector

R. Harrison (✉)
Faculty of Arts, The Open University, Milton Keynes, UK
e-mail: rodney.harrison@gmail.com

S. Byrne et al. (eds.), *Unpacking the Collection*, One World Archaeology,
DOI 10.1007/978-1-4419-8222-3_3, © Springer Science+Business Media, LLC 2011

taste and indigenous agency, and the ways in which we might develop a micro-cosmic view of colonialism and cross-cultural engagement through an analysis of a series of objects featured in curio dealers' catalogues. Through this window into ethnographic souvenir markets, and the entangled agency of both indigenous people and collectors, we might begin to explore broader issues of colonial identities, indigenous agency and the role of objects in mediating and constructing colonial encounters.

In this chapter I consider some ideas which have been put forward by Tony Bennett with regard to the application of Bruno Latour's work to museums, and in particular the ways in which Actor-Network Theory (ANT) allows one to conceive of networks of connection between the 'field' and colonial metropoles, and how both might be transformed by the circulation of new objects, technologies and/or techniques for their distribution within this network. In doing so, my aim is to connect these with some of the concepts I have previously worked on associated with networks of material agency based on the work of anthropologist Alfred Gell (e.g. Harrison 2006, 2010) to develop a picture of the conceptual chain of connections between souvenirs, indigenous people, tourists, collectors and the colonial 'project' more generally. I focus on the late nineteenth and early twentieth century Sydney-based curio dealers Tost and Rohu (later Tyrells Museum) as a case study to help develop an understanding of the broader networks and relationships between these curio sellers and the movement of objects from colonies via a process of souveniring back to the colonial metropoles, and the ways in which ideas which influenced the governance of indigenous populations were transmitted back along the same networks. I also want to consider the role of the catalogues themselves as agents within an alternate actor-network which comprises indigenous people, curios, collectors and museums, and the idea that the process by which curios are assembled together in new ways at a distance from their context of production might also transform the colonial metropole and its conception of itself.

Material Culture and Colonialism

Colonialism has generally been seen to be distinct from other forms of cultural contacts in terms of the unequal power relations that characterise colonial systems (e.g. Gosden 2004; Given 2004; Silliman 2005). This fact has meant that the agency of indigenous peoples in colonial encounters has tended to be downplayed in the analysis of colonialism (a point made by several chapters in edited volumes by Torrence and Clarke 2000b and Russell 2001a). Nicholas Thomas (1994) argues that the colonial project and colonial discourses are in fact a disparate and diverse set of ideologies, rather than a unitary phenomenon. Thomas is particularly concerned in situating the idea of colonialism within the socially transformative projects of both colonisers and colonised. His book, *Entangled Objects* (1991), takes for its case study colonialism and material culture exchange in the Pacific. On the colonial peripheries, material culture forms a conduit for cross-cultural negotiation. Eschewing theories of creolisation, once popular in colonial studies, Thomas discusses processes of creative recontextualisation or re-authorship as objects move between colonisers and colonised. In this context, the significance of material objects in social life is critically important, and Thomas draws our attention both to the way in which westerners used the artefacts of the colonised, as well as the way in which the colonised re-authored and recreated 'western' objects (see also Thomas 1999). Objects are therefore not what they were made to be, but what they become in the process of creative recontextualisation. In colonial contexts, social identity is fluid and fashioned out of appropriation and exchange: the colonial construction of difference is paradoxically intimately related to knowledge and experience of the colonised 'Other'. Colonialism is not to be understood through the 'colonial discourse', but through the historical specificity of local encounters and the entanglement of material objects on the colonial periphery (Gosden and Knowles 2001).

Thomas (1994) argues for a radical reworking of the anthropological project—one that examines colonialism through

> localised, practically mediated expressions, through projects constituted through discursive agency rather than by individual historical actors or dehistoricised discourses .... an "anthropology of colonialism" cannot situate "the colonial" as an external object of study; this lack of comfortable distance from the power structures and the discourses being analysed seems appropriate, given the continuing energy of various colonial forms, such as those of settler primitivism (1994: 192).

It is the lack of coherence of colonial discourses that creates a space for creative subversion and re-authoring (an idea which resonates with the work of Homi Bhabha (e.g. 1994) and the application of postcolonial theory to archaeology more generally; e.g. see Liebmann and Rizvi 2008). This chapter then seeks to take a fine-grained local approach to the study of colonialism and colonial representation through the study of the engagements of indigenes, settler colonists and others in the production and trade in souvenir objects in colonial contexts. To date, very few studies of the lived experience of colonialism have emerged which operate at this level (but see Given 2004; Torrence 1993, 2000; Gosden and Knowles 2001).

Actor-Networks and the Local

This emphasis on the 'local' and the role of material culture in negotiating the 'social' finds reflection in the raft of current approaches to the study of organisations and society which are gathered under the label 'Actor-Network Theory' (ANT) (e.g. Latour 1993, 1999, 2005; Law 2008; Law and Hassard 1999; see further discussion in Byrne et al. Chapter 1). Bruno Latour (2005) notes that the term 'social' within the social sciences has come to mean both a process of assembling groups of people as well as a type of material, arguing that the social sciences should not be concerned with establishing the correct frame of reference for understanding social relations, but should be concerned with tracing networks of connection. He terms this approach the 'sociology of associations', showing how the social becomes traceable only where it is actively transformed. He suggests that we should not assume priority or primacy within this process of tracing networks of connection, but should instead assume social processes are 'flat' (Latour 1993) and without hierarchy. In ANT this notion is sometimes associated with a position of radical symmetry in which humans and non-humans are not treated differently in the process of tracing the actor-network (Latour 2005); hence not only humans but also objects and other non-humans might be thought of as actors or agents in tracing these networks of association.

This discussion calls to mind the important work of anthropologist Alfred Gell (1994, 1996, 1998), who has been cited widely within the field of material culture studies to argue the active role that objects can play in social relations between humans. However, I have argued elsewhere (Harrison 2010) following the critique of Leach (2007) that while Gell's anthropological theory of art is useful for describing the *social* agency of objects, it cannot be used to describe the *material* agency of objects, as it places primary agency only in the hands of human actors who are seen as the ultimate starting point in the chain of agent–patient relationships he describes. In relation to the study of indigenous objects in museum collections, this aspect of Gell's anthropological theory of art means it is only possible to focus on the agency of indigenous producers (Harrison 2010). While this is often the aim of such analyses (e.g. Harrison 2006), I want to broaden my viewpoint here to examine not only the agency embodied in the manufacture of an artefact but also the ways in which curios and other collected objects might produce innovative reactions and interactions in their varied networks of exchange. It is only when we effectively admit that an artefact might have primary agency of its own that we can use the distinctive life histories of material objects to generate innovative critical positions and alternate models of the efficacy or agency of objects themselves (see further discussion in Harrison 2010). Such an apparently radically perspectivist approach to material culture finds reflection in the work of a number of scholars across the social sciences who wish to push our understanding of the relationships between 'people' and 'things' (e.g. Viveiros de Castro 2004), blurring these categories in a way which is consistent with indigenous, totemic or animistic ontologies (e.g. Harvey 2006; Alberti and Bray 2009; Haber 2009; Harrison and Rose 2010).

A number of actor-network theorists differ from Gell in seeing objects as having agency which exists independently of human actors (or in Gell's terms, 'the artist'). Latour uses the term 'actor' or 'actant' to stand for anything which modifies any particular state of affairs. Thinking this way shifts the emphasis from what objects 'symbolise' to the ways in which material objects are involved in particular forms of interactions which create social 'features' such as inequalities in power or networks of social connection. We can trace the creation of these social features by looking to the shifts or movements in which the social becomes visible (or traceable) and new combinations of associations are made available to social groups by looking at the associations which they choose to explore.

Tony Bennett (2010; see also 2005, 2007, 2008a, 2009) has built on the work of Latour to describe the changing role and nature of ethnographic material culture collections in the relationship between museum, field and colony during the late nineteenth and early twentieth centuries as anthropology changed from its 'armchair' to 'fieldwork' phases. Bennett draws on Latour's account of the circulation of reference between field and laboratory based on his analysis of a soil sampling expedition in the Amazon Rainforest (Latour 1999), in which he notes that scientists gained a knowledge of the forest by attaining a distance from it. When collecting in the field, Latour argues that scientists do not see any relationships between the specimens of the field sites from which they are taken. These relationships are only developed once the material is taken back to the laboratory and reassembled in particular ways with material from other expeditions and are considered as a *collection*. Latour goes on to argue that it is not only the specimens themselves but also the forest from which the plants were taken that is transformed as a result of this process, through the actions which are subsequently undertaken as a result of this new conceptualisation of the forest as the sum of these collections and the knowledge which has been produced using them. In the same way that these collections of plant specimens are reassembled into new networks of action in the scientific laboratory, Bennett argues that

> anthropological assemblages … in what they assembled and brought together, provided new templates for both colonial, and in some cases, domestic governance. This involves a consideration of how the materials collected by these expeditions were assembled together, exhibited, circulated, and institutionally processed in ways that shaped new 'working surfaces on the social', formatting it for intervention on the part of new agents, in the context of new kinds of colonial governmental rationalities' (Bennett 2008b: 3).

Drawing on a series of late nineteenth and early twentieth century museum expeditions including the Cambridge Torres Strait Expedition led by Alfred Haddon, Baldwin Spencer's Expeditions in Central Australia in association with Frank Gillen, the work of Frank Hurley, the Jessup North Pacific Expedition led by Franz Boas and the expeditions into French colonies in Africa arranged by the Musée de l'Homme under the directorship of Paul Rivet from 1928 to 1938, Bennett suggests six ways in which the relations between the field, museum and colony were transformed over this period. These include:

(i) The involvement of new sets of agents in the process of collecting, and the development of new actor networks in which the materials that were assembled together from such expeditions were able to become active;

(ii) The role of new technologies of collecting, particularly film and sound-recording, in reorganising anthropological collections into more varied assemblages of artefacts and textual traces;

(iii) The role of these new technologies in reorganising the processes of collection by operating as key players in the actor networks that informed the relations between anthropologists and their 'subjects' within the fieldwork situation as well as their relations to both scientific and popular publics;

(iv) The growing influence of the laboratory sciences on the museum's conception as either itself a laboratory, or as needing to contain laboratories, in which … the

> relations between the constituent elements of anthropological assemblages could be manipulated for scientific and/or governmental purposes;
>
> (v) A strong relationship between . . . a series of (incomplete) transitions in the epistemological frameworks governing the modes of collecting and exhibiting non-Western cultures marked by an (incomplete) break with evolutionary conceptions and an (incomplete) shift to their conception as equally valid synchronous totalities, and . . . the emergence of a post-conquest, post-frontier set of colonial governmental rationalities;
>
> (vi) The development of clear, but limited, backwash effects of these forms of colonial governmentality on the development of new forms of anthropological assemblage orientated toward the governance of the domestic populations of imperial powers (Bennett 2008b: 4).

The value of an approach which focuses on networks of connections between collectors, objects and museums has already been demonstrated by the work of Gosden et al. (2007; see also Larson et al. 2007) and the Relational Museum Project in tracing the history of the collections of the Pitt Rivers Museum. Larson et al. (2007: 211) comment on the usefulness of the term 'network' as a metaphor for 'social and material interactions more generally' in understanding the history of the Pitt Rivers Museum, foregrounding 'patterns in sets of relationships that are beyond normal reasoning, and . . . a spur to more in-depth, nuanced research' (2007: 212). They note that they employ the network metaphor as a methodological tool, rather than a theoretical maxim, but make reference to ANT and the work of Latour in re-invigorating the interest in the agency of objects. Using a relational database, Larson et al. (2007) produce a series of network diagrams to map connections between collectors and donors, individual objects, and various clusters and associations between individuals (e.g. Members of the Royal Anthropological Society who were also donors to the Pitt Rivers Museum), and express the strength of these relationships using statistical techniques. While the sort of network methodology utilised by the Relational Museum Project is certainly appealing, for the purpose of this chapter I am concerned more with the network as a metaphor for interactions or 'shifts' which will allow us, in Latour's (2005) terms, to trace the social while it is being transformed.

Hunting the Gatherers: The Souvenir and the Collection

It is possible to identify two very different kinds of collecting that exist in colonial societies which produced two different mechanisms that stimulated the circulation of indigenous objects (this section after Harrison 2006). The first of these kinds of collection was linked closely with the rise of social anthropology and the colonial project as a whole. 'Systematic' or 'representative' collecting involved the acquisition and classification of representative items of the whole range of material culture from individual 'primitive' cultures. The nature of this kind of colonial field collecting and its relationship with nineteenth and early twentieth century anthropology, and the colonial project in general, has been relatively well studied (e.g. Stocking 1985; Clifford 1988, 1997; Lawson 1994; Griffiths 1996; Thomas 1991, 1999; papers in O'Hanlon and Welsch 2000; Gosden and Knowles 2001; Torrence 1993,

2000; Russell 2001b). F.E. Williams, in an instructional guide on *The Collection of Curios and the Preservation of Native Culture* (1923: 6), distinguished between 'casual' and 'systematic' collection, highlighting the importance of the methodical collection of all items of material culture, in particular, culture areas and their careful preservation in museums in the preservation of indigenous cultures (see further discussion in O'Hanlon 2000). The impetus for developing such collections derived from the historical specificities of Euro-American colonial expansion, and the relationship between natural history collections and newly emerging research in the biological sciences in the early- to mid-1800s in Europe (Herle 1998: 80). Museums were to assemble complete sets of material culture with which to reconstruct the very cultures that they were 'modernising' in the process of collecting them. Fabian (1983) and Clifford (1988: 202) draw our attention to the ways in which the narratives of ethnography rest on an allegory of modernity in which the non-western world is always in decline and ruin, emphasising the project of collecting cultures as one of salvaging the authentic in the wake of the modernisation of the tribal world. These collections were the very essence of a colonial narrative that fossilised indigenous culture by emphasising it as 'pure', essential and un-creolised (papers in Thomas and Losche 1999), but most importantly, vanished, an extinct strata covered over by European invasion and modernity (see Thomas 1999: 109).

Susan Stewart's (1993) work *On Longing: Narratives of the Miniature, the Gigantic, the Souvenir, the Collection* assists us by suggesting that differences between the meaning of such *systematically collected objects* and *souvenirs* lie in the way in which they function within different systems of cultural representation. Systematically collected objects, particularly through their removal from their autochthonous social context and display in the museum, become metaphors for culture and humanity. These artefacts operate within a capitalist 'system of objects' (Baudrillard 1968, 1994) or art–culture system which attributes to them particular kinds of value based on notions of authenticity and aesthetic value (Clifford 1988: 220ff), they are either (and sometimes simultaneously) exemplars of culture or 'art'. The art–culture system constructs itself as an ahistorical realm by the abstraction of objects through their recreated context of orderly display. Somewhat paradoxically, artefacts are *created* as 'authentic' objects through their removal from their historical context and their display within the context of the museum (Clifford 1988: 228). The collection is its own world. It closes itself to the existence of any world outside of itself through its insistent taxonomic recreation of context and reality (Belk 1995).

Souvenirs exist within a very different context to systematically collected objects. Where collected objects are either prominently displayed in a museum or parlour, and 'classified' in an orderly way, the souvenir belongs in the attic, the shoebox, the cellar – places whose context is not tied to function, but to the temporality of the past (Stewart 1993). The primary function of the souvenir is metonymy, not metaphor. Souvenirs, like collected objects, are created through their removal from their original context, but must be restored to that context through reverie or narrative to function as souvenirs. Souvenirs are collected mnemonic devices that function to address the gap between experience and memory – they are 'splinters of memory' (Leslie 1999: 116 in a discussion of Benjamin's work on the souvenir). Souvenirs function for the idealised recreation of a past that is focussed on the individual, and the desire to recreate an 'authentic' experience. The exotic object belongs within the genre of travel writing, and represents a particular form of (colonial) cultural imperialism which seeks to appropriate distance through stressing the intimacy of cultural contact (Stewart 1993: 147). Baudrillard (1968) links the souvenir to the world of childhood and its toys. Souvenirs function as tools with which to represent the life biography of the individual. The emphasis in the souvenir is on the destruction of the context of production in favour of the context of consumption, on the ability of the object to replace *experience* with enforced memory (Leslie 1999: 116).

In a ground-breaking study of the development of Native North American souvenir production in the northeast during the eighteenth and nineteenth centuries, Phillips (1997; see also Phillips and Steiner 1999) demonstrates the significance of a large body of post-contact aboriginal artistic material, challenging the academic negligence of this material as 'inauthentic'. Significantly, she notes the ways in which the production, consumption and circulation of northeastern souvenir art allowed Indigenous North Americans to actively negotiate and rework notions of 'indigeneity' by producing images of themselves which circulated widely in the new colonial world (see also Hays-Gilpin Chapter 8). By producing material which had mass market appeal, Native American tourist art allowed indigenous imagery and craft techniques a persistence in the new colonial world; on the other hand, in buying and sometimes imitating 'Indian' imagery, colonisers and settlers naturalised their own identities as North Americans which allowed them to justify themselves as the rightful heirs and successors to Indigenous Americans. Clearly Phillip's work has important implications for the Oceanic region, but few specific studies of tourist art have been carried out in this geographic area (but see Torrence 1993, 2000; O'Hanlon 1999; Gosden and Knowles 2001; papers in Herle et al. 2002; Taçon et al. 2003; Gosden 2004; also see Torrence and Clarke Chapter 2; Davies Chapter 4; Philp Chapter 12).

Tost and Rohu Curio Dealers/Tyrells Museum: A Case Study

The early history of Sydney-based curio dealer Tost and Rohu has been well documented in terms of the role of women taxidermists in colonial Sydney (University of Sydney 2008). Jane Tost and her daughter Ada Rohu were professional taxidermists who worked in Australia between 1856 and 1900. Coming from a renowned family of English taxidermists, Jane Tost immigrated with her family to Tasmania in 1856, working on a casual basis for museums in Hobart and Sydney, having previously worked on taxidermy assignments for the British Museum. Jane's daughter Ada also took up the family craft, and together they founded a taxidermy business in Sydney in 1872, which operated from 1872 to the 1930s, first trading under the name 'Tost and Coates Fancy Work Depot and Taxidermy Studio', and in 1881 with Ada's marriage to the naturalist Henry Rohu, under the name 'Tost and Rohu'. Despite their critical success in taxidermy which won them a number of awards and prizes at exhibitions between 1860 and 1893, towards the end of the nine-teenth century, Tost and Rohu became increasingly involved in the sale of furs and curio items (University of Sydney 2008). This has been attributed to the influence of Henry Rohu, who was a naturalist involved in the collection of ethnographic objects, and who collected ethnographic objects from northern Australia from the 1870s (University of Sydney 2008; Davies 2002: 84).

By 1901, Tost and Rohu had developed into a curiosity shop with a museum in the space upstairs and was managed by Willis B Coates, Ada's son from her first marriage (University of Sydney 2008). At this time, it was trading under the name 'Tost and Rohu Taxidermists, Furriers, Tanners and Island Curio Dealers', noting:

> We hold the largest stock in Australia of genuine Native Implements and Curiosities from all parts of Australasia and the Pacific Islands. Land and Sea Shells in every variety. Carved Emu Eggs, Boomerangs, Fur Skins and Mats, Lyre Bird Tails and other beautiful Souvenirs (Advertisement in 1901 edition of Sands Directory [Sands 1901]; see Fig. 3.1).

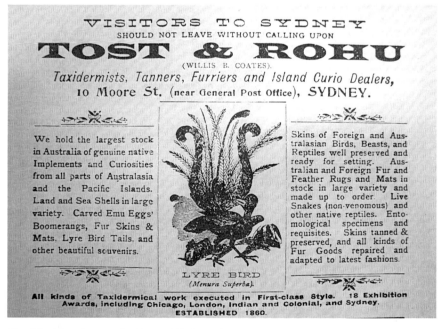

Fig. 3.1 Advertisement for Tost and Rohu which appeared in the Sands Business Directory in 1901 (Courtesy of the Australian Museum Research Library)

In August 1923, the collections of Tost and Rohu were purchased by bookseller James Tyrell, owner of Tyrells Bookshop and Antique Dealers. The curio shop and museum subsequently traded under the name 'Tyrells Museum' (Tyrells Museum

1929). The curio business seems to have been phased out of Tyrells' operations by the late 1930s.

A series of catalogues were produced by Tost and Rohu in the early 1920s (Tost and Rohu n.d. a, n.d. b), and an extensive catalogue documenting what appears to be its complete ethnographic collection following its acquisition of the Tost and Rohu collection was produced by Tyrells Museum in 1929 (Tyrells Museum 1929). The catalogues, alongside advertisements placed in Sands Sydney Business Directory and the Australian Museum Magazine (see Figs. 3.1 and 3.2), show that the principle market for the curio dealer was a souvenir market of tourists and amateur collectors. The catalogues describe aspects of the collection alongside detailed descriptions of the objects and their role in indigenous societies. The emphasis is on the *peculiarity* of the objects and their particular association with the indigenous cultures of Australia and the Pacific Islands.

> We have absolutely the greatest and most complete collection of genuine Australasian and Island Curios, in the World, the extent and variety of this unique collection, comprising, as it does, Native Weapons, Implements, Ornaments (Personal, Ceremonial, and Magical), and the many other curiosities peculiar to the Savage in his native element, gathered from all parts of Australia and the innumerable Islands of the South Pacific . . . all purchases will be carefully packed (free) and forwarded to any part of the world (Tost and Rohu n.d. a: 2).

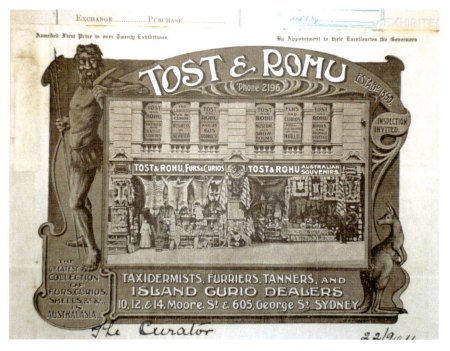

Fig. 3.2 Detail of letter dated 1919 showing letterhead with photograph of Tost and Rohu Museum and Show-Rooms with the sign 'Australian Souvenirs' (Courtesy of the Australian Museum Research Library, Australian Museum Archives, AMS 9: 1911/T26)

The fact that Tost and Rohu and Tyrells Museum were targeted at the tourist market at such an early date is itself a revelation. We tend to think of tourism, particularly in the Australasian region, as a relatively recent phenomenon, however as various Australian historians have noted, there was an early tradition of tourism both from Great Britain as well as within Australia (White 2005). Indeed, production of souvenirs for trade began almost as soon as permanent European contacts were established in the region, well before the 'collecting craze' began, as demonstrated by McBryde's (2000) study of cross-cultural material exchanges at Port Jackson in New South Wales in the late eighteenth and early nineteenth centuries and O'Hanlon's (1999) work on 'man-catchers' from New Guinea in the nineteenth century. This long history of interest in the exchange of indigenous material goods as souvenirs, coupled with a reasonable volume of official visitation from Great Britain up until the time of Federation (and to a lesser extent after Federation) meant that there was a burgeoning tourist market in Sydney in the late nineteenth and early twentieth centuries. Alongside the international mail order market to collectors, museum curators and antiquarians, this sustained the curio business for Tost and Rohu and Tyrells Museum over the course of more than 70 years.

The Catalogues

Three sale catalogues from Tost and Rohu and Tyrells Museum have been located. The first two catalogues are undated but appear to have been produced in the early 1920s (Tost and Rohu n.d. a, n.d. b). The third catalogue was produced by Tyrells Museum in 1929 following the acquisition of the Tost and Rohu collection (Tyrells Museum 1929). In this chapter, I focus on the 1929 Tyrells Museum catalogue as it is the most detailed and allows a quantitative analysis of the objects which were being made available for sale.

The Tyrells Museum catalogue, *Australian Aborigines and South Sea Islanders Implements, Weapons and Curios*, is a lavishly illustrated 40 page catalogue which lists over 551 ethnographic items for sale, along with original photographs of 'Australian Aboriginals, also the Natives of New Guinea, Solomon Islands, Tonga, Fiji, Samoa, New Hebrides and other islands', books related to Australian and Pacific natural history and ethnology, postcards, and collections of 'bird skins' (Fig. 3.3). The catalogue is composed of descriptions of a series of numbered artefacts, organised according to location (Fig. 3.4). It is illustrated throughout with images from what is now known as the Tyrell Collection (Fig. 3.5). This consists of 7903 glass plate negatives taken by Charles Kerry (1857–1928) and Henry King (1855–1923), who ran two of Sydney's most important photographic studios in the late nineteenth and early twentieth centuries. Study of Tyrells and Tost and Rohu correspondence indicates that this collection was offered for sale to the Australian Museum by Tost and Rohu on at least two occasions. The collection was ultimately bought by James Tyrrell in 1929 alongside the ethnographic collections. The collection was kept intact and eventually sold in 1980 to Australian Consolidated Press,

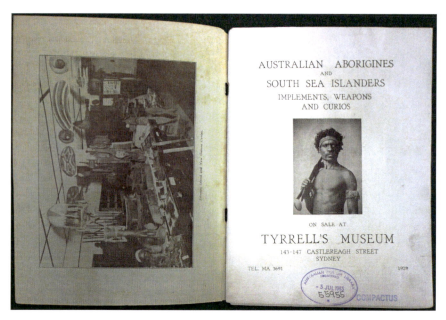

Fig. 3.3 Inside front cover of *Australian Aborigines and South Sea Islanders Implements, Weapons and Curios* (Tyrells Museum 1929, courtesy of the Australian Museum Research Library)

Fig. 3.4 'Interior of Tyrrell's bookshop and a fish shop in Sydney, ca. 1925' (Courtesy of the Buchanan Family and the Mitchell Library, State Library of NSW, PXB 365)

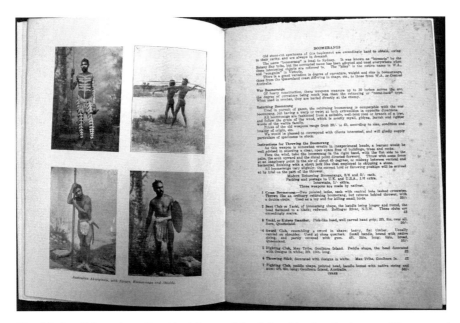

Fig. 3.5 Detail from *Australian Aborigines and South Sea Islanders Implements, Weapons and Curios* showing use of Charles Kerry photographs to illustrate text (Tyrells Museum 1929, courtesy of the Australian Museum Research Library)

who donated it to the Powerhouse Museum in 1985. These photographs were produced for sale as prints or postcards, so their role in the catalogue is twofold—to advertise the postcards for sale and also to make connections between the objects described and the indigenous people featured in the photographs.

The catalogues draw together the natural and cultural world through the placement of images such as mounted moths or platypi opposite lists of ethnographic objects, emphasising the natural and cultural collections as inherent outcomes of the same process of colonial assembling. The tendency for museums to reassemble and 'naturalise' ethnographic objects by way of display has been noted by many authors (e.g. Griffiths 1996; Russell 2001b). This process is also clear from the way in which Tost and Rohu, for example, displayed animal skins alongside ethnographic artefacts as 'Australian Souvenirs' in their shop window display (see Fig. 3.2). However, we should not assume that this would be the norm. Prior to the acquisition of the Tost and Rohu collection, for example, Tyrells Museum seems to have functioned primarily as a bookshop and antique dealer, which is reflected in their mode of display of ethnographic objects amongst the bookshelves in the image shown in Fig. 3.4. The display and sale of animal and bird skins alongside the ethnographic collection seems to relate more to Tost and Rohu as a business than to be a function of the colonial curio dealer in general terms, although it seems significant that both ethnographic objects and animal and bird skins became subsumed within the class of souvenir in the context of this shop and that this idea came to dominate the mode of representation within the Tyrells Museum catalogue.

The catalogue lists most items for sale individually, alongside a price and description, however in some cases where large numbers of individual items are held, the objects are not listed individually and a guideline price range is listed instead. Table 3.1 shows the attributed provenance of individual artefacts listed in the catalogue, in the order in which they are listed. The figure for Australia is almost certainly lower than the actual number of artefacts held, as several artefact classes (boomerangs, shields, message sticks, spears, spear throwers, glass and stone Kimberley points, fire sticks, millstones, 'Chilara' headbands and pearl shell/clam shell pendants) are not listed individually. Indeed, it appears from the number of boomerangs shown in the catalogue itself that many boomerangs were available for sale at Tyrells Museum (see Fig. 3.6). Nonetheless, the table gives a reasonably good indication of the geographic 'spread' of items for sale, with the bulk from Australia, British New Guinea, the Solomon Islands and Fiji.

Table 3.1 Provenance of items listed for sale in *Australian Aborigines and South Sea Islanders Implements, Weapons and Curios* (Tyrells Museum 1929)

Provenance	Number (n)	Percent (%)
Australia	104	18.87
NZ	26	4.72
Fiji	53	9.62
Samoa	6	1.09
New Guinea	194	35.21
Solomon Islands	76	13.79
New Caledonia	7	1.27
New Hebrides	8	1.45
Trobriand Islands	6	1.09
Admiralty Islands	27	4.90
New Britain and New Ireland	15	2.72
Santa Cruz	6	1.09
Gilbert Island	7	1.27
Matty Island	13	2.36
Other	3	0.54
Total	551	100

It is possible to break the individual artefact types into various 'classes' of artefact to get an impression of the nature of the objects available for sale in the catalogue (see Table 3.2). While weapons, including spears, clubs and paddles are the most dominant items in the collection (at around 32%), items of body adornment, including masks, headbands, armbands and other items of clothing and body decoration make up the next highest class of items offered for sale (at 25%). Tools, including adzes and stone axes, make up the third most numerous class of object offered for sale at around 14%. Other items including items of religious paraphernalia, musical items (drums, pipes), containers (including Kava bowls) and textiles make up the bulk of the remainder of the items available for sale in the catalogue.

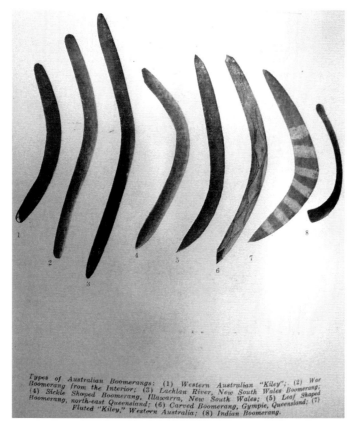

Fig. 3.6 One of the few pictures of artefacts in the catalogue showing 'Types of Australian Boomerangs' in *Australian Aborigines and South Sea Islanders Implements, Weapons and Curios* (Tyrells Museum 1929, courtesy of the Australian Museum Research Library)

Table 3.2 Number of 'types' of items listed for sale in *Australian Aborigines and South Sea Islanders Implements, Weapons and Curios* (Tyrells Museum 1929)

Type	Number (n)	Percent (%)
Body adornment	138	25.05
Weapons/paddles	174	31.58
Tools	79	14.34
Carved wooden items	37	6.72
Religious paraphernalia/Musical items	40	7.26
Containers	25	4.54
Textiles	32	5.81
Other	26	4.72
Total	551	100

Table 3.3 Numbers of most numerous items listed for sale in *Australian Aborigines and South Sea Islanders Implements, Weapons and Curios* (Tyrells Museum 1929)

Artefact type	Number (n)	Percent (%)
Boomerang*	7	1.27
Bull roarer	3	0.54
Shield*	20	3.63
Club	82	14.88
Spear*	26	4.72
Adze/Adze blade/Axe	34	6.17
Necklace	38	6.90
Shell armband	30	5.44
Pearl/Clam shell ornament*	21	3.81
Paddle	36	6.53
Comb	16	2.90
Feather/string/flax bag	13	2.36
Forehead ornament/mask	17	3.09
Wooden bowl	19	3.45
Other	189	34.30
Total	551	100

Those marked with an asterisk (*) include artefact classes which were available in such high numbers that they were not listed individually in parts of the catalogue

Table 3.3 lists the most frequently occurring individual items of material culture listed in the catalogue and their contribution by percentage to the overall total number of items for sale. Several of these items, such as boomerangs, are not always listed individually, so their percentage contribution has to be considered an underestimate. Indeed, a list of those items which are shown to be 'too numerous to mention' individually in the catalogue probably represents a list of the most popular sale items, including Australian boomerangs, shields from Australia and Melanesia, spears from Australia, Melanesia and the Pacific, and pearl shell and clam shell ornaments. Carved wooden clubs and paddles make up the most numerous classes of individually mentioned items, along with shell necklaces of different types.

There is, as would be expected, an inverse relationship between the cost of individual items and their frequency of occurrence within the catalogue. The cheapest items in the catalogue include 'modern' Australian boomerangs (3/6 to 5/–), stone and glass Kimberley points (5/– each), Trochus shell bracelets (5/– each) from New Guinea and the Admiralty Islands and shell armbands from the Solomon Islands (5/–1 to 10/– each). The most expensive individual items for sale included Kava bowls from New Guinea at a price of £10 and a 'rare feather money belt' from the Santa Cruz Islands for £50. Indeed, particular items must have remained continuously in stock, as in 1911 Tost and Rohu advertised 'special offers' on their letterhead paper of 'Boomerangs at 1/6, Nulla Nulla at 2/6, set of bow and arrows at 2/6 and woomerah at 3/6' (Australian Museum Archives, AMS 9: 1911/T28).

Interactions Between Tost and Rohu, Tyrells Museum and the Australian Museum

Archives relating to the purchase and exchange of items between Tost and Rohu, Tyrells Museum and the Australian Museum are held by the Australian Museum in Sydney. Unfortunately, to date it has been impossible to locate archives relating to the sale of objects from Tost and Rohu to tourists and collectors which would allow the sort of network analysis performed by Gosden et al. (2007) and Larson et al. (2007). However, by focussing on the nature of the interactions between the Australian Museum and Tost and Rohu and Tyrells, as well as the network itself and the role of curio objects within it, it is possible to explore the nature of the associations between various forms of colonial souvenir and the place of the curio and curio seller as an alternate node in the network of relations mapped out by Bennett (2008b, 2010). Before moving on to discuss this alternate actor-network and the nature of the interactions which it embodies, I will describe the archives and the objects themselves in more detail.

The Australian Museum Archives holds copies of correspondence and artefact schedules which document a number of purchases and exchanges made with Tost and Rohu and Tyrells Museum over the period 1872–1930. This correspondence documents not only successful exchanges but also requests from Tost and Rohu for particular items to purchase or exchange from the Museum and offers of objects for sale by Tost and Rohu and Tyrells which were subsequently rejected. The letters are summarised in Table 3.4. Requests from Tost and Rohu include a 'Tasmanian Wolf', 'Kangaroo and Emu skins', 'fishing hooks, boomerangs, lime knives', 'Aboriginal and South Sea Island skulls, Platypus specimens, an Eagle, old returning boomerangs', 'post cards' and 'stuffed specimens'. In one exchange they received 26 boomerangs and a stuffed Wedgetailed Eagle, while in another they received a number of shell fish hooks, boomerangs and lime knives. Items offered for sale to the Museum include skulls and other skeletal remains from Papua New Guinea and Australia. Purchases of large numbers of items were made by the Museum in 1923 (at the time that Tost and Rohu closed their business) and 1929, but reasonably regular purchases and exchanges occurred throughout the period 1872–1930. The items requested for purchase and exchange from the Museum to Tost and Rohu and Tyrells again seem to reflect those items in most demand within the shops, being boomerangs, fish hooks and lime knives, although it seems interesting that nulla nullas, woomerahs, spears and clubs were not requested. This might indicate that sufficient supplies of these objects were generally available direct from the curio dealer's network of buyers. The correspondence with the Museum reveals that Tost and Rohu received items from a wide network of semi-professional field collectors, antiquarians and enthusiasts who would either ship material to the seller on request or offer the items for sale in person at their shop. Clearly, some of these field collectors were the same as those used by the Australian Museum and other museums, however, it appears that the network represented by these sources was far larger and more diverse, taking in not only those who traditionally dealt with museums but also members of the general public and amateur collectors and antiquarians, as well as other curio sellers.

Table 3.4 Summary of correspondence between Australian Museum and Tost and Rohu/Tyrells Museum offering specimens for sale or exchange

Date	Offered for sale	Purchased	Requested	Exchanged
1872	85 Bird specimens	Yes	–	No
1878	3 American Squirrel skins	Yes	–	No
1890	Mummy	No	–	No
1895	Various ethnographic items (unlisted)	No	Tasmanian Wolf	No
1898	Lizards	?	–	?
1904	Three skulls	Yes	–	?
1909	Wooden Sarcophagus containing chief's skeleton and model of chief's house	Yes	–	?
1910	Maori cloak, ceremonial board, clam shell armlets, Kangaroo Rat	No	Kangaroo and Emu skin	Yes
1911	Maori carvings	No	–	No
1911	Aboriginal remains from Gunnedah	No	–	No
1911			Fishing hooks, boomerangs, lime knives	Yes
1913	Gilbert Island helmet	Yes	–	No
1914	Old guns	No	–	No
1919	35 Ethnographic specimens from the Markham district	No	–	No
1919	Portraits of Aboriginal people and Tapa cloth given to M Vardy by Premier of Tonga in 1918	No	–	No
1920	12 Clubs, boomerangs, paddles etc.	Yes	–	No
1923	Large ethnographic and osteological collection, 144 items	Yes	–	No
1924	14 Ethnographic items	No	26 Boomerangs and 1 stuffed Wedgetailed Eagle	Yes
1925	–	No	Aboriginal and South Sea Island skulls, Platypus specimens, an Eagle, old returning boomerangs	No
1926	–	Yes	Postcards	No
1927	–	No	Stuffed specimens	No
1929	Large ethnographic collection (148 items) offered for sale	Yes	–	No
1929	Large photographic collection by Charles Kerry and Co	No	–	No
1929	Bird skin collection of 171 'skins'	No	–	No
1930	Mineral collection	Yes	–	?
1930	Negatives from collection of Pacific missionary Dr G Brown	Yes	–	No

Information is based on Australian Museum Archives Purchase Schedules Series 55 item reference numbers 22/1912, 4/1923 and 3/1924; Exchange Schedules Series 62 item reference number 47/1910; Correspondence Series 10 item reference numbers 727, 78.1 and 78.12; and Correspondence Series 9 item reference numbers 1904/T24, 1907/R40, 1907/794; 1907/T3, 1907/795, 1909/T37, 1909/912, 1910/T2, 1910/23, 1910/T41, 1910/836, 1911/16, 1911/T26, 1911/28, 193/T34, 1913-9/9/13, 1914/T40, 1920/T11, 1920/T31, 1920/T36, 1923/T29, 1923/48, 1924/T3, 1924/T12, 1924/T29, 1925/T3, 1925/T13, 1925/T21, 1926/T50, 1927/78, 1929/27, 1929/43, 1929/78, 1929/435, 1930/193 and 1930/572

Amongst the items purchased by the Australian Museum, it currently holds 118 ethnographic objects acquired from Tost and Rohu over the period 1886–1925 and at least 21 items purchased from Tyrells Museum between 1911 and 1930 (note the catalogue lists 42 items from Tyrells in total, a number of which have been de-accessioned). These objects are incredibly diverse, ranging from Australian stone axes and boomerangs to Melanesian clubs and skeletal material. The objects themselves attest to their advertisement and sale as curio items, many of them still having shop sale or price stickers adhering to them (see Fig. 3.7). The geographic spread of items from Tost and Rohu held by the Australian Museum reflects the general spread of items from the Tyrells Museum catalogue, with the bulk of the material coming from Melanesia and Australia (see Table 3.5), as does the spread of material across the various classes of item (Table 3.6). The most numerous items held by the Australian Museum which were acquired from Tost and Rohu and Tyrells are clubs, paddles, boomerangs and various head and arm ornaments. Again, this spread of items is similar to that shown in the catalogue overall.

Fig. 3.7 Clam shell adze head from Matty Island purchased from Tost and Rohu in 1923, showing Tost and Rohu Museum sticker (The Australian Museum E028233, photograph taken by the author, courtesy of The Australian Museum)

Curio Sellers as an Alternate Node in the Colonial Museum's Actor-Network

An analysis of the objects in the collection which derive from purchases and exchanges with Tost and Rohu and Tyrells Museum demonstrates the ways in which these curio objects were involved in the reassembling and reformulation of colonial governmental knowledge practices which Bennett (2008b, 2010) discusses with reference to ethnographic collections. For example, the shark's tooth flaying knife from Queensland (E9947) which was purchased from Tost and Rohu in 1901 formed

Table 3.5 Provenance of Tyrells and Tost and Rohu items held in the Australian Museum ethnographic collections

Area	Locality	Number of items	Percent
Australia	Australia	34	24.46
Torres Strait	Torres Strait	4	2.88
Melanesia	PNG/Gulf	24	17.27
Melanesia	New Britain	8	5.76
Melanesia	Admiralty Islands	7	5.04
Melanesia	Santa Cruz Islands	1	0.72
Melanesia	New Caledonia	6	4.32
Melanesia	New Hebrides	15	10.79
Melanesia	Solomon Islands	2	1.44
Melanesia	Matty Island	16	11.51
Melanesia	St Matthais Island	2	1.44
Micronesia	Caroline Islands	5	3.60
Micronesia	Gilbert Islands	3	2.16
Polynesia	Savage Island	3	2.16
Polynesia	Hawaii	1	0.72
Polynesia	New Zealand	3	2.16
Other	Other	5	3.60
	Total	139	100.00

Table 3.6 Number of 'types' of items of Tyrells and Tost and Rohu items held in the Australian Museum ethnographic collections

Type	Number	Percent
Body adornment	35	25.18
Weapons/paddles	56	40.29
Tools	26	18.71
Carved wooden items	6	4.32
Religious paraphernalia/Musical items	3	2.16
Containers	5	3.60
Textiles	2	1.44
Other	6	4.32
Total	139	100.00

the subject of an article by Etheridge in the *Records of the Australian Museum* in 1902 (Etheridge 1902), while the shovel from NSW purchased in 1923 (E28274) was featured in the same journal in a section of an article by Thorpe in 1928 on 'Aboriginal scoops or shovels' (Thorpe 1928) (see Fig. 3.8). Here we see an illustration of the circulation of reference discussed by Bennett in which objects are assembled together and 'institutionally processed' in ways that shaped new forms of interaction between objects, allowing for intervention on the part of new agents, in

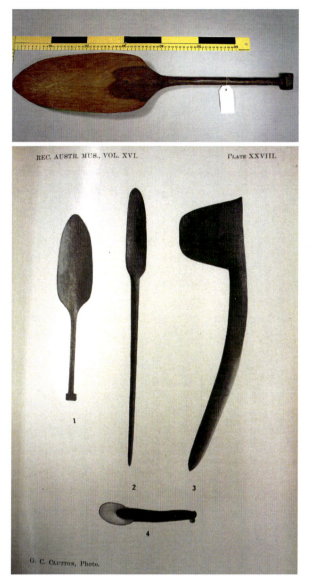

Fig. 3.8 NSW wooden shovel E28274 purchased in 1923 from Tost and Rohu (above, photograph taken by the author, courtesy of The Australian Museum) and the image of the shovel featured in Thorpe's article in *Records of the Australian Museum* in 1928 (below, labelled '1', courtesy of the Australian Museum Research Library)

new colonial contexts. We also see evidence of objects moving through the Museum, being institutionally processed, and then reformulated as curios or souvenirs through sale or exchange to the curio seller, for example the 26 boomerangs which Tyrells Museum received in exchange in 1924.

Souveniring and Creating Empire

In the same way in which Stewart (1993) suggests that souvenirs should be understood to relate to personal memory and are used to recreate a sense of self through object-centred life history telling, I suggest that at a collective level, colonial souveniring might be understood as part of a process of creating a new conception of Empire. It is worth reflecting on the spaces where many of these souvenirs came to rest—in collections displayed with other souvenirs in halls, billiard rooms and libraries in Britain and elsewhere throughout the colonies (see further discussion in Torrence and Clarke Chapter 2). In the same way that Bennett (2008b, 2010) suggests relationships between museum objects are only developed once the material is taken from the field and assembled in new ways with material from other expeditions and considered as a *collection*, souvenirs also cease to function until they are taken back 'home' and made to tell a story about individual travel. The nature of these souvenirs—in particular, the close association of natural and ethnographic objects with books, and the wide geographic provenance of these items which focuses almost exclusively on the British colonies—can subsequently be *reassembled* and reformulated to tell a story of the dominance of Empire within the colonies. These souvenirs represent 'splinters of memory' (c.f. Leslie 1999) of the colonial world. Curio sellers are nodes in a network that connected colonial outposts with colonial metropoles as distribution points not only for objects but also for *ideas* about Empire, indigenous people and the natural world. Such objects not only re-enforced ideas of technological superiority and power but also helped to shape and create a vision of Empire and the fundamentally *material* basis of colonialism.

It is clear that such souveniring not only created the Empire 'at home' but also created 'the colony' among expatriate collectors in Australia, who also collected souvenirs and ethnographic artefacts and displayed them within the home (e.g. Griffiths 1996). At the same time that these objects were being used to create Empire in the metropolis, a new conception of the colony and the colonised was also being produced by the same material process of souveniring and collection. The movement of souvenirs from one colony to the next re-enforced the idea of the Empire as a vast colonial network through which objects travelled, ideas were transferred and governance enacted. Rethinking the process of souveniring and collection using this network metaphor shifts our focus away from the acts of production to the new formulations of colonialism which were being enacted both at the peripheries of Empire as well as at its centre.

Future Directions: Indigenous Agency and Colonial Curios

The study of the catalogues and correspondence between the Australian Museum and Tost and Rohu/Tyrells Museum allows us to identify a number of objects which could be considered to be 'mass produced' colonial curios in the same way that Kimberley Points can (Harrison 2004, 2006); that is they were produced by indigenous people in large enough numbers to meet an external curio market which extended beyond practical demand. These include boomerangs, nulla-nullas, woomerahs, bows and arrows, *Trochus* and clam shell armbands and bracelets, clubs, shields and spears. We might expand this list to include other popular items from the catalogue such as pearl and clam shell pendants and lime knives and gourds. A more detailed focus on the contexts of production of these objects would allow us to determine the extent to which their manufacture might be considered to conform to the model shown to exist with reference to Kimberley Points in Australia and to attempt to track in more details some of the networks of trade and exchange which existed in the local areas in which these objects were produced.

Clearly if material culture and technology constitutes a form of mediation between people and the world, colonial material cultures have a critical role to play in helping us to understand the lived experience of colonialism, the ways in which power is mediated and subverted and the agency of indigenous people in colonial encounters. The concept of indigenous agency acts as a fulcrum for this investigation, and while the role of market feedback in changes in artefact form, for example, is clearly an important area of research, the focus on agency also allows a more detailed study of producers and the contexts of production, an area which has generally been overlooked in museum studies (Torrence 1993, 2000; Byrne et al. Chapter 1).

It is important that any future research attempts to unpack the dichotomy between the two categories of collection and souvenir which previous work on collecting as a colonial phenomenon has established. Clearly, individual souvenirs and collected objects may shift between these two contexts of function of metonymy and metaphor in colonial society. Collections of souvenirs may be donated to museums to form the basis of museum collections and/or move out of academic favour and be sold by museums into private collections, while people who were once amateur collectors may later become museum curators. Museums themselves are clearly diverse, and are established under different circumstances with different collection philosophies. While it has only scratched the surface, this chapter has begun to uncover a picture which is far more diverse, and also far more interesting, and one which may shed more light on the agency of indigenous people in colonial encounters. In turn, such studies can be used to theorise more broadly and to contribute to existing work on the nature of ethnographic objects and their relationship with forms of colonial governance (Bennett 2005, 2007, 2008a, b, 2009, 2010). The relationship between *local* objects and *global* contexts must form the basis for such an analysis, as suggested by the work of Latour (2005) and ANT more generally.

Conclusions

As Gosden (2004: 6) notes, 'colonialism is the major cultural fact of the last 500 years, and to some extent of the last 5000 years, although it is said we now live in a post-colonial world … we are still wrestling with the economic, intellectual and social consequences … by looking at the varying forms power can take we can

learn much about the past and unlearn much about the present'. Contemporary settlers and indigenous people throughout Australasia and the Pacific live each day with
the economic and social consequences of a colonial past; indeed, colonial processes
should be seen as continuing in the modern world (a point made rather eloquently
in Torrence and Clarke 2000a). As such, an understanding of colonialism is of critical importance in the present, but particularly to the programme of reconciling
indigenous and non-indigenous peoples in a postcolonial world. In the same way
that colonialism continues in contemporary global economic and social processes,
the process of negotiation between indigenous artisans and the non-indigenous souvenir trade market is not one which is locked in the past, but continues in the modern
indigenous art and souvenir market. Understanding the nature of colonial souvenirs
and the varied actor-networks which they formulated in the late nineteenth and early
twentieth centuries has the potential to reveal the 'prehistory' of this art market,
which may in turn help us better understand not only colonial processes but also contemporary negotiations between collectors, souvenir markets and indigenous people
in the postcolonial world.

Acknowledgements I thank Robin Torrence, Stan Florek, Rose Docker, Barrina South, Vanessa
Finney and Leone Lemmer for their assistance with access to archival material and collections at
the Australian Museum and for facilitating permission to publish archival images and photographs
of objects from the Australian Museum collection. I also thank Di Jackson at the State Library of
NSW for facilitating permission to publish images from the Mitchell Library collection, and the
Buchanan Family for waiving the usual reproduction fees. I thank Tony Bennett for permission to
make reference to his unpublished conference paper 'Making and Mobilising Worlds: Museum,
Field, Colony and the Circulation of Reference'. Like many other chapters in this volume, this
chapter was originally presented in the session 'Unpacking the Collection' at the Sixth World
Archaeological Congress in Dublin in 2008. I thank Sarah Byrne, Robin Torrence, Anne Clarke
and all the participants in the session for their helpful comments on revising the conference paper
for publication.

References

Alberti, Benjamin and Tamara L. Bray
    2009 Introduction to Special Section 'Animating Archaeology: Of Subjects, Objects and
    Alternative Ontologies'. *Cambridge Archaeological Journal* 19(3): 337–343.

Baudrillard, Jean
    1968 *Le Système des Objects.* Gallimard, Paris.
    1994 The System of Collecting. In *The Culture of Collecting: From Elvis to Antiques—Why
    do we Collect Things?*, edited by John Elsner and Roger Cardinal, pp. 7–24. Melbourne
    University Press, Melbourne.

Belk, Richard
    1995 *Collecting in a Consumer Society.* Routledge, London and New York.

Bennett, Tony
    2005 Civic Laboratories: Museums, Cultural Objecthood and the Governance of the Social.
    Cultural Studies 19(5): 521–547.
    2007 The Work of Culture. *Cultural Sociology* 1(1): 31–47.

2008a *Anthropological Assemblages: Producing Culture as a Surface of Government*. CRESC Working Paper No. 52. Centre for Research on Socio-Cultural Change, The Open University, Milton Keynes.

2008b Making and Mobilising Worlds: Museum, Field, Colony and the Circulation of Reference. Unpublished seminar paper for the CRESC Museums and Social Transformation Workshop, University of Manchester, 14th March 2008.

2009 Museum, Field, Colony: Colonial Governmentality and the Circulation of Reference. *Journal of Cultural Economy* 2(1–2): 99–116.

2010 Making and Mobilising Worlds: Assembling and Governing the Other. In *Material Powers: Cultural Studies, History and the Material Turn*, edited by Tony Bennett and Patrick Joyce, pp. 188–208. Routledge, London.

Bhabha, Homi
1994 *The Location of Culture*. Routledge, London and New York.

Clifford, James
1988 *The Predicament of Culture*. Harvard University Press, Cambridge, MA.
1997 *Routes: Travel and Translation in the Late Twentieth Century*. Harvard University Press, Cambridge.

Davies, Susan
2002 *Collected: 150 Years of Aboriginal Art and Artefacts at the Macleay Museum*. The Macleay Museum, University of Sydney, Sydney.

Etheridge, Robert J., Jr.
1902 An Aboriginal Knife. *Records of the Australian Museum* 4(5): 207–208.

Fabian, Johannes
1983 *Time and the Other: How Anthropology Makes its Object*. Columbia University Press, New York, NY.

Gell, Alfred
1994 The Enchantment of Technology and the Technology of Enchantment. In *Anthropology, Art and Aesthetics*, edited by Jeremy Coote and Anthony Shelton, pp. 40–67. Oxford University Press, Oxford.
1996 Vogel's Net: Traps as Artworks and Artworks as Traps. *Journal of Material Culture* 1(1): 15–38.
1998 *Art and Agency*. Oxford University Press, Oxford.

Given, Michael
2004 *The Archaeology of the Colonized*. Routledge, London and New York.

Gosden, Chris
2004 *Archaeology and Colonialism: Cultural Contact from 5000BC to the Present*. Cambridge University Press, Cambridge.

Gosden, Chris and Chantal Knowles
2001 *Collecting Colonialism: Material Culture and Colonial Change*. Berg, Oxford and New York.

Gosden, Chris and Frances Larsen with Alison Petch
2007 *Knowing Things: Exploring the Collections at the Pitt Rivers Museum 1884–1945*. Oxford University Press, Oxford.

Griffiths, Tom
1996 *Hunters and Collectors: The Antiquarian Imagination in Australia*. Cambridge University Press, Melbourne.

Haber, Alejandro F.
  2009 Animism, Relatedness, Life: Post-Western Perspectives. *Cambridge Archaeological Journal* 19(3): 418–430.

Harrison, Rodney
  2004 Kimberley Points and Colonial Preference: New Insights into the Chronology of Pressure-flaked Point Forms from the Southeast Kimberley, Western Australia. *Archaeology in Oceania* 39(1): 1–11.
  2006 An Artefact of Colonial Desire? Kimberley Points and the Technologies of Enchantment. *Current Anthropology* 47(1): 63–88.
  2010 Stone Artefacts. In *The Oxford Handbook of Material Culture Studies*, edited by Dan Hicks and Mary C. Beaudry, pp. 515–536. Oxford University Press, Oxford.

Harrison, Rodney and Deborah Bird Rose
  2010 Intangible Heritage. In *Understanding Heritage and Memory*, edited by Tim Benton, pp. 238–276. Manchester University Press in association with the Open University, Manchester and Milton Keynes.

Harvey, Graham
  2006 *Animism*. Columbia University Press, New York, NY.

Herle, Anita
  1998 The Life Histories of Objects: Collections of the Cambridge Anthropological Expedition to the Torres Strait. In *Cambridge and the Torres Strait: Centenary Essays on the 1898 Anthropological Expedition*, edited by Anita Herle and Sandra Rouse, pp. 77–105. Cambridge University Press, Cambridge.

Herle, Anita, Nick Stanley, Karen Stevenson, and Robert L. Welsch (editors)
  2002 *Pacific Arts: Persistence, Change and Meaning*. University of Hawaii Press, Hawaii.

Larson, Frances, Alison Petch, and David Zeitlyn
  2007 Social Networks and the Creation of the Pitt Rivers Museum. *Journal of Material Culture* 12(3): 211–239.

Latour, Bruno
  1993 *We Have Never Been Modern*. Harvard University Press, Cambridge, MA.
  1999 *Pandora's Hope: Essays on the Reality of Science Studies*. Harvard University Press, Cambridge, MA.
  2005 *Reassembling the Social: An introduction to Actor-Network Theory*. Oxford University Press, Oxford and New York.

Law, John
  2008 Actor-Network Theory and Material Semiotics. In *The New Blackwell Companion to Social Theory* (3rd Edition), edited by Bryan S. Turner, pp. 141–158. Blackwell, Oxford.

Law, John and John Hassard (editors)
  1999 *Actor Network Theory and After*. Blackwell, Oxford.

Lawson, Barbara
  1994 *Collected Curios: Missionary Tales from the South Seas*. McGill University Libraries, Montreal.

Leach, James
  2007 Differentiation and Encompassment: A Critique of Alfred Gell's Theory of the Abduction of Agency. In *Thinking Through Things: Theorising Artefacts Ethnographically*, edited by Amiria Henare, Martin Holbraad and Sari Wastell, pp. 167–188. Routledge, London and New York.

Leslie, Esther
  1999 Souvenirs and Forgetting: Walter Benjamin's Memory-Work. In *Material Memories: Design and Evocation*, edited by Marius Kwint, Christopher Breward, and Jeremy Aynsley, pp. 107–22. Berg, Oxford.

Liebmann, Matthew and Uzma Z. Rizvi (editors)
  2008 *Archaeology and the Postcolonial Critique*. AltaMira Press, Lanham, MD.

McBryde, Isobel
  2000 'Barter ... Immediately Commenced to the Satisfaction of Both Parties': Cross-cultural Exchange at Port Jackson, 1788–1828. In *The Archaeology of Difference: Negotiating Cross-Cultural Engagements in Oceania*, edited by Robin Torrence and Anne Clarke, pp. 238–277. Routledge, London and New York.

O'Hanlon, Michael
  1999 'Mostly Harmless'? Missionaries, Administrators and Material Culture on the Coast of British New Guinea. *Journal of the Anthropological Institute* 5: 377–397.
  2000 Introduction. In *Hunting the Gatherers: Ethnographic Collectors, Agents and Agency in Melanesia, 1870s–1930s*, edited by Michael O'Hanlon and Robert L. Welsh, pp. 1–34. Berghahn Books, New York and Oxford.

O'Hanlon, Michael and Robert L. Welsch (editors)
  2000 *Hunting the Gatherers: Ethnographic Collectors, Agents and Agency in Melanesia, 1870s–1930s*. Berghahn Books, New York and Oxford.

Phillips, Ruth B.
  1997 *Trading Identities: The Souvenir in Native North American Art from the Northeast, 1700–1900*. McGill-Queen's University Press, Washington, DC.

Phillips, Ruth B. and Christopher B. Steiner (editors)
  1999 *Unpacking Culture: Art and Commodity in Colonial and Postcolonial Worlds*. University of California Press, Berkeley.

Russell, Lynette (editor)
  2001a *Colonial Frontiers: Cross-Cultural Interactions in Settler Colonies*. Manchester University Press, Manchester.

Russell, Lynette
  2001b *Savage Imaginings: Historical and Contemporary Constructions of Australian Aboriginalities*. Australian Scholarly Publishing, Kew, VIC.

Sands, John
  1901 *Sands Sydney, Suburban and Country Commercial Directory for 1901: Comprising amongst other Information, Street, Suburban, Country, Commercial and Miscellaneous Lists*. J. Sands, Sydney.

Silliman, Stephen W.
  2005 Culture Contact or Colonialism? Challenges in the Archaeology of Native North America. *American Antiquity* 70(1): 55–74.

Stewart, Susan
  1993 *On Longing: Narratives of the Miniature, the Gigantic, the Souvenir, the Collection*. Duke University Press, Durham and London.

Stocking, George W.
  1985 *Objects and Others: Essays on Museums and Material Culture*. Wisconsin University Press, Madison, WI.

Taçon, Paul S.C., Barrina South, and Shaun Hooper
    2003 Depicting Cross-Cultural Interaction: Figurative Designs in Wood, Earth and Stone from
    South-East Australia. *Archaeology in Oceania* 38(2): 89–101.

Thomas, Nicholas
    1991 *Entangled Objects: Exchange, Material Culture and Colonialism in the Pacific.* Harvard
    University Press, Cambridge.
    1994 *Colonialism's Culture: Anthropology, Travel and Government.* Polity Press, Cambridge.
    1999 *Possessions: Indigenous Art/Colonial Culture.* Thames and Hudson, London.

Thomas, Nicholas and Diane Losche (editors)
    1999 *Double Vision: Art Histories and Colonial Histories in the Pacific.* Cambridge University
    Press, Cambridge.

Thorpe, William W.
    1928 Ethnological Notes No. 1. *Records of the Australian Museum* 16(5): 249–253.

Torrence, Robin
    1993 Ethnoarchaeology, Museum Collections and Prehistoric Exchange: Obsidian tipped
    Artefacts from the Admiralty Islands. *World Archaeology* 24: 467–481.
    2000 Just Another Trader? An Archaeological Perspective on European Barter with Admiralty
    Islanders, Papua New Guinea. In *The Archaeology of Difference: negotiating cross-cultural
    engagements in Oceania,* edited by Robin Torrence and Anne Clarke, pp. 104–41. Routledge,
    London and New York.

Torrence, Robin and Anne Clarke
    2000a Negotiating Difference: Practise Makes Theory for Contemporary Archaeology in
    Oceania. In *The Archaeology of Difference: Negotiating Cross-Cultural Engagements in
    Oceania,* edited by Robin Torrence and Anne Clarke, pp. 1–31. Routledge, London and
    New York.

Torrence, Robin and Anne Clarke (editors)
    2000b *The Archaeology of Difference: Negotiating Cross-Cultural Engagements in Oceania.*
    Routledge, London and New York.

Tost and Rohu
    n.d. a *Australian Aboriginal Curios.* Wait and Bull Printers, Sydney.
    n.d. b *Australian Aboriginal Boomerangs.* Radcliffe Press, Sydney.

Tyrells Museum
    1929 *Australian Aborigines and South Sea Islanders: Implements, Weapons and Curios on Sale
    at Tyrell's Museum.* Tyrells Museum, Sydney.

University of Sydney
    2008 *Most Curious and Peculiar: Women Taxidermists in Colonial Sydney.* http://www.usyd.
    edu.au/museums/whatson/exhibitions/ctaxidex.shtml, accessed 27th May 2008.

Viveiros de Castro, Eduardo
    2004 Exchanging Perspectives: The Transformation of Objects into Subjects in Amerindian
    Ontologies. *Common Knowledge* 10(3): 463–484.

White, Richard
    2005 *On Holidays: A History of Getting Away in Australia.* Pluto Press, North Melbourne.

Williams, Francis E.
    1923 *The Collection of Curios and the Preservation of Native Culture.* Anthropology Report
    No. 3. Port Moresby Government Printer, Port Moresby.

Chapter 4
Plumes, Pipes and Valuables: The Papuan Artefact-Trade in Southwest New Guinea, 1845–1888

Susan M. Davies

Abstract Drawing on the Papuan collections held in three Australian museums, this chapter uses documented trading encounters between westerners and peoples of the southwest coast and Fly River estuary to help uncover indigenous agency embedded within collections. The case study shows how a methodology which combines an analysis of museum collections, historical sources, ethnographic studies and oral histories can provide new information about how this trade evolved in southwest New Guinea during the second half of the nineteenth century. The results highlight the importance of the social networks that lay behind choices about whether objects were either offered to or withheld from the early explorers and traders.

Introduction

At the beginning of the nineteenth century, south eastern New Guinea was a vast land unknown to the Western world, its coastline only vaguely known from the reports of French and English navigators from the late 1760s (Moore 2004:106). Foreign interest in the region gathered momentum after the British settlement of Australia in 1788. British attempts to find new and safer shipping routes from Australia to Asia during the first half of the nineteenth century led to a series of hydrographic surveys of neighbouring Torres Strait. From 1845 this survey was extended to include the south coast of New Guinea and by 1850 most of the coastline had been laid down on British Admiralty charts. One outcome of the British Royal Navy's charting of south eastern New Guinea was that contact with the region's indigenous peoples led to trade in cultural artefacts. A similar 'passing trade' is associated with the contact history relating to Torres Strait Islanders and westerners from the 1790s (Mullins 1992, cited in McNiven 2001:175). There are also parallels to the trade in indigenous 'curiosities' evident elsewhere in the Pacific in the 1700s

S.M. Davies (✉)
Independent Scholar, Arundel, QLD, Australia
e-mail: susiedavies@optusnet.com.au

S. Byrne et al. (eds.), *Unpacking the Collection*, One World Archaeology,
DOI 10.1007/978-1-4419-8222-3_4, © Springer Science+Business Media, LLC 2011

and 1800s, a feature of contact between Pacific Islanders and passing European vessels (Hooper 2006; Waite 1987).

Trade in cultural items also features prominently in the contact history between Papuans and westerners during the second half of the nineteenth century. On the surface, this trade may appear merely as a way in which Papuans mediated their contacts with outsiders. Certainly, trade was a negotiating medium, but to view indigenous trade only as a response to a particular situation denies the benefit that indigenous peoples derived from their trading encounters with westerners. Consideration needs to be given to the impact foreign goods had on indigenous material culture, economies and trade (Moore 1998: 258–259). This is especially the case in New Guinea, where extensive trade routes had long connected coastal peoples to those living inland and on offshore islands, a range of objects, including valuables, circulated through well-established networks. These created a set of mutually dependent relationships which were re-affirmed over time. Increasing contacts with westerners and their material goods from 1870 led Papuans to establish new types of social and trading relationships, especially with frequent visitors such as missionaries and traders, some of whom later settled in New Guinea.

Entangled within this web of interdependency were the various goods traded by Papuans, many of which are now held in museum collections. These artefacts may be seen as symbolic of the types of interactions which occurred between Papuans and westerners. Viewed in this way, museum collections are a rich archive, a potential source of information about cross-cultural contact and the nature of the Papuan trade in south eastern New Guinea in the 1800s. However, extracting indigenous agency from museum collections is difficult as indigenous artefacts collected in the nineteenth century are often limited by either non-existent or inadequate documentation. Historical records associated with trade are also challenging because the accounts penned by the likes of missionaries, explorers and naturalists provide only one side of the trading encounter. Despite these shortcomings, Gray (1999) has shown that it is possible to use historical records to piece together a picture of trade and contact between local islanders and westerners in the Bismarck Archipelago during the 1800s.

This chapter suggests that when taken together with the presence or absence of artefacts in museum collections, historical sources are very important for shedding light on the changing patterns of the artefact-trade with westerners in nineteenth century Papua. This case study, focused on the south western coast of New Guinea, demonstrates that when studied in conjunction with regional ethnographic studies and oral histories, historical sources comprise a powerful source for uncovering indigenous agency embedded within museum collections. Layers of social networks between individuals and communities emerge. The case study shows that these social relationships played a key factor in the artefact-trade with westerners. For example, the exchange of material goods between western collector and Papuan trader was often facilitated by the presence of a third party, such as a 'chief' or an indigenous interpreter. The social relations which existed between Papuans from different places enabled westerners to obtain artefacts. Thus, social relations, between and among Papuans, as well as those established between collector and trader, underpin the artefact-trade.

The Study Area

The southwest coast and the Fly River estuary (Fig. 4.1), a region with a well-documented history of contact with westerners, provide a suitable study area (Jukes 1847, Chester 1870b; Macleay 1875b; D'Albertis 1881; Strachan 1888). First contact with westerners appears to begin around 1845. At this time, social relations consisted of fleeting offshore encounters between Papuans and the British surveying vessel, HMS *Fly*. Subsequent contacts date from 1870, with most interactions involving the Kiwai-speaking peoples of Mokatta (a small village which lay at the mouth of the Katow River) and Kiwai Island (the largest island in the Fly River estuary). Indigenous material culture from the region is well represented in museum collections. The British Museum (London), Australian Museum (Sydney), Macleay Museum (University of Sydney) and the Queensland Museum (Brisbane) provide

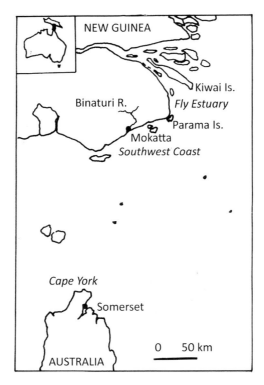

Fig. 4.1 Map of the southwest coast and the Fly River estuary area of New Guinea. (Drawn by Peter White)

a representative example of artefact types collected from the region between 1845 and 1888.

A better understanding of the kinds of objects held in museum collections is gleaned from a reconstruction of the basic range of indigenous material culture in use during the collection period (Appendix 4.1). The objects listed in Appendix 4.1 have been extracted from various sources, particularly indigenous vocabularies gathered by Chester (1870a), Hargrave (1875) and MacGregor (ARBNG 1889–1890). These vocabularies, however, offer no information about the indigenous value of objects. Values have been deduced from data reported in the major ethnographic study undertaken in the region by the Finnish anthropologist and sociologist Gunnar Landtman between 1910 and 1912 (Landtman 1927, 1933). Establishing the relative value of objects is important because their absence or under-representation in museum collections may be taken as a sign of indigenous agency.

Regional Trade Relations

Papuans from the southwest coast and Fly River estuary shared extensive cultural and trading links with neighbouring Torres Strait Islanders; these connections were in existence long before contact with westerners and continue to the present day. A range of customary trade articles are known to have moved from New Guinea into Torres Strait and vice versa. The principal items provided by Papuans were canoes, drums, cassowary and bird-of-paradise feather ornaments, boar tusks, woven bands, belts, mats and weapons (bows and arrows) while Torres Strait Islanders supplied ornaments made from shell, especially pearl shell and conus shell (Moore 1984; Lawrence 1994). These components of customary exchange are important to the present study because Papuans traded some of these same objects with the British in 1845 and with other westerners who arrived in 1870.

Contact and Trade with Westerners Before 1850

The earliest documented contacts between westerners and Papuans on the southwest coast and Fly River estuary appear to date from 1845 when the British vessel HMS *Fly* charted the western side of the Gulf of Papua. The *Fly*'s first encounter with Papuans appears to have occurred near the mouth of a large river (probably the Fly River) where it met three small single outrigger canoes coming from the New Guinea mainland. One of the crew sent out in a dingy to 'communicate' with the Papuans exchanged a hatchet for a bow and arrow, some cocoa-nuts and a small turtle (Jukes 1847 :I 213–214). As the *Fly* continued its survey of the western shores of the Gulf of Papua, subsequent contacts with Papuans were generally less harmonious. The ship's naturalist, Joseph Beete Jukes described the fresh water arms and channels of the rivers as 'swarming . . . with hostile inhabitants' (Jukes 1847 :I 243). Attempts to land and explore were usually met with overt hostility and chance meetings with people in canoes were frequently marked by fear and confusion, with both sides unable to communicate in a common language. An encounter with a canoe in the Papuan Gulf recorded by J.B Jukes vividly illustrates the cultural context.

> As we could not induce them to come alongside, we fastened a hatchet to a breaker, and set it adrift. They pulled for it, but seemed cautious of approaching it, and when they did, they poked it, and turned it over and over with their paddles, as if they feared some hidden danger. At last they espied the hatchet, which they took off, but let the breaker go, although bound with iron hoops. They passed the hatchet from one to the other, and examined it, and at last seemed to comprehend its use, as they set up a shout, and waved it aloft in the air to the other canoes coming up. Its possession, however, instead of inducing them to commence peaceful trade, seemed only to excite them instantly to attack people having such valuable articles. They paddled towards us instantly, cast loose their arrows, adjusted their bows, and very shortly began to shoot at us (Jukes 1847 :I 281–282).

J.B. Jukes's narrative of the voyage of HMS *Fly* provides surprisingly little evidence of trade with Papuans. Significantly, on occasions where trade did take place, the British appear to have been offered local customary trade articles, such as bows and arrows (Jukes 1847 :I 213–214; see Lawrence 1994: 366–367 for types of bows and arrows traded from New Guinea into Torres Strait). While the choice of trade articles offered was perhaps determined by the location of contact (at sea), later historical evidence indicates a similar pattern of trade, suggesting that it was those types of artefacts which Papuans chose to trade with westerners possibly because they were produced in large numbers for local exchanges.

Arrival of New Traders from 1870

A new wave of foreign traders arrived on the southwest coast in 1870. Pacific Islanders and others associated with the Torres Strait pearl-fishing industry arrived first. Their boats visited the coast between Talbot Island (Boigu) and the Fly River seeking fresh food supplies (pearl shell reefs had been 'discovered' off Warrior Island (Tutu) in 1869) (Chester 1870b: 6; Mullins 1994: 74). A small party of westerners, believed to be the first to visit New Guinea since 1845, made a brief visit to the southwestern coastal village of Katow in September 1870. Positive reports of their visit led London Missionary Society (LMS) representatives to visit the same village in the following year. Two LMS mission stations established in the same area in 1872 were short-lived (Murray 1876: 455–456). Natural history collectors and explorers followed. The gentleman-scientist William John Macleay (later Sir) arrived on the barque *Chevert* in July 1875. His party of collectors spent almost 2 weeks collecting scientific specimens around the Katow River region (Macleay 1875b). Not long afterwards, the British explorer Octavius C. Stone joined with the LMS missionary Samuel MacFarlane to explore the Baxter River (Mai-Kussa) (Stone 1875–1876). In 1875, MacFarlane, Henry Chester and the Italian naturalist Luigi D'Albertis explored the Fly River; D'Albertis made further explorations of the Fly River in 1876 and 1877 (D'Albertis 1881:II). Regardless of their ambitions, the foreigners brought large quantities of 'trade' with them; tobacco, cloth, glass

Table 4.1 Sample list of 'Trade' articles taken to southwest coast and Fly River between 1870 and 1885

1870a, b Henry Chester	1875 *Chevert* expedition	1885 RGSA expedition
Tobacco, matches, pipes	–	–
	Tobacco	3 boxes (191 lbs) Tobacco, plus a quarter-tierce of a kind known as 'Trade or Missionary twist' Tobacco. 10 gross Matches 3 gross Pipes 4 cwt Salt
Tomahawks, Knives etc	–	–
Tomahawks	Metal adze and axe blades	5 dozen Hatchets
Knives	Machete blades	4 dozen Pocket knives, assorted $\frac{1}{2}$ dozen Sportsman's knives 3 dozen pairs Scissors 6 dozen Iron table spoons 2 dozen Fishing lines 100 dozen Limerick fish hooks Quantity of Iron – sheet and hoop 3 cwt Galvanized iron wire
Glass trade beads	–	–
Red and white [glass] trade beads	Multi-stringed, small glass trade beads (red, white and blue); Necklaces of single strings of large glass beads (various colours)	19,500 Beads, assorted
Cloth etc.	–	–
Turkey Red (Cloth)	Turkey Red (Cloth) Mirrors (pictures)	5 pieces 'Turkey Red' calico 3 gross Zinc mirrors 2 pieces (121 yards) Prints, 'Island Fancies' 2 pieces (96 yards) Scarlet Saxony flannel 5 dozen Island handkerchiefs 4/1/2 dozen Cricket and boating caps 4 dozen Fancy garters

Sources: Chester 1870a:1; Surplus *Chevert* trade goods in Macleay Museum (accessioned under ET 84.172); *Instructions issued by the Royal Geographical Society of Australasia, the New Guinea Exploring Expedition*, Sydney 12 June 1885, p. 72 and Everill (1885:241)

beads, mirrors and metal implements (iron adze and axe heads) were used to trade for food, natural history specimens and artefacts (Table 4.1).

At first, westerners recruited Torres Strait Islanders to act as navigators, guides and interpreters. Often engaged in pairs, these individuals directed westerners to the New Guinea mainland, particularly to coastal villages with which they had kinship and trading linkages. Despite the attraction of the Fly River (generally regarded as the gateway into the interior), it was the smaller Katow River (Binaturi) which received the first western visitors in September 1870, the former Somerset-based police magistrate Henry Chester among them. Chester's (1870b: 1–2) account of his visit to Katow highlights the role Torres Strait interpreters played in mediating first contact situations.

> Not more than five or six men were visible and they were making off into the bush on our landing, but came towards us on hearing the interpreter call out in their language. The chief whose name was Mino recognised the latter and embraced him with great warmth, the rest then 'scarped hands', first with Kairer (the interpreter) and afterwards with us; . . . One man carried a stone club, and Mino had a trade tomahawk, the rest were unarmed, but all had the bamboo knife and cane loop slung round the neck or thrust into the gauntlet [bamboo beheading knife and head carrier]. It was some time before we could convince them we intended no harm; Mino in particular trembled violently although he made a great effort to appear at ease. After presenting each man with a broad strip of Turkey red [cloth] which they seemed to prize very much, we told them we had come to trade, and wished to be on friendly terms, but if they preferred fighting we were quite prepared. This was said by the advice of the interpreter, and led to a disclaimer on their part of any but the most friendly intentions.

The party of foreigners that visited Katow on 22–23 September 1870 comprised of four westerners, including Henry Chester and William Banner (manager of the pearling station at Warrior Island (Tutu) in Torres Strait). Twenty Pacific Islanders and two Warrior (Tutu) interpreters were also part of the group. Chester, in particular, had come well prepared for trade, having left Somerset, Cape York (Northern Australia) in mid-September with 'a quantity of tomahawks, knives, red and white beads, Turkey Red and tobacco to trade with the natives for weapons and ornaments' (Chester 1870a: 1). Although Chester's account suggests that while villagers were keen to trade their food produce for such goods, they appeared to have been reluctant to part with their material culture.

Chester (1870b: 2) found the 12 houses in Katow village destitute of women, children and possessions. The interiors of the houses appear to have been stripped of belongings although Chester discovered and removed some articles which he found hidden in the palm-leaf roof of the largest dwelling: the dried head of a cassowary; a wooden headrest; a quantity of powdered lime; and several human-jaw armlets (Chester 1870b: 3–4). In fact, the only cultural artefact which Chester acquired through trade during his visit to Katow in 1870 appears to have been a large drum which he discovered hidden in the scrub as he wandered through the plantations at the rear of the village. When Chester showed Mino the drum in the bush, 'he made signs not to take it, but appeared satisfied on being given a tomahawk [iron trade tomahawk] in exchange' (Chester 1870b: 5). While it is not known what sort of drum Chester obtained in 1870, the ethnographic literature suggests that the *warupa* and *buruburu* types made in this part of New Guinea were traded into Western Torres Strait (Haddon 1894: 39; Vanderwal 2004: 265). Drums were also exchanged locally among Papuan communities (Landtman 1933: 68; Vanderwal 2004: 265). Some drums, such as those given individual names by their owners,

were highly valued items (Landtman 1927: 46; Vanderwal 2004: 265). While indigenous exchange values for drums are not known, the exchange of a drum for a trade
tomahawk is probably a sign that the exchange was significant, especially when one
considers the important role that western trade goods had assumed within regional
trade networks and communities by the early 1870s.

Western Trade Goods and Their Impact on Regional Trade

Opportunities for Papuans of the southwest coast and Fly River estuary to obtain
western trade goods before 1870 were limited. Though contact with HMS *Fly* in
1845 may have yielded the odd tomahawk or piece of cloth, the main source of
western goods was via trade with other Papuans or Torres Strait Islanders, especially the latter who had experienced sporadic contacts with westerners from the
early 1790s. Similarly, the wrecks of vessels which littered Torres Strait may have
provided another source of metal, but Kiwai stories recorded by Gunnar Landtman
suggest that initially villagers left such items to decay on the beach because they
believed they belonged to the spirits of the dead (Landtman 1917: story 497, told
by Gamea, son of Mino of Mowatta). More than 30 years earlier, the missionary William Wyatt Gill (1875: 16) had also been informed that Papuans viewed
Europeans as 'Malakai': 'ghosts' or 'spirits'.

The establishment of *beche-de-mer* and pearl-fishing industries in the Torres
Strait in the 1860s stimulated the flow of western goods through Torres Strait-New
Guinea customary trade networks. Henry Chester's visit to the pearling station on
the Torres Strait island of Warrior (Tutu) in September 1870 provides evidence of
this trade and its extension into New Guinea. Chester (1870a: 2) reported to the
Colonial Secretary in Brisbane that peoples of Warrior Islander (Tutu) procured
their canoes and weapons from New Guinea, 'in exchange for shells and the knives
and tomahawks procured from Europeans'. Ethnographic information gathered by
Navigating-Lieutenant E.R. Connor of HMS *Basilisk* in 1873 supports Chester's
remarks about the movement of European trade articles through indigenous trade
networks (Connor in Moresby 1875: 2–6).

The increasing flow of western trade articles, like cloth, metal goods and glass
beads, into Papuan coastal villages during the second half of the nineteenth century impacted on language, material culture and trade. For example, a vocabulary
of about 37 words recorded at Katow by *Chevert* expedition-member Lawrence
Hargrave (1875; 3 July 1875) included indigenous words for European items (e.g.
rope, knife, gun, canvas, calico and handkerchief). Customary exchange rates were
also disrupted; perhaps the most striking example of this is supplied by the canoe
trade, which dominated trade among and between coastal Papuans and Torres Strait
Islanders. By 1905, canoes in southwest New Guinea could be bought entirely
with European trade store goods instead of the usual customary shell ornaments
(Lawrence 1994: 275, 278–279). Subtle changes occurred to material culture as
well. For example, strips of Turkey-red trade cloth and glass trade beads were

Fig. 4.2 Headdress (*daguri*). Cassowary feathers, plant fibre and red trade cloth, 28 × 22 cm. Attributed to the *Chevert* Expedition, 1875 (Courtesy of the Macleay Museum, University of Sydney, ETA.614)

increasingly used to embellish cassowary-feather ornaments and other cultural items (Fig. 4.2). While changes to objects are to be expected as villagers experimented with new materials, the Papuan desire to obtain foreign goods for ornamentation or other purposes appears to have been an important factor in their subsequent trading contacts with westerners.

The Artefact-Trade with Westerners, 1875–1885

The traffic of western goods through indigenous trade networks and trade with outsiders (e.g. pearl shellers) appears to have resulted in changes to the way in which Papuan villagers responded to the visits of foreigners. The accounts of missionaries, explorers and naturalists who visited the southwest coast and Fly River estuary between 1875 and 1885 provide important evidence of this change, showing how some villagers welcomed, or at least tolerated, the visits of outsiders. These records also show an eagerness on the part of villagers to obtain foreign goods. In fact, the demand for such items appears to have stimulated the Papuan artefact-trade with westerners.

Historical sources indicate that from 1870 Torres Strait pearl shell fishers were fairly regular visitors to coastal villages like Mokatta (Katow) where the locals obtained a variety of European goods through trade, including tobacco, cloth, wool and iron implements (D'Albertis 1881: II 18). Oral tradition also records the visits by pearl-fishers. For example, an old Mawatta story reports that Pacific Islander, Malay and Yam Islander pearling crews sought food (Landtman 1917: 540–541; Lawrence 1994: 303). While the pearl shellers are known to have traded tobacco for food (a small piece of tobacco was exchanged for ten coconuts or a bunch of bananas), it is likely that they also traded for Papuan objects. The settlement of Somerset (Cape York, Northern Australia) which serviced the pearl shell fishing industry was described by a visitor in 1874 as, 'a sort of emporium of savage weapons and ornaments' (Landtman 1917: 540–541; Thomson 1885: I 541).

In July 1875, the barque *Chevert*, a three-masted sailing ship with around 30 men on board, spent almost 2 weeks anchored a couple of miles off the mouth of the Katow River (Binaturi). One unnamed 'gentleman' recalled the *Chevert*'s first offshore encounter with villagers on 3 July 1875:

> At 8 this morning, two canoes came alongside – the largest about 30 feet long, with outriggers on one side only. The chief (by name, 'Mino'), dressed, and his son (a boy of about 12) were in one canoe; the rest, about thirty, were naked, except some strips of worsted [smooth woollen cloth] in the ears, and a few had ornaments of pearl shell round their necks. They brought some cocoanuts and taro, which they readily parted with for tobacco. The size of the ship seemed to astonish them (*Sydney Morning Herald*, 18 September 1875, p. 5).

A visit to the village of Mokatta revealed more villagers adorned with European trade articles. The *Chevert*'s engineer, Lawrence Hargrave observed that the ears of villagers were ornamented with 'a fringe of beads or wool' (Hargrave 1875; 3 July 1875). The Italian naturalist Luigi D'Albertis, who visited Mokatta a few months later, noted that wool was obtained from the Torres Strait pearl shell fishers and that Mokatta villagers substituted red wool for the red-dyed grass normally worn in the ears as ornaments (D'Albertis 1881 :II 18). While Mokatta villagers were clearly using European trade goods (wool, cloth and beads) for personal adornment, historical sources suggest that they still adhered to their traditional attire, with the men lacking clothing (Fig. 4.3) and the women wearing grass skirts about 12 inches in length (Hargrave 1875, 3 July 1875; Macleay 1875b). The reference to Mino (also known as Maino) as 'dressed' upon meeting the *Chevert* is the only time that any villager is described as wearing European clothing and is perhaps explained by the fact that Mino had just returned from a few weeks' cruise on the missionary vessel, *Ellengowan* (Macleay 1875b).

European trade goods appear to have been eagerly sought after during the *Chevert*'s stay off the Katow River (Binaturi) in 1875. The logbook of the *Chevert* reveals that shooting and trading parties regularly went ashore during the ship's stay, the trading parties returning with a range of ornaments, implements and weapons. There is also evidence that villagers were responding to the foreigners' interest in acquiring natural history specimens and were actively collecting specimens (e.g. reptiles and insects) and were adding these to their trade offerings (*Chevert* logbook, 7 July 1875).

While interactions between Mokatta villagers and *Chevert* expedition members were friendly, the latter were to experience hostility when they tried to explore the hinterland. The reason was that the exploratory party had sent no prior warning to villages in the interior of their impending visit. Apparently, locals would never visit their friends in another village without sending a messenger first. The only time that locals dispensed with the protocol was during warfare. Subsequent overtures from the bush people to get their coastal friends to join with them to attack the foreigners were unsuccessful. Matters were largely resolved by Mino, who sent one of his men to the inland chiefs with presents (Petterd 1876). A party of armed 'bush natives' that congregated on the beach a couple of days later were also pacified by 'presents'. Macleay (1875a; 7 July 1875) noted in his journal that 'these [presents] served to be a considerable desire to trade among them, but they were very wild & timid'.

Fig. 4.3 Two unidentified villagers with bows and arrows, probably taken at Mokatta village, southwest coast, New Guinea, 1875 (Photograph taken by Captain A.A.W. Onslow, *Chevert* Expedition, 1875. Album of views, illustrations and family photographs, 1857–1879, compiled by William Macarthur, Sir William Macarthur Papers, ML PXA 4358/1, p. 33. Courtesy of the Mitchell Library, State Library of New South Wales)

Subsequent interactions with the 'bush' people living further up the Katow River were positive. The bush people were described as very friendly and were keen to obtain tobacco, tomahawks, knives and brightly-coloured cloth (Macleay 1875b).

During the 10 days (2–12 July 1875) that the *Chevert* remained at its anchorage off the Katow River (Binaturi), a miscellaneous collection of weapons, implements and ornaments were collected by W.J. Macleay and others from the vessel. These included cassowary-feather ornaments and boar-tusk armlets, items which were part of local exchange networks (such objects were traded into Torres Strait). Lawrence Hargrave, who travelled on the *Chevert* as engineer, also collected a 'pillow' and a 'pipe' (probably a wooden headrest and tobacco-smoking pipe) from Mokatta village during the *Chevert*'s stay (Hargrave 1875; 10 July 1875). Tobacco-smoking pipes from this region were usually made from lengths of bamboo and often heavily decorated with intricately incised patterns (Landtman 1927: 42–43). While there are no historical references relating to the exchange of tobacco pipes between Papuans and Torres Strait Islanders, A.C. Haddon's reference to the 'Papuan pipe' used in Torres Strait implies that they were traded (Haddon 1901–1935, Report, 1912: 141). Indeed, a tobacco pipe collected at Darnley (Erub) Island in Torres Strait in c. 1844–1845 by J.B. Jukes and now in the British Museum is remarkably similar to one from the Fly River area collected by members of the Royal Geographical Society of Australasia (RGSA) in 1885 (QM E8638; the pipe collected by Jukes is the smaller pipe illustrated in Jukes 1847: I 165; BM Oc1846, 0731:2). The stylistic similarity between the two pipes suggests that some of those collected from Torres Strait may have originated from the Fly River area, perhaps through customary trade.

While historical sources such as those relating to the *Chevert* Expedition illuminate the nature of the Papuan artefact-trade with westerners at a particular period in time, tabulation of museum collections (Appendix 4.1) confirms the general pattern of trade which emerges through the historical record: that is, Papuan villagers offering particular objects for trade (e.g. bows and arrows, plumed body ornaments and pipes). Significantly, many of these were articles made for customary exchange with other Papuans and Torres Strait Islanders. Equally striking is the under-representation, or complete absence, of valued articles (e.g. dogs' teeth necklaces and shell ornaments), the latter comprising items which Papuans received through trade with Torres Strait peoples. This feature is mirrored in the historical record which suggests that Papuans were selective in their trade and were reluctant, and sometimes even refused, requests to trade objects which appear to have been valued highly.

Indigenous Valuables

The lack of trade in valuables is an important issue that merits further discussion. Nineteenth century documentary sources suggest that certain types of objects were highly valued by Papuans from the southwest coast and Fly River estuary. Perhaps the most telling indication of this are the failed attempts by westerners to procure some artefacts and the protracted negotiations required to obtain others. Significantly, some artefact types are absent or under-represented in museum collections. These include the very objects which naturalists, missionaries, government officials and ethnographers indicate were highly valued: shell ornaments, carved human figures and objects associated with head-hunting (e.g. beheading knife, head carrier and tally sticks). Their scarcity in museum collections provides a measure of their high value to indigenous groups. Some objects such as the bamboo beheading knife, like family heirlooms, were precious items to be passed down through generations. Moreover, the withholding of certain objects is a clear sign of indigenous agency by Papuan villagers.

Ornaments, especially those made from conus and pearl shell, were reputedly prized by groups from southwest New Guinea. No pearl shell neck ornaments were collected during the *Chevert* expedition even though W.J. Macleay and others made reference to them (Macleay 1875b; Petterd 1876). The reason for their omission is perhaps explained by expedition member W.F. Petterd (1876) who noted that 'necklets of pearl shell formed into a crescent shape are much worn and prized'. Such precious objects are unlikely to have been offered for trade. Moreover, there is evidence that in some places locals were removing shell ornaments from their body before interacting with westerners, possibly to avoid requests for these valuables to be sold. For example, Luigi D'Albertis (1881: II 18) noticed that some Kiwai Islanders removed their pearl shell neck ornaments before coming on board the *Ellengowan* to trade food and ornaments.

The importance of conus shell ornaments in the district was noticed by British New Guinea's first colonial administrator, Sir William MacGregor, on his first visit to Kiwai Island in 1889 where he found that the 'most prized decoration' was the polished end of a 'conical shell ... worn suspended from the neck.' He reported that 'Good specimens they will not sell at any price' (ARBNG 1889–1890:41). One of the most highly valued ornaments of the Kiwai Papuans in the entire district appears to have been a conus shell armlet called *mabuo*; Landtman noted that one *mabuo* armlet formed 'a considerable part of the price of a bride or a canoe' (Landtman 1927:26; Landtman 1933:34). Obtained in exchange from Torres Strait Islanders as full or part payment of a canoe, the *mabuo* armlet was still valued highly by Kiwai Papuans in the early twentieth century. For example, Landtman, who spent two years living among the Kiwai people in 1910–1912, was unable to procure a single example for his own collection (Landtman 1927: 26; Lawrence 1994: 358). The high value set on pearl shell and conus shell ornaments explains their under-representation in the Australian museum collections analysed for this chapter.

Carved anthropomorphic figures, often referred to as 'idols' in the literature, were another category of object which was valued and thus difficult to obtain. A fascinating example of this is associated with a carved figure which the Australian Museum purchased from Captain John Strachan in 1886 (Fig. 4.4). Strachan appears to have made three separate visits to New Guinea between 1874 and 1885, with explorations of Strachan Island (Tuj or Buji) being the focus of his travels in 1885 (Strachan 1888). While exploring the mainland east of the Mai-Kussa River in that year, Strachan was guided to a village named Goua (Gowa) by Chief Tamea (Gamea, son of Mino of Mokatta) and the LMS teacher Annu, both from Mokatta village (Strachan 1888: 148–149). At the eastern end of Goua village, Strachan noticed a 'huge ochre-covered idol' at the entrance of a large house which seemed to be guarded by two 'priests'. Strachan resolved to obtain the carved figure named 'Seegur':

> I determined, if possible, to secure this object of native devotion. I therefore began assid-
> uously to cultivate the acquaintance and make the friendship of the priests, to whom I
> presented knives, and tobacco and other trivial articles. Having in some measure gained
> their confidence, through the interpretation of the teacher, I made a proposal to purchase
> the god, which overture seemed to astonish them, and they distinctly replied that under no
> circumstances would they part with him. I then enumerated the large number of articles
> which I was prepared to give in return for the idol, and the teacher told them of all the axes,

Fig. 4.4 Anthropomorphic figure, probably from Goua village, acquired by Captain John Strachan in 1885. Wood and pigments, 142 × 18 cm (Photo by Ric Bolzan, courtesy of the Australian Museum, Sydney, B10092)

> tomahawks, cloth and tobacco that would be forthcoming provided they were willing to part with the hideous object, which I took care to explain could do them no good (Strachan 1888: 150).

Despite offering vast amounts of trade, Strachan left the village without the prized carved figure. However, the figure was later purchased for Strachan by Annu and Tamea, whom Strachan had empowered to negotiate on his behalf. They managed to obtain two 'smaller idols' as well. However, the sale of the figures, particularly 'Seegur', caused a huge disturbance amongst the Goua, Massigari and Koonini peoples who had tried to prevent 'Seegur' being carried away. Strachan later met with the tribes concerned and tried to pacify them with presents of trade, tobacco and promises of sending them a teacher (convert) like Annu (Strachan 1888: 154–155). Strachan's purchase appears to be one of the earliest such carved figures collected; he later sold 'Seegur' to the Australian Museum along with nine other 'New Guinea Curios' for £20 (Australian Museum Purchase Schedule 7/1886; Strachan 1888: 156).

Appendix 4.1 shows that carved anthropomorphic figures are extremely rare in Australian museum collections. The circumstances surrounding the collection of such items by Strachan in 1885 suggest that others which may be found in museum collections are more than likely to have been removed without the knowledge of villagers, or if they were obtained through trade, are likely to have been acquired with an immense amount of pressure from interpreters, missionary representatives and the like. This pattern is repeated elsewhere in south eastern New Guinea. For example, E.G. Edelfelt, a Swedish collector-trader based at Motu-Motu in the eastern Papuan Gulf in 1886–1887, is known to have negotiated with villagers for 6 months before he was able to obtain an important carved figure that resided in a men's house, eventually securing it for a large quantity of trade (Edelfelt 1892: 25–27).

Objects associated with head-hunting represent types of valuables which Papuan villagers refused to trade with westerners during the early contact period. Examples of this appear in the literature from 1875, the Fly River explorations of Samuel Macfarlane, Henry Chester and Luigi D'Albertis providing one of the earliest references. The group was guided by Maino and Auta (headmen or 'chiefs' of Mokatta and Ture-Ture villages, respectively). D'Albertis was particularly fascinated by Maino, describing him as 'the most entertaining person we had on board' and listened avidly to his stories of the country and people they were to visit. At one point, Maino described how easy it was to cut off a man's head with a bamboo knife, informing D'Albertis that, 'he himself had cut off thirty-three heads in this manner' (D'Albertis 1881: II 17). This tally correlates closely with the 'about thirty human heads' which D'Albertis saw 'suspended like trophies' hanging outside Maino's house (D'Albertis 1881: II 10). Maino proceeded to take out of his bag 'a collection of pieces of wood and old tips of arrows, which he arranged before us in a row. Every one of these represented to us a murder – to him a deed of valour' (D'Albertis 1881: II 17). D'Albertis was especially keen to obtain the 'precious collection' of tallies but Maino 'contemptuously rejected the equivalent' which D'Albertis offered in exchange for them (D'Albertis 1881: II 17). Maino's response is particularly revealing for it shows that some highly valued objects could not be procured through trade. Appendix 4.1 shows that there are no documented tally sticks originating from this part of New Guinea in the museum collections studied.

Equally valued was the bamboo beheading knife with notched tallies (Fig. 4.5). An implement used to sever the heads of slain enemies but plain in appearance, it seems that westerners did not realise the significance of the bamboo knife for some time. In 1845 the *Fly*'s naturalist Joseph Jukes referred to the Papuan bamboo knife and cane loop 'always observed slung at the backs of the natives, the use of which we could not make out' and later noticed the same objects among Erub Islanders in Torres Strait who told him their function and said that they obtained them from 'Dowdee' or New Guinea. Jukes dismissed the concept of their use in head-hunting entirely, conjecturing that the knife was used for extracting sago-palm and the cane loop to hold the 'junk of the palm' (Jukes 1847 :I 277–278).

When Henry Chester visited Katow in 1870, he too appears to have been initially unaware of the function of 'the bamboo knife and cane loop slung round the neck or thrust into the gauntlet' which he observed on villagers (Chester 1870b: 1–2). Luigi

Fig. 4.5 Beheading knife
with a suspension loop of
European cloth. Bamboo,
cloth, plant fibre, red ochre
and shell, 41 × 5 cm
(excluding attachments).
Collected from the Fly or
Strickland Rivers during the
RGSA Expedition in 1885
(Courtesy of the Queensland
Museum, E10050)

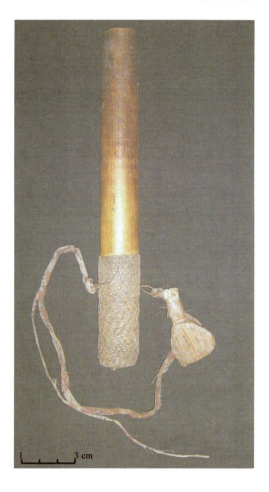

D'Albertis was provided with graphic details of how the knife was used by Maino of
Mokatta village in 1875. Although D'Albertis appears to have acquired an example
during his Fly River explorations, it was unlikely to have been procured through
trade (D'Albertis 1881: II 17; 1881: I 305, No. 21). In the early 1900s, the role of
the bamboo knife and cane loop was described in a paper about Kiwai Islanders by
the missionary James Chalmers (1903: 123). Further information was gathered by
A.C. Haddon (1912: 199–200) who noted that the notches on the handle of knives
were a tally of the number of heads cut-off. In the 1920s, the missionary Baxter-
Riley (1925: 272) discovered that the beheading knife was still held in high esteem;
his efforts to procure the renowned head-hunter Adagi's beheading knife from his
son were futile, leading him to write that the son 'will neither sell nor barter it'.
Baxter-Riley questioned the son as to why he wished to keep his father's beheading
knife and recorded his reply.

> I want to give that beheading-knife to my boy, so that he may know what a great man his grandfather was. I have not got the heads he took to show him, but the marks my father made on the knife are there and are a witness that he cut off a lot of heads. It would not be much use my telling the boy what his grandfather had done. He might not believe me, but if I give him the knife, and he sees the notches, he will believe (Baxter-Riley 1925: 272–273).

Appendix 4.1 shows that the beheading knife and head carrier are absent from the museum collections studied. A beheading knife collected by J.B. Jukes in 1845 was plundered from a deserted village in the vicinity of Goaribari Island (Kikori River delta area) in the Papuan Gulf and not procured through trade (Jukes 1847: I 276–278; illustrated 277; BM Oc1846,0731.15). The same would appear to be the case for the bamboo knife collected from the Fly River area during the RGSA expedition in 1885, now held in the Queensland Museum (QM E10050; see Philp 2007 for a discussion of the collecting methods in relation to the RGSA expedition). While the very plain appearance of these objects may have made them less attractive to uninformed collectors, their scarcity in museum collections may be taken as a sign that villagers were deliberately withholding them from trade. A similar pattern is seen in Torres Strait, where the beheading knife and head carrier were also highly valued. For example, in 1888–1889 and 1898–1899, A. C. Haddon collected only one beheading knife and three head carriers out of more than 700 objects in Torres Strait (see Moore 1984: nos. 125, 174, 711 and 712).

The Trade in Trophy Skulls

Human skulls were another item which villagers were initially unwilling to trade with westerners. Often seen suspended from poles outside houses or inside men's longhouses, these were trophy skulls: that is, the skulls of enemies slain in fighting (D'Albertis 1881: II 12–13; Beardmore 1890: 461; Landtman 1927: 254–268). Most foreign visitors to south western coastal villages were probably aware that trophy skulls were valued items. For instance, W.F. Petterd (1876) noted that for locals the possession of a number of human skulls of their enemies was the 'greatest treasure of the people'. Petterd (1876) reported that Katow villagers were 'reluctant to part with them and do not like to see them handled or examined'. Despite clear signs that villagers were unwilling to trade their trophy skulls with westerners, this did not deter some Europeans like Henry Chester and Luigi D'Albertis who plundered human remains from villages during the course of their travels (D'Albertis 1881: II 10–13; 38–40; 100–102).

Though an active indigenous trade in trophy skulls was reportedly in existence in southwest New Guinea during the early 1900s, it appears that westerners were initially excluded from this trade (Chalmers 1903: 123; Baxter Riley 1925: 271–272). Perhaps the reason for their exclusion is that human trophy skulls were valued possessions as a testimony of an individual's status as a warrior. The missionary James Chalmers explained the importance of possessing trophy skulls.

They have no marks of distinction as at the east [south-east coast], where bravery has tattoo marks. The skull [of slain foe] is secured, the more skulls, the greater the honour. No young man could marry, as no woman would have him, without skulls. Often a family would leave, and go far away for a length of time, and then return with skulls-perhaps all of them were bought–so that it might be said they had skulls. Sometimes a young man would go to friends at a distance, say Mawata, or Tureture, and would remain there for many months, and on his return home would have several skulls, which he bought from or through his friends, but on reaching his village would put on a solemn and sacred air, and, although in confidence to his relatives only, it was soon known by all in his tribe he was a great brave, and the lady he loved would soon be his (Chalmers 1903: 123).

Chalmers' comments related specifically to Kiwai Islanders and his writings indicate that canoes were often 'given in exchange for a skull' (Chalmers 1903: 123). It is highly likely that the skulls of the 'bushmen' formed part of the indigenous skull trade between Papuans of the southwest coast and Fly River estuary. For instance, in the 1870s, Henry Chester and Luigi D'Albertis were both told that the trophy skulls at Mokatta village were those of 'bushmen' (Chester 1870b: 3; D'Albertis 1881: II 12–13). Trophy skulls of the Tugeri (Marind-amin) who lived beyond the Dutch border and who were enemies of some Torres Strait Islanders and Papuans of the southwest coast would undoubtedly have been highly sought after as well. The Tugeri (Marind-amin) are said to have fought with the people of Sabai, Dauan, Boigu and the Kiwai-speaking Papuans in the 1800s, decimating villages and their populations in their raids and driving Kiwai-speaking peoples progressively eastward (Strachan 1888: 131–132, 142). They were also feared by the Keraki people of the Morehead River area (Young and Clarke 2001: 132). Sir William MacGregor reported on the Tugere (Tugeri) in his *Annual Report* for 1889–1890.

Mention was made of the Tugere pirates. Of these people extremely little is known . . . . But this much is certain, that they are warlike and numerous, that they come round the coast from the west in large canoes without outriggers before the north-west wind and return with the advent of the south-east . . . . As this is the season at which they may be expected the whole coast, including the Queensland islands of Sabai, Dauan, and Boigu, are in a state of terror (ARBNG 1889–1890: 68).

The last recorded fight between the Tugeri and the Kiwai is thought to have occurred in around 1888 when the Tugeri raided the Kiwai village of Kadawa (a village less than a mile from Mokatta), killing a European man named Martin (ARBNG 1889–1890: 67–68). More than 100 years later, anthropologist David Lawrence recorded a similar story which was told to him by Kanai Tura of Mawatta village. This story tells of a Tugeri raid during which the Tugeri 'leader and great chief' named Para killed a European and cut off his head (Lawrence 1994: 412; Story No. 10, Death of Para). Para was in turn killed and beheaded by Kaire of Mawatta village and his hair is said to be still kept by the descendants of Kaire (Lawrence 1994: 412). This story indicates that Tugeri skulls were of high value. Along with skulls of the New Guinea 'Bushmen', Tugeri skulls were probably traded locally along the southwest coast and possibly into Torres Strait.

Historical sources suggest that the Papuan trade in human trophy skulls with westerners developed slowly during the 1870s, most likely in response to increasing European interest in such items. For example, although Luigi D'Albertis found it 'impossible' to obtain any of the human skulls he saw hanging up outside houses at Mokatta village in 1875, there were occasions where he managed to coerce villagers into trading trophy skulls (D'Albertis 1881: II 10–13). A typical example is provided by his visit to Para village (Sumaut), Fly River estuary, in late 1876. Forcing his way into a longhouse, D'Albertis noticed numerous human skulls hanging from a pole. His request to purchase some of them was met with refusal. Undeterred and aided by Dawan (an interpreter from Mokatta), he managed to induce the men inside the longhouse into trading three human trophy skulls in exchange for a woollen blanket, knives, hatchets, mirrors and glass beads. This transaction highlighted how social connections between Papuans from different villages could influence the outcome of trade.

By the mid-1880s some villagers were freely offering to trade human skulls with westerners, some of which appear to have been trophy skulls. Significantly, it is the villages of Mokatta and Tureture, reportedly the very places where Kiwai Islanders could obtain trophy skulls in the early 1900s, where such acquisitions could be made. An account of a visit to Turi-turi village (Tureture) in 1885 by Captain John Strachan provides an example of how such trade ensued.

> As we entered the village, the women came crowding out on the platform eager to purchase looking-glasses, handkerchiefs, and other finery, for which they exchanged their combs, plumes made of Paradise feathers, work bags, and other articles of native industry. To the old chief I presented a tomahawk and by him was asked if I wished to purchase 'some man's head'. I asked to see them. He returned to his house and came out followed by two men carrying a string of human skulls well smoked, grim and ghastly, attached to a piece of bamboo . . . I purchased three, which were presented to medical gentlemen of scientific proclivities in Sydney (Strachan 1888: 166–167).

While it was possible for westerners to obtain occasional trophy skulls in the 1870s and 1880s, the trade may have decreased after British colonization. In 1889, after a visit to Kiwai Island Sir William Macgregor wrote that 'effort will be made to have them [the skulls] buried and convince these people that white men do not deal in human heads, or use such trophies' (ARBNG 1889: App. E: 39). The advent of British administration might have impacted the Papuan artefact-trade with outsiders as village life became more and more regulated (a government station was established at Mabudawan on the southwest coast in 1891), but this is outside the sphere of the present study. The types of contact after 1888 were different from those which occurred between Papuans and missionaries, naturalists and explorers in the two decades before colonization.

Discussion and Conclusions

This chapter shows how an intensive study combining information from historical sources and museum collections can be used to extract information about the nineteenth century Papuan artefact-trade with westerners. Analysis of both types of evidence reveals a distinct pattern of trade, with articles of indigenous customary exchange featuring in some of the early trade between Papuans and westerners.

More striking is the under-representation or complete absence of valued goods in museum collections. This important finding only becomes evident through a focused investigation of both collections and historical sources. Valuables, such as shell ornaments, beheading knives, head carriers, tally sticks and carved anthropomorphic figures are largely absent from collections. Withholding valuables from trade is perhaps the most conspicuous indication that Papuan villagers actively controlled the types of artefacts collected by westerners (see also Torrence and Clarke Chapter 2).

Noticeable is the small proportion of women's objects represented in collections in the time period under review, possibly a reflection that the major participants in trade, both trader and collector, were usually men. While one could expect more men's objects to be yielded in such circumstances, a more complex scenario is suggested by the fact that women and young girls were often hidden from view entirely in the early contact period, unable to interact with foreigners, let alone participate in trade (e.g. Chester 1870b; Macleay 1875a, 3 July; Murray 1876: 456). Though historical sources suggest that by the mid-1880s women had become active participants in the artefact-trade, this may have been confined to villages like Mokatta and Tureture, which had experienced a great deal of contact with outsiders (see Strachan 1888: 166–167 for an example of women trading artefacts at Tureture in 1885).

Many of the trading encounters related in this chapter reveal that the social networks formed between Papuans from different communities was an important determining factor in the ability of westerners to procure artefacts through trade. Consider for example the *Chevert* expedition-members' interactions with Mokatta villagers and in particular with 'chief' Mino, who helped facilitate the party's successful introduction to the 'bush' people of the interior. The role that certain individuals, such as Mino, played in mediating contact and trade with other Papuan communities is clearly evident. Mino personally guided Henry Chester around Katow village in 1870, received LMS representatives at his village in 1871 and welcomed the *Chevert* in 1875. He acted as a guide and interpreter on Macfarlane's explorations of the Fly River in 1875 and accompanied Luigi D'Albertis in a similar capacity on his explorations of the Fly River on the *Neva* in 1876. The assistance which Mino (Maino) rendered the *Chevert* expedition was later remembered by W.J. Macleay who later named an insect after him (*Cicindela maino*).

While kinship and trading relations connecting Papuan communities facilitated the artefact-trade with westerners, the relationships established between western visitors and Papuan traders were also important. A key example is provided by the circumstances associated with Captain John Strachan's acquisition of a carved anthropomorphic figure in 1885. Although Strachan's initial offer of vast amounts of trade for the figure were declined, his own relationship with Tamea ('chief' of Mokatta) and Annu (LMS teacher at Mokatta) helped him to secure the object. The Tamea–Annu pair later purchased the object on his behalf.

Another interesting feature which emerges from the study of historical sources is that the prospect of acquiring western trade goods was an important motivating factor for Papuans in the artefact-trade with westerners. While foreign goods were often appropriated for personal use or ornamentation of the body or material culture, the economic benefits following the trade-on of these items was probably substantial since their value presumably increased the further they travelled from their source of collection. Future studies which detail and track the modification of so-called 'traditional' material culture to include foreign trade goods may further illuminate this matter.

The findings from this study illustrate how different types of data can be utilised to reconstruct the role of social networks in shaping trade patterns between communities in southwest Papua and western traders, explorers and missionaries in the 1800s. While trading artefacts was but one of the many ways in which Papuan villagers tried to negotiate their encounters with westerners during the latter part of the nineteenth century, focused studies of the trade and its various components have the capacity to provide further insights into how Papuans responded to the visits of westerners and their increasing demands for their souls, local products, artefacts and land.

Acknowledgements   This chapter has evolved out of the research undertaken at the Macleay Museum as a recipient of the 2007 Macleay Miklouho-Maclay Fellowship. Curatorial and library staff working at the Australian Museum, Macleay Museum, Queensland Museum and Powerhouse Museum are thanked for their assistance in providing access to collections as well as locating photograph and archival sources, in particular, Jude Philp, Rebecca Conway, Melanie Van Olffen, Vanessa Finney, Imelda Miller and Jill Chapman. I am also grateful to Paul Tacon for his comments on a draft of this paper, while Peter White is thanked for assisting with the production of a map at short notice. I am especially indebted to Robin Torrence and Annie Clarke for their encouragement and instructive comments on drafts of this chapter.

Appendix 4.1 Indigenous artefact types from the southwest Coast and Fly River estuary recorded in vocabularies or other historical sources between 1870 and 1888 compared to contemporary museum collections (Australian Museum (AM), Macleay Museum (MM) and Queensland Museum (QM))

English name	Indigenous name	Source	Locality (general or known collecting locality)	No. in museums	Notes
Adze, wooden (for sago making) or steel	*Oto*	MacGregor 1889	New Guinea	–	–
Armlet, rattan	*Tootahai*	Chester 1870a, b	New Guinea	64 (various types of woven armlets)	Rattan armlets are well represented in collections but are largely unprovenanced. Likely to have been collected in either New Guinea or Torres Strait.
Armlet, plaited	*Tusase*	MacGregor 1889	New Guinea	See above	Possibly the 'rattan' type armlet referred to by Chester (1870a, b).
Armlet, shell	*Mabuo*	MacGregor 1889	New Guinea	–	Described by Landtman (1927: 26) as the most valuable shell ornament among the Kiwai Papuans. Obtained through trade from Torres Strait.
Armlet, with Job's –tears (i.e. *coix lachryma-jobi*)	*Piuri*	MacGregor 1889	New Guinea	3	Also worn in Torres Strait but may originate from New Guinea D'Albertis (1881:II 32) saw *coix lachryma-jobi* in cultivation in the Fly River area in 1875.
Armlet, boar tusks	*Boromo-kokai*	Landtman 1927	Katow, New Guinea	4	One labelled example in MM; others attributed on basis of style and method of construction. Landtman (1927: 26) describes this ornament as common in the Kiwai district.
Armlet, made from human lower jaw and worn in the dance	*Bahgoo Bago*	Chester 1870a, b D'Albertis 1881	Katow, New Guinea	–	In 1870, Chester obtained several armlets of this type, found hidden in a house at Katow village. In 1875, D'Albertis saw similar armlets at the same village (then known as Mokatta) and suggested they had been removed from skulls he saw hanging as trophies in the village. He noted that they were ornamented with feathers (D'Albertis 1881:II:10).
Arrow, plain	*Mora*	Chester 1870a, b	New Guinea	50	Arrows are not often described in museum collections making it difficult to ascertain the type or quantity. Arrows made in New Guinea were traded into Torres Strait. Four 'man-arrows' are included in the total of 50 (MM).

Appendix 4.1 (continued)

English name	Indigenous name	Source	Locality (general or known collecting locality)	No. in museums	Notes
Arrow, light reed	*Taera* *Tere*	Chester 1870a, b MacGregor 1889	New Guinea	?	–
Arrow, barbed	*Eeana*	Chester 1870a, b	New Guinea	?	–
Arrow, broad headed	*Soocorri*	Chester 1870a, b	New Guinea	?	–
Axe	*Kabi*	MacGregor 1889	New Guinea	–	–
Axe, stone	*Warikabi* *Daunomu* *Emaaiiopu*	MacGregor 1889	New Guinea	–	MacGregor gives three different names for stone axes.
Basket	*Heeta* *Hee-tar*	Chester 1870a, b Hargrave 1875	New Guinea	1	One basket is in the QM (type unknown).
Basket – small and fine plait (*titi*); of coconut leaves (*sito* or *sito titi*)	*Titi* *Sito* *Sito titi*	MacGregor 1889	New Guinea	?	See above.
Bag (trade bag)	*Baika*	MacGregor 1889	Kiwai/New Guinea	2	2 bags from Kiwai area in QM (type unknown).
Bamboo, for water	*Oho marabo*	MacGregor 1889	New Guinea	–	–
Bow, bamboo	*Gagari* *Gar-gi-re* *Gagari* *Gagare*	Chester 1870a, b Hargrave 1875 MacGregor 1889 Landtman 1927	New Guinea	5	Bows made in New Guinea were traded into Torres Strait. Uncertain where these examples were collected but likely in New Guinea rather than Torres Strait. For a description of bows see Landtman (1927: 27–28). There are possibly more bows in collections (unlabelled).
Bow String	*Wadda* *Wada*	Chester 1870a, b MacGregor 1889	New Guinea	?	–
Carving, Turtle, wood with goa seed pod attachment	–	–	New Guinea	1	–

Appendix 4.1 (continued)

English name	Indigenous name	Source	Locality (general or known collecting locality)	No. in museums	Notes
Carving, Anthropomorphic figure	Seegur	Strachan 1888	Goua Village	3	Large figure in AM (B10092). Location of other two smaller figures collected by Strachan is unknown.
Cassowary feather bundles	?	–	Katow	4	4 bundles; appear to have been bundled for trade (these types of ornaments were traded into Torres Strait).
Cassowary feather, dance ornament?	?	–	Katow?	1	Possibly a dance ornament, similar to some worn in Torres Strait but which were obtained from New Guinea.
Club, wooden club like head of bird	Weider	Chester 1870a, b	New Guinea	–	Type not mentioned by MacGregor (1889) or Landtman (1927).
Club, stone	Gooboo	Chester 1870a, b	New Guinea	–	Highly valued. Landtman (1927: 31) describes the gabagaba
	Gabagaba	MacGregor 1889			club as 'one of the most esteemed weapons of the Kiwai'.
Club, star club	tumanababa	MacGregor 1889	New Guinea	–	–
Club, round disc	gugi	MacGregor 1889	New Guinea	–	–
Canoe	Paer	Chester 1870a, b	New Guinea	–	–
	Ka-be-de-roo	Hargrave 1875			
	Pe	MacGregor 1889			
Canoe Decoration	Gope	Landtman 1927	Fly River	1	See Landtman 1927: 49.
Cage (bird's)	Wowogo moto	MacGregor 1889	New Guinea	–	–
Chest Ornament, crescent of pearl shell	Nahaer	Chester 1870a, b	New Guinea	–	Landtman (1927: 25) noted the local name for this type of chest
	Nese gege	MacGregor 1889			ornament as nese or miri and stated that it was obtained from coastal villages in Daudai (district of New Guinea facing Torres Strait) and from islands in Torres Strait.
Coconut cloth	Sugu	MacGregor 1889	New Guinea	–	–
Coconut drinking nut	Oi	MacGregor 1889	New Guinea	–	–

Appendix 4.1 (continued)

English name	Indigenous name	Source	Locality (general or known collecting locality)	No. in museums	Notes
Comb	*Ipogi*	MacGregor 1889 Landtman 1927	New Guinea	–	Landtman (1927: 25) notes that combs (*ipogi*) were carved from single pieces of wood and were common throughout the Kiwai district. There are possibly examples in collections without documentation.
Conch	*Tuture*	MacGregor 1889	New Guinea	–	–
Cord (rope)	*Karai*	MacGregor 1889	New Guinea	–	–
Cord, of split creeper	*Sawaivi*	MacGregor 1889	New Guinea	–	–
Cross belts, worn at dances (of straw)	*Gabigabi*	MacGregor 1889	New Guinea	–	–
Curiass of cane	*Bata*	MacGregor 1889	New Guinea	–	Possibly associated with people further up the Fly River. In 1876 D'Albertis found body armour in a deserted house (Alice River, north-west branch of the Fly River) (D'Albertis 1881:II 125).
Dagger, of cassowary bone	*Uriosoro*	MacGregor 1889	New Guinea	1	One example in MM without documentation; could originate from another part of southern New Guinea.
Dance ornament (Carved head of bird used in the dance)	*Warree*	Chester 1870a, b	New Guinea	1	One example in QM. Landtman (1927: 48) noted that there was a great variety of dance sticks and other wooden objects used in association with dances.
Dogs' teeth, necklace Dogs' teeth, cross-belts	*Genaiyo* *Genaio*	Chester 1870a, b MacGregor 1889	New Guinea New Guinea	–	Landtman (1927: 26) describes the 'string or necklace of dogs' teeth' (*genaio* or *gesa*) as one of the 'most valued ornaments' among the Kiwai-speaking Papuans.

Appendix 4.1 (continued)

English name	Indigenous name	Source	Locality (general or known collecting locality)	No. in museums	Notes
Drum	*Gunmar Gama Gama-ia* or *Warupa Buruburu*	Chester 1870a, b MacGregor 1889 Landtman 1927 Landtman 1927	New Guinea	4	One 'large' drum collected by Chester in 1870 (possibly the *gunmar* type). Two drums in QM are *warupa* and *burburu* types respectively. One drum from the Fly River area in AM (type unknown). Landtman (1927: 43) notes that the *gama-ia* type drum was also known as *warupa* (in Saibai language). By the early 1900s the *gama-ia* or *warupa* type was no longer made in the Mawata district; the *burburu* type introduced from Budji (village near the mouth of the Mai kussa River) had become popular (Landtman 1927: 43).
Ear ornament, shell	*Gargee-era*	Chester 1870a, b	New Guinea? [Torres Strait?]	7	Chester does not indicate shell type. Seven pearl shell ear ornaments originating from either Torres Strait or New Guinea were collected by Capt. Onslow c. 1875 (now at MM) (illustrated in Edmundson and Boylan (1999, Plate 6). They are in the shape of birds, anchors, etc. and similar to some collected by A.C. Haddon in Torres Strait in 1898 (Moore 1984, Plate 37, No. 322). Similar ear ornaments also appear to have been worn in New Guinea. Landtman (1927: 25) refers to ear ornaments 'of pearl shell in the shape of anchors . . . sometimes worn at dances'.
Ear ornaments, of worsted, twine etc	*Sosugoru*	MacGregor 1889	New Guinea	–	–
Fish-catcher, of wicker-work	*Gonia*	MacGregor 1889	New Guinea	–	–
Fish-hook	*Irisina tudi*	MacGregor 1889	New Guinea	–	–
Fishing line	*Areedhga*	Chester 1870a, b	New Guinea	–	–
Forehead ornament 'Fillet of pearl shell'	*Epoor-ee wee*	Chester 1870a, b	New Guinea?	–	Elsewhere Chester refers to this type of forehead ornament being worn by men from Warrior (Tutu) in Torres Strait (Chester 1870a).

Appendix 4.1 (continued)

English name	Indigenous name	Source	Locality (general or known collecting locality)	No. in museums	Notes
Gauntlet, to protect wrist from bow-string	*Ahdeega Adigo*	Chester 1870a, b MacGregor 1889	New Guinea	6	Also worn by Torres Strait Islanders. One example in MM is without documentation and may have been collected in Torres Strait; it is ornamented with tufts of red and black wool. Five examples in QM may be associated with the RGSA Expedition and therefore not obtained through trade.
Girdle	*Bata, bagi*	MacGregor 1889	New Guinea	–	–
Gourd	*Tidi*	MacGregor 1889	New Guinea	–	–
Groin Shell	*Medahaera*	Chester 1870a, b	New Guinea	–	Two examples in QM, collected during RGSA expedition in 1885 are likely to have been obtained beyond the Fly River estuary and not through trade.
Headdress, of feathers	*Dahgoorie*	Chester 1870a, b	New Guinea	16	Cassowary-feather head-dress (*daguri*) made in New Guinea were traded into Torres Strait. Landtman (1927: 24) describes them as the most common ornament in the whole district (Kiwai).
Headdress, Black plumes	*Daguri*	MacGregor 1889			
Headdress, of ray of white feathers	*Madia wowogo*	MacGregor 1889	New Guinea	–	–
Headdress, ten feet high, of feathers	*Madia wowogo pasa*	MacGregor 1889	New Guinea	–	–
Head ornament, rattan (helmet type)	?	D'Albertis 1881 Haddon 1912	New Guinea [Fly River Estuary]	1	D'Albertis 1881(II: 21) saw 'helmets' like these on men in the Fly River estuary in 1875. Haddon (1912: 38-39) noted that they were used in warfare and originated from New Guinea. The example in MM is labelled 'New Guinea'.
Head-rest ('wooden pillow')	*Eraho*	Chester 1870a, b	Katow, New Guinea	–	Although there are no examples in museum collections studied, Chester took a 'wooden pillow' from a house at Katow and Lawrence Hargrave collected an example from the same village (then known as Mokatta) in 1875.

Appendix 4.1 (continued)

English name	Indigenous name	Source	Locality (general or known collecting locality)	No. in museums	Notes
Head-carrier ('Loop for heads')	*Gurrara* *Garaoro*	Chester 1870a, b Landtman 1927	New Guinea	–	See Landtman (1927: 32).
Hook, wooden, to hang things on	*Tutuopu*	MacGregor 1889	New Guinea	–	–
Knife, bamboo	*Ooera* *Uere*	Chester 1870a, b Landtman 1927	New Guinea	–	Highly valued. According to Landtman (1927:32), 'Old beheading knives are looked upon in great awe; in time of peace they are kept in the men's house, close to sacred posts carved with human figures'.
Leglets and armlets of twine	*Sageri*	MacGregor 1889	New Guinea	–	–
Lime bottle	*Amiopuru*	MacGregor 1889	New Guinea	–	–
Lime spoon	*Toka*	MacGregor 1889	New Guinea	–	–
Mask	?	Landtman 1927	Fly River and Bampton Island	3	Landtman (1927: 48) notes several types of masks being used in the Kiwai district. Of the masks represented in museums, one was collected from the Fly River and another from Bampton (Parama) Island in the 1870s. The third has no location.
Mat	*Tabaro*	MacGregor 1889	New Guinea	–	–
Mourning Dresses	*Sagere*	Edge-Partington (Series 2:177, No.1)	New Guinea	4	Held in MM. Type also known in Torres Strait; uncertain where these were collected although members of the Chevert expedition reported women in mourning at Mokatta in 1875.
Necklace, wallaby incisors	?	Landtman 1927	Strachan Island	1	Landtman (1927: 26) notes that wallaby teeth necklaces came from Budji (a village near the mouth of the Mai Kussa River).
Nut, used as rattle in dances	*Sia*	MacGregor 1889	New Guinea	–	–
Paddle	*Ibee* *Hibe* *Aibi*	Chester 1870a, b Hargrave 1875 MacGregor 1889	New Guinea	–	–

Appendix 4.1 (continued)

English name	Indigenous name	Source	Locality (general or known collecting locality)	No. in museums	Notes
Petticoat	*Wapa*	MacGregor 1889	New Guinea	5	Women's 'grass' petticoats were traded from the Fly River estuary in the early 1900s (Beaver 1920: 75).
Pendant, of shell (Conus shell) worn from neck	*Bidi-Bidi* *Bibidibi*	Chester 1870a, b MacGregor 1889	New Guinea	2	See Landtman (1927: 26). Chester (1870a, b) described this ornament as 'common' but MacGregor (1889) indicates that this type of ornament (made from the ground down base of cone shell) was valued by Kiwai Islanders. Two examples in the MM were collected before 1882 and are without documentation (they may have been collected in Torres Strait where they were known as *dibidibi*).
Pipe, bamboo Pipe, tobacco	*Marahba* *Tar-rook* *Waduru*	Chester 1870a, b Hargrave 1875 MacGregor 1889	New Guinea (Mokatta, and Sumaut)	5	Another pipe (not held in any museum collection) was collected at Mokatta by Lawrence Hargrave in 1875.
Pipe, Bowl of	*Ahteroop*	Chester 1870a, b	New Guinea	?	Bowls of pipes are often missing in museum collections.
Rattle, seed-pod (goa-nut)	?	Edge-Partington	Katow River area	1	Edge-Partington (Series 1:322, No. 3 – 'Rattle used in beating the bush in pig hunts', Katau River).
Rope of Vines	*Yopo*	Chester 1870a, b	New Guinea	–	–
Rope Rope, plaited rope	*Kari* *Pou bari, isisira*	MacGregor 1889	New Guinea	–	–
Shield	*Gope*	MacGregor 1889	New Guinea	–	According to Landtman (1927: 49) *gope* boards were used as canoe decoration (see above).
Spear (fish)	*Tete*	MacGregor 1889	New Guinea	–	–

Appendix 4.1 (continued)

English name	Indigenous name	Source	Locality (general or known collecting locality)	No. in museums	Notes
Torch, of coconut leaf	*Pida*	MacGregor 1889	New Guinea	–	–
Turtle spear	*Wappoo*	Chester 1870a, b	New Guinea	–	–
Washboards of canoe	*Kowtah*	Chester 1870a, b	New Guinea	–	–
Tally Sticks	?	D'Albertis 1881	Southwest Coast	–	A set of tally sticks in the MM are without documentation but could originate from New Guinea.

Appendix 4.1 has been compiled from indigenous vocabularies gathered by Chester (1870b), Hargrave (1875) and MacGregor (ARBNG 1889–1890). Chester's vocabulary consisted of 180 New Guinea words spoken between Talbot Island (Boigu) and the Fly River which he appears to have obtained from Papuans living on Darnley (Erub) Island in Torres Strait in 1870. A small vocabulary of 'Kattow words' was obtained by Lawrence Hargrave during the Chevert voyage in 1875 while Sir William MacGregor's 'Aboriginal Vocabulary of Kiwai' appears in ARBNG 1889–1890, pp. 124–130. MacGregor noted that with dialectic differences the Kiwai language was spoken between Kiwai Island and the Mai Kussa River and some 80–100 miles up the Fly River (some of the items on MacGregor's list are therefore probably outside the region under review; e.g. cuirass of cane). This table omits RGSA expedition 1885 material except those items definitely collected at Sumaut (Fly River estuary) where trade is known to have occurred between expedition members and villagers (Everill 1885: 250–251). Most the RGSA collections were obtained further up the Fly or Strickland Rivers, through plunder rather than trade (see Philp 2007). There are 20 RGSA items in the AM without precise collecting localities while the QM holds around 890 items from the expedition (arrows comprised around half this number), most of which are without documentation. Pre-1882 AM material has been extracted from AM Annual Reports and early AM Registers (this material was destroyed by fire in 1882). Only items which appear to have been collected before south eastern New Guinea was proclaimed a British colony are included.

References

Annual Reports on British New Guinea (ARBNG) 1889–1890. British Government, London.

Australian Museum Purchase Schedule 7/1886 (relating to purchase of 10 New Guinea 'Curios' from J. Strachan in 1886), Australian Museum Archives, Sydney.

Baxter-Riley, E.
   1925 *Among Papuan Headhunters*. Lippincott, Philadelphia, PA.

Beardmore, Edward
   1890 The Natives of Mowat, Daudai, New Guinea. *Journal of the Royal Anthropological Institute of Great Britain and Ireland* 19: 459–466.

Beaver, Wilfred N.
   1920 *Unexplored New Guinea*. Seeley, Service & Co., London.

Chalmers, James
   1903 Notes on the Natives of Kiwai Island, Fly River, British New Guinea. *Journal of the Royal Anthropological Institute of Great Britain and Ireland* 33: 117–124.

Chester, Henry Majoribanks
   1870a Account of a visit to Warrior Island in September and October of 1870 with a description of the pearl fishery on the Warrior Reef. Unpublished manuscript, Letter no. 3425 of 1870, QSA COL/A151, Z7607, Queensland State Archives, Brisbane.
   1870b An account of a visit to New Guinea in September 1870 (separate manuscript attached to the account of a visit to Warrior Island in September and October 1870 noted above). Unpublished manuscript, Z7607, Letter no. 3425 of 1870, QSA COL/A151, Queensland State Archives, Brisbane.

Connor, E.R. in J. Moresby
   1875 Recent Discoveries at the Eastern End of New Guinea. *Journal of the Royal Geographical Society of London* 44: 2–6.

D'Albertis, Luigi Maria
   1881 *New Guinea: What I Did and What I Saw*, Volumes 1–2, 2nd ed. Sampson Low, London.

Edelfelt, E.G.
   1892 Customs and Superstitions of New Guinea Natives. *Royal Geographical Society of Australasia (Queensland), Proceedings and Transactions* 7(1): 9–28.

Edge-Partington, James and Charles Heape
   1890–1898 *An Album of the Weapons, Tools, Ornaments, Articles of Dress etc., of the Natives of the Pacific Islands*. Volumes 1–3, Palmer Howe & Co., Manchester.

Edmundson, Anna and Chris Boylan
   1999 *Adorned: Traditional Jewellery and Body Decoration from Australia and the Pacific*. Macleay Museum, University of Sydney, Sydney.

Everill, H.C.
   1885 Letters. In *Special Volume of the Proceedings of the Royal Geographical Society of Australasia,* edited by A.C. Macdonald, J.H. Maiden and T.H. Myring, pp. 240–253. Thomas Richards. Government Printer, Sydney.

Gill, W. Wyatt
   1875 Three Visits to New Guinea. *Journal of the Royal Geographical Society of London* 44: 15–31.

Gray, Alastair C.
    1999 Trading Contacts in the Bismarck Archipelago during the Whaling Era, 1799–1884.
    Journal of Pacific History 34(1): 23–43.

Haddon, Alfred C.
    1894 *The Decorative Art of British New Guinea: A Study in Papuan Ethnography*. Academy
    House, Dublin.

Haddon, Alfred C. (editor)
    1901–1935 *Reports of the Cambridge Anthropological Expedition to Torres Straits*, Volumes
    1–6. Cambridge University Press, Cambridge. (Volume 1, *Ethnography*, 1935; Volume 4,
    Haddon et al, *Arts and Crafts*, 1912).

Hargrave, Lawrence
    1875 Torres Strait and Papua New Guinea Diaries, 25 January 1872–2 February 1876, pp.
    1–38. Relate to the *Chevert* Expedition, Lawrence Hargrave Papers, Powerhouse Museum
    (Sydney), 94/23/1–1/1.

Hooper, Steven
    2006 *Pacific Encounters, Art & Divinity in Polynesia, 1760–1860*. The British Museum Press,
    London.

Jukes, John Beete
    1847 *Narrative of the surveying voyage of H.M.S. Fly, commanded by Captain F.P. Blackwood,
    R.N. in Torres Strait, New Guinea, and other islands of the eastern archipelago, during the
    years 1842–1846; together with an excursion into the eastern part of Java*, Volumes 1–2.
    T & W Boone, London.

Landtman, Gunnar
    1917 *Folktales of the Kiwai Papuans*. Finnish Society of Literature, Helsingfors.
    1927 *The Kiwai Papuans of British New Guinea*. Macmillan, London.
    1933 *Ethnographical Collection from the Kiwai District of British New Guinea*. Commission
    of the Antell Collection, Helsingfors.

Lawrence, David
    1994 Customary Exchange Across Torres Strait. *Memoirs of the Queensland Museum* 34(2):
    241–446.

Log of the *Chevert*, commanded by Capt Charles Edwards, kept by Robert Williams (Chief
    Officer), Macleay Museum, University of Sydney.

Macleay, William John
    1875a Private journal for 1875. Transcription by Dr Woody Horning held in the Macleay
    Museum. Original journal held in Manuscripts, ML MSS. 2009, Mitchell Library, Sydney.
    1875b The Voyage of the Chevert. *Sydney Morning Herald*, 11 October 1875.

McNiven, Ian J.
    2001 Torres Strait and the Sea Frontier in Early Colonial Australia. In *Colonial Frontiers:
    Indigenous-European Encounters in Settler Societies*, edited by Lynette Russell, pp. 175–
    179. Manchester University Press, New York, NY.

Moore, Clive
    1998 Tooree: The Dynamics of Early Contact and Trade in Torres Strait, Cape York and the
    Trans-Fly to 1890, Looking Back to Southeast Asia from the Pacific. In *Lasting Fascinations,
    Essays on Indonesia and the Southwest Pacific to Honour Bob Hering*, edited by Harry
    A. Poeze and Antoinette Liem, pp. 257–279. Monograph No. 2 of the Yayasan Soekarno
    Monograph Series, Yayasan Kabar Seberang/Yayasan Soekarno.
    2004 *New Guinea, Crossing Boundaries and History*. University of Hawaii Press, Honolulu.

Moore, David R.
1984 *The Torres Strait Collections of A.C. Haddon*. British Museum Press, London.

Mullins, Steve
1994 *Torres Strait: A History of Colonial Occupation and Culture Contact, 1864–1897*. Central Queensland University Press, Rockhampton.

Murray, A.W.
1876 *Forty Years' Mission Work in Polynesia and New Guinea, from 1835 to 1875*. James Nisbet & Co., London.

Petterd, W. F.
1876 New Guinea [No. 1]. (W.F. Petterd's account of Katow – relates to the *Chevert* Expedition). *The Mercury*, 19 April 1876, p. 3.

Philp, Jude
2007 The Royal Geographical Society Expedition to the Western Province of British New Guinea in the 1880s. In *Hunting the Collectors: Pacific Collections in Australian Museums, Art Galleries and Archives*, edited by Susan Cochrane and Max Quanchi, pp. 17–31. Cambridge Scholars Publishing, Newcastle.

Royal Geographical Society of Australasia
1885 *Instructions issued by the Royal Geographical Society of Australasia, The New Guinea Exploring Expedition. Sydney 12 June 1885*. F. Cunninghame & Co., Sydney.

Stone, Octavius C.
1875–1876 Discovery of the Mai-Kassa, or Baxter River, New Guinea. *Proceedings of the Royal Geographical Society of London* 20(2): 92–109.

Strachan, John
1888 *Explorations and Adventures in New Guinea*. Sampson Low, Marston, Searle and Rivington, London.

Sydney Morning Herald, 18 September 1875, p. 5.

Thomson, C. Wyville
1885 *Report on the scientific results of the voyage of H.M.S. Challenger, Narrative*, Volume 1, Part 2. H.M.S.O., London.

Vanderwal, R.
2004 Early Historical Sources for the Top Western Torres Strait Exchange Network. In *Torres Strait Archaeology and Material Culture,* edited by Ian J. McNiven and Michael Quinnell, pp. 257–270. Memoirs of the Queensland Museum, Cultural Heritage Series, Brisbane, Volume 3, Part 1.

Waite, Deborah B.
1987 *Artefacts from the Solomon Islands in the Julius L. Brenchley Collection*. The Trustees of the British Museum, London.

Young, Michael W. and Julia Clarke
2001 *The Photography of F.E. Williams, 1922–1939*. Crawford House Publishing in association with the National Archives of Australia, Adelaide.

Part III
Collectors and Nationhood

Chapter 5
Donors, Loaners, Dealers and Swappers: The Relationship behind the English Collections at the Pitt Rivers Museum

Chris Wingfield

Abstract Deriving from research conducted as part of *The Other Within* research project at the Pitt Rivers Museum, this chapter is intended less as a theoretical argument about materiality, agency and identity and more as a methodological contribution. Its intention is to examine and critique, as well as develop the potential of museum databases as a source of information on the relationships that lie behind museum collections. While 'making the museum central' and unpacking the collection 'along the grain' have been advocated, this does not necessarily mean that databases should be taken at face value. They are tools for museum professionals, and the way in which they present information tends to direct attention in particular directions – in the case of the Pitt Rivers Museum to the place of their ultimate origin, and to techniques of manufacture and use. However, alongside this information there remain traces of the donors, loaners, dealers and swappers who have been involved in the wider network out of which the Museum has taken shape. These traces can provide a means to explore and evaluate the complex and diffuse operations of agency in relation to the assembling of the collection.

Introduction

Visitors to the University of Oxford's Pitt Rivers Museum can be fascinated by its thousands of objects, arranged in rows of glass cases or in some instances hanging from the ceilings. Their attention is drawn to the non-human things in the Museum by a combination of theatrical staging and lighting. While the Museum presents itself as a building full of things, in reality, the institution also depends on a great many humans. Some humans curate, conserve and display the things in the Museum, while others have presented them to the museum in the first place. A museum is an excellent example of the sort of assemblage of humans and non-humans, that Bruno Latour (2005) has called an 'actor-network'. While 'network' suggests the

C. Wingfield (✉)
Pitt Rivers Museum, Oxford University, Oxford, UK
e-mail: chris.wingfield@prm.ox.ac.uk

S. Byrne et al. (eds.), *Unpacking the Collection*, One World Archaeology,
DOI 10.1007/978-1-4419-8222-3_5, © Springer Science+Business Media, LLC 2011

complex way in which things are bound together, 'actor' emphasises that these networks have agency – they do things. In this compound term, the dichotomy between structure and agency is neatly dissolved (Latour 2005: 216–218). Agency is widely distributed throughout an actor-network, and it can by no means be assumed that it is necessarily the humans who do things to the non-humans. Alfred Gell's (1998) writings have often been invoked in support of the argument that objects have agency, but his argument has another implication that is less remarked upon, but possibly more significant. This is that humans frequently do not have agency – they are acted upon and according to his terminology, therefore, become patients rather than agents. In Gell's (1998: 7) scheme, what he calls the art-object can as easily be a human as a non-human. As anyone who has read Gell's book will know, attempting to get to grips with the implications of distributed agency can lead to a bewildering array of increasingly complex flow diagrams. However, what can be taken from these theoretical discussions is that agency is widely spread, and is mediated by each of the nodes in the network through which it flows. Locating agency in museum collections then, may be a question of tracing a network of these mediators, through which collections are made to do things.

The Pitt Rivers Museum database is not unlike the rest of the Museum in that it focuses one's attention on the non-human objects, with one record allocated to each. At the top of the main display screen in prominent bold type is the accession number, and below that is the place the object comes from with any associated cultural group. The next categories describe the type of object, the materials it is made from and its dimensions. Only then, just above a series of longer textual descriptions does the database record a number of categories in which the names of humans connected with the object may be recorded. One of these is for 'Maker' and another for 'Field Collector'. There is also a category of 'Other Owners' for people who have owned the object before it arrived at the Museum. The final role that can be assigned to humans by the Museum database is 'PRM Source' – that is the person or institution from which the Pitt Rivers Museum acquired the object. This might seem to cover all the human hands through which an object might pass between its manufacture and its acquisition by the Museum. However, the data recorded in most of these categories is incomplete. Even for objects in the Museum that have their origin in nearby England,[1] less than 20% of the database records have a maker recorded and well over half of these are plaster casts of church bells personally made by George Phillip Elphick, their collector. If these are excluded, the figure drops to less than one in ten, and many of those are derived from manufacturer's marks imprinted on the objects themselves. Only around one half of the database records include additional information on 'Other Owners'. By contrast, over 99% of the database records

[1] The research underlying this paper took place as part of a three year research project: *The Other Within; An Anthropology of Englishness* funded by the UK's Economic and Social Research Council (RES-000-23-1439) – see http://england.prm.ox.ac.uk/. The project focussed on the Museum's collections from England and developed from a finding from an earlier phase of database-focussed research (*The Relational Museum* – http://history.prm.ox.ac.uk/): that over 30,000 objects from England form around 12% of the total Pitt Rivers Museum collection.

have a clearly identified 'PRM Source'. The further one travels away from their arrival at the Museum, the more obscure the human and transactional history of its objects becomes. A significant reason for this is that the information in the database is mostly derived from the Museum's accession registers. These are a record of the transactions by which an object was transferred to the custodianship of the Museum, so the 'sources' were of prime importance as the partners in these exchanges. Who made a particular object, who owned it beforehand and who collected it in the field are categories that have largely been worked out retrospectively since the database has been in existence.

A great deal of research has been addressed at identifying the field collectors of objects, as distinct from the Museum's 'source' of the material (Petch 2004). The caricature of the ethnographic field collector is a person who has travelled to the place where the thing comes from, perhaps an anthropologist or colonial administrator, who somehow detaches the object from its usual context. Barbara Kirshenblatt-Gimblett (1998: 18) has suggested that 'objects become ethnographic by virtue of being defined, segmented, detached, and carried away by ethnographers'. This would seem to imply that the maker of something might be one person, but its maker as an 'ethnographic object' would be its field collector. During the middle of the twentieth century when both archaeology and social anthropology emerged as distinct enterprises, they increasingly identified themselves as field sciences. Unlike the first generation of professional anthropologists who were employed to work in museums, claims to knowledge made by twentieth century archaeologists and anthropologists were increasingly based on 'time in the field' (Livingstone 2003). While identifying field collectors accords with the twentieth-century focus of the disciplines with which the Pitt Rivers Museum is associated, it also has the tendency of marginalising the museum and locating it away from the action. The field becomes where science is done, discoveries are made and objects are excised or detached, while the museum is just somewhere that things eventually end up.

Arguably, this is also reflected in the prominence the Pitt Rivers Museum database attaches to the place an object is 'from' rather than where it 'is now' or how it has ended up there. Nevertheless, tracing the movement of an object from its place of manufacture to the museum can be a long and complex process involving many stages. This can involve many more transactions and acts of detachment than those characterised as 'field collecting'. They could include the sale or gift of objects by the person who made them, their purchase and sale by local dealers, sales at auction houses, gifts from one collector to another and even an object's inheritance by subsequent generations of the same family. A very large number of objects in ethnographic museums were deliberately made for sale by people in places such as Central Africa (Schildkrout and Keim 1998) and Melanesia (O'Hanlon and Welsch 2000), so the degree to which ethnographic objects are best understood as fragments 'detached and carried away by ethnographers' deserves to be critically assessed (see also Harrison 2006). There have been some instances during the twentieth century when the Pitt Rivers Museum, acting through its employees, actively collected in the field creating a direct exchange relationship with the makers of its objects. However, in most cases the Museum has been connected to the makers of its objects only by long and complex chains of mediators. In these instances, tracking an object back to its maker entails attempting to trace a series of transactions involving many different people as well as multiple acts of detachment. The obscuring effects of some of these can mean that following this trail is no longer possible (Petch 2004). By focussing attention on the 'field' and the 'field collector' as the principle agent of detachment by which an object is removed from its 'authentic' context, the museum obscures its own context, a context of donors, collectors and dealers; of auction sales, bequests and transactions of many different kinds. Arguably the single most important act of detachment in the history of any museum object occurs when it is accessioned by the museum, rather than in some ambiguous and possibly mythical place called 'the field' (Livingstone 2003).

Indigenous Agency and the Postcolonial Field

In many ways, trying to identify indigenous agency by examining museum collections is a similar project to attempting to identify field collectors. While the agency of the original maker of an object in the museum might be 'abducted' (Gell 1998: 13) from the physical form it takes, this agency will often have been heavily mediated by the range of processes and transactions through which the thing has passed since it was made. As the field collector is an important figure in anthropological disciplinary politics, so the indigenous agent is an important figure in postcolonial politics. In characterising the archaeologies that first arose in settler societies as 'colonialist', Bruce Trigger (1984: 360) suggested that they had a tendency to emphasise the 'primitiveness and lack of accomplishments' of indigenous peoples in order 'to justify poor treatment of them'. Trigger also suggested that 'the questions that are asked and the answers that appear reasonable reflect the positions that societies occupy within the modern world-system and change as the positions of countries alter within that system' (Trigger 1984: 368). While the earliest phase of archaeology in settler societies tended to minimise the agency of indigenous people, its more recent phase has tended to maximise it, and this is undoubtedly a useful corrective. Nevertheless, what is retained by 'postcolonial archaeologies' despite their shift in emphasis is the assumption that the focus of study and research should necessarily be on indigenous people.

While ethnographic museums in settler nations tended to focus on recording and displaying material from local indigenous groups, similar museums in England, at the heart of the British empire, frequently attempted to adopt the global or world-oriented focus which Trigger (1984: 363) identifies with what he calls 'Imperialist archaeology'. One consequence of the global focus, at least in the case of the Pitt Rivers Museum, was that the museum not only collected and displayed material that seemed to suggest evidence of 'primitive' forms of life in the Empire's distant colonial possessions but it also collected and displayed similar material from nearer to home. Alongside archaeological and ethnographic material, 'survivals' formed a third and not insignificant category of material collected at the Pitt Rivers Museum. Although the term 'folk' was often used in these contexts, in ways that are similar to the use of terms such as 'native' or 'indigene' in colonial contexts, the terms cannot be substituted straightforwardly. While many 'survivals' originated among the rural and urban working classes, they could also be found among the practices and material culture of the aristocracy and even the urban bourgeoisie. 'Survivals' of more primitive forms, could, it seems, turn up almost anywhere. While it would be possible to seek out working-class agency in an analogous way to uncovering indigenous agency in a settler context, to do so would probably miss the point.

The problem becomes clearer if we consider the problem of identifying the 'field collector' of objects in the Museum that have been collected in England. The conventional definition of secondary collecting used by the Pitt Rivers Museum is obtaining 'artefacts through a non-"native" trader, dealer or auction house' (Petch 2004: 2). Given that the Museum is itself located in England, is staffed by 'natives' and invariably obtains its English collections from 'natives', this distinction between a 'field' collector and a 'secondary collector' becomes immediately unclear, if not irrelevant. Would an English dealer buying an English item at an English market stall, and then selling it to the Pitt Rivers Museum be a secondary collector, a field collector or even a primary field source? The English objects at the Pitt Rivers Museum make it possible to see more clearly the sometimes unhelpful distinctions between native and non-native, and between field and 'armchair' collectors, which are part of the disciplinary heritage of anthropology. In the case of the English market stall described above, the roles imagined for humans by the database categories at the Pitt Rivers Museum are simply too limited and prescriptive to deal with the complex relationships that humans frequently get involved in when dealing with non-human things. In addition, a focus on manufacture and field collecting, the processes in which 'indigenous actors' are most likely to be involved, nevertheless fails to recognise that many of the most complex interactions involving the Museum's collections have taken place during the itineraries the objects have taken between manufacture and the Museum.

Ann Stoler (2009: 47) has recently argued that many studies of colonialism have 'located "structure" with colonizers and the colonial state, and "human agency" with subalterns, in small gestures of refusal and silence among the colonized.' As a consequence, a great deal of work investigating subaltern agency has attempted to read 'against the grain' of colonial conventions. However, Stoler (2009: 50) has argued that '[a]ssuming we know those scripts rests too comfortably on predictable stories with familiar plots'. Instead, she has advocated a 'less assured and perhaps more humble stance – to explore the grain with care and read along it first' (Stoler 2009: 50). In her own work on colonial archives, Stoler (2009: 20) has outlined an approach based on 'archiving-as-process rather than archives-as-thing'. In approaching the operation of agency in relation to museum collections, it seems that there is probably much that could be learned from this approach. Rather than approaching the collection as a source, a site or a thing to be interrogated, it might be fruitful to approach the collection-as-process and attempt to read 'along its grain' at least in the first instance. While ethnographic museum databases may aspire to present information about the 'original context' from which an object has come, this is removed from the museum in both space and time, and can probably only be reached by attempting to trace the network through which the collection has passed. The museum in the present is the inevitable starting point for any such explorations. A first step away from the museum can be taken by interrogating the museum's documentation, which invariably records the immediate source of the items, and the manner in which they arrived. Rather than focussing attention directly on the interface between the native and non-native, indigene and colonialist, it might be helpful to begin with the current location of collections – the museum. Reading museum documentation along the grain makes it necessary to concentrate, at least in the first instance, on the museum's immediate sources of objects, as the first links in the chains of mediators linking the museum to the rest of the world. It may or may not then be possible, depending on the evidence available, to trace these chains back to the original maker of the museum object, but the process will nevertheless reveal a great deal about the network of relationships in which the museum has operated and ultimately from which it has been formed.

Making the Museum Central

Previous research at the Pitt Rivers Museum conducted during the Relational Museum project between 2003 and 2006 aimed to capture a sense of the complex web of relationships that connected many of the humans involved in establishing the collections at the Pitt Rivers Museum (Gosden et al. 2007). This project used database information about the people connected with the collections, as well as further biographical sources in an attempt to investigate the social networks that underlay the creation of the Museum. A formal network analysis was developed by David Zeitlyn at the University of Kent from a database of humans involved with the Museum's collection, resulting in a number of computer-generated network diagrams (Larson et al. 2007). One drawback with this approach was that it treated all connections as being of equal importance (Larson et al. 2007: 236). A single gift of one object might not be distinguished in the resulting diagram from 20 sales totalling thousands of objects (Larson et al. 2007: 220). Connections might have even emerged from the mutual membership of a single learned society and because the diagrams relied on historical research about collectors to constitute some of these connections, the degree of connection relied strongly on the completeness and representativeness of the information available. In addition, the resultant network diagrams only featured individual humans as nodes in the networks. The Pitt Rivers Museum, an institution to which most of the humans were directly connected through donations and sales of material, remained invisible, except through the presence of the humans who worked there.

As noted above, the records in the Pitt Rivers Museum database are effectively a digitisation of a series of handwritten accession books. While the database is object-focussed, having one record per object, this is frequently not the case for the accession books. Instead, what they record are the transactions when objects were transferred to the care of the institution and the legal ownership of 'The Chancellor Masters and Scholars of the University of Oxford'. Looked at in this way, the accessions registers provide a trace of a large number of acts of exchange in which the museum as an actor-network has been involved. It would be possible to redesign the museum database along similar lines so that what it attempted to model was not simply the museum objects themselves, with each record acting as a sort of digital counterpart, but rather the 'collection-as-process'. Rather than creating one record per object, top-level records in a relational database could be focussed on events, such as acquisition by the museum, with each such record connecting a range of human and non-human actors. These actors, brought together in a particular place and time to create the event, might include the objects in the collection but would also be the curators, donors and even the buildings in which the transaction took place. Such an approach would involve treating the museum as a corporate entity in its own right. While there may have been key humans employed by the museum, the Pitt Rivers Museum as a part of the University of Oxford received donations and made purchases as a social actor in its own right. The Museum's accession registers are documents that record the formal reconfiguration of a set of relationships in relation to groups of non-human objects, as legal ownership and responsibility for them shifted from one party to another. The registers also recognise the manner in which this transfer took place, whether through gift, loan, exchange or sale. It has long been recognised that different forms of transaction may be related to different degrees of social distance or proximity (Sahlins 1974). Approached in this way, the accession registers may reveal not only the exchange partners of the museum but also something of the content of the relationships it has had been involved in, and which have ultimately constituted it in its present shape. Focussing on these transactions as key 'acts of detachment', rather than purely on those involved in field collecting means locating the museum itself as a central place in any analysis.

Does Size Matter?

A major problem when considering museum collections as manifestations of complex networks of relationships is establishing whether certain relationships were more significant than others. Many of the statistics about the collections of the Pitt Rivers Museum that have been derived from its database have tended to give weight to collections on the basis on their size – the raw number of individual objects they are composed of (Petch 2006, see http://history.prm.ox.ac.uk/ and http://england. prm.ox.ac.uk/). Collectors have tended to be ranked in tables ordered according to the size of their collections. However, this is partially an artefact of the way in which the Museum database is designed, making it easy to generate queries in terms of numbers of objects and does not necessarily provide an obvious weighting to the relationship of collectors with the Museum. Many of the statistics generated about the Museum's collections, whether from England or worldwide, have resulted in tables that are dominated by stone tools and textiles collections and their collectors. One part of the reason for this is the significance of these items in the history of the Museum, but is partly due to the ease of collecting large numbers of these objects at low cost. However, it is also an artefact of the way in which separate objects are counted by the museum database. Each physically divisible part of an item is counted as a separate object. A pack of cards plus jokers and a box would be recorded as 55 objects by the database. A single lace pillow with associated bobbins from Somerset is recorded by the database as 117 separate objects, meaning that this single assemblage would show up as a total of 117 in any table of statistics. In addition, the number of objects in a particular collection area is at least partially a function of the amount of collections management and research work that has been undertaken. The number of objects in the Museum's collection recorded by the museum databases as being from England has increased significantly since the commencement of detailed research in 2006, as things not previously counted individually or recognised as museum objects (such as photographs) have been added to the total.

As an indicator of the activity of the Museum, statistics dependent on the total number of objects recorded by the database risk masking two different kinds of activity. When assessed in numerical terms, a single acquisition of an extremely large collection could have the same statistical impact as a large number of separate acquisitions of one or two objects. We probably would not suggest that someone who left a single large collection to the Museum at the end of his/her life had the same relationship with the Museum as someone who gave and lent smaller numbers of objects throughout his/her adult life. Nevertheless, this is what tables of donors, listed according to the numbers of objects they are associated with, would tend to suggest. Underlying apparently similarly sized collections can be various patterns of activity that might indicate quite different underlying relationships. Using the number of objects in the database as an indicator of either the museum's activity or of the significance of its relationship with a particular collector would be similar to trying to assess the financial success of the museum's shop by counting the number of coins processed at the till rather than thinking about either their value or the number of transactions that they were generated from.

From Totals to Acquisition Events

In developing an analysis of the collections of Sir John Lubbock, Janet Owen (1999, 2006) has developed the notion of *collecting events* based on discourse analysis (Owen 1999: 288). In determining these, Owen worked not from a database but from two notebooks in which Lubbock recorded the acquisition of 1243 items between 1863 and 1914 (Owen 1999: 284). These functioned in the same way as the Pitt Rivers museum's accession registers, and Owen, in attempting to analyse the changing intensity of collecting activity concentrated not on the total number of objects collected, but on collection events (Owen 1999: 290). These were identified largely on the basis of the catalogue entries as 'single acts of collecting'. She suggests that the 1243 items in Lubbock's collection can be accounted for by 430 collecting events (Owen 1999: 291), with the first 251 objects recorded in Lubbock's notebook forming a single collecting event when a complete collection was purchased from a Danish student, Vilhelm Boye. Although a graphical analysis of Lubbock's 'collecting events' suggests a similar pattern to a graphical analysis of acquisition by the total number of objects, there are also significant divergences. In addition, Owen uses her data to plot different lines on the graph for different methods of acquisition, and while the profile of gifts follows that of general collecting activity, she is able to identify different patterns for purchases and collecting events in the field. Both of these are concentrated for Lubbock in the period 1866–1872 (Owen 1999: 292), which Owen suggests indicates a period of more active collecting by Lubbock, in contrast to the more passive later mode of receiving gifts from friends and colleagues. In the gifts that followed this initial period of active collecting, Owen (1999: 298) has suggested that Lubbock was not the active party and that these gifts became a means of 'reinforcing friendships, status, family ties and networks.'

If it is to be accepted that the Pitt Rivers Museum operates like a 'person' and is a social actor, as suggested above, then it should be possible to treat the Museum's collection as a node in a collecting network in a manner similar to that in which Owen has treated the collection of Lubbock. The Pitt Rivers Museum began with the personal collection of General Pitt Rivers, a human person who was closely connected to John Lubbock. However, after 1884 this became merely the starting point of a new collection which was owned by a non-human person – the University of Oxford – and is paralleled by the way in which Lubbock's collection began with the collection of Vilhelm Boye. There is obviously a question of scale since the collection of the Pitt Rivers Museum is around 300 times the size of Lubbock's and was formed over a period at least twice as long as that in which Lubbock made his own collection. Apart from this, which may simply be a result of dealing with a non-human body, there seems little reason not to approach the Museum's collection in the same way. By treating the Museum as a collecting agent, and a node of exchange in a network of relationships, it should be possible to apply a similar methodology to analysing the formation of its collections. However, given the already established terminological association of the term 'collecting' with field collecting, it seems sensible to refer to these events in relation to the museum as *acquisition events*.

Determining Acquisition Events

As part of *The Other Within* research project, it was decided to attempt a trial of this approach in relation to the collections of English material at the Pitt Rivers Museum. This had the advantage of restricting the analysis to a defined, though arbitrary section of the Museum's collection, as well as allowing a comparison with statistics based on total numbers of objects. The first stage of work was to determine the acquisition events related to these objects. Using this approach, the collection of

3249 stone tools sold to the Museum by Archibald Bell following the death of his father would only count as one acquisition event, immediately reducing the impact of such large collections on the apparent activity suggested by statistical tables based on the total numbers of objects. Unfortunately, the Filemaker database used by the Museum does not have a function for identifying acquisition events. However, as already noted, the accession registers, on which the database is based, group accessions by donor, broadly reflecting the sequence of acquisition events. Most of the Museum's accession numbers have been generated retrospectively on the basis of these groupings in the form *year.acquisition number.object number*. For much of the Museum's collection, the middle number in the sequence provides a key to the acquisition event, as all objects donated at the same time by a single donor should have a single number, starting with 1 at the beginning of each new year and generated sequentially. In addition, the year that begins the accession number places each accession event in a chronological sequence.

Obviously, this is an ideal picture and does not account for occasional instances when single donations may have been recorded in separate batches and so appear to be separate acquisition events. It also assumes that the information recorded in the registers is accurate, but if it is not, this is a limitation of the Museum documentation and not of the approach. For most of the Museum's history, isolating these *acquisition events* is relatively straightforward since accession numbers have been based on the formula described above. However, between 1939 and 1965, the second part of the acquisition number came from the month (1–12), rather than the collection number, meaning that additional work was needed to identify separate acquisition events for acquisitions between these dates. These had to be generated by looking at all records for any given months, and in instances where there are multiple acquisitions from a single source trying to determine by the sequence in which they have been entered whether they represent single or multiple acquisition events. Identifying acquisition events in this way was a fairly laborious process, and it was greatly aided in this case because work by Alison Petch had already identified all the donors of English material to the Pitt Rivers Museum and also created a separate database which only included the objects identified by the database as from England. In addition, a student volunteer, Katy Barrett agreed to spend a period of the summer in 2007 undertaking the initial work of carrying out database searches for each identified source of material and identifying the number of acquisition events they were involved in. This initial work was then followed up with a detailed analysis of those donors who had been identified as being involved in multiple acquisition events, as well as the analysis of the different forms of acquisition events such as loan, exchange and sale. The end result of this data processing has been the creation of an Excel spreadsheet with a row for each source of material. Each row is made up of a number of columns listing the number of acquisition events, the total number of objects donated and also the number of acquisition events involving various forms of exchange such as donations, purchases, loans or exchanges. It has then been possible to interrogate this spreadsheet in various ways in order to produce a range of lists and graphs based on acquisition events, examples of which will be given below.

Analysing Acquisition Events

Using a database of 44,133 objects in the Museum's collection from England, current in September 2007, it was possible to identify 1515 acquisition events involving English objects and 796 different sources of material. A source in most cases is a human identified by the database in the category 'PRM Source'; however, non-human corporations such as other museums are also included in this field. This gives a mean collection size at acquisition of 29 objects and the mean number of acquisition events per source of 1.9. However, these numbers are not particularly revealing since the majority of sources were involved in only a single acquisition event and a very small number were involved in a great many. Henry Balfour, the Museum's first curator, was the source of material for 104 acquisition events of English material between 1884 and his death in 1939. This is the largest number and a considerable outlier in the distribution (Fig. 5.1). The next highest number of acquisition events associated with a single source is only 36, which relates to Francis Knowles, an early student at the Museum who continued to volunteer there for most of his life. It should be noted that these are events in which Balfour and Knowles were the source of the material, and not events in which they participated on behalf of the Museum. While Balfour might act as an agent of the Pitt Rivers Museum when receiving donations from other sources, or even in purchasing material, in these 106 instances the Museum has recorded that Balfour as a legal person

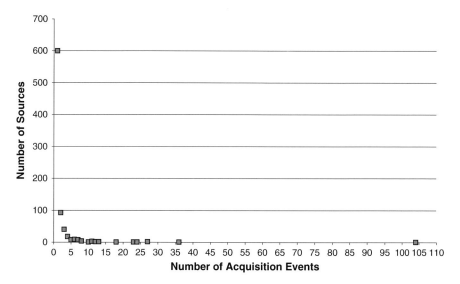

Fig. 5.1 Distribution graph showing the number of 'sources' participating in a given number of acquisition events. The extreme point on the Y-axis shows that 75% of sources were involved in a single acquisition event, while Henry Balfour, the Museum's first curator who was involved in 104, marks the extreme point on the X-axis

in his own right was the exchange partner in a transaction involving the Museum. At times, it seems Balfour was the agent, making the Pitt Rivers Museum do things, while at other times, when he operated as an employee, it was he who was made to do things by the Museum. This finding seems to justify using acquisition events as a measure of the relationship that different persons had with the Museum, since Balfour's relationship was extremely close and much of his own personal and professional identity was derived from his association with the Museum which lasted for most of his life.

For all 796 sources, the median number of acquisition events is 1 and the median value for mean collection size per acquisition is 2 objects. Mean collection size is calculated by dividing the number of objects derived from a source by the number of acquisition events they were involved in. Here again, the distribution plotted in Fig. 5.2 shows that the vast majority of individuals have a mean collection size of 1 – meaning that most sources only transferred a single object to the care of the Museum. Again there are two considerable outliers, Archibald Bell who sold the Museum over 3000 English objects collected by his father in a single transaction and Augustus Henry Lane Fox who donated over 6000 objects from England as part of two acquisition events that formed the founding collection of the Museum, giving a mean collection size close to Bell's. Both donations were predominantly made up of large numbers of archaeological items which has meant that both donors have featured prominently in tables of donors arranged by the number of objects they transferred to the museum. Whereas Balfour's close connections with the museum in Oxford are suggested by the 106 events when he was the source of English material

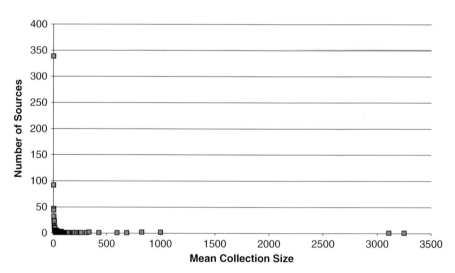

Fig. 5.2 Distribution graph showing the mean collection size against the number of sources. The extreme point on the Y-axis marks the position of most sources of material who donated a single object to the Museum, while the two extreme points on the X-axis mark the positions of Archibald Bell and General Pitt Rivers himself

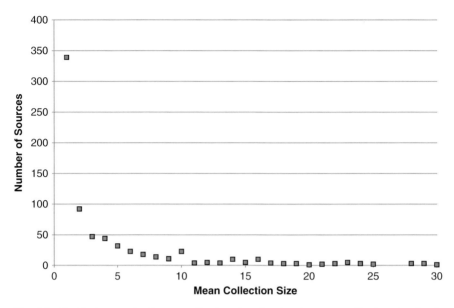

Fig. 5.3 Distribution graph of mean collection size showing the mean collection size for the bottom 90% sources of material (effectively showing *bottom left-hand corner* of Fig. 5.2)

for the Museum, Pitt Rivers' involvement in only two acquisition events suggests that his relationship with the museum that bore his name in Oxford was limited following its foundation.

Figure 5.3 focuses on the lower end of Fig. 5.2 showing that 90% of the 796 sources of material had mean collection sizes under 30. It also suggests that over half of the sources of the English objects in the Pitt Rivers Museum have been involved in transactions that only involved one or two objects. Figure 5.1 suggests that in most cases these would also have been one-off contacts. On the basis of these figures, we can surmise that for most sources of English material at the Pitt Rivers, their relationship with the Museum was short-lived, involved little cost to themselves and was probably reasonably insignificant to the whole of their lives and the range of other relationships and transactions in which they engaged. Their agency in relation to shaping and forming the collection of material from England held by the Pitt Rivers Museum was, it seems fair to conclude, fairly minor.

A Measure of Relationships

While the one-off nature of the majority of transactions with the Pitt Rivers Museum may suggest very weak relationships and little agency on the part of many of the Museum's sources of material, focussing on acquisition events makes it easier to identify those sources for whom the relationship with the Pitt Rivers Museum may have been more significant, because of the large number of acquisition events

Table 5.1 Comparison of ranking by acquisition event and collection size

Top 20 sources of English objects ranked by collection size

Rank	Source	Number of objects donated	Number of acquisition events	Ranking by acquisition events
1	Augustus Henry Lane Fox Pitt Rivers	6,215	2	104
2	Henry Balfour	3,315	104	1
3	Archibald Colquhoun Bell	3,249	1	197
4	Francis Howe Seymour Knowles	2,172	36	2
5	Oxford University Museum of Natural History	1,510	12	11
6	J.H. Tucker	1,381	2	105
7	Eustace Fulcrand Bosanquet	1,282	5	37
8	T.J. Carter	1,146	13	8
9	Damian Webb	1,000[a]	1	198
10	Anselm Cramer	1,000[a]	1	201
11	Trustees George P. Elphick	828[a]	1	200
12	Catherine E. Parsons	828	1	201
13	Margaret F. Irvine	826	10	15
14	Estella Louisa Michaela Canziani	776	11	12
15	Alfred Schwartz Barnes	773	24	5
16	James Reid Moir	755	7	20
17	Ipswich Museum	672	2	106
18	Patricia M. Butler	672	2	107
19	Ellen Ettlinger	600	1	202
20	Beatrice Mary Blackwood	581	18	7

Top 20 sources of English objects ranked by acquisition events

Rank	Source	Number of objects donated	Number of acquisition events	Ranking by collection size
1	Henry Balfour	3,315	104	2
2	Francis Howe Seymour Knowles	2,172	36	4
3	Alexander James Montgomerie Bell	114	27	53
4	Sydney Gerald Hewlett	375	20	25
5	Alfred Schwartz Barnes	773	24	15
6	Stevens Auction Rooms	545	23	21
7	Beatrice Mary Blackwood	581	18	20
8	T.J. Carter	1,146	13	8
9	Kenneth Page Oakley	60	13	80
10	Edward Burnett Tylor	164	12	39
11	Oxford University Museum of Natural History	1,510	12	5
12	Estella Louisa Michaela Canziani	776	11	14
13	George Fabian Lawrence	239	11	31
14	J. Bateman	59	11	82
15	Margaret F. Irvine	826	10	13
16	Edward Lovett	55	8	86
17	Cecil Vincent Goddard	20	8	137
18	Oliver H. Wild	18	8	147
19	Harold St. George Gray	15	8	168
20	James Reid Moir	755	7	16

[a]These figures are estimates

in which they were involved. It seems likely that those who were involved in more acquisition events may have had qualitatively different relationships with the Museum, since the relationships existed for longer and were able to develop more of a history and with that a sense of mutual expectation. In addition, frequent contact in the form of acquisition events might be seen as suggesting a more personally active role in the formation of the collections at the Pitt Rivers Museum, suggestive of a greater degree of influence and agency. While for many human and non-human sources, a one-off donation to the Pitt Rivers Museum was a very minor part of the multiple transactions that made up their social lives, for others their relationship with the Museum was longer lasting and composed of a series of transactions over a considerable period of time. As a means of comparing the insights from total numbers of objects associated with an individual, and with acquisition events, it is possible to juxtapose two lists of names related to the English collections at the Pitt Rivers Museum. The first is ordered according to the number of objects donated. The second is ranked according to the number of acquisition events a source was involved in. Both lists include columns for the total number of objects as well as the number of acquisition events associated with the source and also a ranking from the complete other list. The lists include the top 20 entries for each way of ranking the sources (Table 5.1).

There are nine sources that appear in both lists, suggesting a certain amount of overlap between them. There is obviously some correlation between the number of acquisition events and the total number of objects transferred to the Museum by these events, but this is by no means a clear and straightforward one. Henry Balfour and Francis Knowles who top the list when ranked by acquisition events also appear in the top five when ranked by total collection size. However, General Pitt Rivers who tops the list when ranked by collection size drops to around 100 when considered by the number of acquisition events. This reinforces what has been suggested by archival research – that Pitt Rivers' relationship with the Museum was not as close or sustained after it had been established in Oxford. Arguably, Pitt Rivers did not have much of a relationship with the Pitt Rivers Museum itself, but instead had a relationship with the University of Oxford as a non-human person, from which the Pitt Rivers Museum was generated.

Acquisition Events and Forms of Exchange

In compiling lists of sources, ranked by the number of acquisition events in which they were involved, it became clear that certain types of relationships led to certain names featuring fairly near the top of the list. One grouping was of humans such as Balfour, who had been personally involved in the institution either as staff, students or volunteers. Related to this group are institutions such as the University Museum and Ashmolean Museum which have been corporately linked to the Pitt Rivers through the University of Oxford. Another group involved in regular acquisition events were dealers such T.J. Carter and J. Bateman, who sold material to the Museum. A non-human dealer, Stevens Auction House, is ranked as the sixth most frequent source of English material. Because of this observation, it seemed likely that more regular sources of material would also show a higher proportion of forms of exchange other than donation, which is the most common transaction by which the Museum has received objects. This entailed identifying all sales, loans and exchanges of English material as well as the total number of acquisition events already identified.

Table 5.2 shows a comparison of the proportions of acquisition events made up from donations, purchases, exchanges, loans and transfers, respectively. For all acquisition events, donations make up around 77%, but this figure is over 80% for acquisition events involving sources of material for one event only, whether of single or multiple objects. Interestingly, it is nearly 85% for sources of material involved in between two and five acquisition events. The figures that stand out most relate to the 36 sources involved in six or more acquisition events (just over 4% of the 797 sources of English material). For these, donation makes up between 60–66% of events, depending on whether Henry Balfour is included or not. One might suggest that this difference could be accounted for by dealers, since if they stood to gain financially from the transactions, it might encourage them to be regularly involved in acquisition events with the Museum. This makes up part of the story since the percentage of purchases rises from 17 to 28% of acquisition events for this group which includes seven known dealers for whom purchase is the major form of their acquisition events. Two institutions, the Ashmolean and University Museum account for the increase in transfers, since they were involved when responsibility changed for different aspects of the collections of the University of Oxford. However, there are also significant increases in loans with smaller increases in the percentage of exchanges. Henry Balfour, Beatrice Blackwood and Harold St. George Gray, all at one time employed at the Pitt Rivers Museum, loaned as well as gave material to the Museum. Alongside dealers, University museums and staff members, this list of the 36 most regular sources of English material for the Pitt Rivers includes another significant sub-group. This is made up of 'amateur antiquarians', all individuals who frequently had another source of income, such as teaching or church ministry. These 17 individuals appear to have been in regular contact with the Museum, and active in adding

Table 5.2 Comparison of forms of exchange

Sample	Number of sources		Donations		Purchases		Exchanges		Loan		Transfer	
All events	796	100%	1,166	77.0%	257	17.0%	12	0.8%	53	3.5%	27	1.8%
Single object events	309	39%	256	82.9%	48	15.5%	1	0.3%	3	1.0%	1	0.3%
Multiple object events	487	61%	911	75.8%	209	17.4%	9	0.8%	48	4.0%	25	2.1%
Single events	600	75%	487	81.2%	99	16.5%	1	0.2%	9	1.5%	4	0.7%
Multiple events	196	25%	680	74.6%	158	17.3%	9	1.0%	42	4.6%	22	2.4%
Multiple events < 5	160	20%	357	84.8%	49	11.6%	4	1.0%	3	0.7%	8	1.9%
Multiple events > 5	36	4.5%	323	65.9%	109	22.2%	5	1.0%	39	7.7%	14	2.9%
Multiple events > 5 without Balfour	35	4.4%	233	60.4%	109	28.2%	5	1.3%	25	6.5%	14	3.6%

to its collections, but the acquisition events in which they were involved seem to have been fairly varied. Sydney Hewlett, a schoolmaster is unusual in that over half the acquisition events he was involved in were purchases (62%), but besides selling the Museum material, he also loaned and donated things to the collection. Edward Lovett, a bank clerk and folklorist sold material to the Museum on four occasions, exchanged on three and donated once. This seems to fit with the range of Lovett's activity in relation to a range of collections such as the Wellcome Collection (Hill 2007). Francis Knowles, a former student at the Museum and a long-term volunteer sold material on nine occasions, exchanged material twice, loaned once and donated on 24 occasions. This range of forms of exchange seems to suggest the complexity of the relationships between these figures and the Museum as well as the large number of acquisition events in which they were involved over a period of time. Noteworthy among these amateurs are a number of women; Estella Canziani, Margaret Irvine, Patience Watters and Anna Barrett-Lennard who were all predominantly donors, but were most active in the middle part of the twentieth century when Beatrice Blackwood was also most active at the Museum, suggesting a gendered dimension to the networks involved in supplying the Museum with material. Having been identified by this method of analyzing the Museum's database, female and amateur collectors became a significant additional strand of archival and historical research, suggesting that statistical and database driven research can become the spur to new avenues of more qualitatively focussed work.

Transactions Over Time

Because acquisition events can be easily allocated to a year, it is relatively easy to plot the number of acquisition events over a time range to give an indication of the changing activity of the Museum, just as Janet Owen did for the collection of John Lubbock. Figure 5.4 is an attempt to capture a sense of the changing activity in relation to the English collections at the Pitt Rivers since its foundation, by plotting the number of acquisitions per decade. The pattern of acquisition events relating to objects from England shows a marked decline in the second half of the twentieth century. For comparison, a line has been plotted on a second Y-axis which shows the total number of English objects collected in each decade. Although this also shows a falling away of activity in the second half of the century, a number of peaks and troughs appear in this line that are different from the activity as suggested by acquisition events. This is presumably caused by small numbers of donations involving large numbers of objects, such as that of Pitt Rivers in the 1880s and Archibald Bell in the 1920s. These mask what appear to be relatively low levels of activity at the Museum when measured in terms of acquisition events. Figure 5.5 showing total acquisition events and purchases is not unlike that produced by Janet Owen for the collection of John Lubbock; showing an early peak in activity followed by an overall dropping away alongside a decline in deliberate acquisition through purchasing. The most surprising feature of this graph, however, is the large peak in activity in relation to the 1940s, which interrupts the otherwise apparent decline.

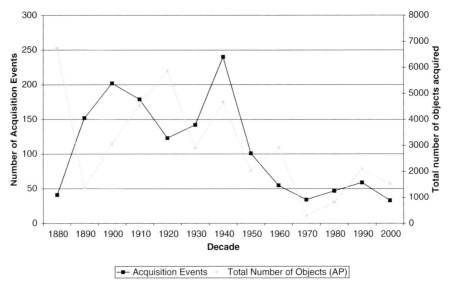

Fig. 5.4 A comparison of the total numbers of objects from England by decade and the number of acquisition events involved by decade

Figure 5.6, by plotting acquisition events for each year between 1930 and 1960, makes it possible to see that the real peaks for acquisition events involving objects from England occurred during the years of the Second World War, between 1939 and 1945 (Pitt Rivers Museum 2010). Obviously, this was a period when there was

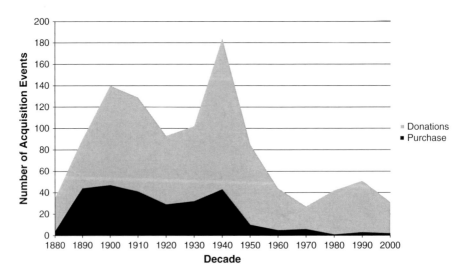

Fig. 5.5 A comparison of acquisition events involving donation and purchase by decade

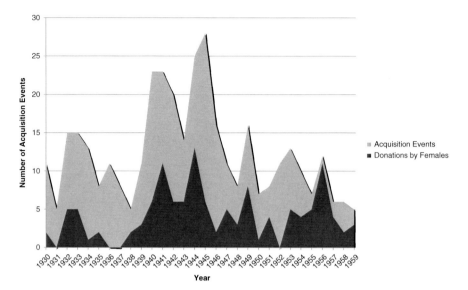

Fig. 5.6 Acquisition events by year between 1930 and 1960 including those involving female donors

a sense of threat to aspects of English life because of the threat of invasion, as well as the aerial bombardment. However, it was also a period in which rural life was radically transformed because of the intensification of agriculture as a result of the problem of relying on imported food supply. It seems to have been a period in which attitudes to Britain as a nation and England as a country were radically reconfigured. Nevertheless, the vast majority of English objects acquired by the Museum during those years were not the ancient stone tools which had dominated collecting in the first half of the twentieth century, but were rather items of domestic life, many of which had been in the custody of women. A second plot on Fig. 5.6 shows acquisition events involving female donors and this makes it clear that their activity was significant in bringing about this apparent peak in activity, and much of this collecting seems to have involved the same network of female collectors already mentioned. A profile of Folk Museums and Collections in England published in *Folklore* in March 1945 stated that:

> The Pitt Rivers Museum (University of Oxford), noted for its Ethnological collections, has always collected British and other Folk material as part of its Ethnological Collections and is now making a special effort to increase and develop its department of British and European Arts and Crafts (Banks 1945).

This is one of the only statements expressing a deliberate attention by the Museum to focus on British as opposed to overseas materials, and it certainly seems to match the evidence of an increase of this type of material in the collections at this time. However, the location of this statement is extremely significant, since the Folklore Society seems to have been a key point of contact for many female collectors, including Beatrice Blackwood. What may be more significant when considering the collections of the Pitt Rivers Museum is that the society held many of its meetings during the war in Oxford, rather than in London, and these may have become a social focus for a group of women spending their war years in Oxfordshire. While it might be possible to understand this shift towards female collectors of domestic objects at the Pitt Rivers in relation to the death of Henry Balfour in 1939, and a shift in the balance of power at the Museum, it would be shortsighted to deny that there was also a wider shift in focus towards local 'folk' material in museums across the country in the years that followed the Second World War, much of which became increasingly identified in subsequent years as Social History (Kavanagh 1993). While it has been suggested above that 'the questions that are asked and the answers that appear reasonable' (Trigger 1984: 368) may have changed in settler archaeologies due to shifts in their position in the world system, it seems that a similar shift may have taken place in relation to the collecting practices of many museums in Britain at around the time of the Second World War. The Pitt Rivers Museum, unlike many British museums, did not reposition itself as a Social History museum, or dispose of its ethnographic collections during the post-war decades. However, the contribution of its global collections to answering the sorts of questions that seemed most relevant in post-war Britain certainly seems to have declined, making the English 'folk' collections assume an additional significance.

Conclusions

Museum databases are commonly used on a day-to-day basis to provide contextual information about objects, as well as for collections management tasks. Their use as a research tool, as a means of 'unpacking the collection,' is relatively recent and little explored. The work underlying this chapter has been carried out as part of *The Other Within* research project at the Pitt Rivers Museum in Oxford, which focussed on the Museum's English collections. The project developed from a statistical finding of earlier database research during the Relational Museum Project which suggested that museum contained over 30,000 objects from England accounting for around 12% of the overall collection. This chapter should have demonstrated some of the ways in which insights and work carried out as part of the earlier project has been developed and extended. Statistical findings derived from the interrogation of databases seem to have a useful function in directing attention to areas that can be fruitfully explored through a range of other methods. One of these has been the development of a methodology based around acquisition events, described above, which has again pointed the way to further areas that have benefited from additional research and analysis: the role of museum employees, dealers and female collectors and the period around the Second World War.

This chapter is intended less as a theoretical exploration of materiality, agency and identity and more as a methodological contribution to examine and critique, as well as develop the potential of museum databases as a source of information on the relationships that lie behind museum collections. While 'making the museum central' and 'unpacking the collection' 'along the grain' have been advocated, this does not necessarily mean that databases should be taken at face value. They are tools for museum professionals, and the way in which they present information tends to direct attention in particular directions – in the case of the Pitt Rivers to the place of their ultimate origin, and to techniques of manufacture and use. However, alongside this information, traces are retained of the donors, loaners, dealers and swappers who have been involved in the wider network out of which the museum has taken shape. These traces can provide a way to explore and evaluate the complex and diffuse operations of agency in relation to the assembling of the collection. When removing museum collections from crates and boxes following transportation, it makes sense to first remove the items that were packed last. This is the same method an archaeologist would tend to excavate a stratified site in order to gain a sense of the processes by which it had been formed. In attempting to unpack museum collections and understand the operation of agency in relation to the processes of assemblage by which they have been formed, it seems sensible to begin by examining the manner and means of their acquisition by the museum.

References

Banks, M. M.
    1945 Folk Museums and Collections in England. *Folklore* 56(1): 218–222.

Gell, Alfred
    1998 *Art and Agency: An Anthropological Theory*. Clarendon Press, Oxford.

Gosden, Chris, Frances Larson, and Alison Petch
    2007 *Knowing Things: Exploring the Collections at the Pitt Rivers Museum 1884–1945*. Oxford University Press, Oxford.

Harrison, Rodney
    2006 An Artefact of Colonial Desire? Kimberley Points and the Technologies of Enchantment. *Current Anthropology* 47(1): 63–88.

Hill, Jude
    2007 The Story of the Amulet: Locating the Enchantment of Collections. *Journal of Material Culture* 12(1): 65–87.

Kavanagh, Gaynor
    1993 History in Museums in Britain: A Brief Survey of Trends and Ideas. In *Social History in Museums: A Handbook for Professionals*, edited by David Fleming, Crispin Paine, and John G. Rhodes, pp. 13–26. HMSO, London.

Kirshenblatt-Gimblett, Barbara
    1998 *Destination Culture: Tourism, Museums, and Heritage*. University of California Press, London.

Larson, Frances, Alison Petch, and David Zeitlyn
    2007 Social Networks and the Creation of the Pitt Rivers Museum. *Journal of Material Culture* 12: 211–239.

Latour, Bruno
  2005 *Reassembling the Social: An Introduction to Actor-Network Theory*. Oxford University
       Press, Oxford.

Livingstone, David N.
  2003 *Putting Science in its Place: Geographies of Scientific Knowledge*. University of Chicago
       Press, London.

O'Hanlon, Michael, and Robert Louis Welsch
  2000 *Hunting the Gatherers: Ethnographic Collectors, Agents and Agency in Melanesia,
       1870s–1930s*. Berghahn, Oxford.

Owen, Janet
  1999 The Collections of Sir John Lubbock, the First Lord Avebury (1834–1913): 'An Open
       Book?' *Journal of Material Culture* 4(3): 283–302.
  2006 Collecting Artefacts, Acquiring Empire: Exploring the Relationship between
       Enlightenment and Darwinist Collecting and Late-Nineteenth Century British Imperialism.
       Journal of the History of Collections 18(1): 9–25.

Petch, Alison
  2004 Collecting Immortality: The Field Collectors who Contributed to the Pitt Rivers Museum,
       Oxford. *Journal of Museum Ethnography* 16: 127–139.

Petch, Alison
  2006 Counting and Calculating: Some Reflections on Using Statistics to Examine the History
       and Shape of the Collections at the Pitt Rivers Museum. *Journal of Museum Ethnography*
       18: 149–156.

Pitt-Rivers Museum
  2010 Acquisition Events: Comparison Over Time. http://england.prm.ox.ac.uk/englishness-
       acq.events7.html. Accessed 15 August 2010.

Sahlins, Marshall
  1974 *Stone Age Economics*. Tavistock Publications, London.

Schildkrout, Enid, and Curtis A. Keim
  1998 *The Scramble for Art in Central Africa*. Cambridge University Press, Cambridge.

Stoler, Ann Laura
  2009 *Along the Archival Grain: Epistemic Anxieties and Colonial Common Sense*. Princeton
       University Press, Princeton, NJ.

Trigger, Bruce G.
  1984 Alternative Archaeologies: Nationalist, Colonialist, Imperialist. *Man New Series* 19(3):
       355–370.

Chapter 6
The Bekom Mask and the White Star: The Fate of Others' Objects at the Musée du quai Branly, Paris

Alexandra Loumpet-Galitzine

Abstract This chapter focuses on the visual remaking of emblematic objects from museums of primitive art by advertising campaigns, with particular reference to posters for the Musée du quai Branly in Paris. As museums have increasingly delegated advertising to commercial agencies, the image of 'Other's' objects constitutes a new arena of translation. These objects, and the ideas generated by them, emerge as important foci for understanding the structuring of various gazes, and the authority and manipulative power of the museum. An analysis of the representations of a helmet mask from the microstate of Kom in West Cameroon Grasslands, now housed in the Musée du quai Branly, exemplifies the metamorphosis of meanings and virtues of Others' objects, their symbolic location, growing personalization and potential for transformation, as well as the ambiguous position which contemporary museums assume in relation to them. The effects of advertising are explored through the notions of 'ravissement' (in French meaning both capture and enchantment) and 'exile' of objects.

Introduction

Modern museums are much more than simple containers. Through special exhibitions or openings they become objects themselves: for example conceptual objects; objects of architecture, interior design; scenography; and, finally, new subjects of research for anthropology. The most important changes in the museum landscape in the last 10 years have been the attempts of museums to become more innovative, transparent and ethical both to reaffirm the legitimacy of heritage processes and to respond to a more diverse modern audience. Museums have also acquired a new status within the culture industry: particularly in terms of clientelization of the public, marketing strategies, media communication and touristic management of reified traditions (Bouju 1995; Clifford 2007; Guerzoni and Troilo 2001). This is especially

A. Loumpet-Galitzine (✉)
University of Yaounde, Yaounde, Cameroon; Asia-Pacific Network, CNRS-FMSH, Paris, France
e-mail: loumpet.galitzine@gmail.com

S. Byrne et al. (eds.), *Unpacking the Collection*, One World Archaeology,
DOI 10.1007/978-1-4419-8222-3_6, © Springer Science+Business Media, LLC 2011

the case where whole collections of ethnographic artefacts have been re-imagined as art objects (Grognet 2005; Jamin 1985, 1998), as happened in the case of the transfer of the Museum of Mankind collections to the British Museum (2000–2001), of the Musée de l'Homme collections to the Musée du quai Branly (2005–2006), and also arguably in the development of National Museum of the American Indian in Washington DC. In this chapter, I will focus on how this process of re-imagining and transformation of ethnographic collections is also expressed through advertising media surrounding the opening of a new museum, in this case the Musée du quai Branly in Paris, France.

From Artefact to Masterpiece: The Metamorphosis of Museum Objects

The notion of object 'metamorphosis', as André Malraux termed it, is commonly used in the Musée du quai Branly conferences (Dufrêne and Taylor 2009) to signify the new status and values of objects and museums, notably their transformation from ethnographic artefacts to art objects. This metamorphosis is also achieved by a process of refashioning the meaning of objects by way of visual and written media. Central to this process is the active role of advertising. Advertising prioritizes particular information content and it seeks and directs the attention of the viewers through the use of typographical signifiers, graphics and geographical icons that emphasize or nuance particular aspects of objects and their meanings. The message is guided, acts as a 'dispositio' (Peninou 2001), imposes an authority on the 'mise en scène' and develops new networks of meaning. In all cases, the use of advertising is a political act.

The increasing place of communication in museums has been analyzed by a number of authors (e.g. Benhamou 2004; Lambert and Trouche 2008; Maigret and Macé 2005; Vivant 2008; Werner 2005). Accordingly, this chapter focuses in detail on one particular aspect of this process – the visual remaking of emblematic museum objects as representations. In doing so, it follows the approach developed by Igor Kopytoff (1986), and is informed by studies concerning the consumption of signs following Roland Barthes (1970) and Jean Baudrillard (1981) and more recently, as developed in art history (Didi-Huberman 1990, 1997, 2009; Stiegler 2008; Weigel 2008). This new visual discursiveness, that assigns additional roles to collected objects, is initiated by museums, but its construction is largely external, often delegated to marketing and advertising agencies (Vivant 2008). The multiplicity of media in those advertising campaigns (e.g. flyers, posters, newspapers, advertisements on buses and in metro and railway stations) integrates the museum into both the broader spheres of everyday life and private domains. The image, as well as the system it synthesizes, thereby constitutes a new arena for translating the missions of museums and a meeting point between museums and new audiences from different social groups. These new media form a 'coalescence of framing and imagination' (Didi-Hubermann 2009) by developing and diffusing what Roland Barthes (1970) termed a 'mythology'. In this way, they create a historically determined mode of language and communication that is presented as being natural and 'true'. From this perspective, the analysis of images of objects emerges as a major analytical framework for understanding the structuring of various gazes, their authority and manipulative powers, identifying them as sites of metamorphosis and transformation.

In this chapter, the re-orientations of relations between signifiers and signified will be analyzed primarily through representations of a helmet mask, originally from the micro-state of Kom in West Cameroon Grasslands and now in the Musée du quai Branly in Paris, but the analysis is also extended through additional examples. Although my study focuses particularly on the Musée du quai Branly, I am not merely adding to the previous critiques amply developed elsewhere (e.g. Dupaigne 2006; Clifford 2007; Price 2007). The question is not about whether or not the Museum is pursuing a colonialist agenda, as different scholars have argued, but how the advertising media participate, with the Museum's agreement, in a more general system of elucidation of different questions, including representation of cultural difference and colonial history. With few exceptions (e.g. Dias 2002), in France this material has more often been studied by semiologists than anthropologists. In this perspective, due to the controversies that preceded and followed its opening and the ambiguity created by the opposition between aesthetical and anthropological approaches, the Musée du quai Branly provides an excellent case study of the tensions at work in most western institutions devoted to the 'Other'.

The premise of this chapter is that there is a paradox inherent in the modes of translation commissioned by the Musée du quai Branly, one that could probably be extended to all the museums that have changed the status of their collections from ethnographic artefacts to art objects. The 'metamorphosis', announced by a discourse of rupture, claims a new autonomy of formerly ethnographic objects through their integration into the new asset category of 'Art'. This action does not necessarily imply a 'new birth' (Grognet 2005), however, but works by the accumulation of omissions. Consequently, the change in object status cannot be reduced to a binary opposition ('primitive art' vs. 'anthropology', or 'scientists' vs. 'curators'). Instead it creates a permanent conceptual conflict resulting from the supposed originality of the new museum, in the same way that modernity must invent primitivism. The implicit field of ongoing conflict between two concepts presented as antithetical is therefore an operating strategy, regularly updated by the controlled reference to personalities able to legitimise the new approaches. This implicit statement is constructed as symbolic violence, as defined by Pierre Bourdieu and Loïc Wacquant (1992), both by the opposition created and by the representations themselves. By playing constantly with the implicit nature of old presuppositions, rejected a long time ago by the scientific community, the curators, as new masters of the objects, nonetheless take the risk of delegating to advertising agencies an uncontrolled but powerful influence over the 'virtues' of the objects, in the sense given by Baudrillard (1981: 15). This act binds them to the way things are 'spoken' and always transformed into something else. Roland Barthes has already stressed the 'finiteness' of super-natural objects (Barthes 1970: 151); Mary Douglas and Baron Isherwood

(2008 [1979]: 14) noted their 'concreteness' when they acquire the value of consumer goods. Fred Myers (1998) and James Clifford (1988, 1997) have shown how familiarity with museum objects helped shape perceptions of non-western identity. This raises the question of whether, in the western eye, some kinds of objects embody these potential attributes of metamorphosis better than others.

The Locations of Objects

In two advertising campaigns during 2006 that announced the opening of the Musée du quai Branly, the M&C Saatchi GAD agency depicted four non-western objects, which were blown up to giant size and superimposed so as to appear to occupy the spaces of three iconic Parisian squares. On the Place Vendôme, a ministerial neighbourhood hosting jewellery stores and the Ritz hotel, first a Chimu gauntlet from Peru and, later, a bell from a Thai temple, replaced the column commemorating Napoleon's battle of Austerlitz, itself inspired by the Trajan column in Rome. On the Place de la Concorde, described by Wikipedia (2010) as 'the most significant creation of the Enlightenment in the capital', an Easter Island Moai obscured the obelisk of Luxor (Fig. 6.1). Finally, on the Place de la République, a Bekom helmet-mask from Cameroon (Fig. 6.2) was substituted for the bronze statue of the Republic created by the Morice brothers (1883). The statue is dressed in antique clothing and

Fig. 6.1 Poster entitled 'Cultures are meant to dialogue' announcing the opening of the Musée du quai Branly, Paris, May 2006, M&C Saatchi GAD (© 2010 Musée du quai Branly, Paris, courtesy of Patrick Gries/Valérie Torre/Scala, Florence)

Fig. 6.2 Poster entitled 'Cultures are meant to dialogue' announcing the opening of the Musée du quai Branly, Paris, May 2006, M&C Saatchi GAD (© 2010 Musée du quai Branly, Paris/Scala, Florence)

is surrounded on its pedestal by allegorical representations of Liberty, Equality and Fraternity.

The locations selected by the M&C Saatchi GAD agency are key referential sites for French identity, and as such they deliver a subliminal message of progress from a conquest to harmony and a Republican equality. They are also intersections, presumably open to dialogue, that symbolically stress the promised transparency of the Museum. The objects are neither ethnographic nor artistic, but are immediately recognized through the contrast with their surroundings as exotic and non-western, although indications of their origins and functions are missing. A 'natural' opposition between fine eighteenth century Haussmann buildings and exotic movable objects stresses the importance of the capital city and highlights the modern nation-state as a showcase. The aim of the advertising agency was indeed to present Paris as a 'jewel box', an aim strengthened in the poster by the African mask being placed on a pedestal (see Fig. 6.2). From this perspective, the highly exaggerated monumentality of non-western objects emphasizes the massive scale of the presumed difference between modernity and primitiveness.

In all, then, this campaign uses seven objects, three of which are absent, but highlighted by their absence. One of these hidden objects, the obelisk of Luxor in the Place de la Concorde, is itself non-western and is currently displayed as a trophy of French power (it was indeed a 'gift', highly prized by France, from the viceroy Mehemet Ali in 1831) and French technological know-how (through its transport from Luxor and re-erection in Paris in 1833). The replacement of the obelisk therefore helps to legitimize the western appropriation of things as 'normal', by rooting this practice in the nation-state's deep past, and offers the opportunity to distinguish between already integrated non-western objects versus those that are still completely alien. Ambivalently, this replacement also insists on alleging equality among all the works. As asserted by Jacques Kerchache (1990), a French primitive art dealer and one of the conceptual architects of the Musée du quai Branly, 'The masterpieces of the world are born free and equal' (see also Guichard 1999). The question raised by the image concerns the expression and the visual representation of this proclaimed equality.

The four non-western objects used in the images are characterized by their disproportionate size in relation to their surroundings. This contrast simultaneously draws attention to, and dramatizes, their incongruity. Since all except one are anthropomorphic, the viewer feels that they are immediately recognizable. Paradoxically, the identification of a common humanity for 'us' and 'them' serves to emphasize their differences. In contrast, the resemblance is immediately denied by size and ornamental patterns: for example the massive and schematic appearance of the Moai; the distinctive decorative patterns covering the Chimu gauntlet; and the 'African' stereotype of the Bekom mask (bulging eyes, large nose and open mouth, filed and evulsed teeth). Devoid of their contextual and functional references, each of these artefacts, derived from widely geographically and temporally separated cultural areas, emphasizes the implicitly ritual nature of their identity as fundamentally distinct from the 'showcase' that receives them. These differential and intrinsic identities are sufficient to justify the relevance of a museum devoted to all the primitive arts, well enough known so that it is not explicitly noted in the posters or in the name of the Museum.

If the name finally selected, 'Musée du quai Branly,' has been interpreted as a sign of embarrassment on the part of its founders, it also shows the importance of anchoring the new institution in a clearly identified spatial setting. 'Territory of Primitive Arts' was the claim of one online museum poster. A recent poster confirmed the metaphorical importance of claiming a particular space. The picture shows a small African statue seen from behind and facing the Museum and the immense Eiffel Tower photographed from below. The accompanying text proclaims 'In 2010, the world docked at quai Branly' (Musée du quai Branly 2010a, see also 2010b). Significantly, the wording does not have the Museum as open to the world, but the world must come to Paris, in a one-way relationship between the centre and its imagined peripheries.

Looked at another way, these anthropomorphic objects are fragmented by the posters (a head, a torso, a hand) and represent the great range of primitive bodies exhibited in the Museum. This dismemberment in the city is symbolic of both a significant and yet intrinsic incompleteness as well as a primitivism that are both contrasted to the small silhouettes of indifferent bystanders. It is interesting to note that none of these Others' objects raise – even symbolically – the curiosity of passersby. This indifference illustrates that the objects' new location is far more important than their properties. The values of the objects disappear in favour of the celebration of the exhibition, and ultimately, of the will of the State.

At first glance what these posters imply is a double inclusion of the 'Other'. At the same time they proclaim the new status of the object. Since they are now in the museum showcase of the French capital, they also forefront the radical 'out-of-placeness and other-timeness' (Fabian 2006) of non-western objects. This leads to a normative perception of 'otherness' or, more precisely, to a confirmation of the difference, an oxymoron of inserting them into a controlled place. An analysis of the poster with the Bekom mask will more precisely demonstrate how an image of an object has been manipulated to correspond to this discourse.

A Bekom Mask in Paris

Significantly oversized within the poster, because in reality it only measures 34 cm, the Bekom mask, which has been depicted in the Place de la République in Paris, introduces an additional element to the general message discussed above (Fig. 6.2). The formal characteristics of its exposed face as it overlooks the site highlight the final component of a western perception that I propose to call the 'ravissement', preserving the double meaning of the word in French as both 'appropriation' and 'enchantment': in other words, fear. Saskia Cousin and Galia Tapiero (2006) indicate the 'rather terrifying' character of a mask that appears to have been specifically chosen for this very trait. Fear, which also has an implicit sense of risk, together with fascination, is a recurring element in an imagined savagery, many traces of which can be found throughout the Musée du quai Branly. For instance, a catalogue published in the year of the Museum's opening and signed by the Museum's head of museology is titled 'You fear, you marvel. Musée du quai Branly, acquisitions 1998/2005' (Viatte 2006). I will return later to the implications of this use of familiarity, particularly through a personal pronoun.

The disturbing aspect of the mask is reinforced both by its red mouth and the graphic manipulation that has deliberately elongated the neck. These are the first signs of a formal reinvention that is required to deliver the message of fear. Deprived of its raffia collar and its costume and without any reference to its original context, the 'mask' is presented as beheaded. Ruth Philips (2009) recently pointed to the lack of a local term for 'mask', along with the importance of the complete costume for the Sande. The example from Sierra Leone is also valid in the kingdom of Kom and more generally in the Cameroon Grasslands. Without its collar and other indications of its original function or provenance, the object is no longer a 'real' mask in the western sense, nor is it really a statue. So its image is doubly intermediate, like its new status, drawing the viewer's gaze to focus on its facial expression. This particular facial expression was also placed on the cover of a children's magazine on primitive art, published for the opening of the Musée du quai Branly, in which changes of colour and contrast, as well as the median line dividing the face accentuate the intended scary appearance of the image (Fig. 6.3).

The commentary by the online sales catalogue for the book is in itself indicative of the effectiveness of a message widely repeated throughout the media, and of

Fig. 6.3 Cover 'Dada
Magazine' for children, 'Les
arts premiers', special issue
number 120, June 2006
(Courtesy of Dada Magazine)

which the poster is a part: 'An issue specifically dedicated to Primitive Art, long
devalued and treated as ethnological curiosities' (Médiatheque Benjamin-Rabier
2010). Use of the phrase 'ethnological curiosities' is perhaps the clearest way to
express the specific mechanism of reduction and superposition of meanings. The
new message is obviously juxtaposed against the past 50 year's work of cultural
anthropology, assigning pejorative sense to an ethnography by including it in the
same category of perceptual misunderstanding as that of explorers and missionaries.

The apparent lack of information concerning the origin and function of the
'mask' on the poster (Fig. 6.2) is particularly interesting. Cousin and Tapiero (2006)
reported that after repeated requests, the Museum's public relations department
finally described the object as a 'hunting mask from Cameroon'. This error is significant in several ways. Firstly, it is actually a helmet-mask of a noble from the
kingdom of Kom (Bekom being the plural) from the West Cameroon Grasslands
that was used in ceremonies of secret societies that bring together peers of the same
rank. The nobility here are linked, in the Grasslands as elsewhere, to the royal family or to a hereditary distinction conferred by the king. It is therefore possible to
point out the unintentional irony that presides over the symbolic displacement of the
object put in the place of a statue representing the Republic and on a pedestal commemorating, by various sculptures in relief, historical events such as, inter alia, the
storming of the Bastille fortress, the abolition of the monarchy and the proclamation
of the Republic.

A second factor is more significant. This mask comes specifically from the Kom
kingdom, an area perhaps best known in the museum world through accounts of
the theft and eventual repatriation of the *Afo-a-Kom* statue. Statues such as this,
effigies of royal ancestors sculpted by kings, are fundamental to dynastic links and
social cohesion. The *Afo-a-Kom* statue was stolen from a storage hut near the Royal
Palace in 1966 and subsequently recovered from the United States and returned to

Cameroon in 1973. Given ceremonial honours at the airport, it was exhibited to the public in the capital for several weeks before being returned to its owners, who reinstated the statue's sacred status through various ceremonies. This first international collaboration following the International Convention on World Heritage (UNESCO dated 1972) is a famous case that is regularly cited by the International Council of Museums and UNESCO's World Heritage Fund (Merryman, Elsen and Ulrice 2007: 363–366; UNESCO 2010). It also marked the beginning of the awareness in Cameroon of notions of cultural heritage which were closely observed by other African countries. The Bekom mask in the poster is thus situated at the intersection of different parallel, and yet compatible, changes: from local significance to a national cultural property (for Cameroon, international specialist organizations), from ethnographic subject (scientists) to an object of Cameroon, African or primitive art (for collectors and museums, potential buyers) or to a commodity (dealers, illegal trade).

The use of a mask from the kingdom of Kom by the advertising agency, with the approval of the Museum, is not only a misunderstanding that signals a worrying absence of consultation with experts of that country or any consideration of the role of such objects in local culture or as part of their national cultural heritage but also indicates a process of commodification of a cultural object that is authenticated by choosing it for the poster, its particular form, and by the authority of the Museum. This choice seems quite awkward in the light of controversies surrounding the acquisition of different objects for the Pavillon des Sessions at the Louvre, the forerunner of the Musée du quai Branly, including questions about how the Bekom mask was acquired. In particular, controversies about the acquisition of the Nok figurines from Nigeria are summarised by Maud Guichard (1999).

This mask belonged to the private collection of Dr. Harter (1928–1991). He was a leprosy specialist who lived for nearly 33 years in Cameroon and claimed on the basis of various publications to be a great specialist in the art of the region. Harter's collection was acquired in Cameroon during the colonial period as 'gifts' in exchange for medical care given to Grasslands kings. Fifty-three pieces bequeathed to the Museum of African and Oceanic Arts during his lifetime were incorporated into the Musée du quai Branly, with the remainder sold publicly in 1995. The Museum offers a 'privileged place' (Musée du quai Branly 2010c) to the collection, particularly because the donor's will specifies that it must be exhibited in its entirety and that individual objects cannot be loaned for temporary exhibitions. The poster image contradicts the status of the single object that is embedded in a regional collection. Given its collection history, it is perhaps even more understandable that origin and provenance are not provided.

While the object representative of the African continent comes from the donation of a private collection, the Chimu gauntlet was acquired from a professional dealer. Only the Moai of Easter Island was collected during a scientific mission (Museum of Natural History and National Museum of Man, Mission Alfred Metraux). This point is difficult to confirm because the catalogue of the Musée du quai Branly does not include the Moai used in the poster image and the only similar example in the collection has no bust. It is thus possible, but has not been verified with certainty, that the poster was created from a photograph or a photomontage of two different objects, or from an object and a photograph.[1]

The absence of information about the origin and function of the Bekom mask is therefore neither accidental nor the result of ignorance by the advertising agency. On the basis of the frequent use of the mask on postcards (where it is shown in profile), in activity reports and booklets, the Bekom mask is commonly used to represent the Museum. How it is described, however, varies with the public being addressed. A search for 'Bekom Mask' on the Museum's website produces at least three results. Firstly, it appears in the catalog of the collections. In addition to the usual details of origin and date (Bekom, Cameroon, twentieth century), materials and inventory number, the mask is described as follows: 'Helmet mask representing the head of a noble with ornate headdress, separated in two curly parts (raffia cap). Hole in the middle of the mouth, rectangular hole at the top of the skull. Native restoration on the left side of the neck at the base of the head. Hardwood with glossy black patina.' No indication about its function is provided (Musée du quai Branly 2010d).

Secondly, under public programs 'Promenades à la carte', it becomes a 'Mask JU-JU – Cameroon, Bekom' with the following comments. 'This mask was worn like a helmet on top of the head. It represents a noble wearing a cap knitted in the form of small cylinders of tied yarn. The mask appears in public to reinforce public order' (Musée du quai Branly 2010e). A gradual loss of descriptive accuracy is replaced here by new functional data. 'Juju' is a generic term in any area of Grasslands that designates objects of high efficacy that are therefore dangerous to the uninitiated. The term is also frequently used when the informant does not know or does not want to provide more details. The mention of its 'police' function is no more adequate than that of a 'hunting mask' given by the Museum's public relations department mentioned above. Both are inaccurate and incomplete. Similar objects from the same area are alternately referred to in the catalog of collections as 'masks' or 'heads', their local designation when they are combined with costumes. In the Museum itself, the Bekom mask is displayed in a large showcase among several others and is not especially distinguished.

Finally, in the catalog of images ('iconothèque') on the Musée du quai Branly website, the Bekom mask appears as a 'poster' but lacks any information about its origin or function (Musée du quai Branly 2010f). Only the creation date, sponsor, name of two photographers and the advertising agency are mentioned. These three different representations reinforce the semantic plasticity of the object called 'mask'. In all cases, variation in the way it is represented creates an 'insignificant' object compared to the glance that defines it, stressing that the representation of the mask belongs to its current owners, with no more direct link to the former producers, in other words, the appropriation process. This difference in values remains incomplete, however, until we examine two other key elements of this first advertising campaign.

---

[1] This remains a hypothesis. See catalogue No. 71.1935.61.1 http://www.quaibranly.fr/cc/pod/recherche.aspx?b=1&t=1. There are, however, similar photographs in the library.

Time and Place of Dialogue Between Cultures

In the poster, the Bekom mask is accompanied by two separate phrases each headed by an asterisk: '*The museum opens in June 23, 2006' and the assertion '*Cultures are meant to dialogue.' As shown in Figs. 6.1 and 6.2, the star asterisk and the phrase 'Cultures are meant to dialogue' clearly do not have the same status since the first is a sign. They are not equally readable and do not have the same visual impact, but both provide important information about the role of the 'Other' in this new French national museum. The order of entries is also different in the two examples presented. For the Moai repositioned in the Place de la Concorde (Fig. 6.1), the assertion 'Cultures are meant to dialogue' appears in large print in a dominant location. The positions are reversed for the Bekom mask poster that announces the opening date of the Musée du quai Branly (Fig. 6.2). In both cases, the address of the website included under the statement of the Museum's opening provides a redundant statement of the locality. In the two alternate phrases, the assertion draws one's attention, partly because it seems to acquire a prescriptive character in relation to the image, and partly because it somehow appears to have an opposite and ambiguous meaning: How can 'cultures' (not people) be 'meant to dialogue?' How do they interact through objects? Price (2007) and Clifford (2007), among many others, emphasize the obvious absence of balance between a museum that contains no western material culture and a 'dialogue' between objects and potential audiences. The question 'Who sets the rules of the game?' (Cousin and Tapiero 2006) is therefore purely rhetorical.

My discussion of dialogue is not fully meaningful until one examines a second statement which has been used on all documents by the Musée du quai Branly since its opening. 'The place where cultures dialogue', again provides a symbolic way to claim territory, but also designates the Musée du quai Branly as a place where dialogue is effective. 'Cultures dialogue' and do interact in a manner visually identified by an advertisement for an annual pass, 'Unlimited time for dialog' that depicts an African object from Bansoa kingdom from the Grasslands of Cameroon – another donation from the collection of Dr. Harter (Fig. 6.4).

In addition to its emphasis on ethnic diversity, the poster advertising the pass presents the equivalence of different entities involved in the dialogic experience; that is persons and anthropomorphic objects. The positions of the individuals depicted are significant (Fig. 6.4). It is notable that the man does not have a specific origin: He is not African, but 'merely' non-European. He comments and seems therefore to hold a form of authority on the subject and the object. He stands in an enclosing and protective position, surrounding his wife and daughter with his hand on the shoulder of his son. His genuine smile is shared by his children. In contrast, the European woman holds her head slightly on one side and therefore is making a serious observation. Two attributes of a shared identity between human and objects are underlined: one between the man and the primitive statue whose eyes are the same level, and the other between the woman and the female statue. As the product of this 'cultural dialogue', the children symbolically belong both to the couple and the object. This specific family audience, portrayed with casual clothes, confirms the

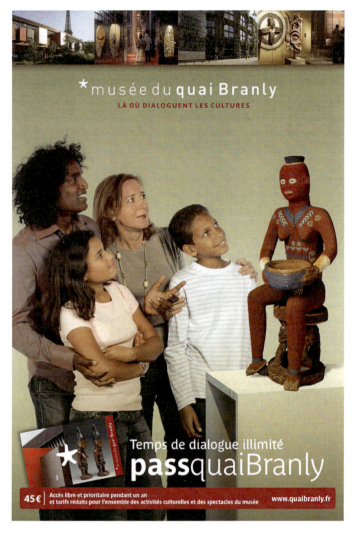

Fig. 6.4 Advertisement for an Annual Pass to the Musée du quai Branly 'Temps de dialogues illimité' ('Unlimited time for dialog'). Poster 138,72 0 138,72 0,00 (1) (© 2010. Musée du quai Branly, Paris, courtesy of Patrick Gries/Valérie Torre/Scala, Florence)

intended intellectual and social goals of the Museum. This example shows that 'cultures' interact in the Museum at different levels and dialogue includes both people and objects. This principle of equivalence does not imply, a priori, an equal status, but involves an on-going transformation of the status of the object. Established as the equivalent of one person, the work of art itself becomes personalized in a new way.

The Object-Person

In general, from the beginning of the Musée du quai Branly project, it has been possible to observe an increasing personalization of the object. The use of personal pronouns has given body and voice to the object, ever since the advertising campaign 'I'm here' announcing the opening of the Louvre's Pavillon des Sessions in 2000 prefigured the Musée du quai Branly (Dias 2002). There are many examples of the ambiguity that breaks down boundaries between the animate and inanimate, as I have already described elsewhere (Loumpet-Galitzine 2008, 2009). For example, the poster of the exhibition 'Objects wounded' (18 June – 16 September 2007) shows a face mask and the scar of a repair, and booklets for targeted audiences are illustrated by presumably representative objects, such as a woman with a newborn child for family visits, a pair of 'teen' statues for 18–25 year-olds, and a grey statue (covered with kaolin or ashes) for seniors.

But the most significant example is a speech supposedly given by the symbol of the Musée du quai Branly, the 'Chipicuaro' statuette that is delivered in the first person on the museum website. It is reproduced here in its entirety.

> *I am* the emblem and logo of the Musée du quai Branly, but I reside at the Louvre Museum, or to be more precise, at the Pavillon des Sessions, within a stone's throw of the Porte des Lions.

> Because *I am* a masterpiece, I earned this place in the temple of Art, among other masterpiece sculptures from Africa, Asia, Oceania and the Americas.

> I came into being in the mountains in Central Mexico and my name comes from an archaeological site that is partly covered with the Lerma River's water.

> I am said to be associated with a funeral rite in connection with soil fertility and the earth's annual cycle of death and rebirth. Indeed, *I am always present*: a great ceramic statue with generous curves, enchanting the eye with my modern design and vivid colours. The red of my array, which is embellished with black, beige or white designs, has not lost any of its brightness, as if the painter and sculptor had employed all of his artistic expertise and standards to bring me to life. And although I am 25 centuries old, *I am still extraordinarily full of vitality*. [italics are mine] (Musée du quai Branly 2010g).

The increasing humanization of the object goes far beyond the personalization process previously noted by Sally Price (2006: 127), who stressed the 'quasi-subject' status of the primitive art masterpiece. More interesting, however, is that these words do not belong to a narrative invented by the Museum, but come, as research by Brigitte Derlon and Monique Jeudy-Ballini (2008) has demonstrated, from the habitual vocabulary of art dealers and collectors among whom eagerly-sought objects acquire a true individuality. The common terminology of museum and art dealers and collectors reveals that they share a common perception of aesthetics which is recognized and valued by the Museum, and is embedded in the posters. One notable effect is the transformation of French cultural anthropological knowledge into another discourse. Such a strategy by the Museum offers no new serious consideration of the peoples whose cultures are represented in the Museum. Thus constructed, the discourse is closed by its internal dialectics.

In this perspective, the aesthetic choice of the latest exhibitions does not imply an aestheticization of the producers, or even an aesthetic viewpoint on the Other transformed into a new category of object, as it is involved, for instance, in the website of the National African Museum in Washington DC where the invitation 'Explore the collection' is imposed on the photograph of a smiling young African girl wearing kaolin patterns, done during a local performance (National Museum of African Art 2010). Instead, it shows a transfer of human qualities to the object. Embodying the humanity of the Other, the object-masterpiece, self-referential, becomes humanly framed, conjured into existence and depersonalizing the real human being in its favour. It seems much easier to deal with the object of an anonymous Other, rather than directly with the real Other.

In the specific social context of the opening of the Musée du quai Branly, which was preceded by violent clashes in the suburbs of the capital where many immigrant families live, the discourse relayed by magazines such as *Paris-Match* helps create an image in which there is an ongoing substitution of unwanted people by celebrated and self-celebrating objects. The Musée du quai Branly is then, logically, described as an 'asylum', transforming France into a 'welcoming land' (*Paris Match*, June 2006). An authorized and non-confrontational migration of this type was suggested by the French primitive art dealer Pierre Amrouche in June 2006. 'If it goes to nations that recognize it (. . .) the object "mask" begins a new life. It's a sort of migrant. When one is no longer beloved in one's country and is deprived of social status, one goes where one is recognized' (Amrouche 2006).

The increasing humanization of objects also involves a break in the ontological order, extending the first circle of determinism conceived in an evolutionist perspective between peoples and primitive art so that the producers are no longer considered as primitive while their objects still are. The second break further distinguishes between producers of objects and their descendants. The 'first art' becomes to them just as foreign as to others. At a second level, the humanization of objects also opposes the cultural mix of assimilated immigrants – now included in the 'time of dialogue' – to the people imagined intact, 'root' or 'source' populations, non-migrant owners of the absolute authenticity. The legitimacy of such communities is regularly used as a touchstone, for example in the presence of Australian Aboriginal people at the opening ceremonies of the Museum.

The Efficacy of the Ambiguous Sign

This similarity in status between some people and some objects encompassed in their primitive community gives us an opportunity to return to the poster campaign, and to analyze a final element: the star asterisk. The star runs through the Museum's representations of objects in all formats. It appears as a logo in the early advertising campaigns for the Pavillon des Sessions at the Louvre in 2000 and plays, on a first reading, the function of a star asterisk, a typographical sign with conventional reference. The star is then seen twice, close to the object and before the museum's statement. Due to its formal anthropomorphic pattern, this five-pointed star appears to correspond to the form of Chipicuaro ceramic mentioned above. Most often white, but also black, red or contrasted to an object, the star contrasts with its background and is therefore immediately noticeable, although its size is relatively modest.

In posters and other museum materials the star asterisk sign is commonly located slightly above the head of an object, this being generally anthropomorphic. In recent years, however, its position has often moved down to eye level. It can also be placed, when appropriate, in the middle or on the side. In any case, this star comes with all the museum objects and sometimes with a photograph of a landscape or setting, where it emphasizes the 'spirit' of a performance (for example, shamanic) appropriate to the Museum's project. Very interestingly, more and more frequently, the star asterisk is affixed to photographs of foreign artists: that is to representations of contemporary individuals invited to perform for the Museum visitor's gaze.

The use of the asterisk, of smaller size, appears invariably as '*Musée du quai Branly'. Early on, it was placed at the bottom of the poster, as for example in the Bekom mask poster campaign, but since the opening it has been situated at the top of the page. Placed under the name of the Musée du quai Branly is the assertion 'The place where cultures dialogue' (which remains written in French in the English and Spanish versions of the website). The reference is present in all communications. In stark contrast, the star is absent from representations of persons or objects not belonging to the Museum.

Understandably, the star asterisk acts also as a 'brand', reiterating the ownership of objects and events belonging to the 'collections' and as part of the mission of the museum. It helps to designate certain types of objects as Others' objects and certain types of acts as Others' acts and also integrates them into the generic notion of 'primitive arts', introducing an implicit statutory discrimination. The poster for the exhibition 'The aristocrat and his cannibals' (23 October 2007–13 January 2008), devoted to Count Festetics Tolna's travels in Oceania (Musée du quai Branly 2010 h), significantly affixes the star on indigenous objects/representations and not near the photograph of the count which appears in black and white. In a still more striking effect, the star legitimates the affinity between 'primitive' people and objects, particularly in the poster for the exhibition, entitled 'D'un regard, l'Autre', developed by another advertising agency (Fig. 6.5).

Placed above the word 'Other' (Fig. 6.5), the star makes clear, if need be, the thematic subject of the Museum by combining representations of human beings and objects. The subtitle 'from Renaissance to the twentieth century: Africa, America, Oceania' does not explain the presence of representations of an anatomical model of a European woman at the centre of the image, nor of a European prehistoric man at the lower right. It is possible to deduce, however, that they are both European 'Others', in time and gender, and also that they serve to accentuate their difference from other 'Others'. The prehistoric European man is also the only one to be presented beyond the torso, and he is opposed, through a line of sight, to the representation of a strangely oriented black man's head. It is also possible to point out that the different faces presented do not cross the viewer's gaze, unlike the objects.

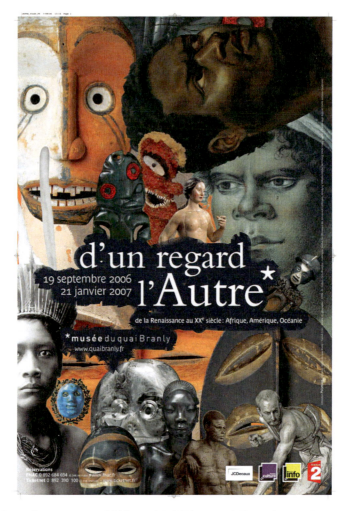

Fig. 6.5 Poster for temporary exhibition entitled 'D'un regard, l'Autre' ('At a glance, the Other'), September 19, 2006 to January 21, 2007. Curator: Yves Le Fur. Paris, Musée du quai Branly (© 2010. Musée du quai Branly, Paris/Scala, Florence)

Finally, it is significant that this is one of few posters, possibly the only one, where the statement 'The place where cultures dialogue' has been omitted.

The association between a particular group of people and a star sign is reminiscent enough in the light of recent world history to lead us to avoid certain questions about their potential effects (although the shape and colour used by the Musée du quai Branly are clearly different from the yellow star imposed in medieval Europe and re-used by German Nazis during World War II). But how can we not believe that, through the employment and dissemination of such a sign in mass media, the star does not point toward a discriminatory perception of the Other far beyond the

Museum's symbolic territory.[2] Recent analyses of posters and museum publicity in France have demonstrated the imperialism of signs (Dias 2002; Murphy 2009). So, is the Musée du quai Branly star simply an unintended coincidence?

A final example perfectly describes the ideological uses and implications of the white star. Figure 6.6 is a poster designed for a very recent exhibition, entitled

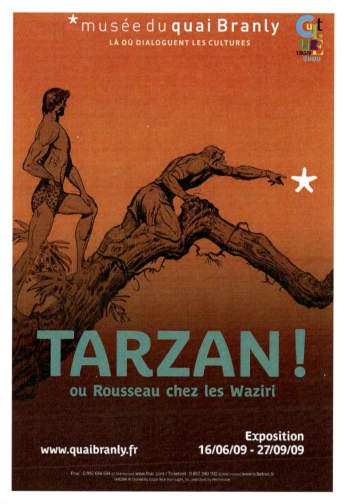

Fig. 6.6 Musée du quai Branly. Poster of the exhibition 'Tarzan! ou Rousseau chez les Waziri' ('Tarzan! or Rousseau in Waziriland'), June 16 to September 27, 2009. TARZAN[TM] and EDGAR RICE BURROUGHS[TM] owned by Edgar Rice Burroughs, Inc. and Used by Permission (© 2010. Musée du quai Branly, Paris, courtesy of Patrick Gries/Valérie Torre/Scala, Florence)

---

[2]When I have presented this hypothesis at various academic seminars, the students have reacted in different ways, either by approval, or by violent rejection. The strength of reactions in all cases is in itself significant.

'Tarzan! ou Rousseau chez les Waziri'. In the press kit for the exhibition the chairman of the Musée du quai Branly underlines the importance of myths as a 'collective dream and the nucleus of the identity of people.' Furthermore, this precise imagery is aimed, to 'all those who dream of a reinvented elsewhere' (Musée du quai Branly 2010i). 'A reinvented 'elsewhere' which can also be echoed in a field close to the museum: that is tourism.

Increasingly, museums and tourism share a common rhetoric, articulated around the concept of 'escape' (Ciarcia 2001; Grognet 2008; de l'Estoile 2007; Olu 2008). Similarly, museums are part of a new 'experience', in which the focus is on the commercialization of experience rather than goods and services. From the program 'Invitation au voyage' to the 'Globe-trotters workshop', the Musée du quai Branly offers to 'disorient without confusing' (Lavalou and Robert 2006: 56) and find enjoyment in a new 'Other distant place' that is legitimized and made safe by the Museum (Musée du quai Branly 2010j). This chapter is not the place for a more detailed analysis of this correlation, including its spatial architecture which, with its vast white hall and ramp access to the collections, resembles an airport. But the abolition of the presumed distance between oneself and an idealized Other also makes possible one's temporary replacement, as shown by different packages offered by travel agencies: for instance the tour called 'I will be a Masai' proposed by Terra Natura (2010). By purchasing the travel – real or symbolic – the visitor acquires the ability for a time to stand 'instead of' the Other – an ultimate fantasy of appropriation – and then to return to the sources which commodify the whole diminished experience of the Other, that is to say, his or her irreducible difference.

Objects in Exile

Ultimately, the dream of a 'reinvented Other', whose artistic status has been enhanced and is therefore attractive to a broad audience is precisely the purpose of the visual message of advertising campaigns, thus an invitation to participate in the 'ravissement' process. The poster featuring a Bekom helmet-mask in the centre of a place representing a historic cross-roads (Fig. 6.2) legitimises an inevitable and unavoidable gaze, affirming clearly that there is no other way of looking. In examining changes from this early poster to the recent one of 'Tarzan!' (Fig. 6.5) – with the apeman's deictic position of the hand – a principle of exhibition emerges, the purpose of which is not to present formal knowledge, but to offer the right to reshape the meanings of objects.

This double lack of interest in the history of the objects and of the producers, who are increasingly not invisible but transparent and symbolically replaced by the frame of objects and by a western showcase for them, can be termed 'exiling'. Exile entails presupposing a form of destitution through particular state historicities that are founded on distinct temporalities, but also different periods of life (pre-exile, exile, post-exile) and differentiated spaces and places of existence, often in parallel (Loumpet-Galitzine 2009: 621). In this particular case, exile also implies a specific 'mise en abyme' process of standing between the two worlds of the western Self and the Other but only seeing an infinite reproduction of one's own image. This is reinforced in the Musée du quai Branly by the design of the permanent exhibition, in which the window reflections accentuate a mirror effect, allowing one to admire the objects and one's own image simultaneously.

Obviously, these new frames create new networks of meaning surrounding the objects in the Museum: that is to say, they are transformed into a new heritage. By its etymology and its usage in this case, the concept of heritage is ambivalent. As another way of describing cultures, using an apparently neutral term associated with the Museum objectives, this new concept is also an attempt to include uniqueness within a universal category of Otherness and in the epistemological field of modern western art and history. Heritage is obviously not reducible to the past, nor solely to 'primitive' art, but it transforms de facto participation in history into a commodity, thereby reducing cultural diversity involved in the 'dialogue' to a small part of its products.

In his 'Bichon among Negroes', a short chapter of *Mythologies* which analyzes the journey in Africa of a young couple of artists with their 2-year old son, Bichon, published in *Paris-Match* magazine in 1957, Roland Barthes (Barthes 1970: 114) recalls a few components of the French 'petit-bourgeois' myth of the 'Negro'. He points to heroism without goals, ethical demonstrations receiving their culmination only in advertising, and romantic places. Concerning the particular case of Musée du quai Branly, I would add to these a new romanticism of the organic. With its jungle projected onto the windows, its green facade and garden, the Musée du quai Branly's architecture and rhetoric not only implicitly oppose nature to culture but also include in its mission the ethics of sustainable development and return to Nature, both in the sense of 'human nature' and of core values of nature. Presented as particularly dependent on its ecosystem, primitive art becomes, in effect, a kind of 'organic' and simplified art that might appeal to new and valued audiences.

Could a museum of primitive art escape from this not exclusively French 'Bichon syndrome'? Probably not as long as the notion of primitive art, and its exclusive aesthetic approach, remains so ambiguous. All the elements included in the advertising posters tend to reveal the current incapacity of this and some other museums to even consider a diversity that would escape inequality and, consequently, are unable to communicate uniqueness other than by the 'assertion of a paternalistic generosity through an act of inclusion', as discussed by Annie Coombes (1999: 654). In this perspective, the inessential translation, in Benjamin's sense (Benjamin translated by Lamy & Nouss 1997: 13), of Other's artefacts by advertising contribute to the general object system, as Baudrillard (1968: 194) pointed out, and becomes an autonomous object by itself. This is a double determination which, when concerning the Other's object and, de facto, the Other him or herself, urgently calls for what Barthes (1970: 17) well termed a 'semioclasty'; that is, a deconstruction of signs.

Acknowledgements   I am very grateful to Robin Torrence for help in transforming this chapter from French to English. Many thanks also to Rodney Harrison for help with editing and obtaining permissions to publish the images in this chapter.

References

Amrouche, P.
    2006 L'Afrique "pourrait racheter des objets". http://www.rfi.fr/actufr/articles/077/article_ 44043.asp, accessed 30 May 2006.

Barthes, Roland
    1970 [1957] *Mythologies*. Le point Seuil, Paris.

Baudrillard, Jean
    1981 *Le Système des Objets*. Denoël-Gonthier, Paris.

Benhamou, F.
    2004 *L'Économie de la Culture*. La Découverte, Paris.

Bouju, J.
    1995 Tradition et Identité. *Enquête, Usages de la Tradition*. http://enquete.revues.org/ document313.html, accessed 27 July 2010.

Bourdieu, Pierre, and L. Wacquant
    1992 *Réponses, pour Une Anthropologie Réflexive*. Seuil, Paris.

Ciarcia, G.
    2001 Croire aux Arts Premiers. *L'Homme* 158–159: 339–351

Clifford, James
    1996 [1988] *Malaise dans la Culture, l'Ethnographie, la Litérature et l'Art au XXème Siècle*. Ensb-a, Paris.
    1997 *Routes: Travel and Translation in the Late Twentieth Century*. Harvard University Press, Cambridge.
    2007 Quai Branly in Process. *October* 120: 3–23. http://www.mitpressjournals.org/doi/pdf/10. 1162/octo.2007.120.1.3, accessed 27 July 2010.

Coombes, Annie
    1999 L'Objet de la Traduction: Notes sur "L'Art" et l'Autonomie dans un Contexte Post-Colonial. *Cahiers d'Études Africaines* 155: 635–658.

Cousin, Saskia, and Galia Tapiero
    2006 Dialogue des Cultures? *EspacesTemps.net*. Mensuelles 13.06.2006, Paris. http:// espacestemps.net/document2037.html, accessed 27 July 2010.

De l'Estoile, B.
    2007 *Le Goût des Autres, De l'Exposition Coloniale aux Arts Premiers*. Flammarion, Paris.

Derlon, Brigitte, and Monique Jeudy-Ballini
    2008 *La Passion de l'Art Primitif, Enquête sur les Collectionneurs*. Gallimard, Paris.

Dias, N.
    2002 Une Place au Louvre. In *Le musée Cannibale*, edited by M.O. Gonseth, J. Hainard, and R. Kaehr, pp. 15–30. Musée d'Ethnographie, Neuchâtel.

Didi-Huberman, Georges
    1990 *Devant l'Image. Question Posée aux Fins d'Une Histoire de l'Art*. Minuit, Paris.
    1997 *L'Empreinte*. Centre Georges Pompidou, Paris.
    2009 Imaginer, Disloquer, Reconstruire. In *Histoire de l'Art et Anthropologie*. INHA/Musée du quai Branly, Paris. http://actesbranly.revues.org/193, accessed 27 July 2010.

Douglas Mary, and Baron Isherwood
    2008 [1979] *Pour Une Anthropologie des Biens de Consommation, le Monde des Biens*. Translated by M. Benguigi. Institut Français de la mode. Éditions du Regard. Paris.

Dufrêne, Thierry, and Anne-Christine Taylor
    2009 By way of introduction. In *Cannibalismes disciplinaires,* edited by Thierry Dufrêne and Anne-Christine Taylor. INHA and Musée du quai Branly ('Actes de colloques'), Paris. http://inha.revues.org/2713, accessed 27 July 2010.

Dupaigne, Bernard
    2006 *Le Scandale des Arts Premiers.* Fayard, Paris.

Fabian, Johannes
    2006 *Le Temps et les Autres: Comment l'Anthropologie Construit son Objet.* Translated by B. Müller and E. Henry-Bossoney. Originally published 1983. Editions Anacharsis, Toulouse.

Grognet, Fabrice
    2005 Objets de Musée, n'avez-vous donc qu'une vie? *Gradhiva* 2-2005: 49–63, Paris. http://gradhiva.revues.org/473, accessed 27 July 2010.
    2008 Du Sens perdu de l'Autre et du Semblable. *L'Homme* 185–186: 455–477.

Guerzoni, G., and G. Troilo
    2001 Pour et Contre le Marketing. In *L'Avenir des Musées*, edited by Jean Galard, pp. 135–154. Éditions de la Réunion des musées nationaux, Paris. http://www.mcsaatchi.com, accessed 27 July 2010.

Guichard, Maud
    1999 On Line Bibliography and Newspaper Articles, Review about the Nok Figures of the Louvre Museum. http://www.globalstudies.gu.se/digitalAssets/809/809871_Maud_Guichard_Appendices.pdf: pp. 74–79, accessed 27 July 2010.

Jamin, Jean
    1985 Les Objets Ethnographiques sont-ils des Choses Perdues? In *Temps Perdu, Temps Retrouvé, Voir les Choses du Passé au Présent*, edited by R. Kaehr and J. Hainard. Musée d'Ethnographie, Neuchâtel.
    1998 Faut-il Brûler les Musées d'Ethnographie? *Gradhiva* 24: 65–69.

Kerchache, Jacques
    1990 *Les Chefs d'Œuvre du Monde Entier naissent Libres et Égaux.* Adam Biro, Paris.

Kopytoff, Igor
    1986 The Cultural Biography of Things: Commoditisation as Process. In *The Social life of Things: Commodities in Cultural Perspective*, edited by Arjun Appadurai, pp. 64–91. Cambridge University Press, Cambridge.

Lambert, Emmanuelle, and Dominique Trouche
    2008 L'Exposition mise à nu par ses Visiteurs, même? *Semen,* N.S. 26. http://semen.revues.org/8451, accessed 27 July 2010.

Lamy, Laurent, and Alexis Nouss
    1997 L'Abandon du Traducteur: Prolégomènes à la Traduction des "Tableaux Parisiens" de Charles Baudelaire. In *Walter Benjamin's Essay on Translation: Critical Translations,* edited by Alexis Nouss. *TTR: traduction, terminologie, rédaction* 10(2): 13–69.

Lavallou, A., and J. P. Robert
    2006 *Le Musée du quai Branly.* Le Moniteur/Musée du quai Branly, Paris

Loumpet-Galitzine, Alexandra
    2008 Objets en Exil; les Temporalités Parallèles du Trône du Roi Njoya (Ouest Cameroun). In *Les Temporalités de l'Exil.* Poexil, Université de Montréal 15–17 February 2007. http://www.poexil.umontreal.ca/events/colloquetemp/actes/Alexandra.pdf, accessed 27 July 2010.

2009 Displaced objects, Objects in Exile? Changing Virtues of Cameroon's Grassfield Objects in the West. In *Crossing Cultures: Conflict, Migration and Convergence,* edited by Jaynie Anderson, pp. 621–624. Melbourne University Press, Melbourne.

Maigret, Éric, and Éric Macé (editors)
2005 *Penser les Médiacultures. Nouvelles Pratiques et Nouvelles Approches de la Représentation du Monde.* Armand Colin/INA, Paris.

Médiatheque Benjamin-Rabier
2010 *Bibliographie Jeunese.* http://abcd.ville-larochesuryon.fr/lrsy/files/afr_jeux_soc.pdf, accessed 27 July 2010.

Merryman, John H., Albert E. Elsen, and Stephen K. Urice
2007 *Law, Ethics and the Visual Arts.* 2nd ed. Kluwer Law International, Alphen aan den Rijn, The Netherlands.

Murphy, Maureen
2009 Du Champ de Bataille au Musée: les Tribulations d'Une Sculpture Fon. In *Histoire de l'Art et Anthropologie.* INHA/Musée du quai Branly, Paris. http://actesbranly.revues.org/213, accessed 27 July 2010.

Musée du quai Branly
2010a No title. http://www.dreamon.fr/medias/projet/minivisuel/format_long_quai_branly_projt2_thumb_255_127_1.jpg, accessed 18 May 2010.
2010b Ymago-Musee du quai Branly. http://ymago.quaibranly.fr/, accessed 20 May 2010.
2010c Permanentes colecciones-África. http://www.quaibranly.fr/es/collections/permanentes-colecciones/africa.html, accessed 20 May 2010.
2010d Bekom mask. http://www.quaibranly.fr/cc/pod/resultats.aspx?b=1&t=1, accessed 20 May 2010.
2010e Mask JU-JU – Cameroon, Bekom. http://www.quaibranly.fr/fr/collections/promenadesalacarte/masques.html?tx_fepromenadealacartet3_pi1[uid]=83, accessed 22 May 2010.
2010f Poster. http://www.quaibranly.fr//cc/pod/recherche.aspx?b=2&t=1, accessed 20 April 2010.
2010g The Chupicuaro. http://www.quaibranly.fr/cn/collections/the-chupicuaro.html, accessed 5 June 2010.
2010h l'Aristocrate et ses cannibales. http://www.quaibranly.fr/fr/programmation/expositions/expositions-passees/l-aristocrate-et-ses-cannibales.html, accessed 15 April 2010.
2010i TARZAN! ou Rousseau chez les Waziri. Exposition dossier. http://www.quaibranly.fr/uploads/tx_gayafeespacepresse/MQB_DP_TARZAN.pdf, accessed 15 April 2010.
2010j Invitation au voyage. http://www.quaibranly.fr/fr/programmation/invitations-au-voyage.html, accessed 5 May 2010.

Myers, Fred
1998 Question de Regard. Les Expositions d'Art Aborigène Australien en France. *Terrain* 30: 95–112.

National Museum of African Art
2010 *Explore the Collection.* http://africa.si.edu/collections/index.html, accessed 2 July 2010.

Olu, Elsa
2008 L'Argument Culturel du "Touristique", l'Argument Touristique du Culturel, Symptômes de 'la Fin du Muséal'. *Téoros* 27(3): 9–17. http://teoros.revues.org/63, accessed 27 July 2010.

Peninou, Georges
2001 Des signes en publicité. *Études de communication.* 24: 15–28. http://edc.revues.org/index986.html, accessed 27 July 2010.

Philips, R.
2009 The Mask Stripped Bare by Its Curators: The Work of Hybridity in the Twenty First Century. In *Histoire de l'Art et Anthropologie*. INHA/Musée du quai Branly, Paris. http://actesbranly.revues.org/336, accessed 27 July 2010.

Price, Sally
2006 *Arts primitifs; regards civilisés*. Originally published 1989. Ensb-a., Paris.
2007 *Paris Primitive. Jacques Chirac's Museum on the Quai Branly*. Chicago University Press, Chicago, IL.

Stiegler, Bernd
2008 'Iconic Turn' et Réflexion Sociétale. *Trivium* 1. http://trivium.revues.org/index308.html, accessed 27 July 2010.

Terra Natura
2010 Terra Natura. http://www.terranatura.fr, accessed 27 July 2010.

UNESCO
2010 Guidelines for the use of the standard form concerning requests for return or restitution. http://unesdoc.unesco.org/images/0007/000720/072071EB.pdf, accessed 27 July 2010.

Viatte, G.
2006 *Tu fais Peur, tu Émerveilles. Musée du quai Branly, acquisitions 1998/2005*. Musée du quai Branly – RMN, Paris.

Vivant, E.
2008 Du Musée-Conservateur au Musée-Entrepreneur. *Téoros* 27(3): 43–52. http://teoros.revues.org/82, accessed 27 July 2010.

Weigel, Sigrid
2008 Les Images, Acteurs Majeurs de la Connaissance. À Propos de la *poiesis* et de l'*episteme* des Images Langagières et Visuelles. *Trivium* 1. http://trivium.revues.org/index319.html, accessed 27 July 2010.

Werner, Paul
2005 *Museum, Inc.: Inside the Global Art World*. Prickly Paradigm, Chicago, IL.

Wikipedia
2010 Place de la Concorde. http://fr.wikipedia.org/wiki/Place_de_la_Concorde, accessed 27 July 2010.

Chapter 7
Agency, Prestige and Politics: Dutch Collecting Abroad and Local Responses

Pieter ter Keurs

Abstract European collecting abroad was more than simply a cultured activity of the elite and a search for beautiful things. Instead, collectors have always worked within national and local political and economic networks. This chapter discusses the various roles of local communities, politicians and middlemen in the process of Dutch collecting in early nineteenth century Indonesia and the Mediterranean. In that period, European nationalism led to unprecedented desires for the expansion of horizons through travel and the collection of trophies from outside Europe. This was partly a search for the roots of European culture (related to the Romantic Movement) and partly triggered by status and prestige, but economic reasons were also important. Although local incentives to participate in this drive to collect were usually not documented, we can begin to identify reasons why local informants engaged with collectors.

> *... it makes more sense to conceptualize cultural developments not as a linear progression from faith to reason but as a dialectical encounter between a culture of feeling and a culture of reason*
>
> *(Blanning 2007: XXVII).*

Introduction

The history of collections and collecting has recently received ample attention in anthropological discourse (e.g. Thomas 1991, 1994; Gosden and Knowles 2001; Shelton 2001; ter Keurs 2007). European collecting abroad was more than a cultured activity of the elite and a search for beautiful things. In the early nineteenth century, collecting was also closely related to politics, to nation building and to the collector's personal, 'romantic' search for adventure and prestige. Both in their countries of origin and in the areas where they searched for objects, the collectors were also part of economic networks. Sometimes the political reality frustrated the collecting activities, but at other times it stimulated them. In all cases the local population, in particular the leaders, had a say in what was and was not collected. And,

P. ter Keurs (✉)
Department of Collections and Research, National Museum of Antiquities, Leiden,
The Netherlands
e-mail: p.terkeurs@rmo.nl

S. Byrne et al. (eds.), *Unpacking the Collection*, One World Archaeology,
DOI 10.1007/978-1-4419-8222-3_7, © Springer Science+Business Media, LLC 2011

often unconsciously, the collectors' choice of objects must have been manipulated by local people.

To illustrate these general points, I will focus on early nineteenth century Dutch collecting in the Netherlands East-Indies (modern Indonesia) and the Mediterranean (Italy, Tunisia and Egypt). In both cases the political and ideological context of this particular period in European history provided the background for the collecting activities and determined to a large extent the thoughts and practices of the collectors. The particularities of specific regions may have been important as well, but a better understanding of the rapid developments in European politics and the changes that took place in the history of ideas is crucial to get a clear view on what actually happened in that important period to European collecting.

The cultural and political context of the late eighteenth and the early nineteenth centuries provided the stimulus for the different kinds of collecting that took place in such different regions as Indonesia and Egypt. Collectors and collecting activities will never be well understood unless we try to comprehend the urge that triggered collecting in that particular period. There are of course general, very human reasons for wanting *to possess* things. The psychology of the human mind can no doubt say sensible things about that. However, here I will look into the culture and politics of collecting within a particular historical setting.

The Advent of the Nineteenth Century

There is some justification for using the year 1798 as the beginning of the nineteenth century. It is the year in which General Napoleon Bonaparte invaded Egypt. The French revolution had shocked European politics and evoked fear among the ruling classes of the various European centres of power. The invasion of Egypt was the first clear sign of General Bonaparte's megalomaniac aspirations. In 1804, he would crown himself Emperor Napoleon and then continue to dream of stepping in the footsteps of Alexander the Great (Strathern 2007: 3, 29) by conquering most of Europe. He would finally be halted in Russia in 1812 and receive a definite blow at the field of Waterloo in present-day Belgium in 1815.

No doubt Napoleon's invasion of Egypt was guided by personal ambitions. His secretary Bourrienne claims to have heard the following words from his master as a comment on the failing government of the *Directoire*.

> I ought to overthrow them and make myself king; but the time has not come. I would be alone. I want to dazzle the people once more . . . We will go to Egypt . . . My glory is slipping from my grasp, tiny Europe has not enough to offer . . . (cited in Strathern 2007: 31).

Militarily and politically the Egyptian campaign did not bring the success Napoleon was hoping for, but he did dazzle the people of France. One of the most striking aspects of the whole campaign is that Napoleon brought a large group of scholars with him to Egypt. He recruited them mainly from the Institute of France, of which he was a member himself. Immediately after the conquest of Cairo, the Institute of Egypt was founded to introduce modern western science in the area (Strathern

2007: 191–203). The idea of progress by means of research based on Enlightened rationalism was clearly present and used for ideological as well as political purposes. Many people were indeed convinced that the democratic ideas of the French revolution, combined with rationally improving our knowledge of the natural and cultural environments, would finally lead to better living conditions for all people, including the poor. Napoleon wanted to change Cairo into a modern city and started to reorganize many Egyptian institutions, at the same time showing respect for the local Islamic leaders who remained in Cairo after the French conquest. The scientists worked to achieve Napoleon's idealistic goal, which of course also furthered his political ambitions and those of his closest aides.

Although 'bringing civilization' was regularly mentioned as one of the aims of the occupation of Egypt, documenting the cultural history of the area became one of the most fascinating and spectacular activities of the expedition's scholars and artists. Napoleon's famous words to his soldiers before the Battle of the Pyramids show that he was very well aware of the historic depth of Egyptian culture: 'Soldiers, forty centuries of history look upon you!' (Fig. 7.1). However, the big surprises came when a part of his army moved south to follow the Mamelukes who were fleeing from the invincible French. The Pyramids of Gizeh had already been impressive, but what the soldiers saw in the south defied all imagination. Large temples with enormous stone statues and mysterious reliefs and texts, until then largely unknown to the outside world, surprised and impressed soldiers and artists such as Vivant Denon (1802), who later wrote about his adventures in Egypt. Together with the 23 volumes of *Description de l'Égypte* (1809–1828), compiled by the many scholars and artists who were in Egypt with General Bonaparte, Denon's book was one of the most influential publications derived from the campaign. Where Denon's report gave an artist's impression of Egypt, the *Description* is 'consciously modeled upon

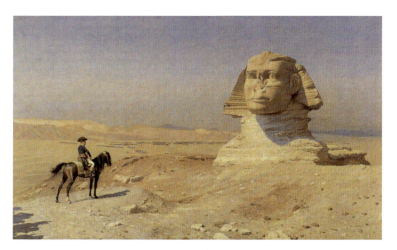

Fig. 7.1 Bonaparte before the Sphinx. Painting by Jean-Léon Gérome (1824–1904) (Photo by Victoria Garagliano/© Hearst Castle®/ CA State Parks)

the great French *Encyclopedie* of the previous century, the work that was seminal in spreading the knowledge, ideas and culture of the Enlightenment.' (Strathern 2007: 424). The material witnesses collected during the Egyptian campaign can still be seen in the Louvre and in the British Museum (after their defeat the French had to leave parts of the collections to the British), including the famous Rosetta stone with the text that enabled Jean-Emile Champollion to decipher old Egyptian hieroglyphs.

The politics of power, the challenges of war and the striving for more status and prestige went hand in hand with the ideals of the Enlightenment. Bonaparte's Egyptian campaign is a good illustration of all the contradictions that are characteristic of the end of the eighteenth and the beginning of the nineteenth century. For two decades, war and peace, destruction and construction (e.g. in architecture and art) and ideals and less elevated practices determined the political agenda. Europe was in an uproar until 1815 when stability returned and a new conservatism, based on fear of another revolution, became dominant in politics and cultural life. However, throughout the nineteenth century 'Egyptian things' were part of European decorative styles and a renewed interest in the Orient became an integral part of European culture. Egyptian antiquities became desired objects whose quest reached unprecedented intensity in the first decades of the nineteenth century.

In a way, Napoleon's Egyptian adventure is also an introduction to another important element of nineteenth century history: colonialism. The French occupation of Egypt in 1798 did not lead to a long period of French rule – defeated by the English, the French were forced to leave Egypt – but European military involvement in non-European cultures, often resulting in political control of the region, became regular practice in the course of the nineteenth century.

To understand the cultural context of early nineteenth century collecting, it is not sufficient to describe important political events of the time. The end of the eighteenth century also witnessed an important development in the history of ideas. The German historian of philosophy Rüdiger Safranski dated the beginning of this development to 17 May 1769 when the young protestant priest Johann Gottfried Herder (1744–1803) left his flock in Riga and boarded a ship loaded with cargo for the French town of Nantes. When leaving Riga, Herder is supposed to have said: 'My only intention is to get to know better the world of my God' ('Meine einzige Absicht ist die, die Welt meines Gottes von mehr Seiten kennenzulernen') (cited in Safranski 2009: 17). Herder wanted to make a new start and used the boat trip back to western Europe to rethink many of the 'issues' of life that had haunted his mind for some years. Throughout his life he remained faithful to the thoughts he had during the boat trip and he influenced some of the major intellectuals of eighteenth-century Europe. Soon after his arrival in France, Herder had a meeting with Johann Wolfgang von Goethe (1749–1832) in Strasbourg and he would greatly inspire the young author.

There was a need for alternative ways of thinking. The last decades of the eighteenth century was the heyday of enlightened rationalism, since many people were convinced that rational study would eventually lead to a better world. Knowledge and understanding of the natural world improved enormously in that period and it only seemed logical that our comprehension of human society would follow this general model. The idea of progress was crucial to this mindset. It was assumed that research would lead to understanding and finally to improvements in all fields of human activity. This idea was supposed to be universally valid, no matter where you applied it. Napoleon justified the invasion of Egypt along these lines. However, it was Herder who challenged the idea of universality. He recognized the importance of local cultural traditions and studied local legends, myths and language diversity. Inspired by Herder's ideas, the first generation of Romantic writers visited the countryside, read and wrote about the diversity in European cultural traditions and documented folk stories (e.g. Safranski 2009). Opposition to Napoleon's imperialism provided extra impetus to this movement. Europe had submitted to Napoleon's will and particularly in Germany, where military resistance had long been futile, alternative forms of resistance evolved.

Another source of inspiration for the Romantics was Johann Georg Hamann (1730–1788). Although he was a personal friend of Immanuel Kant, who with his three *Kritik* (Critics), originally published in 1781, 1788 and 1790, can be seen as the ultimate example of enlightened rationalist ideology, Hamann's ideas were quite different from those of Kant. This is best characterized by Isaiah Berlin, the historian of ideas who has given Hamann his proper place in history.

> Hamann rose in revolt against the entire structure of science, reason, analysis – its virtues even more than its vices. He thought the basis of it altogether false and its conclusions a blasphemy against the nature of man and his creator; and he looked for evidence . . . in the empirically . . . perceived facts themselves, in direct observation of men and their conduct, and in direct introspection of his own passions, feelings, thoughts, way of life (Berlin 2000: 272–273).

The tensions between Enlightenment and Romanticism, between universalism and particularities, between classifications and feelings, and European nationalism paired with a strong political and military involvement in non-European regions set the stage for collecting in the first half of the nineteenth century, as illustrated in my two case studies.

Collecting in the Netherlands East-Indies

European history greatly influenced collecting in the Dutch colony, the Netherlands East-Indies. Until 1800, the trading company *Verenigde Oost-Indische Compagnie* (V.O.C.) had ruled the archipelago that is now known as Indonesia. Usually translated as Dutch East Indies Company, the name literally means 'United East-Indies Company', referring to the unification of previously competing companies. It represents the first multinational company in this early stage of the development of global capitalism. In the seventeenth century, Dutch traders were interested in making a profit and not primarily concerned with colonization. Their power play with local rulers aimed at getting the best deals to monopolize trade in the archipelago in order to gain the highest possible profit, a strategy that worked extremely well in the seventeenth century and into the eighteenth century. Although the Netherlands became a powerful country capable of outmanoeuvring the Portuguese and the Spaniards and engaged in fierce competition with the British, its dominance did not last. Due to bad management and corruption, the V.O.C. lost money and was declared bankrupt on 31 December 1799. From that date onwards, all the V.O.C. possessions in the East Indies became property of the Dutch state, one could say that the Dutch political colonialism of Indonesia formally began on 1 January 1800.

At that time Europe was in an uproar, since Napoleon's rise to power had become a threat to other European states. The French forced the Dutch Republic to become a satellite state of France. In 1806, Napoleon gave a definite blow to Dutch independence by appointing his younger brother Louis Napoleon (1778–1846) King of the Netherlands. As a result, the British occupied the Netherlands East-Indies, which had been under very weak Dutch control since the bankruptcy of the V.O.C. Sir Thomas Stamford Raffles, generally known as the founding father of Singapore, became Governor of the archipelago. During his short reign, Raffles stimulated scholarly research, and in particular, research on the antiquities of Java. The recently rediscovered impressive temples of Indonesia's Hindu–Buddhist past triggered the imagination of the colonial officers and the colonial government began to document systematically the remains of the past. Raffles's book *History of Java*, published in 1817, bears witness to that. After 1815, when Napoleon was defeated and the British were forced to leave the archipelago to the Dutch again, this policy of stimulating an interest in Javanese antiquities, and in general in Indonesian cultures, was taken over by the returning Dutch. The Batavian Society for Arts and Sciences (founded in 1778 by a V.O.C. officer) was to play a key role in scientific research in the colony. And all this was given an extra stimulus by the new King William I (1772–1843).

After the Napoleonic era, the map of Europe was redrawn during the Congress of Vienna (1814–1815). To counterbalance the possibility of a recovering and newly powerful France, the politicians of Europe created a United Kingdom of the Netherlands, north of France. For the first time in history, the northern and southern Netherlands were united in one Kingdom, with a clear aim of making it a strong national state. The new King was very well aware of the possibility that expansion would lead to an increase in status and prestige for the new state and for himself. Besides building a powerful colonial empire, part of his policy was the creation of three national museums in Leiden (National Museum of Antiquities (1818), National Museum of Natural History (1820) and National Museum of Ethnology (1837), at that time not yet seen as a general ethnographic museum, but as a museum that consisted of the Japanese collection of Philip Franz von Siebold). In 1820, William I also founded the *Natuurkundige Commissie* (Natural Science Committee), whose task was to conduct research in order to improve knowledge about the Dutch colonies. Members of the Natural Science Committee would become the main collectors of ethnographic objects in the first half of the nineteenth century. Collecting antiquities would be a slightly different story. First, I will consider ethnographic collecting by Committee members and then discuss the acquisition of antiquities.

Motivated either by Dutch nationalism, scientific curiosity, a search for adventure and/or status and prestige, the members of the Natural Science Committee did not have an easy life in the East Indies. Salomon Müller (1857), the only European member of the group who survived the expeditions (1828–1836), wrote in the introduction of the Natural Science Committee's formal report that his colleagues Zippelius and Van Raalten died on Timor, Macklot lost his life on Java in 1832 during a revolt of the Chinese and Van Oort died in 1834 on Sumatra (Temminck 1839–1844: 9). Apart from the search for antiquities on Java, the more isolated areas of the archipelago needed to be mapped and documented (particularly the eastern part of the colony which included the Lesser Sunda Islands (now Nusa Tenggara), Celebes (now Sulawesi), the Moluccas (now Maluku) and the west part of New Guinea (now Papua)). Later Sumatra also became an important area for study.

It is striking to read how little contact the expedition members had with the local population. In Salomon Müller's (1857) notes on the expeditions (including accounts by his deceased colleagues), there are hardly any references to the local people whom they met and to the exact circumstances of collecting. The following typical citations show how the local people remain vague and impersonal, without names or a personality of their own (translated from Dutch):

– 'some of them offered us colored mats of split rattan, and some living fishes' (Müller 1857: vol. 1, 174).
– 'in Lontontoer we bought some rattan mat clothing of Dayak men and women, weapons and decoration' (Müller 1857: vol. 1, 221).
– 'some things were accepted by the local leaders with pleasure: salt and *arak* (rice wine) commodities that are much desired but scarce and expensive in the interior' (Müller 1857: vol. 2, 132).

The expedition sometimes had to overcome great difficulties, since the circumstances of travel were not easy and medical care for tropical diseases was inadequate. Apart from the Dutch scholars and artists who died during the trips into the interior, an unspecified amount of local helpers never returned, although the latter are hardly mentioned by Müller.

Traders or colonial officers already living in the region were crucial for the expeditions. The help of the *Resident*, a high ranking colonial officer, on Timor (visited in 1828) was greatly appreciated (Müller 1857: vol. 2, 82), but the contacts with the local leaders did not always go well. On September 30 the expedition had to run away 'suddenly and without order' (vol. 2, 185) as a result of a quarrel with or among local rulers. Under such circumstances one can hardly expect systematic collecting.

A clear example is the expedition's visit to the south coast of New Guinea (see also ter Keurs 2007: 10). First of all the expedition members made it clear that they claimed the area for the Dutch as a civilizing power. The local people showed a 'total lack of respect for persons and property' (Müller 1857: vol. 1, 105) and were, therefore, obvious targets for the European 'Enlightened' view to civilize all other people.

However, the interaction between the local people and the visiting Dutch expedition members was difficult. The Moluccan interpreters could not understand the local language (it must have been the language of the Marind Anim) and communication was limited to gestures and gift exchange.

It was only when leaving at sunset that things got out of hand. The Dutch wanted to return to their boat anchored at some distance from the coast, when the local people intervened. Apparently, they did not want the Dutch to leave. After some time, arrows were fired and some people were wounded. This initiated the use of firearms to frighten the local people. It worked. The local people ran away in fear and left some spears on the beach. These were promptly taken to the boat and sent to Batavia and the Netherlands as 'collector's items' (Müller 1857; vol. 1, 58). This event illustrates the haphazard collecting resulting from such difficult circumstances. Systematic collecting of ethnographic objects was impossible. This particular case makes clear that collections compiled in such a way portray less about the role of material culture in the societies that were visited and more about the relationships between the new visitors and the local people than about the local culture itself.

The last part of Müller's (1857) notes describes types of objects, such as clothing, weapons, houses etc., but there is nothing more on the context of the collecting activities. How did they obtain the objects? Did they pay for them? What types of objects were collected and what was not collected? It is very difficult to get a clearer picture of the ethnographic collecting activities of the members of the Natural Science Committee expeditions. There are references of exchange of objects for tobacco, but the actual nature of interaction is unclear.

We can, however, get an impression of the collecting process from the collections themselves. When the Natural Science Committee started its activities, the ethnographic museum (which would later become the National Museum of Ethnology) in Leiden did not yet exist. Therefore, it was also unclear what could be done with the objects collected. The Batavian Society of Arts and Sciences (Jakarta) established in 1778 was given a new stimulus by Raffles, but there was not yet a clear policy about what to do with ethnographic objects. The members of the Natural Science Committee appear to have considered the ethnographic objects as private property. Most, including Salomon Müller, were natural scientists and concentrated on collecting animal and plant species which were sent to the National Museum of Natural History in Leiden (now Naturalis). Ethnography was a sideshow and the objects were probably seen more as souvenirs than as sources for systematic research. For example, after Henrich Christian Macklot was killed during a Chinese revolt on Java in 1832, his collection was not sent to the Batavian Society or to the Royal Cabinet of Rarities in the Hague, but was considered as private property and returned to his family in Europe. The family then sold it to Philip Franz Von Siebold, the founding father of the Museum of Ethnography (at that time called *Japansch Museum Von Siebold*). Von Siebold integrated the Macklot collection in his own collection. Later he numbered it in the same sequence as the Japanese objects he had collected himself in Japan. Salomon Müller's collection was purchased by the Museum of Ethnography in 1864, although the objects had been collected during official, government sponsored, expeditions.

Looking at the objects in the collections made by Macklot and Müller, one is struck by the fact that neither seems to contain important masterpieces, statues or any other – according to western standards – spectacular pieces (e.g. Fig. 7.2). Objects of great ritual importance are also missing from the two collections. This does not imply that the objects were devoid of importance to the local people from whom they were obtained, but it seems likely that they sold or exchanged objects that were easy to replace. Thomas (1991) has shown that objects collected by European collectors in the Pacific were 'entangled' within local cultural values and norms and systems of trade. It is most likely that a similar situation occurred in the Lesser Sunda Islands but the Dutch collectors had no idea of the local contexts. It is also likely – at least in the beginning of the nineteenth century – that the most important ritual objects were not shown to the European visitors and therefore they could not be obtained. In fact, many of the objects collected by Macklot and Müller show no signs of use whatsoever. Although we cannot prove it beyond doubt, many objects may have been newly made; maybe even especially made

Fig. 7.2 Coconut spoon, collected by Salomon Müller. National Museum of Ethnology, Leiden, Inv. no. 16–564 (Photo by Ben Grishaaver, courtesy of the National Museum of Ethnology)

for the approaching expedition. Unfortunately, the evidence remains circumstantial. However, it is beyond doubt that the knowledge the collectors had of the cultures where they worked was very limited. They must have been highly dependent on local middlemen, such as colonial officers, missionaries, traders, local leaders or other cultural brokers.

The Quest for Antiquities

After the Napoleonic period in Europe initiated a new political climate characterized by the increasing importance of national states and, as a consequence, more competition among these states, political colonialism, often supported by military strength, became a powerful driving force in the nineteenth century. The Netherlands particularly concentrated on the Indonesian archipelago to consolidate a commanding position in international politics and trade. However, the Dutch were not in a position to successfully compete everywhere against powerful competitors such as the English and the French; for them the profits of the 'golden' seventeenth century were definitely over. Since the new King William I was very keen on creating and promoting a strong nation that would not be overlooked in European politics, it is, therefore, not a coincidence that the Dutch National Museum of Antiquities was founded by William I in 1818, only 3 years after the Battle of Waterloo decisively ended the French dominance in Europe.

After the fall of Emperor Napoleon, the quest for antiquities and the fascination for the Orient would become strong forces behind the European urge to travel, discover and collect. In his impressive *The Pursuit of Glory,* Blanning observed that during the seventeenth and eighteenth centuries:

> [t]he shift in Europe's demographic centre of gravity was momentous. Late medieval and Renaissance Europe had been dominated by the Mediterranean. ... Yet by the eighteenth century, northerners were coming south as if to a museum, their admiration for its past exceeded only by their contempt for its present (Blanning 2007: 45).

Soon after the beginning of the nineteenth century, when the new balance of power in Europe was installed, the European nation-states competed for the treasures from that large 'Mediterranean museum' referred to by Blanning. However, the urge to acquire antiquities for the glory of the nation-state was not limited to the Mediterranean area. As Hoijtink (2009) observed, the fascination for the Orient went further east than ancient Mesopotamia. The English had their own Orient in British India and the Dutch discovered the importance of ancient Hindu–Buddhist culture in Java. So, when the new National Museum of Antiquities unfolded its collecting policy, Hindu–Buddhist sculpture from the Netherlands East-Indies was explicitly part of the corpus of 'desired goods'.

> When the antiquarians learned, in the nineteenth century, about the discoveries of hoards of antiquities, they considered that Javanese soil must obviously yield a constant flow of these objects. The Javanese brought the antiquities, whether newly found or deriving from family

estates, to the Europeans. These constituted a new class of buyer, and the Javanese traded their antiquities for European coins, a new means of exchange and a direct way of acquiring prosperity (Lunsingh Scheurleer 2007: 77).

Most antiquities were not collected on the site of origin itself. Often, some inter-mediary phase had already precluded the purchase of an object by a European. The same can be said of the collections of Roman, Greek and Egyptian antiquities that the new museum acquired.

Caspar Reuvens (1793–1835) was brought to the attention of the King as a young man and was promptly appointed director of the National Museum of Antiquities in Leiden and the first Professor of Archaeology in the world. He was highly energetic, had a classical education and had studied the impressive classical and Egyptian collections in Paris. Reuvens appeared to be the right man for the job. Starting with a relatively small collection from the University of Leiden, he expanded the museum collection in a short period of time. His main strategy was to work with agents in the field. Using his good relations at the Ministry and a direct link to the King, he was able to react fast and become a central figure in the international network of connoisseurs and art dealers. Reuvens' most important agents worked in Tunisia, Italy and Greece, but he also secured very important Hindu–Buddhist statues from Java. In 1819, three statues from the thirteenth century kingdom of Singasari were sent to Leiden and in 1823 the famous statue of the Buddhist goddess *Prajnaparamita*, (Fig. 7.3) now an internationally acclaimed masterpiece, arrived in Reuvens' museum. Other important pieces followed quickly. We should consider that '[b]y 1800 a large number of antiquities were no longer in their original place'

Fig. 7.3 The Buddhist goddess of supreme wisdom, Prajnaparamita. This statue was returned to Indonesia in 1978. It is now part of the collections of the National Museum of Indonesia, Jakarta (Courtesy National Museum of Indonesia, Inv. no. 1403–1587)

(Lunsingh Scheurleer 2007: 83). Many statues had already been taken to private homes, to become part of family *pusaka* (heritage objects), or to decorate gardens of colonial officers.

The Governor of East Java, Nicolaus Engelhard, was particularly important as an intermediary between the field and the Museum. As Governor (from 1801 to 1808), he travelled in East Java and searched for antiquities in the area. He also commissioned artists to document sites and objects and many of the statues he found were transported to his garden in Semarang (Fig. 7.4).

Fig. 7.4 The Ganesha statue of Singasari (East Java, thirteenth century) (Courtesy of National Museum of Ethnology, Leiden, Inv. no. 1403–1681)

Since then his reputation has been that of a robber of antiquities, but actually he was repri-manded not for removing them from the site, but for keeping them for himself. Engelhard then donated the two guardians, Durga Killing-the-Buffalo-Demon, Ganesha, the bull Nandi and Bhairawa, to King William I of the Netherlands (Lunsingh Scheurleer 2007: 86).

For the time being Reuvens succeeded in convincing the authorities that Hindu–Buddhist remains from the East Indies had to be sent to the Museum of Antiquities in Leiden and not to the Royal Cabinet of Rarities in The Hague (Halbertsma 2003: 36–37). His main argument was that if the people who produced the objects no longer exist, it was justifiable to call the objects 'antiquities'. Therefore, they belonged in a museum of antiquities and not a museum of ethnology.

There is no doubt about categorizing as antiquities the artefacts of peoples which either no longer exist, or have changed completely due to foreign occupation or a change in religion (Reuvens cited in Halbertsma 2003: 36).

Naturally this categorization gave rise to much discussion in the Dutch museum world, but it would take until 1903 for the Hindu–Buddhist collection to be transferred to the National Museum of Ethnology in Leiden. Although Reuvens suddenly died in 1835, still young, his energy and political insights fixed the ideas about dividing collections among the museums in the Netherlands for many decades.

Agents in the Mediterranean

How exactly were the collections of Classical and Asian antiquities formed in Reuvens' time? How did he operate in the feverish atmosphere of early nineteenth century national competition in order to obtain the desired East Indian, Egyptian, Greek and Roman antiquities?

In the Netherlands East-Indies, the Dutch had a monopoly over collecting, but in the Mediterranean, the British and the French were fierce competitors and had the better starting positions. Like his foreign competitors, Reuvens used agents in the field to obtain collections. His most active agents were I.B.E.A. Rottiers (1771–1857) (see Bastet 1987 and Halbertsma 2003) and J. E. Humbert (1771–1839), whom I discuss below (Fig. 7.5). Both conducted archaeological fieldwork, surveys and excavations, but their main importance lies in the fact that they had large personal networks of traders, collectors, diplomats and local leaders. These networks were used to obtain various important collections of antiquities for the Leiden museum.

Fig. 7.5 Jean Emile Humbert (1771–1839). Anonymous drawing (Courtesy of Leiden University Library, Inv. no. PK-T-3054)

Jean Emile Humbert's family was of Swiss Huguenot origin. Although he was born in The Hague, Jean Emile was never able to write a letter in good Dutch. He probably spoke French at home and since he spent many years of his adult life in French-speaking areas, his written Dutch never improved. He was trained as military engineer, but refused to take up active service in the army of the new Batavian Republic, created in 1795. Instead, in 1796 he moved to Tunisia to serve the local ruler Hamouda Pasha Bey and to help with the construction of a harbour. This was the beginning of a long stay in Tunisia during which he developed good relationships with the Pasha and the Dutch consul Antoine Nijssen, in whose house he also lived (Halbertsma 2003: 72). In 1801, Humbert married Nijssen's daughter Thérèse.

Together with the exiled Italian Count Camillo Borgia, Humbert made several trips to the interior of Tunisia, documenting ruins, inscriptions and antiquities. Just after Borgia returned to Italy in 1817, Humbert found four Punic stelae and some fragments with inscriptions. He decided to excavate further and found the first Punic remains postdating the destruction of Carthage (Halbertsma 2003: 75–76). In 1819, he decided to return to the Netherlands to claim his place in the Dutch military hierarchy and to sell his collection of antiquities. While away from home, his daughter died from the plague and all his possessions had to be destroyed. All that was left were his wife's jewellery and his collection. In February 1821, he met Reuvens for the first time and a long cooperation began.

Reuvens asked Humbert to return to Tunisia to buy objects from Utica (known to be available on the market), to start excavations at Carthage and to collect Punic material. In 1822, Humbert's first action was to revitalize his relationship with the Bey by offering gifts and at the same time asking for permission to collect antiquities and start excavations (Halbertsma 2003: 81). In return, the Bey asked Humbert to do some engineering work for him. Humbert immediately began negotiating the purchase of a superb collection of Roman statues, from Utica. Despite competition from the English and the Danish consuls, the collection was secured for Reuvens' museum.

Humbert's excavations in Tunisia never lasted long and consisted mainly of digging long trenches. Apart from digging, Humbert was also engaged in preventing other competing excavations. He successfully prevented the Danish consul, Christian Falbe, from doing archaeological work in the area by spreading the rumour that the Danish team had found an important treasure and kept it hidden from the authorities. Consequently, they were immediately ordered to stop the excavation. Falbe would never forgive him (Halbertsma 2003: 84). This incident clearly illustrates the fierce national competition in the quest for antiquities.

After Tunisia, Humbert lived for long periods in Italy. His experiences in Italy were perhaps even more illustrative for the manner in which the European nation-states obtained their collections. We know of several occasions when Reuvens urged his agent not to stay too long in Italy, but to continue his trip to Tunisia, since objects could still be collected for reasonable prices, but on several occasions Humbert showed a certain reluctance to leave Italy that he did not always explain fully to his boss in Leiden. From archive sources (Halbertsma 1995: 63–64) we know that the

Dutch consul in Tunisia saw Humbert as a threat, since he suspected that Humbert had the ambition to take his job, but he wanted his own son to succeed him. As far as we know, Humbert never communicated this to Reuvens, but it must have been important for Humbert to avoid a confrontation with the consul. Some years later Humbert again remained in Italy, against the wishes of Reuvens. This time there was a woman involved. Humbert, whose first wife had died some years earlier, apparently had a relationship with the daughter of one of his Italian friends. He probably hoped to have a family life again, but all was in vain. He was not allowed to marry her since she was a Catholic and he was a Protestant. Personal circumstances apparently determined to a large extent Humbert's travel plans (Halbertsma 1995: 152–154).

The important cause for Humbert's prolonged stays in Italy was that he used this time profitably to expand his network of local art dealers and collectors, thereby becoming a serious competitor for art agents of other European countries. Humbert became the personal friend of the trade agent Giuseppe Terrini and through him met all the important traders in Egyptian and Classical art. Through this network, he also became friendly with Champollion and Rosselini, two well-known experts in Egyptian art, but at the same time Humbert's competitors.

At that time the Armenian Jean d'Anastasy was one of the most important collectors of Egyptian antiquities, only to be surpassed by the Englishman Salt and the Italian Drovetti (Schneider 1985: 17–19). d'Anastasy was a businessman using Italian trade companies to trade Egyptian grain for Swedish iron with the support of Pasha Muhammed Ali, the ruler of Egypt. He was given the title Consul of Sweden and Norway, providing a convenient way to entangle economic and political relationships. The Egyptian objects of d'Anastasy were put on the market by the Italian trade company Tossiza in Livorno, and the two agents Francois Barthow and Francesco Castiglione were authorized to negotiate prices with the European art agents roaming around in Livorno. Humbert negotiated with them for nearly a year, supported by the Dutch ambassador in the Vatican, Johann Reinhold. They succeeded in lowering the price for the Anastasy collection from 400.000 francs to 230.000 francs and they cleverly outmanoeuvred competitors such as Champollion. In 1828, the collection of d'Anastasy was bought by the Dutch state, thereby giving the National Museum of Antiquities in Leiden one of the best Egyptian collections in the world (Fig. 7.6). This was a great victory for Caspar Reuvens.

Reuvens went to great length to explain how d'Anastasy obtained the objects. He knew that Muhammed Ali had given the monopoly over the trade in Egyptian antiquities to Salt and Drovetti. These two (also consuls) were central figures in the early nineteenth century trade in Egyptian objects, but they were also competing against each other. How then could d'Anastasy build up such a good collection? Reuvens found that he had made accidental discoveries on sites that were seen by Salt and Drovetti as less important (Fig. 7.7), purchased from Arabs who did not need special permission to dig and bought from Salt and Drovetti as well as from Boghoz, a Minister in Mohammed Ali's government (Schneider 1985: 20).

Fig. 7.6 The double statue of
Maya and Merit. Maya was
the Minister of Finance and
the Interior during the reign
of Pharao Tutanchamon.
Merit was his wife (Courtesy
of National Museum of
Antiquities, Leiden, Inv. no.
AST 3)

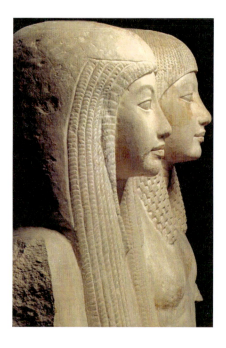

Fig. 7.7 In 1986, the grave of Maya and Merit was rediscovered by an excavation team of the
National Museum of Antiquities and the Egypt Exploration Society. The grave is now restored
(Photo by Pieter ter Keurs, 2010)

These case studies show that Reuvens' agents in the Mediterranean obtained important collections through intermediaries. In turn, they operated within a complex field of trade and politics. Sometimes personal circumstances accidentally helped them acquire objects that are still seen as aesthetic masterpieces today. While these objects are powerful silent witnesses of ancient times, they also portray the story of modern collecting.

Concluding Remarks

In this chapter, I have used the history of early nineteenth century Dutch collecting in Indonesia and in the Mediterranean to unveil the role of scholars, agents, local politicians and middlemen and the complex networks in which they operated to obtain desirable objects. In that period, European nationalism drove an unprecedented expansion in travel and the collection of trophies from outside Europe. This was partly a search for the roots of European culture (stimulated by the Romantic Movement) and partly triggered by status and prestige, but the desire for economic profit was also eminent. In short, it was a complex situation not only on the demand side of the story but also on the supply side. Although local incentives to participate in this drive to collect were usually not documented, we can begin to get an idea of the political or economic reasons local informants had for co-operating with the collector.

The Dutch cases make it very clear that collecting was never a one-way activity involving only a collector's drive to search for interesting, beautiful and unique things. The producers and the middlemen who manipulated the market also played key roles. Collecting objects is rarely just grabbing what you can get – although this certainly did happen – but more typically it was a complex phenomenon embedded in local and international politics. As a consequence, collections are embedded in politics and therefore do not give us an objective, value free picture of the cultures they originated from.

Acknowledgements I would like to thank Professor Ruurd Halbertsma for the discussions we had about Jean Emile Humbert and Anne-Solène Rolland for her work on Müller's texts. I also thank the anonymous reviewers of an earlier version of this chapter who made some sensible remarks for improvement.

References

Bastet, Fréderic L.
  1987 *De Drie Collecties Rottiers te Leiden*. Rijksmuseum van Oudheden, Leiden.

Berlin, Isaiah
  2000 *Three Critics of the Enlightenment. Vico, Hamann, Herder*. Edited by Henry Hardy. Princeton University Press, Princeton, NJ.

Blanning, Timothy C.W.
  2007 *The Pursuit of Glory. Europe 1648–1815*. Penguin, London.

Denon, Vivant
    1802 *Voyages dans la Basse et la Haute Égypte pendant les Campagnes du Général Bonaparte.*
    P. Didot, Paris.

Description de l'Égypte
    1809–1828 *Description de l'Égypt ou recueil (publié par Jomard) des observations et des
    recherches qui ont été faites en Égypt pendant l'expedition de l'armée francaise.* Imprimerie
    Imperiale, Paris.

Gosden, Chris and Chantal Knowles
    2001 *Collecting Colonialism. Material Culture and Colonial Change.* Berg, Oxford.

Halbertsma, Ruurd B.
    1995 *Le Solitaire des Ruines. De Archeologische Reizen van Jean Emile Humbert (1771–1839)
    in dienst van het Koninkrijk der Nederlanden.* Rijksmuseum van Oudheden, Leiden.
    2003 *Scholars, Travellers and Trade. The Pioneer Years of the National Museum of Antiquities
    in Leiden, 1818–1840.* Routledge, London.

Hoijtink, M.
    2009 *Caspar Reuvens en de Musea van Oudheden in Europa (1800–1840).* Unpublished Ph.D.
    dissertation, University of Amsterdam.

Lunsingh Scheurleer, Pauline
    2007 Collecting Javanese Antiquities. The Appropriation of a Newly Discovered Hindu–
    Buddhist Civilization. In *Colonial Collections Revisited*, edited by P. ter Keurs, pp. 71–114.
    CNWS Publications, Leiden.

Müller, Salomon
    1857 *Reizen en onderzoekingen in den Indischen archipel, gedaan op last de Nederlandsche
    Indische regering tusschen de jaren 1828 en 1836.* 2 vols. Frederik Muller, Amsterdam.

Raffles, Thomas, S.
    1817 *History of Java.* 2 vols. Black, Parbury and Allen and John Murray, London.

Safranski, Rüdiger.
    2009 *Romantik. Eine Deutsche Affäre.* Carl Hanser, Munich and Vienna.

Schneider, Hans D.
    1985 *De Laudibus Aegyptologiae. C.J.C. Reuvens als verzamelaar van Aegyptiaca.* Inaugural
    Lecture. Rijksmuseum van Oudheden, Leiden.

Shelton, Anthony A. (editor)
    2001 *Collectors: Expressions of Self and Other.* The Horniman Museum and Gardens, London
    and Museu Antroplógico da Universidade de Coimbra, Coimbra.

Strathern, Paul
    2007 *Napoleon in Egypt. ' The Greatest Glory'.* Jonathan Cape, London.

Temminck, C.J.
    1839–1844 *Verhandelingen over de Natuurlijke Geschiedenis der Nederlandsche Overzeesche
    Bezittingen door de Leden der Natuurkundige Commissie in Indië en andere Schrijvers.*
    3 vols. S. en J. Luchtmans en C.C. van der Hoek, Leiden.

ter Keurs, Pieter (editor)
    2007 *Colonial Collections Revisited.* CNWS Publications, Leiden.

Thomas, Nicholas
    1991 *Entangled Objects. Exchange, Material Culture and Colonialism in the Pacific.* Harvard
    University Press, Cambridge.
    1994 *Colonialism's Culture: Anthropology, Travel and Government.* Polity Press, Oxford.

Part IV
Communities and Collections

Chapter 8
Crafting Hopi Identities at the Museum of Northern Arizona

Kelley Hays-Gilpin

Abstract The Hopi of Northern Arizona are renowned for their arts, particularly katsina dolls, pottery, silver overlay jewellery and basketry. Hopi objects began to enter museum collections and curio markets in large numbers in the 1880s, and have made their way into museums all over the world, by means of galleries, traders, collectors, tourists and individual commissions. The Hopi collections at the Museum of Northern Arizona (MNA) are unique because MNA has long taken an active and collaborative role in developing Hopi arts. In the 1930s, MNA curators suggested new jewellery techniques to Hopi artisans; they also supported traditional basketry and textile styles and promoted both revival and innovation in pottery making and katsina doll carving. Hopi artists accepted some of the Museum's suggestions but developed each art form in their own directions. Over time, the Museum's role has shifted from one of paternalism to one of collaboration including education, production, marketing and research that focuses on Hopi history and cultural values. Study of MNA collections and associated documentation, and discussions with Hopi artists, show that Hopi art emphasizes the makers' social identities at many levels – ethnic group, village, clan, membership in ritual associations, gender and age. Sometimes these identities are clearly signalled and can be 'read' once a viewer learns how to recognize them; sometimes they are apparent only when information about objects' individual biographies has been recorded. Presenting the internal diversity of Hopi identities to the public, and preserving this record of diversity for future Hopi generations, is especially challenging in the museum setting.

Museum of North Arizona and the Hopi Tribe

All art has a tendency to degenerate – to go downhill; it needs jacking up and practical encouragement. This is just the movement we are trying to start; we have no desire to step on anyone's toes. We are scientific and artistic; not commercial (Mary-Russell Ferrell Colton, 1930, letter to museum trustees in Colton 1930a, Allen 1984: 69).

On the 5th and 6th of July 2008, the Museum of Northern Arizona hosted its 75th Hopi Festival of Arts and Culture. This event began in 1930 as the 'Hopi

K. Hays-Gilpin (✉)
Department of Anthropology, Northern Arizona University, Flagstaff, AZ, USA; Museum of Northern Arizona, Flagstaff, AZ, USA
e-mail: kelley.hays-gilpin@nau.edu

S. Byrne et al. (eds.), *Unpacking the Collection*, One World Archaeology,
DOI 10.1007/978-1-4419-8222-3_8, © Springer Science+Business Media, LLC 2011

Craftsman exhibition' (no shows were held during the war years, 1943–1946). Museum founders Harold Colton, a biologist, and Mary-Russell Ferrell Colton, a professionally trained artist, wanted to encourage the survival of Hopi arts and crafts (see Mangum and Mangum 1997: 69, 76–77). Early on, the Coltons focused on encouraging Hopi artisans to produce pottery, textiles and baskets for sale to tourists, traders and MNA. They soon turned their attention to jewellery, then katsina doll carving and painting. Attending the festival is now a tradition in Hopi families; many artists who attend today remember coming to the festival as children. The Museum of Northern Arizona thus has a unique relationship with the Hopi Tribe (although many indigenous communities in North America have stopped using the term 'tribe', the Hopi use the term in their official name).

Before detailing MNA's long relationship with members of the Hopi Tribe, I will explain where this small, regional museum fits in a larger context of relationships between Native American communities and museums in North America. The Coltons founded MNA in the 1920s in a conscious effort to counter the dominance of large museums based in the eastern United States, such as the Smithsonian Institution in Washington, D.C., the American Museum of Natural History in New York and the Chicago Field Museum. By the 1920s, these and many European museums had engaged in 50 years of 'salvage ethnography' and archaeological excavations that removed hundreds of thousands of objects from the Southwest and shipped them far away where most local people, European-American and Native alike, would never see them. The Coltons, and other wealthy immigrants to the region such as Harold Gladwin, who founded Gila Pueblo in central Arizona and William Fulton, who established the Amerind Foundation in southern Arizona, began to conduct scientific research and collect objects for the benefit of their local communities and the nation. They intended for objects and knowledge to stay close to their sources; researchers and tourists would come to them. But like the distant behemoths they wished to challenge, MNA and the others operated under European-American frameworks of scientific knowledge, ownership and control. These paradigms contrast significantly with indigenous views which are based in inherited and earned rights to proprietary knowledge and accompanying responsibilities for correct use and transmission of knowledge (Isaac 2007). All these museums collected sacred objects as well as objects of everyday use, made photos and recordings of religious activities and wrote down descriptions of ceremonies that should neither, in the Native view, have been fixed in permanent media nor removed from their source communities. Karen Coody Cooper (Cherokee Nation of Oklahoma) writes, 'Some people say American Indians should be grateful to museums for having saved so many American Indian cultural items. In some cases, some American Indians are indeed grateful. But, in other cases, there has been great disappointment.' For example, museums have exchanged objects, sold items to private dealers or failed to prevent thefts, thereby 'denying American Indians the opportunity to view or possess things that could be culturally important to them' (Cooper 2008: 83).

Civil rights protests throughout the United States and Canada in the 1960s and '70s included American Indian assertions of rights to have a voice in how museums treated the remains of their ancestors, sacred and ceremonial objects, and knowledge. They won the right to take active roles in presenting the histories and identities of their communities (Cooper 2008). Most museums that held American Indian collections appointed Native advisory boards, some of which included community cultural experts in program planning, and many Native communities established tribal museums or museum-like cultural or heritage centres. Passage of the American Indian Religious Freedom Act in 1979 drew attention to sacred and ceremonial items in museums, but it was not until the passage of the Native American Graves Protection and Repatriation Act of 1990 that all museums that received Federal funding or tax-exempt status were forced to engage in dialogue with source communities. Federally recognized tribes became eligible for Federal funding to help facilitate repatriation. Tribes won rights to operate casinos on tribal lands, some opened successful casinos and some directed profits to tribal museums and cultural centres. Although the Hopi and Zuni tribes have the right to open casinos, they have consistently rejected gambling on the grounds of traditional values.

By 2008, over 200 museum-like operations were being run by and for tribes in Canada and the United States (Cooper 2008: 137). By some definitions, this would include a small, privately-owned museum run by a handful of Hopi individuals as a visitor centre aimed at orienting tourists to Hopi history and material culture. The Hopi tribal government has worked on plans for a tribal museum that would serve both community members and outsiders for decades, and at this time of writing there are no firm plans in place. In contrast, the government of the neighbouring Navajo Nation founded the Navajo Nation Museum in 1961 as a one-room orientation for tourists with one staff member, and in 1998 emerged in a beautiful new building that serves the largest Indian Reservation in the United States with exhibits, cultural programming, library and archives (http://www.navajonationmuseum.org/). Its development was delayed for nearly a decade because the new building was strongly identified with an outgoing tribal President, and the incoming administration felt it needed to establish its own signature projects. The Zuni tribe developed its A:shiwi A:wan tribal museum over a period of about 20 years with a long series of planning projects. Perhaps learning from the Navajo experience, Zuni reached a decision to keep the museum separate from the tribal government so that it would be truly owned by the community, and not be identified with particular politicians or political factions (Isaac 2007). The current MNA-Hopi partnership presents a 'third way' – not a tribal museum, not a completely 'outsider' museum. This partnership rests on a unique history that includes a founding focus on cultural arts as well as history and archaeology, a long-standing practice of hiring Hopi employees, and programming that went well beyond collecting and displaying Hopi objects to tourists and other outsiders.

The Museum of Northern Arizona did not merely collect objects produced by Hopi artisans but also took an active role in shaping what was produced, marketed and collected. In turn, Hopi artists used the MNA and their artwork to assert their social identities at many levels, ethnic, village, family, clan and individual. In particular, they were interested in differentiating themselves from the Navajo people who surrounded and outnumbered them.

The Hopi live in 12 farming villages in the high desert of northern Arizona. Today, they number about 12,000. Many still speak their indigenous Uto-Aztecan language in addition to English. One village, Hano, was founded in 1700 by Tewa-speaking immigrants from what is now New Mexico. The Hopi-Tewa still maintain a distinct ethnic identity, and many Hopi-Tewa women are renowned potters. Each autonomous village is governed by traditional religious leaders. Traditional leadership roles, ritual knowledge and responsibilities, land tenure and certain social roles are passed down the generations in matrilineal clans. Many Hopi people identify themselves first by clan, then by village and last as 'Hopi', a term that refers more to an ideal way of life than an ethnic or political identity, although the word has come to encompass many meanings. Most Hopi villages also send elected or appointed representatives to a tribal council, a structure imposed by the US government. Today, the Hopi Cultural Preservation Office serves as the arm of tribal government that brokers relationships among tribal members, researchers, museums and government agencies in attempts to foster continuity in language, arts, traditions and sacred places on and off the reservation.

Over the past 80 years, MNA has helped to shape the general public's view of Hopi ethnic identity through promotion of arts and crafts. For example, many museums in the western United States have Native American art fairs that include Hopi artists, but only MNA has an exclusively Hopi show (as well as Navajo, Zuni and Hispanic fairs). The Hopi tribe has contributed to the identity of MNA, through the activities of Hopi employees, artists and scholars. In 2005, the Museum and the tribal government signed a formal Memorandum of Understanding that has moved the relationship from paternalism to collaboration and reciprocity (Museum of North Arizona 2005). By facilitating discussion and presentation of Hopi traditional histories, language preservation and contemporary Hopi use of archaeological data, and by assisting the Hopi Tribe in curating its collections until it can develop its own tribal museum, MNA has become an active participant in shaping the way future generations will understand what it means to be Hopi. For example, MNA currently cares for two archaeological collections excavated on the reservation and a collection of Southwest Indian fine arts donated to the tribe. MNA and the Hopi tribe are currently partnering on a long-term exhibit planning project. Hopi and non-Hopi museum professionals have held public discussion forms and interviewed nearly 40 Hopi consultants about permanent and travelling exhibits that will explain the Hopi world to outsiders in Hopi voices, and provide educational programs for Hopi families and school groups. When asked whether Hopi people would welcome such exhibits in a non-Hopi owned museum, one Hopi consultant said, 'of course! Hopi families have been coming to MNA for generations and we feel this is *our* museum.' In this chapter, I will explain how the varied and changing relationships between MNA and Hopi artisans have shaped the Museum's extensive collections of Hopi jewellery, pottery, baskets, textiles and katsina dolls (Fig. 8.1). The histories of making, collecting and interpreting are dynamic and distinct for each category but some common themes are discernable.

Fig. 8.1 Hopi arts on display: coiled and wicker basketry, a woven belt, kachina dolls, pottery and jewellery (Photo by Milton Snow, 1946–1950. Northern Arizona University Cline Library item 26974, call number HCPO.PH.2003.1.HC5.8. Courtesy of the Hopi Cultural Preservation Office)

Hopi Silver Jewellery

Hopi silversmithing began in the late nineteenth century, but was undifferentiated until the 1940s from that made by their Navajo and Zuni neighbours. In 1938, MNA founders and curators began to help Hopi smiths develop a distinctive style. Mary-Russell Ferrell Colton wrote a letter to 18 Hopi silversmiths to tell them 'of our plan to improve Hopi silver and to assist Hopi smiths' (in Wright 1977: 40). She pointed out that Hopi smiths received low prices for their work because tourists did not know the difference between hand-made jewellery and mass-produced machine-made work. New government programs were beginning that would help to identify and mark 'genuine' Indian arts. She wrote:

> Navajo silver, Hopi and Pueblo silver, is very much alike, most people cannot tell the difference. Hopi silver should be entirely different from all other Indian silver, it should be *Hopi*, silver using only Hopi designs. . . .The Museum proposes to help the Hopi silver smiths in this way. First, we are making a set of designs for silver, using certain Hopi designs in a new way. . . .We hope that these designs will help the Hopi smiths to understand what we mean by asking them to use one of the Hopi designs, which has not been used for silver before, and that they will then begin to make their own Hopi designs (Colton in Wright 1972: 42).

Fig. 8.2 Design for a silver
and turquoise bracelet,
presented to Hopi
silversmiths by the Museum
of Northern Arizona (MNA).
Goache painting by Virgil
Hubert, Assistant Curator.
Catalog number C2405
(©2010 Museum of Northern
Arizona)

Virgil Hubert, assistant curator of art at the Museum, who was not Hopi, produced
a set of drawings and paintings of jewellery that would require many different
silverworking techniques by borrowing designs from Hopi pottery, basketry and textile designs (Fig. 8.2). Mary-Russell Colton researched the Federal Government's
hallmark guidelines, established by the Indian Arts and Crafts Board to assure
authenticity in Indian arts and insisted that smiths use hallmarks along with Hubert's
designs. A few Hopi smiths, notably Paul Saufkie, began to use the designs, but only
four artists submitted work that Colton felt was up to standards for the 1939 Hopi
Craftsman Exhibition at MNA. Their pieces were sold and she continued to encourage the program she called the 'Hopi Silver Project' (Mangum and Mangum 1997:
100–102).

During World War II, smiths could not obtain materials. Most Hopi men went to
war, were imprisoned as conscientious objectors or had to do extra work at home to
make up for those who were gone. After the war, men needed work that would help
their families survive in an increasingly cash-based economy. Making jewellery was
one option.

Fred Kabotie, a well-known Hopi artist, showed Saufkie's work and his own
designs to the director of the Federal Indian Education program and proposed silversmithing classes for veterans. Classes began in 1947 with Kabotie and Saufkie
as instructors (Fig. 8.3). Veterans received training, tools and living expenses for
the 18 month course. Instructors and students used the MNA designs, augmented by
ones from other Hopi arts, and their own original designs (Figs. 8.4 and 8.5). They

Fig. 8.3 Paul Saufkie instructs a student at Oraibi High School (Photo by Milton Snow, 1944–1950. Northern Arizona University Cline Library item 29099, call number HCPO.PH.2003.1.HC5.64. Courtesy of the Hopi Cultural Preservation Office)

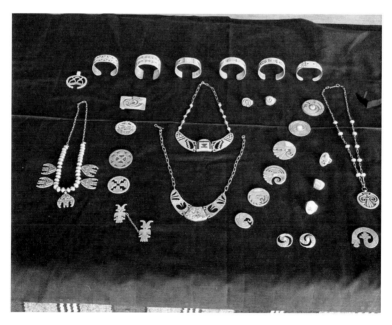

Fig. 8.4 Hopi silver overlay jewellery, based on designs elements from Hopi pottery and basketry provided by MNA curator Virgil Hubert (Photo by Milton Snow, 1944–1950. Northern Arizona University Cline Library item 26980, call number HCPO.PH.2003.1.HC5.14. Courtesy of the Hopi Cultural Preservation Office)

Fig. 8.5 Sketches with 'suggestions for jewellery designs' based on painted pottery (Photo by Milton Snow, 1944–1950. Northern Arizona University Cline Library item 26972, call number HCPO.PH.2003.1.HC5.7. Courtesy of the Hopi Cultural Preservation Office)

started using a variety of different techniques and over time, the appliqué technique suggested by the Museum gave way to the overlay technique. In Kabotie's own words, 'Overlay jewellery is made from two layers of flat silver. The under layer is a solid piece; the upper layer bears designs which have been cut out. The two pieces are soldered together' (Kabotie 1950: 1).

When the veterans' program ended in 1949, smiths had no way to get additional materials and tools, so some of them formed the Hopi Silver Craft Guild, which obtained a government loan for supplies and equipment. Later, it was legally incorporated as a non-profit organization (Kabotie 1965). The Guild built its own workshop and store, and flourished through the 1970s. It still exists today, but is largely inactive. Some think the Guild's inactivity is due in part to its own success – a number of prosperous silver artists have built their own shops and clientele. Yet its main competitor in the 1960s and 70s was HopiCrafts, a shop founded by brothers Wayne and Emory Sekaquaptewa of Third Mesa. Both HopiCrafts and the Guild thrived in that era, and the competition between the two workshops seems to have raised the overall technical quality of Hopi silverwork and promoted diversity in design. Early on, Hopi silversmiths worked in groups in the formal teaching and mentoring programs practiced by both the Guild and HopiCrafts, and now they tend to work as individuals who sometimes mentor a small number of students. Many have their own workshops and some have their own retail shops.

Hopi silver has come to express Hopi ethnic identity even though it was a new technology, kick-started by outsiders who at first told Hopi silversmiths what to do

Fig. 8.6 Fred Kabotie instructs the Hopi veterans' silversmithing class. The group is discussing how to adapt designs from the traditional brocade manta (shoulder blanket) to jewellery (Photo by Milton Snow, 1944–1950. Northern Arizona University Cline Library item 27314, call number HCPO.PH.2003.1.HC5.39. Courtesy of the Hopi Cultural Preservation Office)

and how to do it. The Museum's intervention diverted Hopi jewellers from reliance on a larger, pan-Southwestern Indian jewellery tradition to distinctly Hopi designs that came from other media, primarily women's basketry and pottery and men's textile arts (Figs. 8.5 and 8.6). Some Hopi men began to draw on archaeological sources – prehistoric pottery and petroglyphs. While materials and techniques came from outside, designs came from inside Hopi culture and developed from there as a result of Hopi efforts. Hopi choices of designs reflect concerns that are still current today: the unique trajectory of Hopi history and the diverse ethnic composition of Hopi communities – clan symbols, migration symbols and use of ancestral designs newly brought to light by archaeologists and museums (Fig. 8.7) (see Bernardini 2005; Colwell-Chanthaphonh and Ferguson 2006).

Hallmarks, Clan Symbols and Clan Knowledge

The hallmarks smiths used to identify their work (a practice encouraged by the Museum and the Guild) were sometimes based on artists' initials, but more often on clan symbols (Figs. 8.7 and 8.8). These symbols also became one of the most popular sources of designs (Figs. 8.8 and 8.9). Jewellers proudly point out their own clan symbols, inherited from their mothers, and also those of their fathers and other

Fig. 8.7 Hopi veterans' silversmithing class, displaying clan symbols used as jewellery designs and as hallmarks (Photo by Milton Snow, 1944–1950. Northern Arizona University Cline Library item 27301, call number HCPO.PH.2003.1.HC5.32. Courtesy of the Hopi Cultural Preservation Office)

relatives, both blood relatives and ceremonial godparents. The clans, including Sun, Sun Forehead, Bear, Spider, Snow, Water House and Tobacco, let each smith design his own version of a clan symbol as a hallmark (Fig. 8.7). For example, one Bear clan member depicted a bear's face and another used a bear track; one Water House clan member depicted a cloud, and another a tadpole.

Hopi clan symbols are not just convenient ways to identify individuals or their artwork. Clanship is at the heart of Hopi ethnic identity. Hopi men who could not write their names in English signed government documents with clan symbols in the nineteenth century, not with stereotypical Xs (Fewkes 1897). Clan identities and clan symbols continue today, and are key to understanding the Hopi world. Clan knowledge and responsibilities pass from uncle to nephew, and to some extent from mother to daughter. Initiation into religious societies passes from ceremonial sponsors to initiates, and additional knowledge and responsibilities are acquired that way. When men have the right to know the clan histories of their sponsors, as well as their own clan histories, knowledge is transmitted across generations, but it also remains dispersed within each Hopi community. No individual or family has the ritual information that comprises a complete ritual cycle for any village, which ensures that community members stay connected. Sharing clan histories and ritual knowledge too widely dilutes knowledge, disrupts distribution of social and ritual responsibilities and highlights potential contradictions and conflicts. Dispersed knowledge

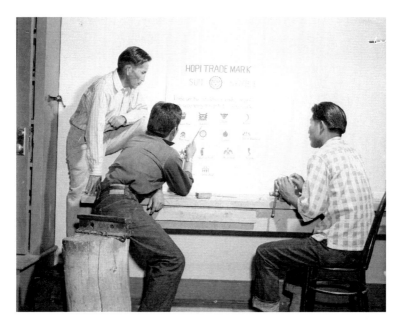

Fig. 8.8 Fred Kabotie, left, teaching GI silversmithing class use of traditional Hopi design in modern jewellery. Here, they examine designs and hallmarks based on clan symbols displayed below the Hopi Silvercraft Guild's sun symbol trademark (Photo by Milton Snow, 1944–1950. Northern Arizona University Cline Library item 27309, call number HCPO.PH.2003.1.HC5.35. Courtesy of the Hopi Cultural Preservation Office)

Fig. 8.9 Hopi silver overlay bracelet with sun design. The sun is a clan symbol, but it also became the hallmark of the Hopi Silvercraft Cooperative Guild. Museum of Northern Arizona catalog number E10280 (© 2010 Museum of Northern Arizona)

presents several dilemmas for exhibit planning – what information should be presented? How much information is appropriate? Who should provide it? The symbols used in Hopi jewellery designs and as hallmarks thus serve as a tangible reminder to curators that the Hopi world is deliberately diverse, and curators must take care not to homogenize symbols, meanings or stories. A culturally homogenous presentation of Hopi life and art would be an inaccurate presentation.

MNA's Hopi Jewellery Collection

In spite of MNA's key role in developing a distinctive Hopi jewellery style and selling the work of many Hopi jewellers in its gift show, the Museum collected little Hopi silver for its permanent collections. The current collections manager attempts to fill out the collection by regularly checking online auction sites for Hopi jewellery that is identified by maker and hallmark, with the goal of obtaining at least one piece from each maker insofar as this is possible given the Museum's limited acquisitions budget. Other pieces arrive in the collections through individual donations which are evaluated by a committee who considers each piece's contribution to the existing collection.

Pottery

Hopi pottery traditions are an amalgam of stylistic and technological inheritance from several archaeologically defined regions and local innovations. The first pottery vessels in the region appeared around AD 200 in the form of polished low-fired brownware vessels that looked like pottery from northern Mexico. By the 700s, potters had adapted their techniques to local materials, adopted higher firing temperatures and a decorative style apparently based on small repeated geometric units that first appeared on textiles and coiled baskets. From that time to the late 1200s, pottery styles in the Hopi area consisted of coarse gray cooking pots; brightly coloured red and polychrome bowls, dippers, canteens and seed jars; and black-on-white water jars, dippers and bowls with designs that echo those on loom-woven cotton textiles. Following severe drought, demographic upheavals and widespread migration in the late 1200s, Hopi traditional history recounts a 'gathering of clans' on the Hopi Mesas. Potters on the Hopi Mesas developed a new pottery technology called 'Jeddito Yellow Ware'. Fired with coal at a high temperature (about 1000°C), this ware has a bright yellow colour that is entirely new in the region, but painted designs are very similar to those on red and white slipped pottery from other regions, such as Homo'ovi along the middle Little Colorado River about 100 km to the south and ancestral Acoma and Zuni sites to the east. By 1375, all these areas and potters of the Rio Grande Valley shared an elaborate set of painted designs that included katsina faces, parrots, prayer feathers, cloud and water designs and serpents. After the Spanish *entrada* of 1540, Hopi villages took in refugees from Spanish oppression and other waves of Pueblo refugee immigrants arrived from what is now New Mexico after the Pueblo Revolt of 1680 and the Reconquest of 1692. By 1700, Hopi pottery began to look very much like that of Acoma and Rio Grande Pueblos.

Subsequent population movement among Zuni and Hopi villages in the nineteenth century resulted in Hopi potters emulating Zuni products.

Hopi pottery, then, has a long history of flexibility and change. Archaeologists can look at a fragment of painted pottery from anywhere in Arizona or New Mexico and infer a date within a 50-year interval, using techniques developed in part by Harold Colton and colleagues at MNA (see Colton 1953, 1956).

When Thomas Keam and other Anglo-Americans set up trading posts in Hopiland in the late 1800s, Hopi pots were indistinguishable from those made by Zuni potters. Pottery making was diminishing on Second and Third Mesas, and only First Mesa potters were producing enough pottery for trade. Keam and others encouraged First Mesa potters to copy ancient designs, particularly those of the fifteenth century Sikyatki Polychrome. Several potters worked with Keam and others to develop what has become known as Sikyatki Revival pottery. The most famous potter working in this style was Nampeyo, a Hopi-Tewa woman. Her husband, Lesou, a Hopi, painted many of the vessels that Nampeyo formed and fired. Demand for Sikyatki Revival pottery increased in the early decades of twentieth century, as more visitors arrived by train and took Fred Harvey tours. Ultimately they followed the highway that became the famous Route 66, the Mother Road from Chicago to Los Angeles, which passed within 100 km of the Hopi villages. Unfortunately, as demand for Hopi pottery increased, quality decreased.

In recalling the Museum's role in revitalizing Hopi ceramic arts, MNA librarian Katharine Bartlett recalled,

> By 1920, pottery art had deteriorated in quality in favour of quantity. Every potter was busy turning out as many little curios as possible – ashtrays in the form of cowboy hats was a horrible example – in addition to a few larger pieces for her own use. The quality of black paint had also declined, for it easily rubbed off. (Bartlett 1977: 13)

Mary-Russell Colton resolved to improve Hopi ceramic arts, a central goal of the first MNA Hopi Craftsman exhibition in 1930. She encouraged potters to send their best work, to make pieces in a variety of sizes and shapes and to mark the pottery with their own name or symbol 'in order to establish a reputation for themselves.' Potters complied with her first two edicts, but not the third. Bartlett speculated that 'they didn't use signatures because it is not the Hopi way to draw attention to oneself', but in the MNA Hopi Shows, 'every entry bore a [paper] tag showing the maker's name and village'. She adds, 'in the last few years [mid-1970s] more and more women are signing their works' (Bartlett 1977: 13). Subsequent generations of potters were more amenable to signing their work, and the practice was common by the late 1970s. Like male jewellers, many potters sign with a clan symbol, some with a symbol that referred to a personal name, such as a flower, frog or fawn.

Harold Colton's contribution to the 'improvement' of pottery making, at least in part, consisted of conducting controlled firing experiments with Hopi potters who demonstrated their craft at the annual Hopi exhibition (Colton 1951). He used a pyrometer to measure the maximum temperature in settings with varying proportions of coal and sheep dung. Coal had been the favoured fuel for firing prior to the introduction of livestock by the Spaniards in 1629. Colton's efforts to persuade Hopi potters to include at least some coal fuel met with limited success. Few potters use coal today, even though it is now available free to tribal members from the Peabody Coal Company's strip mine several hours drive north of the Hopi villages. One potter told me, 'it's just so much easier to buy a whole pickup truckload of dung from Navajo ladies who bring it right to the village.'

MNA also educated pottery buyers. Over the last few decades, MNA has produced publications for non-Hopis that explain the Museum's collection of Hopi pottery and how prospective collectors can evaluate, purchase and care for it. One such article recommends that prospective buyers visit the usual 'authorities' (dealers, galleries, publications) to learn how to judge the quality of Hopi pottery, but also advocates visiting the reservation and talking with potters (Hitchcock 1977). In its publications, the Museum tended to define 'quality' in terms of western aesthetics, emphasizing the precision of painted designs as important and identifying the presence of colour variations such as fire clouds as flaws. In contrast, Hopi potters even today emphasize the importance of a warm yellow and orange mottled colouring called 'blush' that indicates that a pot has a living spirit, and that it survived the risky traditional open-air firing process (Charley and McChesney 2007: 87, 89). Hopi potters admire painted designs, and most enjoy doing them, but they are the measure neither of a master potter nor of a masterpiece. Unfortunately, many Hopi potters have bent to pressure from galleries and high-end buyers and now strive to produce precise but rigid designs on pots with uniform colours that seem lifeless to those with more traditional aesthetic standards and preferences.

Likewise, museum advice about caring for Hopi pots may deny them a life of their own. Potters say that pots have always been meant for use. They are made to be used, and should go out into the world as ambassadors for Hopi values, to be loved and enjoyed in the home. But the Museum's publications advise buyers to avoid placing them on a hard surface lest the base get scraped. As this is the location of the signature, when there is one, scratching this emblem of prestige and authenticity might diminish the piece's monetary value. Older Hopi pots in MNA's collection are seldom signed, and often have use-wear on the base. Should contemporary Hopi pots be used by their makers – to hold coins, toothpicks, matches and other household items, or to cook beans in the microwave? Many Hopi potters say 'yes' – pots are both tools and members of the buyer's as well as the maker's family; curators say 'no, they are too fragile.'

MNA's own pottery collection preserves examples of pottery that was made for use as well as for sale to buyers whose most common notion of 'use' was display that did not involve frequent handling. The collection began in 1928, when Lyndon Lane Hargrave collected 41 Hopi pots. Unlike other traders and collectors of the time, Hargrave focused on obtaining large utility jars that families considered to be of no value because newly available metal cans and buckets were lighter and stronger. These storage and cooking jars comprised the Museum's first ethnological collection. In a belated act of salvage ethnography, these jars were meant to capture evidence of a way of life that was rapidly disappearing as Euro-American containers were adopted. MNA added pieces almost every year from the Hopi Craftsmen show starting in 1930; most of these probably had been made for sale. In the mid-1970s,

MNA embarked on a National Endowment for Arts-funded project to catalog the Hopi pottery and published an illustrated description (Allen 1984). At that time, the Museum had 1053 pieces. Over half, 58%, were purchased by the Coltons and Museum staff through direct interaction with potters at their homes or at the Hopi show. Rather than focusing on pottery as a fine art form, MNA's collection policy was to 'show representative examples of what was produced' (Allen 1984: 15).

The Museum regularly added a few pieces from the Hopi Show to its permanent collections until the 1980s; then collecting became sporadic. Due to diminishing finances and rising prices, the Museum could not often afford to purchase Hopi pottery. Museum administrators sometimes purchased items that were broken accidentally and added these to the collection in order to have some record of what kinds of pottery had been on offer. Limited collecting of representative pieces began again around 2003, with the assistance of donor sponsorship. Today there are 1403 objects in the historic period (post-A.D. 1630) and contemporary Hopi pottery collection.

Over the history of the Museum, active influence on Hopi pottery went from a relationship of active efforts to influence what Hopi potters were doing, to an effort focused more on educating buyers, to what is now a relatively passive role of hosting a venue for sale and demonstration of the craft. Future plans are detailed below.

Baskets and Textiles

Hopi basketry is a popular and well-known art form, with many extraordinary women basketweavers working today. Textiles, on the other hand, are becoming scarce although the Museum has over the decades made efforts to encourage weavers, who are almost all men. Basketry and textile production and their use are encoded with deeply important gendered meanings and have critical roles in key Hopi rituals and family life. Hopi weddings, elaborate multi-year affairs, involve exchange of women's baskets and men's textiles, sometimes in large numbers.

Women are responsible for making basketry plaques for weddings and other life-cycle events, as well as for their own ritual sorority performances and community-wide katsina dances. Ritual foods should be properly carried and served on basketry trays or plaques. Basketry style and technology signals village membership – Second Mesa weavers make coiled baskets of fine yucca strips stitched around a spirally bundle of grass. Third Mesa weavers make wicker plaques of dyed rabbit-brush. At least some women in most Hopi villages, including the ones on First Mesa, make plaited yucca leaf 'sifter' baskets (Breunig 1982). All are popular gifts among Hopis and items for purchase in shops, galleries and art festivals. Baskets sometimes serve as a form of currency, in that they can be exchanged for other items and services.

One internal force that supports high quality and continuity in Hopi basketweaving is the spiritual need for a bride to present her groom with a basket plaque that will serve at his death as a vehicle for safe passage to the underworld. The wedding plaque is called 'hawapi', a 'thing for descending upon' (to the under-world). Likewise, the groom's family must provide the bride with her wedding robes, including a white cotton robe that will serve as her burial shroud and her vehicle to reach the land of the dead. Men must also weave traditional textiles such as wide brocade sashes, embroidered kilts and shoulder blankets for ceremonial use. All katsinas wear such clothing, as well as social dancers like Butterfly and Buffalo dancers who perform in the fall and winter, following the spring–summer katsina season. They are, then, worn the year round and also in places other than Hopi vil-lages. Weaving in the New Mexico pueblos has declined even more than at Hopi, and performers there often purchase ritual textiles from Hopi weavers.

Hopi and other Pueblo men who want to take part in ritual performances but cannot weave their own ritual garments must purchase or trade for them, often at great expense. In 1933, Hopi potter Ethel Muchvo wrote to her Boston friend Maud Melville that she was very angry with her husband, Wilfred, for selling all his sheep to 'get the things that they ware [sic] when they dance.' He had decided to reject the Christian missionaries' conversion efforts and resume practice of Hopi katsina reli-gion (Davis 2007: 129). Wilfred Muchvo was an accomplished belt-weaver (Davis 2007: 127), but apparently did not make the requisite kilts, sashes and shoulder blan-kets. Ethel wrote that without the sheep, they would have nothing to sell to get the 'things they needed' for the coming winter. Clearly, for Wilfred, having the right ritual garments was a very high priority. Why, then, did more men not weave? In Wilfred's case, frequent incapacitation due to tuberculosis was a factor; for others, military service, off-reservation wage labour and mandatory attendance at boarding schools interrupted traditional training in weaving and other skills and left little time for weaving in the kiva.

In the 1940s, for a variety of reasons, long-staple cotton and traditional dyes became increasingly difficult for weavers to obtain, and commercial traders did not perceive enough demand to make it worth their while to provide these essential materials to the few remaining Hopi weavers. The Museum stepped in, pur-chasing suitable dyes and cotton for re-sale to weavers (Mangum and Mangum 1997: 74–76, 93). Mary-Russell Colton and botanist Alfred Whiting conducted research on vegetable dyes for both textiles and basketry in an effort to promote self-sufficiency and innovation. Their efforts continued the Museum's benevo-lent paternalism in helping artists research and obtain materials, make guided innovations and market their work.

MNA did not push weavers to sign their work, perhaps because it is difficult to sign a basket or textile. But recently a few basket weavers have developed distinctive finishing techniques that can be recognized as signatures. Not surprisingly, these are often clan symbols. For example, a Corn Clan weaver from Second Mesa put four coloured dot-in-square *'qa'öveni'*, corn markings, in the outermost coil of a basket plaque entered in the 2006 Hopi show, and a lizard Clan member from Third Mesa weaves a tiny lizard shape into the binding of her wicker plaques.

Of the Museum's current relationship with weavers, director Robert Breunig says, 'In recent decades we have not tried to influence the direction or techniques of the art. We have tended to let things evolve. I remember when in the 1970s yucca sifter baskets first had metal rings rather than willow rings. We fretted about whether or not to accept them but eventually did accept them because it was clear that the makers were not going back – the metal rings were considerably easier to work with and gave a rounder sifter' (Robert Breunig personal communication, 2008).

What do contemporary weavers think about the Museum's involvement in their work and the current 'hands off' approach? Feedback from weavers strongly suggests that they like to see items made for sale at shows, and exemplary items displayed in the collections and exhibits. Artists especially enjoy seeing the work of earlier generations, especially their own ancestors. But seeing items that were meant for a specific individual's wedding ceremony now kept in a museum can be emotionally distressing. For example, one Hopi staff member recently pointed out wedding robes in the collection that had feathers attached, signalling that they had been given by a groom's family to a bride and used in a wedding. Why was the robe now in the Museum instead of being kept for its intended use as a burial shroud? Had the bride set aside her family's wishes and sold the robe? Likewise, a basketry plaque given to a groom should be buried with him, not sold or put in a museum. A coiled plaque with corn made for the famous jeweller Charles Loloma by his wife's family was sold to MNA after Loloma's divorce. MNA recently decided not to display it out of concern that Loloma's family members might see it and feel distressed to recall that the late artist's body was buried without this spiritually essential item.

Katsina Dolls

Katsinas are benevolent spirit beings who represent all the good things in life. They live in the San Francisco Peaks, a tall volcanic mountain that overlooks the campus of the Museum of Northern Arizona. Katsinas visit Hopi villages in the summertime in the form of clouds and rain, and dance in the kivas in early spring and in open plazas in the summer. In certain ceremonies, katsinas give dolls to babies and to girls. Dolls are made of the roots of cottonwood, a ritually important tree because it grows near springs and other water sources. Until initiation into the katsina society at about age seven to nine, children are not to know who carves and paints the dolls the katsinas bring. A doll, *tihu,* is a form of prayer, a toy and an educational device. Girls play with them, care for them like babies and hang them on the walls of the home as a reminder of their roles in Hopi life. In the early twentieth century, many men were reluctant to carve katsina dolls for sale, saying it would be 'like selling your children' (Breunig and Lomatuway'ma 1992: 10). Some carvers still feel this way and do not carve for sale, others carve 'traditional' dolls for ceremonies but produce stylized 'sculpture' for sale, and still others make no distinction. Some carvers say any accurate image of a katsina carved by a Hopi is a *tiihu,* appropriate as a gift for a girl (see Pearlstone 2001: 16–21, 35, 59, 61, 167 for direct quotes). Although indigenous artists often create differences in items made for sale and for their own use, practices and voiced opinions among Hopi carvers vary a great deal. The most consistent formal differences between dolls made for sale and as gifts for

Hopi girls are: first, dolls for girls are meant to be hung on the walls of the home, hence they virtually never stand on bases and those made for sale often (by no means always) have a wooden base so they can stand on a shelf; second, those made for girls are never signed because the katsinas give them, not carvers or relatives, and those made for sale are often signed. Carving for sale has grown and diversified over the last century, and MNA has played several roles in this development.

Few objects that might have been katsina dolls have been identified in prehistoric or early historic archaeological contexts and the art form may not have emerged until the nineteenth century (although depictions of katsinas appear in rock art, pottery and kiva murals as early as the AD 1300s). Early katsina dolls in museum collections have fairly simple shapes and are painted with mineral pigments from the local landscape. As metal carving tools and commercial paints became more available, and as demand from traders, collectors and curio shops increased, the dolls became more elaborate, with well-defined limbs and facial features. Hopi families hang dolls on the walls when girls are not playing with them. Non-Hopi buyers preferred to stand them on shelves, so carvers began attaching dolls to small wooden stands (Beaver 1992: 19). The base also provided a convenient surface on which to sign the carver's name and provide the Hopi name of the particular katsina represented. Across the decades of the twentieth century, carvers developed many new styles including impressionistic 'katsina sculpture' and naturalistic 'action' figures that represent katsina dancers. Action figures are controversial among religious leaders – tiny fingernails and dimpled knees signal depiction of a mortal human dressed as a spirit being, not the spirit itself, which is the proper subject of a katsina doll. Not only are uninitiated children supposed to be protected from such allusions to spirit impersonators, they should not see katsina carving demonstrated in public. The process of carving dolls metaphorically evokes gestation and birth, and like weaving, carving is a way for men to fulfil their procreative abilities. For this reason, women traditionally do not carve, and the few women who carve today have been asked to stop by religious leaders. Opinions within the community of carvers are diverse; some women carvers have stopped but some continue to do so (Pearlstone 2001: 51–52).

As with other media, the Museum's role in developing carving for collectors included publication of books and buyers' guides. One of the first is Harold Colton's 1949 guide to systematic classification of 266 different katsinas, inspired by his friend Barry Goldwater's questions about classifying the katsina dolls he collected (Miller 1991: 146). In typical fashion for the mid-century biologist that he was, Colton provides keys to diagnosing the identity of any given katsina doll, but identifying a limited range of head shapes, mouth shapes and eye shapes from which to choose. Colton's taxonomy has little, if anything, to do with how Hopis think about katsinas, who are likely to group them in terms of which time of the year they come, what role they play in public rituals (for example, line dancers, side dancers, runners and clowns), what kinds of spiritual roles they fulfil or which neighbouring group (Zuni, Jemez. Navajo) first introduced that katsina to the Hopi. Former MNA Curator Barton Wright's 1977 *Complete Guide to Collecting Hopi Katsina Dolls* provided a somewhat more culturally sensitive classification. Still, Hopis today are inclined to recall his field research as fraught with mistranslations of Hopi names and provocation of rather vigorous arguments about whether features of particular katsinas were 'correct'. MNA's 1992 *Hopi Katsina Dolls* publication takes a more flexible approach to katsina classification. Author, trader and MNA board member Bill Beaver dedicates several pages to explaining that different katsinas come to different villages, different carvers know different ones and some carved figures are not katsinas at all, but ritual clowns and performers of non-katsina rituals (Beaver 1992).

Perhaps the Museum's role in the development of carving will be best remembered for the Hopi employees who worked at the Museum and carved dolls for sale to visitors, such as Jimmie Kewanwytewa, who in the 1950s was perhaps the first carver to sign his dolls with his initials (Breunig and Lomatuway'ma 1992: 10). By developing personal relationships with MNA staff and visitors and selling directly to them or through the MNA's gift shop, they cultivated an appreciation for the art form that surely contributed to today's international market for a range of carvings, from traditional cradle dolls to action figures to large-scale sculptures.

Most recently, beginning in the 1980s, some carvers – not directly associated with the Museum but with local galleries – have revived an 'old' or 'traditional' style doll that hangs on the wall, has mineral pigments and preserves original contours of its original cottonwood root (Day 2000). This 'revival' was apparently independent of MNA's influence. The revival or 'New Traditional' style developed out of a single carver's memories of the dolls he saw as a small child, not from ones seen in a museum. Manfred Sunsukewa wanted to recapture the emotional response of a Hopi child to dolls that represented awesome and important spirit beings (Day 2000: 12). The style caught on with a few other carvers (see Day 2000, Pearlstone 2001: 166–167) and some traders (Pearlstone 2006). MNA's extensive collection of katsina dolls has virtually no examples of the late nineteenth to early twentieth century dolls that inspired the revival, and very few examples of the revival style dolls. Yet the Museum's gift store sells many New Traditional style dolls.

Conclusions

What patterns can we see in the way traditional Hopi arts have changed over the past 120 years or so, and can we identify influential interactions between individual Hopi artists and MNA programs and personnel? Hopi artists who experienced the most direct interventions by MNA personnel were silversmiths, potters and textile weavers, and to some extent basketweavers, whom Museum personnel encouraged to use vegetable dyes. The Museum appears to have asserted little overt influence on katsina doll carving, and likewise paid little attention to easel painting, quilting and other forms of jewellery such as beadwork which are not derived from traditional art forms. Arts most integrated into traditional Hopi ritual practices and life cycle events are basketry, textiles and some doll carving. Of these, carving has changed the most, but with the Museum apparently exerting more influence on potential buyers than on carvers. Textiles show the least outside influence in terms of designs and techniques, because these are prescribed by ritual requirements. The Museum's role in helping weavers obtain materials may have bridged a difficult economic period and helped the art form to survive until better supply networks developed. Unfortunately, textiles are still the most vulnerable art form due to their relatively high labour costs and steep learning curve. Silverwork shows the most complicated interactions between Hopi artists and MNA personnel, with the Museum's art curator offering specific designs as well as advice about developing distinctive techniques meant to convey a Hopi ethnic identity. Yet here, individual artisans strongly asserted their own clan and individual identities in their choices of designs and hallmarking. Hopi leaders began training silversmiths and developing markets within a few years of MNA's initial efforts.

Overall, the history of MNA's involvement with developing and marketing Hopi art can be summarized as a gradual shift from benevolent paternalism – Museum personnel telling Hopi artists what to do and how to do it – to a concentration on markets and buyers, to a recent emphasis on partnerships. Mary-Russell Colton's earliest writings on the subject seem shocking today, perhaps even racist. For example, in a 1930 Museum newsletter she wrote,

> The art of a people is only of value in as long as it maintains a distinct pure bred character. Like all native people in the process of readjustment, their art has a tendency to absorb the worst rather than the best, from the dominant civilization that surrounds them. It behoves the dominant culture to lend every assistance and encouragement to its native people to maintain the purity of its beautiful peasant arts and bring with it a worthy contribution to the new era (Colton 1930b: 3 and in Mangum and Mangum 1997: 76).

The Coltons tried to help Hopi artists maintain their native 'purity' while at the same time pressuring them to conform to western values such as emphasis on individual artists via signing their work and touting individual reputations, all without critical reflection about their roles as elite outsiders. Good intentions – and we are sure their intentions were benevolent – were enough. Over the years, MNA retreated from its position of power over Hopi artists and turned its attention to educating buyers rather than producers. By the 1980s, many Hopi artists, not only carvers, had achieved economic self-sufficiency. They have college degrees, their own shops and maybe a few helpful patrons. They can choose to work with museums or not. More recently, MNA has served as a culture broker, providing a place for buyers and sellers to meet face-to-face and sponsoring programs to help outsiders understand Hopi art in its own terms.

Currently, MNA aspires to a partner role, but this approach also has challenges. With whom are we partnering? The tribal government's Cultural Preservation Office? Individual artists? Artists who do not appreciate the government's 'culture police' interfering with what crafts can be demonstrated in public or whether women carvers should be allowed to sell their work at the Museum show or shop? When a dispute centres on conflicts between traditional values, such as the proscription on female carvers versus creativity and innovation, how can the Museum avoid the appearance of taking sides? And there is always more than one side. There are village leaders, clan leaders, men and women, young and old, practitioners of traditional religion and Christians and those who practice both. Museums cannot serve all interest groups, and must avoid the appearance of favouritism. MNA is also more complex than it used to be, with multiple curators, gift shop managers, collections managers, cultural and educational programmers, resident artists, docents, and Hopi and Navajo staff members and Trustees.

Future Hopi-MNA plans include efforts to make the Museum's extensive collection more available to contemporary Hopi artists (and other community members), via workshops, shared digital archives and collections tours in MNA's newly opened Easton Collection Center. This 'green' building was designed with comfort for Native community members in mind; advisors from Hopi, Navajo, Yavapai, Apache, Walapai and Havasupai communities took active roles in architectural design. The architect and MNA's director were gratified and relieved to see that all agreed on culturally-appropriate design features, in spite of cultural and political differences. In this endeavour, Hopi participants subsumed their tribal identity within a broader Native American identity (that has also emerged in struggles to preserve the San Francisco Peaks as place that is sacred to 12 tribes). The resulting collections repository is designed to let in natural light (filtered), is made of mostly local natural materials and has views of the San Francisco Peaks. Unlike the old collections building, the new one will not house human remains and funerary objects, at the request of religious leaders concerned about the health and well-being of community members. Hopi visitors will soon be able to examine and handle ancestral pottery without exposure to items that came from graves. In the museum exhibits building, MNA is currently designing exhibits of katsina dolls and carvings that will not include depictions of ritual personages that should not be seen by outsiders or uninitiated Hopi, or should not be displayed at certain times of the year.

The current incarnation of the Hopi Craftsman Exhibition is the Hopi Festival of Arts and Culture, part of the MNA Heritage Program (Museum of Northern Arizona 2009). Artists still enter their work for judging. Some submit work to be sold on commission; many pay a nominal fee for a booth where they can sell directly to festival visitors. Programming not only includes dance, music and demonstrations of arts and food preparation but also 'Heritage Insights' lectures and artist interviews, and craft activities for children. Although some artists complain about booth fees, admission prices and other details, others note that booth fees in other shows are higher and that MNA administration, staff and volunteers clearly make efforts to be friendly and flexible. The Museum makes no profit on the festival, as expenses still outweigh income from admissions, booth fees and commissions. The benefit to the Museum is all in community outreach and publicity; benefit to the Hopi Tribe likewise comes in the form of positive publicity and continuation of what has become a social and cultural tradition for many families.

Collections are the key to maintaining a record of the relationships between the Museum and Hopi artists over time. Unfortunately, collections and documentation are uneven. MNA had a strong hand in shaping Hopi silver overlay jewellery, but has a surprisingly small collection of Hopi jewellery; fortunately, archives, photos and correspondence about the Hopi Silver project survive to tell the story. On the other hand, MNA personnel who worked with Hopi basketweavers to develop vegetable dye recipes saved samples of basketry materials, dye plants and mineral pigments, documenting each sample with its scientific name and provenience. The Museum's herbarium collection increases in importance as some culturally important plants are disappearing from Hopi lands due to drought, livestock grazing, exotic invasive species and soil erosion.

It is difficult to offer practical advice to other museum professionals who would like to collaborate with indigenous communities. Every such effort will be a unique process. Ethnogenesis is everywhere an ongoing process, and even small communities are internally diverse. Developing mutually productive relationships between museums and communities therefore takes time, nurturing and continuity in personnel. Comparing the MNA–Hopi relationship with nearby Zuni Pueblo's museum planning process as detailed by Isaac (2007) reveals similarities in patterns of tensions and contradictions between economic and traditional cultural goals, insiders and outsiders, object-based and process-based exhibition. Maybe the most important thing to say is that we cannot expect to take dynamic, diverse and situational discourse about history and identity and find perfect ways to represent the arts and other material culture of indigenous communities in museum settings. But we can make our museums places where discussion is encouraged, and where there are objects, texts and media on display that are worth discussing. The first step towards relationships that put Native communities on an equal footing with the museum is serious reflection on how the museum's collections, archives, publications and long-term community relationships came to be. This volume moves us all towards that goal.

Acknowledgements   Many thanks to Zena Pearlstone and Dennis Gilpin for much-needed editing and fact-checking, to anonymous reviewers who encouraged me to think about the larger context of this case study and to the Hopi Cultural Preservation Office and Robert Breunig at the Museum of Northern Arizona for guidance and support. Any errors that remain are my own.

References

Allen, Laura Graves
  1984 *Contemporary Hopi Pottery*. Museum of Northern Arizona, Flagstaff, AZ.

Bartlett, Katharine
  1977 A History of Hopi Pottery. *Plateau* 49(3): 2–13.

Beaver, Bill
  1992 Collecting Hopi Katsina Dolls. *Plateau* 63(4): 18–31.

Bernardini, Wesley
  2005 *Hopi Oral Tradition and the Archaeology of Identity*. University of Arizona Press, Tucson, AZ.

Breunig, Robert
  1982 Cultural Fiber: Function and Symbolism in Hopi Basketry. *Plateau* 53(4): 8–13.

Breunig, Robert, and Michael Lomatuway'ma
  1992 Form and Function in Hopi *Tithu*. *Plateau* 63(4): 3–13.

Charley, Karen Kahe, and Lea S. McChesney
  2007 Form and Meaning in Indigenous Aesthetics: A Hopi Pottery Perspective. *American Indian Art* 32(4): 84–91.

Colton, Harold
  1951 Hopi Pottery Firing Temperatures. *Plateau* 24(2): 73–76.
  1956 *Pottery Types of the Southwest: San Juan Red Ware, Tsegi Orange Ware, Homolovi Orange Ware, Winslow Orange Ware, Awatovi Yellow Ware, Jeddito Yellow Ware, Sichomovi Red Ware*. Museum of Northern Arizona Ceramic Series No. 3C. Museum of Northern Arizona, Flagstaff, AZ.

Colton, Mary-Russell Ferrell
  1930a Report to the Board of Trustees. May 8, 1930. On file at the Museum of Northern Arizona, Flagstaff, AZ.
  1930b The Hopi Craftsman. *Museum Notes* 3(2): 1–4. Museum of Northern Arizona, Flagstaff, AZ.

Colwell-Chanthaphonh, Chip, and T. J. Ferguson
  2006 Memory Pieces and Footprints: Multivocality and the Meanings of Ancient Times and Ancestral Places among the Zuni and Hopi. *American Anthropologist* 188(1): 148–162.

Cooper, Karen Coody
  2008 *Spirited Encounters: American Indians Protest Museum Policies and Practices*. AltaMira Press, Lanham, MD.

Davis, Carolyn O'Bagy
  2007 *Hopi Summer: Letters from Ethel to Maud*. Rio Nuevo,, Tucson, AZ.

Day, Jonathan S.
  2000 *Traditional Hopi Katsinas: A New Generation of Carvers*. Northland Press, Flagstaff, AZ.

Fewkes, Jesse Walter
  1897 Tusayan Totemic Signatures. *American Anthropologist* 10(1): 1–12.

Hitchcock, Ann
  1977 A Consumer's Guide to Hopi Pottery. *Plateau* 49(3): 22–31.

Isaac, Gwyneira
  2007 *Mediating Knowledges: Origins of a Zuni Tribal Museum*. University of Arizona Press, Tucson, AZ.

Kabotie, Fred
  1950 Hopi Silver. Manuscript on file, Museum of Northern Arizona archives, manuscript number 13,855
  1965 Letter to Edward B. Danson, Museum of Northern Arizona. On file, Museum of Northern Arizona, manuscript number 66-1-1.

Mangum, Richard K., and Sherry G. Mangum
  1997 *One Woman's West: The Life of Mary-Russell Ferrell Colton*. Northland Publishing, Flagstaff, AZ.

Miller, Jimmy H.
  1991 *The Life of Harold Sellers Colton: A Philadelphia Brahmin in Flagstaff.* Navajo Community College Press, Tsaile, AZ.

Museum of Northern Arizona
  2005 Memorandum of Understanding between MNA and the Hopi Tribe. http://www.musnaz. org/trustees/hopimnamou.html, accessed 30 March 2011.
  2009 Heritage Program. http://www.musnaz.org/Heritage%20Program/Heritage%20Program. htm, accessed 30 March 2011.

Pearlstone, Zena
  2001 *Katsina: Commodified and Appropriated Images of Hopi Supernaturals.* UCLA Fowler Museum of Cultural History, Los Angeles, CA.
  2006 Tsakursovi: The Little Shop That Could. *American Indian Art* 32(1): 58–65, 92–93.

Wright, Barton
  1977 *Complete Guide to Collecting Hopi Katsina Dolls.* Northland Press, Flagstaff, AZ.

Wright, Margaret
  1972 *Hopi Silver: The History and Hallmarks of Hopi Silversmithing.* Northland Press, Flagstaff, AZ.

Chapter 9
Pathways to Knowledge: Research, Agency and Power Relations in the Context of Collaborations Between Museums and Source Communities

Lindy Allen and Louise Hamby

Abstract Museum collections have in recent decades been a pivotal point of reference for indigenous people and source communities across Australia. This chapter seeks to demonstrate how collaborative projects between the museum sector in Australia and Aboriginal people and source communities have created new insights into heritage collections. At the same time engagement with museum collections has provided a focus for Aboriginal people to explore their own history and created an environment that supports the regeneration and maintenance of knowledge and the construction of group identity. In this chapter, we explore the nature of collaborations drawing on case studies from projects involving remote communities in Arnhem Land and Cape York of northern Australia. These projects have focused on collections held by Museum Victoria in Melbourne. We explore the way in which indigenous people have initiated and been a part of engagements with museum collections of images, objects and field material that relate to themselves and their own history. We discuss a research model that promotes the value of museum-based research while giving due recognition to the authority of source communities. In this context, the contemporary museum environment is one of a *contested site* where knowledge is negotiated and a *field site* where both contemporary and historical indigenous agency emerges.

L. Allen (✉)
Indigenous Cultures, Museum Victoria, Melbourne, VIC, Australia
e-mail: lallen@museum.vic.gov.au

L. Hamby
Research School of Humanities and the Arts, Australian National University, Canberra, ACT, Australia
e-mail: lousie.hamby@anu.edu.au

S. Byrne et al. (eds.), *Unpacking the Collection*, One World Archaeology,
DOI 10.1007/978-1-4419-8222-3_9, © Springer Science+Business Media, LLC 2011

Introduction

A significant shift in postcolonial power relations in late twentieth century museum practice in Australia gives due recognition to the authority and epistemologies of source communities, that is descendants of those people from whom the heritage materials in museum collections originate. This is a position that has been formalized in a proliferation of policy frameworks and documents enshrining the principles underlying this paradigmatic shift: for example, *Continuous Cultures, Ongoing Responsibilities – Principles and Guidelines for Australian Museums Working with Aboriginal and Torres Strait Islander Cultural Heritage* (Museums Australia 1993 revised in 2005) and the *National Policy Framework for Aboriginal and Torres Strait Islander Library Services and Collections* (National and State Libraries Australasia 2007). The active lobbying by Aboriginal and Torres Strait Islander people in Australia since at least the 1970s has led to a new curatorial practice that gives recognition to the rights of indigenous people in asserting ownership and control of museum collections (see Bolton 2003; Edwards and Stewart 1980).

The paradigmatic shift is one in which museums wrestle with the moral and ethical issues necessary in redressing the injustices of past practices in museums and the postcolonial experience more broadly. An important discourse surrounding heritage material in museums has emerged where due deference is paid and power and authority are conceded in favour of source communities; and museums become contested spaces as source communities assert their rights to retain control of knowledge and the historical narratives relating to their cultural patrimony. Corn and Gumbula argue that this position needs to underpin all research engagements with source communities.

> Accepting that Yolngu leaders have been and still are equal, if not leading, partners in research endeavours that draw on their hereditary knowledge, rather than casting them as mere sources of data without the capacity to think and engage with others theoretically, is a necessary part of de-colonising and, indeed, humanizing the academic project so that ownership of research processes and their outcomes can be shared by all contributors (Corn and Gumbula 2006: 190).

While the fundamental shift in the power base in favour of source communities is unquestionable, the efficacy of their authority in practice relies on relationships brokered with museums. 'The desire to build trust and to share power are the most important manifestations of a new curatorial praxis which incorporates community needs and perspectives' (Peers and Brown 2003: 1–2). In this chapter, we examine the very nature of these relationships and explore the impetus of source communities in engaging with museums and collections, the primary motivation being a concern for the regeneration and maintenance of knowledge and strengthening of group identity. However, we discuss a collaborative and cross-cultural model that creates a research environment in which meaningful and informed dialogue is fostered and one 'which involves the sharing of skills, knowledge and power to produce something of value to both parties' (Peers and Brown 2003: 4). This methodology allows for the museum to move from a site of friction (see Karp et al. 2006) to a field site where knowledge emerges and merges and new understandings are created.

As a unique and vital set of evidence of cultural practices from their past, museum collections serve as a catalyst to memories, the most powerful of which are drawn from lived experience. Without museum collections it is possible that certain knowledge of incidents or events would never be discussed and perhaps even be forgotten. What serves as a marker or trigger is influenced as much by the knowledge as by interests of the individuals involved, and as a consequence the insights will both vary and be limited by personal histories and experiences. The passage of time has made this an increasingly tenuous situation as most of those involved in these projects are displaced by at least a single generation from those from whom the collections were gained. As such, the process of engagement needs to be essentially organic and able to accommodate the disparate nature of the experiences and issues of concern to source communities.

From the interplay of competing and complementary views and perspectives of heritage collections, born essentially out of an oral tradition, what will surface is a vastly enhanced and reinvigorated knowledge base that can breathe new life into and give new relevance to collections. This chapter provides insights into the way in which a number of source communities in remote parts of northern Australia have sought out collections held at Museum Victoria (MV) in Melbourne, one of Australia's largest cultural institutions with significant historic holdings of ethnographic material. We explore the iterative nature of the process and the discourse that emerges; how ideas are exchanged and how new knowledge and old knowledge emerge and merge. The case studies are drawn from projects undertaken in recent times with Yolngu from Arnhem Land and Pama from Cape York (see Figs. 9.1

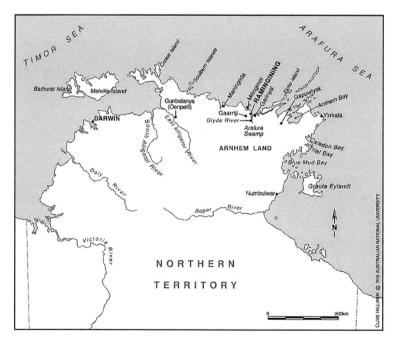

Fig. 9.1 Map of Arnhem Land showing places mentioned in the text

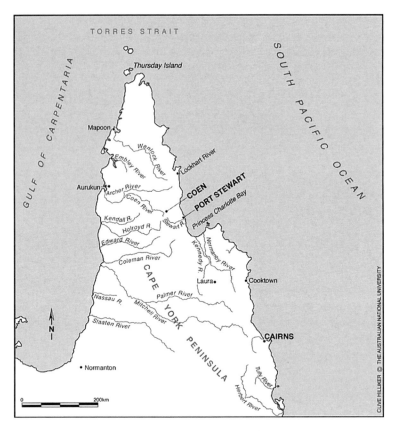

Fig. 9.2 Map of north Queensland showing places mentioned in the text

and 9.2); and focus on material in the Donald Thomson Collection dating from the late 1920s through to the early 1940s. The core of the Collection amassed through-out Thomson's academic career consists of around 7200 artefacts and 11,000 images mainly from Cape York and Arnhem Land (see Thomson 2003; Rigsby and Peterson 2005; Allen 2008). As with objects and images in museum collections generally, those collected and taken by the Melbourne-based anthropologist, Donald Thomson, act as a key reference point for a past that is not too distant and still features largely in some people's memories.

Taking Collections to the Field in Central Arnhem Land

The most effective strategy for source communities accessing their heritage mate-rial is for them to be able to see and handle collections directly either by visiting the museum or by having objects and images taken to communities. In October 2004, the authors selected 26 objects from the Collection to take to Arnhem Land close to 70 years after they were collected. This strategy allowed many more Yolngu to access their cultural patrimony than would have been otherwise possible. The Collection holds great significance for Yolngu and Donald Thomson is generally remembered well and his work is identified as a key legacy of their past. The late Yolngu leader, Gatjil Djerrkura OAM commented on its special significance mainly due to Thomson's images that show 'the parents, grandparents and greatgrandparents of myself and many people living in the area from Milingimbi to Yirrkala today' (Djerrkura 2003: ii).

Objects of body adornment or 'bodywear' (Hamby 2007a: 215) relating to 11 central Arnhem Land clans were selected. The consignment included 5 armbands, 3 headbands, 3 necklaces, 7 skirts/pubic covers and a spindle; collected from Djinba, Djinang/Mildjingi, Ganalbingu, Gupapuyngu, Liyagalawumirr, Liyagawumirr, Rembarrnga, Warramiri, Wulaki and Yan-nhangu clans. The authors collected the objects in their purpose-built crate and drove across unsealed roads to Ramingining in central Arnhem Land with these in the rear of a Toyota Landcruiser. Ramingining Community Education Centre (RCEC) had been planning to run workshops with the authors using objects and images from the Collection as part of an educational program known as the *Gart'tjirkk* Curriculum that focused on the cultural and language diversity of the region. The primary aims of the joint initiative were: (1) the objects would be the focal point of developing and confirming skills and passing on knowledge relating to the making of such objects, (2) the workshop would be fully documented including a visual record made by an MV photographer and (3) the relationship between the Donald Thomson Collection, Museum Victoria and the Ramingining community would be developed further by enhancing the documentation of the material.

Elders in the community looked at the material first followed by secondary students, Yolngu teachers and teacher's aides and the other teachers. The authors worked with the group while they handled and discussed the objects. Enormous interest and great excitement was generated in the community including a group from the Ramingining Women's Centre, who had the responsibility for producing the 'costumes' for the film *Ten Canoes* (de Heer and Djigirr 2006), a project inspired by black and white photographs taken by Donald Thomson in the Arafura Swamp in early May 1937. While it was set in a fictional period 'a thousand years ago' (Vertigo Productions 2006), inspiration for props and costumes came from the objects and images in the Collection (Hamby 2007b). While the level of interest from the community was extremely high, the capacity or confidence for them to discuss the works was mixed, most being comfortable only to engage about material from their own clan or their mother's clan. Discussion focused on who had worn these objects and how they were worn, inspiring reflection on issues of body image and health and well being. The objects and Thomson's photographs were a great source of pride for people as they discussed that everything had been produced from the land, and great care, artistry and industry had been taken in their production. RCEC followed up the workshop by ordering a set of 12 poster-sized prints of Thomson's images to be framed and hung in an extension to the library; and quality photocopies of another 94 images to be used as a resource for cultural programs.

Exploring current knowledge of processes for making items of 'bodywear' was Hamby's research focus on the project (Hamby 2007b), and our expectation was that items be made in response to seeing, touching and discussing these historical works. A *ba̱larra* or *dhirri dhirri*, skirt or pubic cover, was made by a group of women led by the late Elizabeth Lilipiyana Ngumabuy and Daphne Banyawarra Malibirr in response to the historical Liyagawumirr clan example from 1935 from the Collection (Fig. 9.3). The whole process of selecting the tree, stripping the bark and beating it, working it into fibre, constructing the waist band and the body of the skirt and trimming the ends was all captured on video by John Broomfield, Museum Victoria and Marcey Garrawurra, a student at RCEC. Her short documentary *Arnhem Weaving* is included on the *Ten Canoes* DVD.

Fig. 9.3 Elizabeth Lilipiyana Ngumabuy and Daphne Banyawarra Malibirr making a bark skirt at the Ramingining Community Education Centre. Seated on right is Clara Matjandatjpi. Lindy Allen standing on right. 29 October 2004 (Photo by Louise Hamby)

One particular object brought in the consignment turned out to be especially important. This is a *marradjiri* string, a multi-strand feathered string carried by a messenger to bring people together for ceremony. At Garinyal, an outstation at the mouth of the Glyde River, we spoke about this piece with Burinyila Mildjingi and his sister Myall. Their father was the Yolngu leader, Rraywala (c. 1905–1965), who accompanied Donald Thomson across Arnhem Land; and the string collected in 1936 proved to be particularly important at this time, as Burinyila was preparing for his grandson's *dapi* or initiation ceremony. Myall brought the string headband and armband she had been making for this event, explaining that the fibre for the string had come from Gaartji, their mother's mother's country. She pointed to the feathers in the 1936 piece saying, 'just waiting for this one' (Myall Mildjingi 31 October 2004, personal communication). Burinyila identified them as egret, lamenting how hard it is to catch this bird. With Myall, the authors looked at the way the feathers were joined with beeswax forming delicate flower-like tufts; at the overall structure noting exact numbers of strands of feathered strings versus unfeathered strings; and the joints of beeswax separating sections. Objects from the Collection are considered to be evidence of what is 'true' and proper, and so Burinyila wanted the new one to be made the right way instructing his sister to make a faithful copy. Detailed photographs and prints were made for Myall at her request, knowing that our field gear included a colour printer and glossy photo paper for printing out images requested by families.

Burinyila had seen this *marradjiri* string at the Museum. The last time was in November 2002 when he reviewed all Mildjingi clan material in the restricted men's store at Melbourne Museum. Following this, ceremonial material he identified as not being secret or sacred made its transition back into the 'open store'. This included the *marradjiri* string that Burinyila explained represented a 'north wind cloud – long fine cloud [and was] sent to collect all people to come for ceremony.' Moving the Mildjingi objects out of the restricted store was based on his own knowledge, a cultural legacy vested in him over a lifetime spent with his fathers, Rraywala and Makani (c. 1905–1985). At the same time, Burinyila consulted the related notes and documentation written by Thomson, which he, together with a few others, always considers before offering an opinion or his own insights. In fact, for this specific purpose copies of relevant documentation had been included with these objects. At Garinyal, Burinyila deferred to these notes that identified the string as *lunggurrma marradjiri*, literally meaning a *marradjiri* string representing the 'north (-east) wind'. Thomson qualifies this writing that it does not really represent the wind but rather clouds brought by that wind with 'the two arms . . . represent[ing] two small clouds that travel in a different direction (at a distance) from the big one, "him go that way" (pointing to the two sides), "leader one him go this way – ahead" ' (Donald Thomson, handwritten object tag [DT673] 29 September 1936; The Donald Thomson Collection on loan to MV). Burinyila relayed the story about the piece and its connections to clouds and songs, the essence of which was set out in Donald Thomson's notes.

Burinyila commented on its remarkable condition saying that it was 'just like [it was] made yesterday – fresh one.' No documentation exists about who had made it or from whom Thomson collected it, but Burinyila offered information about two close relatives who made these types of strings in days gone by. He elaborated that Makani and Wilandjango were 'artefact make[rs]. . . like bark paintings, string, butterfly net – same as pelican – [and] fish trap' (Burinyila Mildjingi 31 October 2004, personal communication). Burinyila's mention of this distinctive 'butterfly net' is interesting, given his extraordinary familiarity with the Collection. At Gaartji earlier that same year, the authors had conducted an exercise with Burinyila mapping the layout and location of wet-season camps erected there in late 1936 (Fig. 9.4). Thomson also set up his base camp there collecting extensively and documenting in detail the ceremonial activity carried out at Gaartji

Fig. 9.4 Burinyila Mildjingi holds up copies of images taken by Donald Thomson at Gaartji outstation. July 2004 (Photo by Lindy Allen)

over the following months (Fig. 9.5). Writing to his solicitor in February 1937, Thomson (2003: 20) says, 'I have got a great deal of work done – and tons and tons of valuable material.' Burinyila had similarly reflected on the extraordinary legacy left by Thomson telling us, 'He was writing it all down ... and

Fig. 9.5 Donald Thomson at a base camp in central Arnhem Land (Photograph possibly taken by Rraywala Mildjingi, 1937. Donald Thomson Collection. Courtesy of Thomson Family and Museum Victoria)

in the secret ceremony ... so people will know' (Burinyila Mildjingi 19 July 2004, personal communication). Burinyila's awareness of the gaps in the collecting from that time is evident in the comment, 'Donald Thomson didn't get any butterfly nets either at Gaartji' (Burinyila Mildjingi 19 July 2004, personal communication).

Burinyila had previously seen the head ornament of marsupial incisors embedded in beeswax collected at Gaartji in late August 1942. This time he identified it as one made and worn by men and women in the past for the Ubarr ceremony; and like the *marradjiri* string was no longer restricted despite its ceremonial association. Burinyila suggested that it would likely have been 'gifted' at the end of the ceremony with Yolngu retaining half the 'equipment' for the next ceremony when new ones would be made to replace those gifted to Thomson. Tobacco and wire were the main commodities for exchange (Allen 2008: 408–410), but details relating to this ornament are absent other than the place and date of collection and its association with a Djinang speaking clan. Burinyila's suggestion of 'gifting' half the ceremonial cache to outsiders provides a context for how Thomson may have come to collect this piece. The enticement for Yolngu in parting with such objects was because they were 'starving for tobacco' (Burinyila Mildjingi November 2002, personal communication).

Other criteria for the selection of objects taken to central Arnhem Land were materials and techniques used, giving consideration to representing as broad a sample as possible. Objects varied from those made with string spun from vegetable fibre, human hair and possum fur; necklaces and head ornaments that include grass segments, shell, shark vertebrae, fish bone, teeth and feathers into their components; skirts or pubic covers of possum fur string and bark fibre; interlaced armbands made from 'jungle vine' (*Flagellaria indica*) as well as those of cane overwound with possum fur string and wool. Loss of skills is a major concern for Yolngu, including Burinyila and Myall, who made an unsuccessful attempt to make an interlaced armband from this vigorous 'jungle vine' growing near the entrance to Garinyal. The exercise was not totally wasted, as it revealed key information about preparation of the vine. Eventually, Burinyila accepted defeat admitting that the technique was 'too clever' (Burinyila Mildjingi 31 October 2004, personal communication). On a subsequent field trip to southeast Arnhem Land we located the specialist knowledge and skills for making these distinctive armbands surviving with two or three very old women at Numbulwar. Similarly, spinning possum fur into string is another endangered practice, and in fact Thomson recorded only one person doing this. The spindle that Makani used was collected by Thomson and was amongst the objects taken to central Arnhem Land. Burinyila lamented this loss saying 'we used to get that [possum] at Galawdjapin. Poor fella – we can't hear him anymore' (Burinyila Mildjingi 31 October 2004, personal communication). Other Yolngu across Arnhem Land have expressed a similar concern at not having seen or heard possums for many years, but since no one has offered an explanation, the status of this practice may relate to a general absence of this marsupial in Arnhem Land.

Lamalama People Linking the Past with the Future

Our second case study focuses on Lamalama people, a small group of Aboriginal people who live in and around Coen in southeast Cape York. Lamalama are a small group whose traditional lands are on the east coast of Cape York Peninsula, from Massey River in the north to lower Princess Charlotte Bay eastwards to the Normanby River. The descendants of those clans are the Jealous, KullaKulla, Liddy, Peter/Bassani, Salt and Tableland families. They have visited MV at least seven times with each contingent led by the late Sunlight Bassani, whose singular agenda was to access the Donald Thomson Collection. Deputations of Lamalama people have included a gender and intergenerational mix taking advantage of the unique situation for the appropriate transmission of knowledge (Fig. 9.6). Engaging with the Collection provides a remarkable opportunity for elders to share stories and knowledge triggered by seeing, handling and discussing the material collected and the photographs taken at Port Stewart decades ago (Allen, 2005, 2008; Hafner 2005; Hafner et al. 2007). Sunlight Bassani and his wife with Bobby and Daisy Stewart came to Melbourne in February 1990 with two young men and one young woman on a trip organised by Professor Bruce Rigsby for the specific purpose of strengthening Lamalama identity and reinforcing and proving what is the correct 'Lamalama way' with the material in the Collection. Hafner (2008: 262) best explains the importance of this concept and its roots in 'an oral culture in which knowledge is passed down between the generations by the telling of stories that recount the exploits of the Story beings and the Old People, providing a moral universe that describes "the Lamalama way".'

Fig. 9.6 Alison Liddy, Seppi Bassani and Sunlight Bassani (deceased) (background) work with Lindy Allen, Simon Wilmot and Diane Hafner at Melbourne Museum on a pilot project in 2005 to document Port Stewart material collected and images taken by Donald Thomson (Photo by Rosemary Wrench)

In actively pursuing their cultural patrimony, the Lamalama have focused almost exclusively on the Donald Thomson Collection, engaging only in very minor ways with other collections such as the Norman B. Tindale Collection at the South Australian Museum and the W.E. Roth Collection at the Australian Museum. Hafner elaborates on her observations stating, 'people now see it as their responsibility as owners of their country and custodians of traditions to actively pursue this research into the Collection. Indeed, it is as a direct result of their requests that the research proceeds' (Hafner 2008: 259). They have made seven separate visits to Melbourne over almost two decades, and their interests have been almost entirely served by the 500 or so images depicting their 'Old People' camped along the Stewart River; the very same people immortalized by Thomson as the 'Dugong Hunters of Cape York' (Thomson 1934). The exploratory visit in 1990 proved to be a catalyst in restoring confidence within the Lamalama community about themselves and their identity historically as a group. This was part of a larger agenda for the Lamalama, who were, at the same time, forging a pathway simultaneously by pursuing formal title to parcels of land available under Queensland's land rights legislation. Thomson's images were a key part of this being tendered as evidence in Land Court hearings in support of the oral testimonies of Lamalama elders. Sunlight Bassani in particular has blazed this trail and, by engaging in both agendas, simultaneously sought to secure the future for forthcoming generations of Lamalama.

Validation of the knowledge and authority of today's elders has been achieved through visits of around 20 Lamalama people to Melbourne. The images taken by Thomson at Port Stewart have been singularly crucial in aiding and prompting the recall of events and specific customary practices. This has been drawn to a large extent from living memory. The important discoveries made on these visits have affirmed details of a 'proper Lamalama way'. That younger people have visited the Collection under the direct tutelage of elders, for some more than once, has been a deliberate and critical strategy to restore confidence in and renewed understandings of what it means to be Lamalama. A prime example of this is a sequence of images of men catching fish in the Stewart River using large framed nets, *aampa*, and assisted by old men and young children. Sunlight's delight in seeing these images for the first time in 1990 was palpable, explaining to one of the authors that young people hadn't believed him that this was how the Old People caught fish in their time. Their understanding of this was enhanced by being able to see the two framed fishing nets, at least one of which is possibly the same one as that being used in the Stewart River in the photograph taken in 1929. Lamalama elder, Jimmy Peter was very animated about this when he and his daughter came with the most recent contingent of 11 in 2007. He recalled fishing in the tidal reaches of the Stewart River with these nets, and how a scoop formed at its base when cornering the fish in the river's bend. He also identified where the images were taken either in the freshwater section of the river or the salt arm.

These images capture a unique time, one that survives in the memories of the children and grandchildren of these 'Old People'. Photos such as those taken of burial practices have been particularly important in re-establishing and recovering knowledge of the 'proper Lamalama way'. A number of burials were underway at

Port Stewart in May 1928 when Thomson arrived and when he returned the following year. Great interest has been generated when showing images of Old Jimmy KullaKulla and 'Old Charcoal' disposing of bones that had been neatly parceled in a folded and stitched bark container. Descendants of the old KullaKulla man have been especially keen to have copies of these, expressing their genuine surprise at not knowing about this practice or their father and grandfather's involvement. Again these images provide clear evidence of Lamalama ways and 'proof' of the recollections of Sunlight and other elders. Other photos of burial bundles made of large sheets of bark secured with string and set in the forks of trees provoked an interesting memory with one Lamalama elder, who recalled finding his own father in the bush a long way from 'home' and carrying him back home to his country wrapped to be buried in the proper Lamalama way.

Given the tide of history and the enforced removal in 1961 of any remaining families at Port Stewart, the knowledge and experience of these Lamalama ways has survived only with a few elders, but the photographs corroborate their recollections and memories. These sequences and many other photographs have been circulating in the Lamalama community since the first visit by elders to the Collection in 1990, and consequently many individuals have been identified. The main 'boss' for Port Stewart, Monkey Port Stewart or 'Mungi' as Thomson identified him, features strongly, as does his sister's son, Old Harry Liddy, who inherited responsibility for that country.

Another important legacy embedded in the Collection is specialized craft practice, knowledge of which is held and controlled by particular individuals. For example, rainmaking is linked to specific Story Places in Princess Charlotte Bay, where Thomson photographed one such rainmaker and documented his highly guarded craft. The material collected from men's Bora ceremonies held at Port Stewart and involving neighbouring groups has been kept in a separate secure store given its sacred nature. On every visit, Sunlight Bassani reiterated that this material should never be made public. On one occasion when the material had been relocated with all the collections to the Museum's new building completed in 2000, he voiced his grave concern of the dire consequences of not doing the right thing with this material, saying 'I might get sick or you might get sick' (Sunlight Bassani 2002, personal communication). Diane Hafner (2008) writes about Lamalama behaviours being mediated by 'Old People and the Story' and their capacity to mete out punishment accordingly. 'Their actions do not apply exclusively to the Lamalama and may be extended to anyone behaving inappropriately on Lamalama country' (Hafner 2008: 258). Sunlight's declaration reflects his concern that the reach of the 'Old People and the Story' extends beyond Lamalama country and into the museum; or further, that since the part of the museum store where their material is stored constitutes a surrogate for Lamalama country, the same rules apply.

The engagement of Lamalama with objects overall has been less intense but no less important. Despite the wealth of documentation associated with the Donald Thomson Collection, the inevitable first question of whom does an object belong to remains problematic as relevant details are more often absent than present. While concerns may not be vocalized, decisions need to be made as to who has the right to speak about the 'Lamalama way'. That power associated with objects is not confined to men's sacred material became clear during the very first Lamalama visit. The Collection was accessed in the main ethnographic store at the former museum site in Swanston Street. The Lamalama expressed concern at their objects being stored alongside those from the clans living on the opposite side of Cape York; and so an undertaking was given that when the collections were relocated to the new museum, the layout of the collections would take account of the relative locations of these materials. Sunlight Bassani was pleased when he came the next time and saw that the Lamalama material in the new store was no longer contained within the same cabinets as the west coast material. However, he pointed out that cabinets containing the opposing material were situated adjacent to each other, so subsequently the Port Stewart material was again relocated to respond to his ongoing concerns.

Observing protocols relating to the 'Lamalama way' can apply in different ways as became clear when an old Thaypan man, Old George Musgrave, wanted to access the Lamalama material at the Museum. He had to seek permission from Lamalama elders, just as he would if he entered Lamalama country. Very little, if any, Thaypan material has survived, and the core of the material culture collected by Thomson was important to him. His country lies inland and southwest of Port Stewart and the material types of both would have been similar, so the Port Stewart material had a specific relevance to this old man. He was keen to pass on knowledge to his own grandson using the Collection as a focus and consent was given.

The Collaborative Research Model

The value gained from employing a range of strategies to provide direct access for source communities to museum collections, whether inside the museum where the storerooms become 'field sites' or for heritage material taken to source communities and close to their place of origin, should be clear from these case studies. However, the success of working with groups is predicated on good preparation, appropriate consultation and the building of relationships over time – even a lifetime. A collaborative and cross-cultural research framework can ensure the emergence of new meanings and relevance for collections for both the source community and the museum. The case studies reveal that a clear affiliation can exist between source communities, the objects and especially the images. They also demonstrate how museum collections can be the catalyst for dialogue that explores the importance and relevance of the heritage held in museums today and the way in which it can have an immediate relevance: whether it is making costumes and props for a film or remaking an 'authentic' cultural object for ceremony or just reinforcing people's cultural roots.

Central to this model is recognition of the essential tenet that knowledge is embedded in collections. It can be identified from oral accounts fixed within a knowledge base held by members of source communities and it can be measured against and informed by the written record that emerges from the collection itself and museum-based research. Burinyila, as with a number of other senior men and women of similar age and status living in remote northern Australia, draws upon his own existing rich body of cultural knowledge gained from a lifetime of experience and learning from mentors, in his case from his fathers, Rraywala and Makani, and other key individuals like Yilkari (c. 1890–1956), the senior Liyagalawumirr clan leader in Thomson's time. He relies also on the documentation associated with the material and the insights to be gleaned from asking questions of the collections. Such deep intellectual engagement among indigenous people is rarely given due recognition.

Individuals like Burinyila and Sunlight do not represent the generic 'source community', but are key individuals pivotal to these engagements. They emerge with their own strong personal agenda motivated by concerns for forthcoming generations. They demand and respect the context provided by the collectors and researchers and seek out details about museum collections and associated documentation on individual objects and images. They want to know about the collectors themselves and where they went and about specific objects or classes of objects and the materials and techniques used. At the same time, they can identify the people behind the collections: that is, which of their kin collaborated with these collectors and influenced what was collected, as explored in more detail in the next section. Their insights provide important context, such as Burinyila's information that Makani made *marradjiri* strings and was an accomplished artisan. Like their ancestors or Old People, they are experienced in dealing with outsiders.

These elders also know that other key knowledgeable individuals have also accessed the collections and are keen to learn about and share in the insights and views built up over time. They will also confer with and defer to others in their own communities. Working with as many people as possible is a key element of this strategy of collaboration and maximizes opportunities to extend the reach of the collections and, by default, broaden the knowledge base. The fact that these individuals have sought out the collections and confirmed the nature of the material builds confidence that the chance of inappropriate exposure to material is minimized. Their confidence and sophistication in engaging with museums and collections is shared with a handful of elders in remote communities in northern Australia, such as Dr Neparrnga Gumbula, who has collaborated with the authors over a number of years in relation to his own research into Gupapuyngu material in museum collections in Australia and overseas.

Gumbula also recognizes the importance of documenting the knowledge of older people himself (Fig. 9.7). 'When I return [with images] and sit down with the elders, people will feel something. They will get that spirit back. I don't want to see people losing this history' (Gumbula in Gibson 2007: 2). Recognizing the intrinsic link between the two storehouses of knowledge, the archives and the oral record, Neparrnga commented 'people kept it in their mind and passed it on for generations – people [were] recording their [own] history' (Gumbula in Gibson 2007: 2). Neparrnga has recently collaborated with the Macleay Museum in Sydney and as guest curator developed the exhibition, *Makarr-Garma: Aboriginal collections from a Yolngu Perspective* (29 November 2009–15 May 2010). 'This exhibition is part of

Fig. 9.7 Neparrnga Gumbula discusses the interlaced armband from the Donald Thomson Collection with his oldest brother, Baltha Gaykamangu at Garriyak outstation. 31 August 2005 (Photo by Louise Hamby)

my work: the research and promotion of Yolngu history and culture. Makarr-garma is a cultural exchange. Makarr-garma, this is my invitation for people to share in Yolngu understanding, philosophies and Rom (law), and how Yolngu transformed their knowledge through generation to generation' (Gumbula 2009: 4).

Agency in the Formation of Collections

Recognition of contemporary indigenous agency as integral to the future development of knowledge and the relevance of museum collections for the future has been touched on earlier in this chapter; however, historical agency in the formation of these collections is essentially hidden. The engagement of source communities with collections has served to shed light on this issue, as evidenced in the example of Burinyila and the role that his father Rraywala had in the creation of the Donald Thomson Collection. Neparrnga also highlighted the importance of Rraywala after he closely examined Thomson's photographs in his own research on the Collection to identify his own father, let out a long whistle and said, 'his family must be so proud and Burinyila!' (Neparrnga Gumbula 2006, personal communication).

He explained what an extraordinary accomplishment Rraywala had achieved taking himself and Thomson safely across the length and breadth of Arnhem Land. From a Yolngu perspective, he was seeing the importance of Rraywala rather than Thomson.

An important indication of historical Aboriginal agency is found in Thomson's photographs. Over 275 Yolngu have been identified as a result of longstanding research on the images in Arnhem Land. From Thomson's notes, examinations of photographs and learning about specific individuals from their Yolngu descendants and, in many instances, from those who knew these people first hand, it is possible to glean who the main collaborators were likely to have been. The key cultural brokers of this time, mostly men, feature largely in this context. Among these, Rraywala is a legendary figure; however, other well-known individuals emerge. At Port Stewart, Willie and Lena Webb, Harry Liddy and Monkey Port Stewart feature strongly in Thomson's images and in the memories and stories of Lamalama people. Since these individuals usually had a good grasp of English and had previously engaged with outsiders, they were key brokers and collaborators with scientists and collectors; for example, Lena Webb was the cook for Hale and Tindale when they went to Princess Charlotte Bay and collected objects and took photographs in 1927. This was 14 months before Donald Thomson arrived at Port Stewart for the first time. Similarly, William Lloyd Warner was at Milingimbi six years before Thomson. A number of Yolngu appear in both Warner's and Thomson's photographs and key individuals amongst these undoubtedly influenced the collecting practices of both. A comparison of names of people identified in the Thomson photographs with those named in Warner's book (1937) reveals that those who worked with Warner and Thomson were the Djambarrpuyngu men, Balimany #1, Bangalliwuy and Minyipirriwuy; Mildjingi men, Rraywala (Fig. 9.8) and Wilindjango; Gupapuyngu Birrikili men, Dimala and Birrinjawi; Djäwa, a Gupapuyngu Daygurrgurr man; Wangurri men, Binydjarrpuma and Makarrwala, and two women Gutjiringgu, Wobulgarra clan, and Burrmilakakili, a Marrangu woman, wife of Rraywala (Hamby 2008). Harry Makarrwala, however, was the closest to Warner. He played the equivalent role that Rraywala did for Thomson. Indeed, Makarrwala is the only named individual in Warner's photographs.

While it is clear that historical agency and the crossover of individuals with other collectors can be explored mainly through photographs, consideration of oral accounts of events in history from source communities reveals the way in which contemporary Aboriginal knowledge can provide alternative perspectives and historical narratives. An example is the deconstruction of the sequence of images taken by Thomson at Trial Bay in 1942 into a more meaningful and relevant order by Yolngu. These relate to a *makarrata*, a formalized public ordeal held to settle disputes between rival groups. During his own research into Thomson's photographs, Neparrnga, as well as two senior Yolngu men from Blue Mud Bay on a separate visit to the Collection, were able to reconfirm the correct sequence of this famous event in Arnhem Land folklore. Distinctions were made initially about which photographs belonged to which side of the dispute: that is those 'warriors' who belonged to

Fig. 9.8 Songs being
recorded by Warner on wax
cylinders at Milingimbi with
Rraywala Mildjingi observing
on far left. c. 1928 (Photo by
Lloyd Warner.)
Source: Sydney University
Archives, p130_18_61_227,
permission granted by
Burinyila Mildjingi

Binydjarrpuma and Rraywala's 'team' from central Arnhem Land as distinct from
the camp of Djapu leader, Wonggu, from northeast Arnhem Land.

Gawirrin Gumana and Marrira Marawili are elders from Blue Mud Bay and were
children when this *makarrata* took place. During their visit to Melbourne, it was
clear that this event remains a significant event in Yolngu history. These men had
heard it retold many times in their younger days, no doubt from their fathers, both
of whom appear in Thomson's photographs. Both these men were children when
Thomson photographed them in Arnhem Land. Their memories in this instance are
drawn from the first-hand accounts of family members and their own experiences of
other *makarrata* provided a reference point for sorting the sequence of images into
the correct order. Marirra in fact directed the performance of a *makarrata* re-enacted
for the film, *Dhakiyarr versus the King* (Murray and Collins 2005).

Conclusion

The approach discussed in this chapter reveals the critical importance of engaging with source communities and creating dialogue by establishing a cross-cultural
research model whereby source communities, researchers and museums alike play
an active role in the process. It is within this unique environment that old knowledge is rediscovered and new knowledge emerges that subsequently informs our

understandings and creates new meanings that would not otherwise emerge. It is an environment that importantly gives credence to the epistemologies of indigenous knowledge systems with their root in an oral record and the memories of old people. This is a framework that gives due recognition to the power and authority of source communities while recognizing a clear role for museums, particularly in drawing out the knowledge inherently embedded in collections revealed by the application of anthropological and archival research. This model allows for interplay of competing and complementary views and of different ways of seeing and understanding the material in museum collections. What emerges is a vastly enhanced and reinvigorated knowledge base with the potential to breathe new life and vitality into museum collections, giving them a new relevance in the present and securing their relevance into the future.

We have focused on the Donald Thomson Collection because it has served as a singular source of inspiration for a number of communities in remote northern Australia over many decades. Interest in their cultural patrimony is a very familiar situation not just in Australia (e.g. Knowles Chapter 10; McEwan and Silva Chapter 11). However, Donald Thomson's work and his collection particularly provide a key platform for exploring the way in which knowledge emerges and merges, relationships are built, and competing knowledge, interests and perspectives intersect. Engagement with source communities in these projects has allowed for the revision of museum practices and informed systems and protocols for managing collections or specific components of these. These collaborations have confirmed the 'proper way' to manage the Collection; such as the Lamalama agenda to ensure the 'proper Lamalama way'. It is clear that protocols applied equally within the Museum as evidenced by the visit by Old George Musgrave to see the Port Stewart material. The case studies further revealed the intrinsic power and potency of objects and photographs in the Donald Thomson Collection and demonstrated the intrinsic value of museum collections and their capacity to impact on the way in which knowledge and experiences of the past are revealed. They represent a singularly valuable benchmark of the past and as such are used to reconfirm and reclaim knowledge. Access to the collections is mediated by communities and undertaken by those in positions of power or with seniority. Initial and exploratory visits serve to establish confidence as to the actual nature of the material and who can access it; and as elders rarely come without younger people, serve further as a key strategy in engendering pride and strengthening identity.

Many collections in Australia relate to source communities who, like the Lamalama, have been prevented until very recent times from residing permanently on or having access to the county with which they have close ancestral, family or even historical ties. However, the intrinsic importance of these collections is best demonstrated by the value afforded to them in support of land and native title claims and in this museum collections have proved to have a greater relevance than could ever have been anticipated. Such engagements between source communities and museums as shown here have also led to the collections having a new relevance in communities with the agendas of key members of source communities to ensure that knowledge survives into the future for the following generations. This process has further allowed for their versions and interpretations of history to emerge with new narratives, new interpretations and new contexts provided for museums to construct around collections in their role with the broader public.

Acknowledgments This research primarily arises from Australian Research Council (ARC) funded projects: LP0347221 (2003–2006) *Anthropological and Aboriginal Perspectives on the Donald Thomson Collection: Material Culture, Collecting and Identity*, awarded to the Australian National University and a collaboration with Museum Victoria (Lindy Allen, Dr Louise Hamby and Professor Nicolas Peterson); LP0667418 (2006–2009) *Oral Tradition, Memory and Social Change: Indigenous Participation in the Curation and Use of Museum Collections* awarded to the University of Queensland and a collaboration with Museum Victoria and Deakin University (Lindy Allen, Dr Diane Hafner, Professor Bruce Rigsby, Simon Wilmot and Rosemary Wrench); DP0879397 (2007–2011): *Contexts of Collection – A Dialogic Approach to Understanding the Making of the Material Record of Yolngu Cultures*, awarded to the Australian National University (Professor Howard Morphy, Dr Louise Hamby and Phillipa Deveson). Permission to reproduce images was obtained from relevant Yolngu and Pama, the University of Sydney Archives, the Donald Thomson Family and Museum Victoria.

References

Allen, Lindy
>
> 2005 A Photographer of Brilliance. In *Donald Thomson, Man and Scholar*, edited by Bruce Rigsby and Nicolas Peterson, pp. 45–62. Academy of the Social Sciences in Australia, Canberra.
>
> 2008 Tons and Tons of Valuable Material. In *The Makers and Making of Indigenous Australian Museum Collections,* edited by Nicolas Peterson, Lindy Allen and Louise Hamby, pp. 387–418. Melbourne University Publishing, Melbourne.

Bolton, Lissant
>
> 2003 The Object in View: Aborigines, Melanesians and Museums. In *Museums and Source Communities*, edited by Laura Peers and Alison K. Brown, pp. 42–54. Routledge, London.

Corn, Aaron, and Neparrnga Gumbula
>
> 2006 Rom and the Academy Re-positioned: Binary Models in Yolŋu Intellectual Traditions and Their Application to Wider Inter-Cultural Dialogues. In *Boundary Writing: An Exploration of Race, Culture and Gender Binaries in Contemporary Australia,* edited by Lynette Russell, pp. 170–197. University of Hawai'i Press, Honolulu.

de Heer, Rolf, and Peter Djigirr
>
> 2006 *Ten Canoes.* A Film by Rolf de Heer and the People of Ramingining, Fandango/Vertigo Production in association with South Australian Film Corporation, Film Finance Corporation Australia.

Djerrkura, Gatjil
>
> 2003 Foreword. In *Donald Thomson in Arnhem Land*, edited by Donald Thomson, compiled and introduced by Nicolas Peterson, p. ii. The Miegunyah Press, Melbourne.

Edwards, Robert, and Jenny Stewart
>
> 1980 *Preserving Indigenous Cultures: A New Role for Museums.* Australian Government Publishing Service, Canberra.

Gibson, Noel
    2007 Reclaiming the Past Can Be Personal. *Sydney Morning Herald*, Monday April 9: News 2.
        Sydney.

Gumbula, Neparrnga
    2009 *Makarr-Garma: Aboriginal Collections from a Yolngu Perspective*. Macleay Museum,
        Sydney.

Hafner, Diane
    2005 Images of Port Stewart: Possible Interpretations. In *Donald Thomson, Man and Scholar*,
        edited by Bruce Rigsby and Nicolas Peterson, pp. 45–62. Academy of the Social Sciences
        in Australia, Canberra.
    2008 The Past, Present: Lamalama Interactions with Memory and Technology. In *The New
        Boundaries between Bodies and Technologies*, edited by Bianca Maria Pirani and Ivan Varga,
        pp. 250–267. Cambridge Scholars Publishing, Newcastle.

Hafner, Diane, Bruce Rigsby, and Lindy Allen
    2007 Museums and Memory as Agents of Social Change. *The International Journal of the
        Humanities* 5(6):87–94.

Hamby, Louise
    2007a Wrapt with String. *Textile: The Journal of Cloth and Culture* 5(2):208–228.

Hamby, Louise
    2007b Thomson Times and Ten Canoes. *Studies in Australasian Cinema* 1(2):127–146.

Hamby, Louise
    2008 Lloyd Warner: The Reluctant Collector. In *The Makers and Making of Indigenous
        Australian Museum Collections*, edited by Nicolas Peterson, Lindy Allen, and Louise
        Hamby, pp. 355–386. Melbourne University Publishing, Melbourne.

Karp, Ivan, Corinne Kratz, Lynn Szwaja, and Tomas Ybarra-Frausto (editors)
    2006 *Museum Frictions: Public Cultures, Global Transformations*. Duke University Press,
        Durham and London.

Murray, Tom, and Allan Collins
    2005 *Dhakiyarr vs the King*. Film Australia.

Museums Australia
    1993 Revised 2005 *Continuous Cultures, Ongoing Responsibilities*. http://www.
        museumsaustralia.org.au/dbdoc/ccor_final_feb_05.pdf

National and State Libraries Australasia
    2007 *National Policy Framework for Aboriginal and Torres Strait Islander Library
        Services and Collections*. http://www.nsla.org.au/publications/policies/2007/pdf/NSLA.
        Policy-20070129-National.Policy.Framework.for.Indigenous.Services.pdf

Peers, Laura, and Alison K. Brown (editors)
    2003 *Museums and Source Communities*. Routledge, London.

Peterson, Nicolas, Lindy Allen, and Louise Hamby (editors)
    2008 *The Makers and Making of Indigenous Australian Museum Collections*. Melbourne
        University Publishing, Melbourne.

Rigsby, Bruce, and Nicholas Peterson (editors)
  2005 *Donald Thomson, Man and Scholar.* Academy of the Social Sciences in Australia, Canberra.

Thomson, Donald
  1934 The Dugong Hunters of Cape York. *Journal of the Royal Anthropological Institute* 64:237–262.
  2003 *Donald Thomson in Arnhem Land.* Compiled and introduced by Nicolas Peterson. The Miegunyah Press, Melbourne.

Vertigo Productions
  2006 *Ten Canoes Press Kit.* Vertigo Productions, Adelaide.

Warner, William Lloyd
  1937 *A Black Civilisation: A Social Study of an Australian Tribe.* Harper and Brothers, New York, NY.

Chapter 10
'Objects as Ambassadors': Representing Nation Through Museum Exhibitions

Chantal Knowles

Abstract The histories of both the Scottish and the Tlicho Nation in Canada are entwined through the fur trade. The National Museums Scotland (NMS) holds a nineteenth century collection of Tlicho artefacts made by Scots working in Canada. Each nation considers the collection part of its cultural patrimony and heritage. In 2008 when NMS exhibited these artefacts, the individual objects became agents of representation for both nations and their emerging political identities and histories. In discussing the significance of the objects for each nation in the twenty-first century, I examine how two such disparate groups can lay claim to the collection in this way. Through a case study of collecting, interpretations and exhibitions, I will explore artefact agency and the Tlicho perception of 'objects as ambassadors.'

> *It is not artefacts that make a nation; but it is the artefacts made by people and for people that speak most clearly of the quality of that people, be they artists or engineers, peasants or poets, artisans or aristocrats*
>
> *(Magnusson 1989: IX).*

Introduction

This chapter sets out to examine how objects can be agents of representation for individuals and communities, how their use in exhibitions can convey multiple messages of the past and the present and how 'ownership' and responsibility can be mutable and shared. In using the example of a partnership forged between National Museums Scotland (NMS) and the Tlicho Nation (also known as the Dogrib) of the Northwest Territories of Canada, it is possible to examine how museums, communities and individuals invest in objects and create lasting legacies and alternative representations of themselves.

The chapter is informed by three central concepts: multiple agencies (the object and the various individuals and institutions who encounter it); the identification of nation and political identity through the political employment and interpretation of objects; and representation of these nations through display. Firstly, an individual's agency can be read through the material properties and collecting history of

C. Knowles (✉)
Department of World Cultures, National Museums Scotland, Edinburgh, Scotland
e-mail: c.knowles@nms.ac.uk

S. Byrne et al. (eds.), *Unpacking the Collection*, One World Archaeology,
DOI 10.1007/978-1-4419-8222-3_10, © Springer Science+Business Media, LLC 2011

an object (Gosden and Knowles 2001). The act of making, the materials chosen and the sale or gift of the object may be visible in the patina, marks and style of the object, and by studying a series of objects, conclusions about this historical past can be drawn (Torrence 2000). Scholars have also described objects as 'witnesses' (Phillips 2005: 108), 'travellers' (Clifford 1997: 213) that are able to acquire biographical histories. Implicit in these metaphors is the ability of the object to 'act' and impart information to others to tell their own stories and thus 'speak for themselves'. In working with the Tlicho Nation on a series of exhibitions, those mandated to represent the community concerning whether objects should be returned or remain in Scotland state that they were comfortable with Tlicho cultural objects remaining in the Museum and being exhibited there because they would function as 'ambassadors' for their Nation. The Tlicho were satisfied even though the placement of their cultural property within a space in the National Museum of Scotland also situated them very firmly in a Scottish national context, inscribing the objects as agents of Scotland's past and its engagement with the rest of the world.

Forging a Partnership

In September 2002, seven members of the Tlicho Nation visited the National Museums Scotland to view the Tlicho portion of the collection of nineteenth century Dene material housed in the Museum's collections. Dene is used to refer to the language and cultural group in the sub-Arctic and Northwest Territories region of Canada of which the Tlicho are one group. This was a significant moment. These world-renowned collections, widely published and exhibited (Kerr 1953; Clarke and Idiens 1974; Idiens 1979), were being handled for the first time by the descendants of their makers. Over several days the 37 objects were examined. Responses by the Tlicho oscillated between detailed discussion of the sewing, knotting or manufacturing techniques; the telling of stories about how objects were used; and comfortable silences where individuals enjoyed being in the room with the collection and having them to hand. On one occasion the visitors telephoned their families at home in Canada to tell them that they were in Edinburgh holding, touching and spending time with the objects.

As a consequence of the visit and the individuals' responses to the collection, a partnership project was established with the aim of exhibiting the collection in the Northwest Territories so that the whole Tlicho and wider Dene community could share access to the collections. National Museums Scotland agreed to work towards an exhibition that would provide an opportunity for 'knowledge repatriation' to the Tlicho. In providing a materiality to the lived past and sense of cultural continuity, the objects had sparked and inspired discussion and dialogue amongst those who had visited Scotland and helped unlock oral histories. The goal of the new partnership was to expand this experience to the wider community. An exhibition would provide the originating community with physical access to artefacts by placing them in an accessible space where elders and youth would be able to meet and discuss them. For the Tlicho, in particular, making the collection accessible to those at home would provide material substance to the traditional stories of the land and a physical connection between the makers and their descendants.

In order to take forward the aspirations that this first visit had initiated, a steering committee including representatives of the proposed partner institutions, as well as experts with anthropological, archaeological, curatorial and cultural knowledge, was set up to define project aims and explore possible funding. The steering committee comprised John B. Zoe and Rosa Mantla (Tlicho), Gavin Renwick (University of Dundee), Tom Andrews and Joanne Bird (Prince of Wales Northern Heritage Centre, PWNHC), Chantal Knowles (NMS), and Judy Thompson (Canadian Museum of Civilisation). Four years later in October 2006, the exhibition *Dè T'a Hoti Ts'eeda: We Live Securely by the Land* opened at the Prince of Wales Northern Heritage Centre, the Territorial Museum in Yellowknife, capital of the Northwest Territories of Canada and the region containing the traditional homeland of the Tlicho. The exhibition marked the return of artefacts from the National Museums Scotland's Dene collections to the Northwest Territories after an absence of over 150 years. Running for a year, the exhibition was subsequently toured to the Carleton University Art Gallery in Ottawa until December 2007. In May 2008, a new temporary exhibition *Extremes: Life in Subarctic Canada* was opened at the National Museum of Scotland. This exhibition comprised the historical Tlicho collections, supplemented by a new twenty-first century collection made during the course of the project.

It was ultimately the decision to display the collection in the National Museum of Scotland, whose founding principle was to 'present Scotland to the World' (Fig. 10.1), that provoked a reengagement with the idea of political identity and cultural histories and how this is conveyed through the contents of the collection and

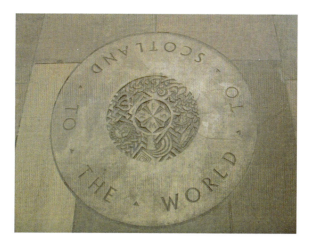

Fig. 10.1 This stone is set into the floor at the point at which the visitor can cross between the twentieth century Museum of Scotland and the original Victorian museum which houses world collections of science, natural history and the arts. The phrase can refer to either museum; one presents 'The World to Scotland,' while the other 'Scotland to the World' (© National Museums Scotland)

the circumstances under which it was assembled. The Museum of Scotland presents Scotland's story to its international audience, and for the temporary exhibition the endeavours of the Scottish diaspora was a key narrative thread in order to relate the material to the rest of the Museum's displays. However, by focussing on the Tlicho story in this space we had to be explicit about the relevance of the collection to this nation's history. The timing of the exhibition was pertinent to this method of interpretation and the stories being told. The successful realisation of the Tlicho's land and self-government claim in 2005 and the relatively recent devolution of the Scottish government in 1999 and the election of the first Scottish nationalist government in 2007 meant that the themes of national identity, self-determination and history were in the minds of those curating and developing the exhibition and many of the visitors.

Two moments in time – the first, a museum-instigated encounter between the Scots and the Tlicho in the fur trading posts of the Northwest Territories at the time of the collection of the artefacts (1858–1862), and the second, in 2008, when the exhibition opened in the National Museum of Scotland – entangle the stories and histories of both nations. The Scots in Canada were there as part of the fur trade. The Hudson Bay Company (HBC) ships returning from London's Thames to Canada would routinely stop at the Orkney Islands to recruit labour, building a labour force for the HBC in Canada that by the 1730s was predominantly Scottish (Williams 1983: 25).

In examining two moments of interaction between the Scots and Tlicho, one historical (fur trade) and one recent (partners in exhibitions), I intend to go beyond the textual histories and examine the relationships that the objects embody. The engagement with the present, past, and the institutions of government and museum has enabled a new interpretation of the collection, imbuing it with different meanings and sentiments. This gave the 'owners', both Tlicho and Scottish, a new way of interpreting and relating to the collection. The objects, by being placed in a public institution, had been transferred from individual ownership to public property. The right of museums to own cultural property has been widely debated; yet, in this partnership, ownership was defined through the Museums' role: it holds artefacts in trust for its public. Museum practice places ownership amongst its stakeholders – those who frequent, use the Museum or have an interest or connection to the collections. From this perspective every Tlicho and Scot has a claim to 'own' the collection and therefore the right to contribute to discussions regarding its care and interpretation. The plurality of 'ownership' allowed for multiple voices and histories to be woven into the interpretation and care of the artefacts.

Material Connections Through Collecting Histories

To consider the formation of the collection in the mid-nineteenth century and the agency of both parties involved, it is necessary to examine their role and vested interest in the transactions of each side: Scots and Tlicho. We can use details of the formation of the collection to get to the heart of indigenous agency in shaping it, the fur trader in assembling it and museum practice in interpreting it. By examining the documentation held by the Museum, comprising lists and correspondence, it is difficult to address the agency of those indigenous owners who offered the items for sale. Yet through understanding the performative relationship that prescribed certain activities in the trade room of the fort or trading post, there is the opportunity to propose some ideas about the shaping of the collection by the indigenous traders at that time. Observations made by modern Tlicho about the workmanship of their ancestors and choice of materials provide useful insights into the makers' agency when responding to the request for artefacts.

The fur trade in Canada began in the seventeenth century on the east coast and expanded westwards as new regions were opened up to the opportunistic French and British companies. Seeking lucrative beaver fur for the European market, trading companies explored different mechanisms of engagement with the indigenous population in order to increase their access to furs. This settled into a pattern of manned trading posts or forts in key strategic areas. Indigenous trappers could visit the forts run by European men known as 'Factors' and exchange or sell furs in return for money or trade goods (Williams 1983: 26–34). The initial contact trading relationships between the Hudson's Bay Company and Dene groups began towards the end of the eighteenth century. By the middle of the nineteenth century the most remote of the Dene groups were involved in the fur trade and had contact with at least one trading post (Helm 2000: 26–27). It was in these trading posts, where many Scots worked, that the Tlicho collection of artefacts was assembled for the Museum.

The relationships between company men and the indigenous population at the forts could be quite formal using a prescribed language and set of protocols. Economic transactions would follow a particular choreography. The pricing of furs was regulated, and all pricing was related to the value of one beaver pelt. Groups of indigenous trappers would come to the post and camp about one day's journey away. From there they sent someone forward to trade. A formal exchange of gifts took place, cementing alliances and reaffirming relationships (Ray 1974: 65). This was a political relationship; the trading room was purposefully unheated, discouraging any prolonged interaction. But over the years, knowledge and trust built between Hudson Bay Company men and the local trappers.

The trading fort's main economic transactions with indigenous trappers were based on the acquisition of fur pelts, and these were exchanged for money and goods such as blankets, guns and food. Thus, a request for artefacts will have been additional to, and distinct from, this providing a new opportunity for trade and broadening the range of items that indigenous communities could offer for sale and therefore increasing their potential for economic gain (Lindsay 1993: xv). Source communities were eager to engage in the sale of artefacts, and this could have been due to not only the widening opportunities for economic gain provided by the request for artefacts but also the lack of rules pertaining to these transactions. In this case prices were potentially negotiable, providing greater opportunities to barter, distinct from the regulated trade of pelts and trade goods.

Artefacts are neither agents in their own right nor are they passive. Rather they are entwined in social interaction (Gosden and Knowles 2001: 22). Canadian fur trading posts were the locales where social relations were formed and maintained through the exchange of objects. Their relationship can be glimpsed over a century later through the presence of the object in a museum. During this time the object has become the locus for a set of stories, a life history, which connects makers, owners, interpreters and others and can be used to elicit local agency at certain moments in time, such as the initial transaction, or at the point of interpretation in a museum context.

In the case of the traded Tlicho artefacts it seems that at the moment of transaction, both maker and collector were satisfied with the outcome. Consequently, modern Tlicho feel the objects were 'fairly traded.' The museum collection can therefore be researched to illuminate the entangled, mutually dependent relationship between two communities. The notion of unequal relationships and unjust acquisitions, which underpins many colonial collections, seems to be absent from this collection.

Examination of the Tlicho collection shows that many artefacts collected by Bernard Rogan Ross, the Chief Trader at Fort Simpson and the main source for the Tlicho material, were new and unused (this is not true of all the NMS Dene and Inuvialiut collections). This suggests that these artefacts were deliberately made and offered for sale, or directly commissioned from the maker. In addition the collection acquired from the Tlicho contains several small-scale models of items one assumes were too large, unwieldy and costly to ship back to Scotland. They include a pair of snowshoes and several hunting bags in miniaturised form (Fig. 10.2).

Fig. 10.2 Model snowshoes. Snowshoes are made to measure, their length made roughly to the shoulder height of the owner. This model pair measure 592 mm in length (© National Museums Scotland)

These were specific commissions, not just taken from a wish list of representative items as compiled by Ross or an opportune acquisition based on something already on offer, but instead a specific request to a selected individual that resulted in a special relationship between maker and collector. This collection is founded on long-term relationships where artefacts were made specifically for sale, or commissioned with specific instructions such as dimensions for the models, or items in stages of manufacture to demonstrate technical process.

Ross was forming a collection in response to a call for material from George Wilson, Director of the new Industrial Museum of Scotland. In his annual report Wilson stated: 'An industrial museum ... cannot be complete without illustrations of the existing state of the useful arts, among the ... nations of the world' (Wilson 1857: 166). His anticipated museum audience and those attending his lectures included many artisans: practical people who made things. Therefore, Wilson was driven to seek out collections from other cultures to form a 'library of techniques'.

Wilson's strategy was to use existing networks, in particular the Scottish diaspora that encompassed the globe through colonial, trading, missionary and explorative enterprises. This network of influential friends became agents for the Museum, encouraging the donation or acquisition of artefacts. Amongst these agents was Wilson's brother Daniel, a professor at the University of Toronto, who put him in touch with George Simpson, a Scotsman and governor of the Hudson Bay Company. A letter requesting specimens and outlining specific collecting criteria was endorsed by Simpson who passed it on to a number of HBC men working at the forts or trading posts (George Simpson to George Barnston, letter, 4 May 1857, Hudson's Bay Company Archives, Winnipeg, B.239/c/10, fo.237d). The collecting guidelines encouraged not only the collection of the everyday but also artefacts in the process of being made providing the process of production, its tools and techniques.

Ross amassed his collection, encouraging other traders and missionaries to contribute and commissioning the Tlicho to fulfil Wilson's collecting agenda. Although there was a list and methodology supplied by Wilson to guide collecting, it is likely that opportunity as well as design formulated the collection's contents. In reviewing the collection in the twenty-first century the overwhelming sense is one of personal, everyday objects that were offered for trade at posts, but not necessarily the best examples of their maker's work. Today several Tlicho seamstresses have commented on the poor quality of the hide used to make two summer outfits in the collection, and there is a general consensus that what was offered for trade was inferior in quality to those made for use by the Tlicho. In reviewing the collection and the objects it comprises, we can glimpse the negotiation and personal agency of some of those involved. For example, Tlicho seamstresses clearly believe this was a clever way of trading, making money, but keeping back the best hides for family use. It is difficult to assess whether this was the case; it may have been that less successful trappers turned to the artefact trade to have access to trading posts goods. The lack of quality of materials may also suggest that the collector was not as knowledgeable about certain indigenous artefacts as others. For example, stone pipes and snowshoes were bought on a regular basis by trading post staff for personal use; therefore, they would be better placed to critically assess their quality before buying them for the collection.

Reframing Tlicho Agency

The moment of collection presents the object as a locus for a network of relationships that crosses Canada and the Atlantic. The journey from land to trading post along trading routes to the Museum creates a series of ties that binds the two communities or nations across time and space. Significant aspects of their histories and cultural biographies may be said to be bound into this network.

A reconsideration of the moment of collection and the relationships between the Tlicho and Scots leads us to examine how the objects have been interpreted for the twenty-first century audiences, whether by museum visitor or Tlicho elder. The two partners, Tlicho Nation and the National Museum, approached their communities differently through the interpretation used in the exhibitions and consequently sought differing responses and outcomes from their audiences. Both parties brought their own invested interest and sense of ownership to the artefacts and aims for the exhibitions, so that the objects themselves became agents of representation for the two nations.

Today the Tlicho Nation, consisting of a population of just over 3000, is settled in four communities across the area known as the North Slave region. In 2005, ten years after the claim was filed and five years after an agreement in principle, the Tlicho won their land claim and right to self-government. In the context of the land claim and the research being carried out within the Tlicho communities, 'traditional knowledge' in the form of oral histories was gathered and recorded. This provided a mechanism to map traditional land use and knowledge of the land to substantiate the historical basis for the land claim.

Early on in this process, Tom Andrews (territorial archaeologist) and John B. Zoe (chief negotiator, Dogrib Treaty 11 Council) elicited a story from an elder, Harry Simpson (interview between Chantal Knowles and John B. Zoe, 15 May, 2008). They learnt that their informant's grandfather had been a keen trader, travelling widely, trapping fur and making or seeking out other desirable goods to trade at the forts. Amongst these goods were stone pipes, a carved stone version of pottery pipes manufactured in Europe at that time. Through further discussion with the elder a location for the source of the stone was determined. The following summer an ethno-archaeological survey was conducted in the area, and two sites with the remains of pipe manufacture were identified. On their return from the field Andrews and Zoe sought historical examples of the trade pipes in museums; their researches brought them to the National Museums Scotland (Fig. 10.3).

The impetus behind reconnecting with these artefacts has a broader context. This tracking of oral histories across the land opened the story book of the Tlicho, which they believe is inscribed on the land and their relationship with it. Reopening this storybook led to the institution of the *Trails of our Ancestors,* an annual trip

Fig. 10.3 Stone pipes in
various stages of manufacture
(© National Museums
Scotland)

involving youth and elders that followed old travelling routes (Zoe 2005). This in
turn prompted the formulation of the Traditional Knowledge Project (Legat 2005),
the collecting of oral histories, all of which reinforced a generational continuity of
land use and knowledge of the land by the Tlicho. This confidence in their association with their land, its centrality to their way of life and life itself meant that the
process of the land claim fed off and into this knowledge.

After uncovering the existence of the stone pipes and the larger Tlicho collection
in NMS and as a consequence of the visit to the Museum by elders in 2002, NMS
curatorial and conservation staff began a series of visits to the Northwest Territories
from 2004 on (Fig. 10.4). These visits provided face-to-face opportunities to discuss
the practicalities of a touring exhibition, potential means of funding and to work
with the elders to research the collection and select objects for the exhibition. Images
of the objects were shared with elders, and each object provided the doorway to a
material memory for the elders. This allowed them to reconnect with their stories.
The objects provide a physical link to the past and their ancestors. In addition to
the personal connection of elders to their ancestors, the objects provided a material
marker, or reference, for the Tlicho community to their land. An intimate knowledge
of the land and the language gives the Tlicho their identity and sense of self. Objects
are inextricably linked to the land by the materials from which they are made and

Fig. 10.4 Chantal Knowles uses photographs to discuss the National Museum's collection with elders of the Gameti community during an initial visit to Canada, May 2004 (© Gavin Renwick)

their use in the landscape. This reference point, as potent as the markers on the land, connected things in the past with stories and people existing in the present.

Whilst the continuity with certain objects had been lost, in that they were no longer made or techniques had changed considerably, the memories they evoked and their connection to the land and its stories remained. Each exquisite object, crafted from the land, affirms the link with the landscape. Amongst the objects that elicited one of the most emotional responses was the largely unassuming willow bark fishing net (Fig. 10.5). These nets stopped being made a long time ago, so few people remembered seeing one, although everyone had heard about them. Large nets, owned by family groups, were placed under the ice in winter, providing access to vital food in a season of scarcity. Many different elders talked of family stories describing how a family's survival had depended on nourishment provided through the net's catch. What was an unassuming object for the Museum, difficult to conserve and harder still to unravel and examine in detail, was not only something that resonated for the Tlicho to a past nomadic life, at times harsh and uncertain, but also something made from the land, made collectively and owned collectively. It represented community and collaboration, winter camps and the knowledge and skills needed to live on the land.

Tlicho connection to land and use of the objects as a way to recreate the past were critical in how they used the objects within the context of a museum exhibition. As we have seen, the modern Tlicho are a confident, self-assured and thriving nation. Their recent successes in winning their land claim and right for self-government have given them a secure base from which to engage with the world. For the Tlicho

Fig. 10.5 Fishing net, willow bark fibre. This net would have to have been kept wet at all times to remain pliable and flexible for use (© National Museums Scotland)

the land is their life. The title of the Canadian leg of the exhibition *Dè T'a Hoti Ts'eeda: We live securely by the land* is explicit (Andrews 2006). Without the land there is no life, and without knowledge and the ability to read the land, its stories and its memories of the past, present and future, the Tlicho will lose their culture, their sense of who they are and their way of life.

In the Yellowknife exhibition, interpretation was minimal. Each case had two labels, the first a personal quote or story from a member of the Dene community to whom the object related and a descriptive label for anyone unfamiliar with the object. In addition, two panel texts, discreetly placed along one wall of the exhibition told the story of the collection's assembly and its journey to Scotland and the other the Dene and Tlicho history. Back in their source community the objects were framed as being of the land and having come 'home', yet the inclusion of a panel about Scotland hinted at the collection's other 'identity', a collection with meaning for the Scottish nation.

Unprecedented numbers of visitors came to the exhibition. The Yellowknife population is 18,000, and the visitor numbers for the exhibition reached 30,000. Although these figures include tourists, there were many repeat visitors. A visitor's book gradually filled with comments often not about the exhibition but the objects themselves. 'It was my culture' wrote one; 'I was moved, it was a spiritual experience. These Dene items are still very alive with Dene culture. Mahsi Cho [thank you] to our ancestors,' wrote another; and 'Good to see our culture preserved for the rest of the world to see'. Many of the comments were therefore about identity and pride, pride in the work of their ancestors, pride in the nation today and pride in the fact that their objects were respected internationally. Each visitor attributed the objects with their own sets of meaning and a new narrative or contemporary agency. The objects had become ambassadors for the nation and symbols of cultural identity, working to give the people a presence and identity on the world stage. This world stage was realised during the special exhibition at the National Museum of Scotland in Edinburgh: *Extremes: Life in Subarctic Canada.*

Nation Building in the Museum

The Tlicho collection has not only participated in nation building among the Tilcho themselves in modern Canada but, surprisingly, has also played a similar role in Scotland, both at the time of its original collection and later in the twenty-first century. In the 1850s, when the Scottish National Museum was amassing a national collection, it wanted to represent Scotland and its relationship with the rest of the world, comparing and learning from other industries around the world. In the claustrophobic life at the HBC trading posts, this was an opportunity for individuals to think of home and make their mark at home, a lasting testimony of their work and life abroad. The Scottish fur traders' response to Wilson's request was patriotic and generous. The material arrived in the Museum in a series of consignments between 1858 and 1862. In total around 240 documented items relating to Dene communities of the northwest and around 180 Inuit artefacts, largely from the Inuvialuit communities from the Mackenzie River area, were deposited at the Museum. One of the collectors, Robert Campbell, wrote '. . .whatever could be procured in this country for the National Museum of Scotland – I am sure that Scotchmen in general in whatever clime they be, will feel it both a pleasure, and honor, to respond to the call' (Robert Campbell to George Wilson, letter, 5 May 1859, Hudson Bay Company Collections supplementary file, Department of World Cultures, National Museums of Scotland, Edinburgh).

The Industrial Museum of Scotland, founded in 1854 and opened in 1866, was extended in 1999 by the addition of a whole new building, the Museum of Scotland. Distinct from the Victorian establishment, which contained natural history collections, science and technology, arts and ethnography from around the globe, it was built with the intention to tell the story of Scotland from its geological beginnings through to the twentieth century. To use the temporary exhibition space in the Museum of Scotland to bring a different nation's story to the Edinburgh public during festival time was a departure for the Museum. As the Museum provides a destination for many international visitors, the displayed collection (which now included the Tlicho's published land claims documents) had to provide the Scottish context for the collection and address Scottish engagement with the Tlicho in the nineteenth and twenty-first centuries, in order that visitors could understand its location in the heart of the Museum of Scotland. Underlying some of the discussion at steering group level between the Scottish curators and the Tlicho representatives was the politics of the countries or nations that were involved. The two dominant partners, the National Museums Scotland, which held the collection, and the Tlicho, whose ancestors had made the collection, both claimed the collection as part of their cultural history or to use a Zoe's words as their 'storybook'.

In order to understand the contemporary usage of the term 'nation' by the two participating communities, it is necessary to look at how the terms emerged in relation to the two populations. For the Canadian First Nations, of which the Tlicho Nation is just one, the term 'nation' was largely interchangeable with 'tribe' for many years. However, in 1975 the Dene Declaration was published, a document that requested the world to recognise the Indigenous Dene as a stateless nation that had a claim on Canada and the right to land. From this moment on the word 'nation' gained ground and became current terminology for describing indigenous communities in Canada (Flanagan 1985: 368). For most the idea of nation, or cultural identity, is predicated on notions of difference between the nation and the 'Other'. Whilst the Tlicho are a stateless nation that can define itself in opposition to the Canadian nation, for Scots the history is different. Once a sovereign state, it is now a stateless nation, defining itself in opposition to other 'nations,' in particular the English. There are resonances between the two communities and their recent political histories, but this does not bring the communities together, make them similar or mean that the artefacts stories would be the same for both sides.

For the Tlicho the objects in the collection are physical manifestations of the history of their engagement with and on the land, embodied by the materials and knowledge with which they were crafted. For the Scots the collection is material evidence of their or Scotland's engagement with the world and their adventurous and enduring spirit. Of particular significance is that the collection comes from Canada, a country where the largest proportion of the Scottish diaspora resides currently.

'Museums negotiate and construct meanings of national identity' (McLean 1998: 244) and not necessarily just their own. In the case of the Tlicho exhibition, the National Museum of Scotland was empowered to tell the story of the Tlicho Nation, something that the Tlicho expected their objects would also do: standing as testament to who they were and who they are today. Representing the Other and ourselves is part of the Museum's role. The way in which we do this is influenced by the cultural and political agendas of the moment. The Tlicho and the Scots both have very specific perspectives on their histories, given their current political and cultural climates.

McLean's research amongst the visiting public to the newly opened Museum of Scotland found that many see the Museum as an 'ambassador' for Scotland presenting a positive image of Scotland's culture and history to the rest of the world (2003: 121). The use of the word 'ambassador' amongst the visiting public in discussing the role of the Museum and the series of stories it conveys echoes Zoe's assurance that the Museum's display of Tlicho objects created ambassadors for his community. This ambassadorial role, played out before an international audience of visitors, whether attributed to objects or the Museum, imbues the space and its contents with an agency that goes beyond the written interpretation compiled by the curator and museum staff. The structure, placement and politics of the museum enhance the influence of the narratives that are written into the exhibition interpretation, providing material evidence or even material influence over the visitor. It shapes their visit and the messages they take home. For Zoe the objects provide the evidence that the Tlicho exist as a nation and community then and now, to an audience that would otherwise have no reason to know of them.

Representations

The notion of the 'objects as ambassadors' for the Tlicho Nation is a compelling one. Exploring this metaphor is an important part of understanding the partnership process, the project's perceived success and the contemporary Tlicho approach to artefacts and their long-term care and display in Scotland. The artefacts were representatives of the Tlicho Nation abroad, and although consulted on the interpretation used in the Scottish exhibition, Zoe and others were willing to let the knowledgeable museum personnel guide the interpretation. The Museum chose to create an exhibition that historically contextualised the Tlicho, placing them in their landscape, environment and culture, and touched upon Scottish links to the community and how the collection came to be so far away from its source community. A final section looked at the political emergence of the Tlicho Nation, their land claim and their recent history and how this had brought the Museum and Tlicho back into contact and created a new collecting opportunity.

Contemporary objects of Tlicho manufacture, including clothing and bags as well as documents and flags that related directly to the land claim and emergence of a nation, were dispersed throughout the exhibition. This additional material, accessioned to the collections of the Museum, was only exhibited at the Scottish venue. The juxtaposition of modern artefacts, such as the bags used to store and keep fresh dried meat, alongside historical ones demonstrated continuity of materials and techniques. The representation of Tlicho history and continuity provided the clear message that the Tlicho have always lived on their land, continue to live on their land and will remain on their land. They adapt to changing times, whether political change or physical changes to the landscape through mineral resource exploitation, but maintain their identity through the inalienable association with the land and the messages or lessons it contains.

This narrative, presented in the exhibition, was supplemented by direct quotes from the Tlicho, both past and present providing opportunities for the stories, both historical and modern to come through. Zoe clearly believed the objects could and should 'speak for themselves,' imbuing them with a contemporary agency. In describing the stone pipes as his favourite objects, he noted:

> ...the most important object to me is the stone pipe ... it represents the landscape and the skill of the people in recognising the type of stones they used, the artwork that went into developing it, the time and patience that it must have taken and the knowledge that had been passed on to the artist in putting it together. ...It is made out of some soft stone material that is a piece of the landscape and it has a stem that is made from a plant that grew out from the landscape as well as the babiche that comes from the animal from the landscape so it has all the elements of the landscape, the vegetation and the animals ... all put into one... (Interview between Chantal Knowles and John B. Zoe, 15 May, 2008).

In the context of the here and now of Tlicho history, the stone pipe can be seen as the summation of what it is to be Tlicho, who they are and their enduring relationship with the land. Yet the same stone pipe also represents Scotland's past, the thirst for knowledge and understanding that prompted the foundation of a museum and informed its early collecting strategy, and the economic opportunities that took Scots abroad.

Conclusion

Museum artefacts have a past and a present, in the same way as do the two nations that claim ownership of them. The nations also have a past and a present that are bound together by the objects. Over 150 years ago the relationship was deemed unequal with Scots being part of the appropriation of land and its exploitation for commercial gain. Today both nations meet over common causes since they find themselves at a point where ownership and the right to self-government are crucial issues. These common concerns created a connection whose presence was periodically felt throughout the recent partnership in creating exhibitions. These were 'nations working together' to address our past and access the knowledge locked within a set of artefacts. The exhibition in Scotland, situated in the Museum of Scotland, a monument to one nation's culture, provided a different take on Scots' past relationships with other cultures and a moment for reflection on them. The exhibition gave the Tlicho an international platform for recognition (artefacts as diplomats or ambassadors). Working together has provided a new, more equal relationship where co-curation, co-care and responsibility are acknowledged and hopefully will continue to thrive.

Just as nations can be associated through the connectivity of the objects and the networks created by the transactions, embracing those connections and reawakening dormant ties have resulted in a reinvigorated collection with new multiple layers of meaning being attributed to the museum artefact and perhaps getting us closer to a sense of the agency of the actors and artefacts, both then and now. This case study shows how museums collections have multiple agencies since each party associated with the collection has imbued the objects with agency and their own sets of meaning. It is up to the museum to unlock these meanings allowing the visitor to engage with objects.

Acknowledgements   The exhibition and associated activities were the culmination of five years of work in partnership with the PWNHC, NMS, the Tlicho Government (formerly the Dogrib Treaty 11 Council) and the University of Dundee. It involved many different people, and all are thanked for their hard work and support. The members of the Steering Committee were vital to the success of the exhibition in both venues, in particular, Gavin Renwick, Tom Andrews and John B. Zoe. This chapter also draws upon research work relating to the Museum's collection and history, in particular discussions with Henrietta Lidchi, Geoff Swinney and Charles Stable. For insight into ideas of Scottish identity, nationhood and the Scots colonial endeavours I am grateful to John Burnett. Jane Wilkinson, Kylie Moloney, Alison Morrison-Low and Jeremy Coote have commented on earlier drafts. I am extremely grateful to the organisers of the session at WAC, Robin Torrence, Rodney Harrison, Sarah Byrne, and Annie Clarke for their help and encouragement in the development of the chapter and in particular Robin Torrence for her encouragement and editorial skills.

References

Andrews, Tom (editor)
  2006 *Dè T'a Hoti Ts'eeda: We Live Securely by the Land*. Prince of Wales Northern Heritage Centre, Yellowknife.

Clarke, A. McFadyen, and Dale Idiens
  1974 *The Athapaskans: Strangers of the North*. National Museum of Man, Ottawa.

Clifford, James
  1997 *Routes: Travel and Translation in the Late Twentieth Century*. Harvard University Press, Cambridge.

Flanagan, Thomas
  1985 The Sovereignty and Nationhood of Canadian Indians: A Comment on Boldt and Long. *Canadian Journal of Political Science* 18(2):367–374.

Gosden, Chris, and Chantal Knowles
  2001 *Collecting Colonialism: Material Culture and Change in Papua New Guinea*. Berg, Oxford.

Helm, June
  2000 *The People of Denedeh: Ethnohistory of the Indians of Canada's Northwest Territories*. University of Iowa Press, Iowa City.

Idiens, Dale
  1979 *A Catalogue of Northern Athapaskan Indian Artefacts in the Collections of the Royal Scottish Museum*. Royal Scottish Museum, Edinburgh.

Kerr, Robert
  1953 For the Royal Scottish Museum. *The Beaver* (June):32–35.

Legat, Allice
  2005 Traditional Knowledge. In *Trails of our Ancestors: Building a Nation*, edited by John B. Zoe, pp. 33–39. Tlicho Government, Behchoko.

Lindsay, Debra
  1993 *Science in the Subarctic: Trappers, Traders, and the Smithsonian Institution*. Smithsonian Institution Press, Washington, DC.

Magnusson, Magnus
  1989 Foreword. In *Wealth of a Nation: in the National Museums of Scotland*, edited by Jenni Calder, pp. 7–9. National Museums Scotland, Edinburgh.

McLean, Fiona
  1998 Museums and the Construction of National Identity: A Review. *International Journal of Heritage Studies* 3(4):244–252.
  2003 The National Museum of Scotland: A Symbol for a New Scotland? *Scottish Affairs* 45:111–127.

Phillips, Ruth B.
  2005 Re-placing Objects: Historical Practices for a Second Museum Age. *Canadian Historical Review* 86(1):83–110.

Ray, Arthur J.
  1974 *Indians in the Fur Trade: Their Role as Trappers, Hunters and Middlemen in the Lands Southwest of Hudson Bay, 1660–1870.* University of Toronto, Toronto.

Torrence, Robin
  2000 Just Another Trader? An Archaeological Perspective on European Barter with Admiralty Islanders, Papua New Guinea. In *The Archaeology of Difference: Negotiating Cross-Cultural Engagements in Oceania*, edited by Robin Torrence and Anne Clarke, pp. 104–141. Routledge, London.

Williams, Glyndwr
  1983 The Hudson's Bay Company and the Fur Trade: 1670–1870.*The Beaver* (Autumn):26–34.

Wilson, George
  1857 *Annual Report of the Director of the Industrial Museum of Scotland* 31 Jan 1857 (for 1856).

Zoe, John B. (editor)
  2005 *Trails of our Ancestors: Building a Nation.* Tlicho Government, Behchoko.

Chapter 11
Seats of Power and Iconographies of Identity in Ecuador

Colin McEwan and Maria-Isabel Silva

Abstract On the Pacific coast of Ecuador, the late precontact Manteño (800–1530 CE) culture is noted for its distinctive corpus of stone seats, stelae and other sculpture. The Manteño seats in particular have long played a key role in Ecuadorian iconographies of national identity in the face of successive waves of conquest and colonial influence – Inca, Spanish and North American. They feature variously on the sculptural frieze on the facade of the National Congress building in Quito and on wall murals in coastal cities such as Manta as an emblem of indigenous cultural achievement. This prominence reflects a charged history, including collecting practices that began with the removal and dispersal of the great majority of the seats from their sites of origin to public collections in Ecuador and abroad, and also into private hands. Their potency as vehicles of both local and national political and cultural agency was effectively diluted – a process that is now being reversed. Beginning in the 1980s, the archaeological excavation of seats in their original architectural contexts at the site of Agua Blanca involved a sustained engagement between professionals and campesinos (rural inhabitants). This in turn led to the adoption of the seat icon to express pride and identity locally and as a powerful symbol of endurance and resistance by national indigenous federations. More recently the conscious appropriation of the past has been extended by the newly elected government of President Rafael Correa, which has incorporated the seats into a reconfigured national political consciousness.

Manteño Stone Seats

From as early as the 4th millennium BC Ecuador's Pacific coast fostered a precocious formative cultural florescence. Subsequent cultural developments maintained an essentially independent trajectory up until the Inca incursions of the late fifteenth and early sixteenth century. Nevertheless, compared to Mexico and Peru, indigenous

C. McEwan (✉)
Department of Africa, Oceania and the Americas, The British Museum, London, UK
e-mail: cmcewan@thebritishmuseum.ac.uk

M.-I. Silva
Museum Centro Civico Ciudad Alfaro, Montecristi, Ecuador
e-mail: mi-silva@illinois.edu

S. Byrne et al. (eds.), *Unpacking the Collection*, One World Archaeology,
DOI 10.1007/978-1-4419-8222-3_11, © Springer Science+Business Media, LLC 2011

Ecuadorian achievements have struggled to find their due place in cultural histories of the Americas as well as in the popular imagination. It is not widely appreciated, for example, that the coastal Manteño Culture (800–1530 CE) successfully forged a powerful confederation of polities known as Señorios that controlled a long-distance maritime trade in sumptuary goods using seagoing balsa rafts. Among the populous coastal towns and inland settlements of this period, two hilltop ceremonial sites in southern Manabí, known respectively as Cerro Jaboncillo and Cerro de Hojas, were an important focus of religious life. Situated on adjacent plateaux, each about 600 m high, they served as the preeminent regional cult centre and the setting for an impressive corpus of stone sculpture comprising seats, stelae and diverse anthropomorphic and zoomorphic subjects.

In this chapter, we will first address the profound dislocation among indigenous societies brought about by the Spanish Conquest, followed centuries later by early collecting practices that entailed the removal of many cultural objects from their sites of origin. We then describe the role played by archaeologists more recently in reconstructing the ceremonial and political settings in which Manteño seats were once used and their significance as indices of indigenous social hierarchy and religious power. We conclude by tracing the reappropriation of the seats by contemporary communities and national politicians alike, as potent symbols of indigenous cultural achievement and prestige.

Conquest, Collapse and the Early History of Collecting

Epidemic diseases introduced by first European contact had a devastating impact on native populations, resulting in the rapid demise of Manteño ports and towns. In 1585, the new Spanish provincial capital of Portoviejo was founded, and the collapse of indigenous social and political institutions was further hastened by forced resettlement implemented in the seventeenth century. By this time most indigenous towns lay abandoned and the hilltop ceremonial centres had long since fallen into disuse. Today little survives in the way of extant ruins to indicate the location, size and layout of the native towns and villages. Modern settlements have developed on, or adjacent to, some of the largest archaeological sites such as Jocay near Manta. As these sites were overrun by urban expansion, mounds have been levelled, terraces destroyed and the pre-Columbian wall foundations frequently 'quarried' for construction materials.

The early colonial accounts make scant specific mention of Manteño stone seats, which is strange considering the number of archaeological examples known to exist. From the mid-nineteenth century onwards the seats began to figure prominently among the archaeological relics and curios acquired in Ecuador by travellers and antiquarians. As readily visible portable objects they became sought-after curiosities – a process best described as 'trophy' collecting. Occasionally a specimen would be brought in to Manta from the hinterlands of Manabí to be gifted or sold to passing merchant seamen and passengers. In ones and twos the seats found their way

Fig. 11.1 Manteño stone seat with crouching human figure reported to have come from Cerro de Hojas, Manabí, and accessioned in 1861 (Am1861,0909.1) (By kind permission of the trustees of the British Museum)

into collections in Ecuador and abroad, including those in major museums in Paris, Vienna, Berlin, Copenhagen, London, Madrid, New York and Chicago as well as smaller regional museums (Fig. 11.1).

Speculation as to their origin and function has ranged from the serious to the fanciful. The first published account of their existence in 1858 is described as follows:

> Two leagues north of Montecristi there are some hills, such as the Cerro de Hojas; this is a low mountain with a flat summit; in this plain there is a circle of seats of stone, no less than thirty in number, each one is a sphinx, above which is the seat with two arms, all of stone well worked, and of a single piece which may be transported (Villavicencio 1858: 101).

This account of the alleged discovery of a circle of seats found on top of the hills gained currency over the years and was further embellished with the claim that a stone table also originally stood in the centre of the circle.

In the early 1880s, the French traveller Wiener visited Manabí noting that

> there are some other broken chairs, four of which could be easily repaired, to be found on a hill eleven leagues and a half northeast of the small port of Manta (Wiener 1880: 178).

A decade later the Ecuadorean historian González Suárez reports that:

> these seats are found in the Cerro de Hojas, placed in a semi-circle, in each one of the platforms on the hill. This comprises a group of broken hills, and on the summit of each one of these were a number of these seats placed around with symmetry (González Suárez 1890–1903: 256).

In the early 1900s, the George G. Heye Foundation (New York) began sponsoring archaeological collecting expeditions to selected regions of the Americas. In 1906, 1907, and again in 1908, Marshall H. Saville, then Loubat Professor of American Archaeology at Columbia University, led a series of exploratory trips to the coastal provinces of Esmeraldas, Manabí and Guayas, Ecuador. His horseback treks took him down long stretches of the coastline with occasional forays inland. On his first visit to Manta in 1906 he observed Manteño stone sculptures that had been brought in from the hills. He returned in 1907 equipped to excavate and explore the other hilltops from which the sculptures were said to have come.

Writing at the conclusion of his first field season, Saville noted the following:

> Careful examination was made of the summit of Cerro de Hojas, and it will be remembered that, in the description of the ruins on the hill mention is made of the numerous house-sites locally known as *corrales* which are found in great numbers. It was in the rooms of these houses that the stone seats were found; and in no case were they observed occupying any regular order, or placed in any way which would indicate their having been around stone tables or in a circle. In fact no large stone slabs are found in any of the ruins, with the exception of small bas-reliefs (i.e. stelae), to be described later. In some rooms only one seat was found, in others two; and sometimes three, four or even five have been discovered in a single house. So far as the Cerro de Hojas is concerned, we must conclude that the story of the ceremonial placing of these seats is a myth (Saville 1907: 24).

Saville recorded a clear association between the seats and the buildings of different sizes that housed them, but the fact that he could detect no 'regular order' is hardly surprising. As portable, highly visible objects, the best intact examples were probably among the first to be removed and would have left no trace of where they once stood. Saville does, however, provide much useful information about the seats and other sculptures that he observed in situ. He then arranged for a substantial number of the seats and other stone sculptures to be removed from Cerro Jaboncillo and adjacent hilltops and shipped back to the Heye Foundation New York (now incorporated into the National Museum of the American Indian, Smithsonian Institution).

The Distribution of Seats at Cerro Jaboncillo

The exceptional concentration of stone sculpture recorded by Saville at Cerro Jaboncillo underlines the preeminence of this site within Manteño culture and its distinctive ceremonial character. Using information extracted from Saville's two-volume publication *Antiquities of Manabí*, together with his unpublished field notes now held in Tulane University Library, it has been possible to reconstruct the location of the seats in something approximating their original topographic and architectural contexts. This is complemented by an analysis of the stelae iconography that helps explain why this hilltop site was revered and its enduring viability and elaboration as a ceremonial centre (McEwan 2004: 341–425; 2011).

Altogether Saville recorded several dozen stone seats in association with some sixteen structures and mounds on and around Cerro Jaboncillo. He observed that the seats sculpted in stone found on Cerro Jaboncillo fall into 'two great classes': one bearing a human figure crouching under the 'U' of the arms of the seat and another with a crouched feline depicted in the same position. The seats were found within, or close to, structures on the valley floor, along the ridge crests of the main spurs and in the architectural complexes on the summit plateau:

> During the summer of 1907, while the work of clearing the *corrales*, and excavating the two large mounds on Cerro Jaboncillo, was being carried on, we visited nearly all the *corrales* on the hill, carefully noting the number and position of seats, and fragments of seats, to determine, if possible, whether there was any fixed arrangements or order of placing them in the *corrales* (Saville 1910: 88).

Despite Saville's claims, precise attributions are not always given for seats discovered or acquired elsewhere on Cerro Jaboncillo, or from other sites. The number and distribution of seats he reports are necessarily incomplete, since an unknown number were spirited away before he began his fieldwork. He included photos of a few structures showing the seats that the expedition came across amidst the undergrowth in the course of working their way up the northern arm of Cerro Jaboncillo towards the summit plateau. Many structures harboured only broken fragments, but there is one where twelve seats remained in place. The main concentrations of seats were found among the three groups of structures on the summit plateau: the 'northern' group, 'mound' group and 'southern' group, respectively:

> There was no definite arrangement, so far as we could determine, and the same holds true of the other undisturbed *corrales*. Where a large number of seats were grouped in a single *corral*, undoubtedly there may have been originally some orderly arrangement around the sides, or even in a circle, but there is no way to verify this presumption at the present time. The two large mounds had formerly a considerable number of seats on their summits, but the greater number have been removed, and we found only the fragments of perhaps a dozen medium-sized seats lying scattered around the mounds. Here there was probably some arrangement in relation to the columns and other sculptures. Seats, bas-reliefs, columns, human figures, and other sculptures are found in the same *corrales,* and must have been placed in some regular order in relation to each other (Saville 1910: 89).

Nearly a century later, Saville's unpublished field notes provided the basis for reconstructing the distribution of the seats among the different architectural complexes (McEwan 2004: 221–224, 229–233, 310–315, 324; McEwan and Delgado 2008). In the meantime, the Manteño seats began to occupy an increasingly prominent role in Ecuadorian public iconographies of identity.

Seats as Symbols

Initially it appeared to Saville that the seats were restricted to a closely circumscribed area within a twenty-mile radius of Cerro Jaboncillo and Cerro de Hojas (Saville 1907: 23). This has now been expanded by modern archaeological fieldwork to embrace most of southern Manabí province and coincides with Manteño territory as indicated by early ethnohistoric accounts and the archaeological presence of Manteño pottery. Together this evidence points to an integrated polity that played an influential role far beyond the territory under its direct control (McEwan 2004: 97–104, 132–134). The Manteño were renowned seafarers and their coastal ports and anchorages such as Jocay located towards the northern limits of their territory, and Sercapez and Salango at the southern extremity, lay at the hub of a far-reaching long-distance maritime trade network that employed large balsa rafts with considerable navigational expertise (Marcos 1977–1978). In a well-known account Pizarro's pilot Bartolome Ruiz made a careful inventory and description of the valued sumptuary goods aboard a raft that the Spaniards encountered as they approached the coast of Ecuador from the north. This trade swiftly disintegrated in the early sixteenth century as a consequence of the disruption and dislocation brought about by European contact. Apart from their immediate interest in whatever gold they could lay their hands on, other materials, such as the prized red *Spondylus princeps* in the form of *chaquira* (shell beads) that fuelled Andean trade and exchange, held little more than curiosity value for the arriving foreigners.

Some coastal products gradually found a market in the international mercantile economy, and in the course of the nineteenth century, crops such as *tagua* (popularly known as 'ivory nut') became a major export. In parallel with this, the history of informal collecting practices, briefly described above, resulted in the removal and dispersal of the great majority of the seats from their sites of origin. They were delivered to collections abroad and also to the anthropological museums of the Central Bank in both Quito and Guayaquil as well as into private hands. This had ambivalent consequences. On the one hand, the process of sundering the connection between object and place effectively diluted the seats' potency as vehicles of political and cultural agency in Ecuador. A few have been on public display, but the majority were consigned to museum storerooms and have languished out of sight for decades. On the other hand the publication of the seats and stelae in Saville's substantial volumes amply illustrated with photographs and line drawings, gained them a newfound visibility within the international archaeological community. They have since become a standard point of reference for all synthesising treatments of both Ecuadorian prehistory and South American archaeology in general, which all draw upon Saville's original illustrations (Meggers 1966; Willey 1971).

Among the local population in and around Manta an awareness of the prominent hilltops and their past associations has always existed. This was tacitly recognised by the location of the early colonial church at the foot of Cerro Montecristi and the positioning of a large stone seat brought down from Cerro Jaboncillo, which for many years occupied pride of place in the small park in the public plaza in the centre of Montecristi (Fig. 11.2). Today the town is best known for the manufacture of 'Panama' hats and fosters a network of long-distance relationships and annual festivals, which draw upon and preserve discernable pre-Columbian elements. These echo the kind of annual pilgrimages that once focused on the hilltop sites.

The Manteño seats gradually began to feature in public iconography deployed as symbols of indigenous Ecuadorian cultural achievement. Many decades after Saville's expeditions, they are depicted in the sculptural frieze on the facade of the National Congress building in Quito created in the 1950s (Fig. 11.3). The frieze portrays a coastal Manteño 'lord' with a conspicuous stone seat used as a prominent visual device to signal his status and authority. He and his entourage are garbed in flowing robes that the sculptor has rendered in a 'neo-classical' style. They carry one style of 'axe' and confront an Inca 'lord' coming towards them bearing a different style of distinctive star-shaped Inca 'battle-axe'. A central figure witnesses

Fig. 11.2 Manteño stone seat
with crouching human figure
which probably came from
Cerro Jaboncillo, Manabí,
and stood for many years in
the plaza at Montecristi
(Photo by Colin McEwan)

and mediates the exchange, the inference being that this was more in the nature of a
'fraternal' greeting rather than 'conquest' and submission.

By the 1960s a modern era of archaeological investigations had begun at the
early formative site of Valdivia, gaining international visibility for Ecuador as the
hearth of one of the earliest ceramic traditions in the Americas (Estrada 1957a, b;
Evans and Meggers 1965). Later during the 1970s, the first systematic archaeological field surveys were undertaken on the Santa Elena Peninsula. Around this time in
coastal cities such as Manta, Manteño seats appear prominently in murals painted
on the walls of public buildings extolling Ecuador's pre-Hispanic cultural achievements. Mural art owes its popularity as a medium for interpreting and representing
political history in Latin America to the Mexican muralists such as Diego Rivera
working in the 1930s. Political mural art subsequently experienced a resurgence in
Central America (especially Nicaragua) in the 1980s, and this undoubtedly stimulated the creation of Ecuadorian murals created both around that time and in recent
years (Fig. 11.4). These reflected a growing imperative to fashion a new narrative
of national identity that acknowledged not only Ecuador's pre-Columbian past but
also recognised its rich ethnic diversity. In the 1980s, the archaeological surveys
were extended to encompass much of what was once the territory of the Señorío of

Fig. 11.3 Sculpted frieze on the facade of the National Congress building in Quito, Ecuador, showing Manteño seat with local lords and warriors 'greeting' an Inca lord (Photo by Maria-Isabel Silva)

Fig. 11.4 Contemporary wall mural in Manta, coastal Ecuador, showing the recreation of a Manteño scene featuring stone seats (Photo by Maria-Isabel Silva)

Salangome in southern Manabí, where the remains of a major Manteño settlement with seat fragments still visible among the ruins were located close to Comuna Agua Blanca (McEwan 2004).

Archaeology and Community at Agua Blanca – Using the Past to Forge the Future

The archaeological site of Agua Blanca is located in the Buenavista Valley about eight kilometres inland at the heart of the *Parque Nacional Machalilla*. In pre-Columbian times, this was an important route connecting inland settlements such as Jipijapa (originally, Xipijapa) via Joa, Julcuy, with those of the Pacific coast. At the neck of the valley lie the ruins of a very large Manteño (800–1530 CE) settlement that takes its modern name from the nearby community of Agua Blanca. Around 500 years ago, this site was the nexus of an alliance of four coastal towns collectively referred to by the Spanish chroniclers as the Señorio of Salongome. In fact, the ruins seems likely to have been those of Salangome itself, the *pueblo principal* (leading town) described in the ethnohistoric accounts as governing the Señorio and a key political and religious centre controlling the southern approaches to Manteño territory (Silva 1983, 1984, 1985). The stone wall foundations of several hundred structures are still visible today scattered across an area of some four square kilometres. The principal architectural complexes reveal a carefully ordered hierarchy of public and residential structures serving a variety of functions. They range from large public buildings up to fifty metres long and twelve metres wide, down to smaller standard domestic dwellings. Comuna Agua Blanca itself lies directly on top of one *barrio* (outlying residential sector) of the archaeological site, and the Manteño wall foundations that underlie the village are clearly visible in places. Sporadic finds of Inca pottery are consistent with the accounts recorded by the Spanish chroniclers of an imperial presence on the coastal mainland complementing the Inca burials that have been found on Isla de La Plata, twenty-five kilometres offshore (McEwan and Silva 1989, 2000; McEwan and van de Guchte 1992).

When the archaeological survey of the Buenavista drainage began in 1978, Agua Blanca was a village of about 50 families organised politically with an elected village president and committee. People lived principally from felling timber for construction, making and selling charcoal, herding goats and cattle plus some hunting. Upon the creation of the National Park in 1979, most of these activities were banned; however, no practical alternatives were offered, resulting in continuous friction between the park authorities and the Comuna. Throughout the recent history of archaeological investigations, Comuna Agua Blanca has played a key role. From its inception, the project employed people in the comuna who gained excavation skills and experience in archaeological survey and topographic mapping, as well as in post-excavation processing of finds (Fig. 11.5). As the project developed, all the main strategic decisions were made after consultation and discussion between the archaeological team and the village committee. In the course of excavations in the late 1980s, many fragments of broken Manteño seats were found both in their original architectural contexts under the debris of collapsed walls (Figs. 11.6 and 11.7) and on the surface amidst the ruins of other outlying structures. These finds represented a vital step in restoring the link between object and setting that enabled us to address where the seats were placed within the overall settlement plan and what they can tell us about Manteño social organisation.

The accidental discovery in 1985 of an intact Manteño stone seat at Agua Blanca galvanised everyone's thinking about the possibility of an archaeological display in the comuna. The seat was initially sold by the finder to a local merchant who, having bought it, then realised that everyone in Agua Blanca was united in demanding that it be restored to its rightful place in the community. He subsequently returned the seat voluntarily and without being recompensed. This pivotal moment provided

Fig. 11.5 Author
Maria-Isabel Silva instructing
the archaeological team at
Agua Blanca in
archaeological excavation
techniques (Photo by Colin
McEwan)

the impetus for securing funding to support the creation of a small Casa Comunal (village hall) display and served as a catalyst by engaging villagers' awareness of the significance of cultural resources for practical ends (see McEwan et al. 2007 for a fuller account; see also Ballesteros 2009 for a broader ethnography of Agua Blanca situating the archaeological project within the life of the community). It stimulated donations of artefacts for display and led to using local labour to create a visitor path around the archaeological site, making it far more accessible. Members of the archaeological team visited other sites and museums, and talks were given in the village hall by visiting archaeologists and others. The archaeological project also helped find support for alternative subsistence activities, including irrigation for family horticultural plots, a tree nursery and a pig project, and one or two villagers found employment as park rangers.

By 1988 plans were made to create a full-fledged site museum, envisaged as a place where visitors could rest before and after visiting the site and learn more about the objects and their cultural context. A museum designer was asked to develop ideas for a building with the active participation of the community. Financial support was sought from the Community Development programme run by the State Oil Corporation (CEPE), which at that time was preparing to lay a pipeline across the valley. Together we decided to promote the use of traditional materials and design, which are more practically and aesthetically suited to the local environment. Tagua

Fig. 11.6 General view of the excavated wall foundations of a Manteño structure at the site of Agua Blanca with the remains of stone seats in situ along one wall and Comuna Agua Blanca in the background (Photo by Colin McEwan)

Fig. 11.7 Close-up of a stone seat in situ at the site of Agua Blanca with the excavated wall foundations of a Manteño structure behind (Photo by Colin McEwan)

palm thatch was used for the roof and the technique of applying 'quincha' (daub) employed to surface the split-bamboo lime-washed walls. Funds were administered by the village president. The bulk of the work was carried out by carpenters from the village and only louvered windows, glass for showcases and photographic work were sourced from outside. The finished building is well suited to assure comfort in the tropical climate, standing on 'stilts' with a steep roof pitch for rain runoff, light and ventilation grills, open porch and external staircases. The entrance porch with a small shop accommodates both local needs and those of visitors. The building was quickly baptised the 'Centro Cultural' and also provided office, storage and accommodation for the archaeological project. The exhibition, which consists of simple glass cube showcases with both excavated and donated artefacts, is organised thematically. It includes an interactive touch table and establishes clear visual links with life in the community today. The seat was adopted as a symbol to represent community pride and identity. This is reinforced by specially made T-shirts bearing the logo 'Rescuing what is ours' with images of natural and cultural heritage. The Casa Cultural opening celebration was timed to coincide with the annual '*encuentro cultural*' (cultural festival) in 1990 in which members of communities from all over Ecuador come for 2 days of talks, music, guided tours of the site, eating and drinking (Fig. 11.8) (Silva and McEwan 1989, 2000; McEwan and Silva 1993; McEwan et al. 1994).

Fig. 11.8 The opening celebrations for the inauguration of the Centro Cultural and Site Museum at Agua Blanca in 1990 (Photo by Colin McEwan)

Subsequent Experience

The creation of the Casa Cultural at Agua Blanca was a signal step in transforming the *Comuna's* fortunes. The number of visitors to the archaeological site rapidly increased along with income from the sale of food, drink, and handcraft goods as well as through guiding, providing accommodation and renting out trail horses. Soon after the site museum and cultural centre opened, a bar and café was built nearby, and later a craft centre was created next to the museum. The annual cultural encounters continued as *Dia de la Raza,* which roughly translates as *Day of Indigenous Pride,* and represents a 'grass roots' alternative to the conventional National Columbus Day holiday on October 12, originally conceived to celebrate the Spanish arrival in the Americas.

In 2005 the cultural centre was refurbished with support from the British Museum, enabling new showcases to be built with bilingual captions and lighting. By 2006, 70% of households in the *Comuna* were engaged to a greater or lesser extent in 'Community Tourism,' which provided an estimated 25% of overall income. In the same year 25 women made and sold craft products. The Archaeology Committee that manages the maintenance and guiding around the site comprised 29 men. In 2008, Comuna Agua Blanca was awarded the inaugural Hernan Crespo Toral prize for the 'conservation, protection, development and dissemination of Ecuadorian heritage.'

All these achievements are positive manifestations of the village's ability to preserve and manage its cultural resources and have increased its confidence and commitment to future improvements. The villagers' newfound expertise is recognised by the National Park administration, which now understands that the human population within the park can be a positive rather than a negative asset. Along with the alternative economic activities, vegetation and bird life are recovering and the Park is now building structures with local materials.

Collectively much has been learned from these experiences: it is vital to work from needs expressed by the community rather than impose unwanted projects; people knowledgeable and proud of their past are less likely to part with objects that represent it; the long-term advantages of preserving and managing cultural resources outweigh short-term gains made by *huaqueros'* (looters) sales; community engagement can make an essential and very positive contribution to heritage management and conservation projects. This modest experience has encouraged the local community to develop responsible attitudes to the conservation of their cultural resources and has contributed to substantial improvements in village life. Moreover the Encuentros Culturales (cultural festivals) have helped forge intercultural ties between indigenous peoples from the highlands and the coast.

Reconstituting Identity – Symbols of Cultural Identity and Resistance

The central symbol chosen for Ecuador's national flag is the distinctive snowcapped profile of Mount Chimborazo – an extinct volcano south of Quito whose massive bulk broods over the surrounding landscape. Chimborazo, for a time thought to be the highest peak in the world, had been projected into international visibility and fame through the illustrated accounts of the travels made by the Prussian naturalist Alexander von Humboldt. Above the mountain on the flag perches a condor; however, any reference to Ecuador's indigenous cultural heritage is conspicuously absent. In truth, few appropriate cultural symbols exist. Most of the best-known archaeological sites in the highlands such as Ingapirca or Rumicucho were built by the Incas. The pre-Inca *tolas* at Cochasqui were eventually accorded due recognition as a manifestation of indigenous cultural prowess (Benavides 2004). The Museos of the Banco Central del Ecuador also adopted a pre-Columbian gold 'sun mask' as an iconic symbol, notwithstanding the confusion generated by the divergent claims concerning its cultural attribution.

The evolving process described in this chapter has proven instrumental in investing the Manteño seats with renewed significance. An indispensable part of the process of recovering meaning has been to restore the link between the objects, their original setting and the people who live there today (c.f. Lumbreras 1974). Seat imagery has been appropriated anew by local communities seeking to define their own vision, values and realities and also adopted by national indigenous federations as a symbol of resurgent indigenous identity and resistance in the face of successive waves of colonisation – Inca, Spanish and North American.

Additional chapters in the individual and collective object histories of the seats continue to unfold. This involves not only the original seats themselves but also a whole new tradition of producing sculpted facsimiles. Both are now effectively being deployed as 'chess-pieces' in a reconfigured national iconography revolving around the figure of the liberal commander and later president, General Eloy Alfaro Delgado. In the late nineteenth century, he led opposition to the entrenched power of church and state, and by the late twentieth century, had become an inspirational figure for the Ecuadorian 'left'. In 2005, a popular poll declared Alfaro to be the most illustrious Ecuadorian of all times. A new mausoleum and civic centre was inaugurated in November 2007 in his birthplace Montecristi. The original stone seat that had occupied pride of place for many years in the central plaza of the town was moved to the Centro Civico Ciudad Alfaro and placed by the mausoleum sarcophagus and statue along with a dozen modern replicas (Fig. 11.9). In the new constitution of 2008, Ecuador was declared a plurinational state, and the following year Cerro de Hojas and Cerro Jaboncillo were officially recognised by President Rafael Correa as 'Patrimonio Nacional' (National Cultural Heritage Sites) and funds allocated for research and development of these sites.

Concluding Remarks

In this chapter, we have described how 'packing' and 'unpacking' the collection has been shaped by paradigmatic shifts in perceptions, attitudes and practices towards the past and to archaeological objects. The initial phase of collecting was a semi-casual, haphazard pursuit leading to the dispersal of Manteño seats to diverse collections in Ecuador and abroad. The subsequent application of scientific method in the early twentieth century witnessed the systematic recording of contextual information but was also used to justify the wholesale removal of objects to foreign institutions. By the end of the century a new community-based approach

Fig. 11.9 The Mausoleum and Civic Centre dedicated to General Eloy Alfaro Delgado in Montecristi encircled by replica stone seats (Photo by Maria-Isabel Silva)

to archaeological investigation began to be implemented. This, in turn, has combined archival and collections research with a discerning field strategy adapted to local circumstances and actively seeking to reaffirm the connection between object, people and place. This has been instrumental in effecting the seats' metamorphosis from abstract icons of a remote past to potent signifiers of social agency and empowerment.

Acknowledgements   Comuna Agua Blanca; Museo Antropológico del Banco Central del Ecuador (Guayaquil); Instituto Nacional de Patrimonio Cultural, Ecuador; Corporación Estatal Petrolífera Ecuatoriano; Servicio Forestal Nacional; Parque Nacional Machalilla; Museo Arqueológico del Banco del Pacífico; Programa de Antropología para el Ecuador; Fundacion Natura; University of Illinois; UCL Institute of Archaeology; The British Council; The British Museum.

References

Ballesteros, Esteban Ruiz
    2009 *Agua Blanca – Comunidad y turismo en el Pacífico ecuatorial.* Ediciones Abya-Yala. Quito, Ecuador

Benavides, Oswaldo Hugo
    2004 *Making Ecuadorian Histories: Four Centuries of Defining Power.* University of Texas Press, Austin.

Estrada, Emilio
    1957a *Prehistoria de Manabi.* Publicacion del Museo V.E. Estrada, 2, Guayaquil.
    1957b *Arqueologia de Manabi Central.* Publicacion del Museo V.E. Estrada, 7, Guayaquil.

Evans, Clifford, and Betty J. Meggers
  1965 *Early Formative Period of Coastal Ecuador: The Valdivia and Machalilla Phases.* Smithsonian Contributions to Anthropology 1. Smithsonian Institute, Washington, DC.

González Suárez, Federico
  1890–1903 *Historia General de la Republica del Ecuador.* Imprenta del Clero, Quito.

Lumbreras, Luis Guillermo
  1974 *La Arqueologia Como Ciencia Social.* Ediciones Histar, Lima.

Marcos, Jorge G.
  1977–1978 Cruising to Acapulco and back with the thorny oyster set. *Journal of the Steward Anthropological Society* 9 (1–2): 99–132. University of Illinois, Urbana.

McEwan, Colin
  2004 *And the Sun Sits in His Seat: Creating Social Order in Andean Culture.* Unpublished PhD Dissertation. University of Illinois, Urbana.
  2011 On Being and Becoming: Ruminations on the Genesis, Evolution and Maintenance of the Cerro Jaboncillo Ceremonial Center, Ecuador. In *Enduring Motives: Religious Traditions of the Americas*, edited by L. Sundstrom and Warren de Boer. University of Alabama Press, Tuscaloosa.

McEwan, Colin, Chris Hudson, and Maria-Isabel Silva
  1994 Archaeology and Community: A Village Cultural Center and Museum in Agua Blanca, Ecuador. *Practicing Anthropology* 16 (1): 3–7. (A condensed version of this article appeared in *Museum (UNESCO)* 178 (45): 42–45).

McEwan, Colin, and Maria-Isabel Silva
  1989 Que fueron a hacer los Incas en la costa central del Ecuador? In *Relaciones Interculturales en el Área Ecuatorial del Pácifico durante la Época Precolombina*, edited by J. F. Bouchard and M. Guinea, pp. 83–95. British Archaeological Reports International Series No. 503. (Reprinted in: Compendio de Investigacions en el Parque Nacional Machalilla, 2000).
  1993 Arqueología y Comunidad: Un Centro Cultural y Museo en la Comuna de Agua Blanca, Ecuador Case Study. In *Interpretación ambiental: Una Guida Practica para Gente con Grandes Ideas y Presupuestos Pequeños*, edited by S. H. Ham, pp. 228–235. Fulcrum Publishing, Colorado.
  2000 La presencia Inca en la costa central de Ecuador y en la Isla de la Plata. In *Compendio de Investigaciones en el Parque Nacional Machalilla*, edited by M. Iturralde and C. Josse, pp. 66–73. Corporación CDC and Fundacion Natura, Quito, Ecuador.

McEwan, Colin, and Florencio Delgado-Espinoza,
  2008 The Late Pre-Hispanic Polities of Coastal Ecuador. In *The Handbook of South Amercian Archaeology*, edited by Helaine Silverman and William H. Isbell, p. 1xx. Springer, New York, NY.

McEwan, Colin, Maria-Isabel Silva, and Chris Hudson
  2007 The Genesis of the Community Site Museum at Agua Blanca. In *Ecuador in Archaeological Site Museums in Latin America*, edited by Helaine Silverman, pp. 187–214. University of Florida Press, Gainesville.

McEwan, Colin, and Marten van de Guchte
  1992 Ancestral Time and Sacred Space in Inca State Ritual. In *The Ancient Americas: Art from Sacred Landscapes*, edited by R. F. Townsend and E. P. Benson, pp. 359–371. The Art Institute of Chicago, Chicago, IL.

Meggers, Betty J.
  1966 *Ecuador.* Thames and Hudson, London.

Saville, Marshall H.
   1907 *The Antiquities of Manabi, Ecuador. Preliminary Report.* Heye Foundation Contributions
   to South American Archaeology, Vol. 1. Irving Press, New York, NY.
   1910 *The Antiquities of Manabi, Ecuador. Final Report.* Heye Foundation Contributions to
   South American Archaeology, Vol. 2. Irving Press, New York, NY.

Silva, Maria-Isabel
   1983 *Toponymic Reconstruction as a Basis for Analysing Social, Economic and Political
   Relationships Among Contact Period Settlements on the Central Coast of Ecuador.* Paper
   Presented at the XI Annual Midwest Conference on Andean and Amazonian Archaeology
   and Ethnohistory, Bloomington.
   1984 *Pescadores y Agricultures de la Costa Central del Ecuador: Un Modelo Socio-economico
   de Asentamientos Precolombinos.* Unpublished MA Thesis. University of Illinois at Urbana-
   Champaign.
   1985 *Dual Division Quadripatition and Hierarchical Organization Among the Manteno
   Polities of late Pre-Columbian Coastal Ecuador.* Paper Presented at the International
   Congress of Americanists, Bogota, July 1985.

Silva, Maria-Isabel, and Colin McEwan
   1989 Machalilla: El Camino de la Integración. *Colibrí*, Revista de la Fundación Natura. Año II
   No. 5, pp. 71–75. Quito, Ecuador.
   2000 Arqueologia y comunidad en el Parque Nacional Machalilla: breve historia y reflexiones.
   In *Compendio de Investigaciones en el Parque Nacional Machalilla*, edited by M. Iturralde
   and C. Josse, pp. 66–74. Corporacion CDC and Fundacion Natura, Quito, Ecuador.

Villavicencio, Manuel
   1858 *Geografia de la Republica del Ecuador.* R. Craighead, New York, NY.

Wiener, Charles
   1880 *Pérou et Bolivie. Récit de voyage suivi d'études archéologiques et ethnographiques.*
   Hachette, Paris.

Willey, Gordon
   1971 *An Introduction to American Archaeology, Vol 2: South America.* Prentice-Hall,
   Englewood Cliffs, NJ.

Part V
Individual Collectors, Objects and 'Types'

Chapter 12
Hedley Takes a Holiday: Collections from Kanak People in the Australian Museum

Jude Philp

Abstract The Australian Museum holds over 1,000 cultural objects from New Caledonia. A quarter of the collection was obtained by a Museum zoologist, Charles Hedley, who visited La Grande Terre on his holidays late in 1897. He collected ethnographic and zoological specimens and organized an exchange of objects with the then Colonial Museum of Noumea. This chapter investigates the historical background to this exchange and the circumstances under which heritage and zoology were given equivalent values and objects and specimens literally swapped.

Introduction

This chapter is concerned with material culture acquired in New Caledonia at the end of the nineteenth century. I will begin by investigating the museum processes that were involved in assembling this Kanak material at the Australian Museum (AM), namely, exchange and field collection. Both kinds of collection relied upon extensive international networks, both formal (between institutions) and informal (between people). I share with the other contributors to this volume an expectation of the continued agency of both the Australian Museum and Kanak people in relation to these collections. That is, I do not see this material as a single stable artefact of the Museum (e.g., 'nineteenth century ethnographic collection', see also Kirshenblatt-Gimblett 1998), but rather these objects 'are alive, have their own 'histories' and 'continue to have agency in the present' (Byrne et al. Chapter 1; see also Geismar and Herle 2010: 40). The history explored here reveals the path of Kanak objects into the Australian Museum, largely drawn from museum documentation. I will first describe exchange as a distinctive and historical museum practice and then discuss the role of the field collector, Charles Hedley, in obtaining Kanak material for the Australian Museum. As described by Bronwyn Douglas for texts (Douglas 1998: 162), I argue that objects 'need creative, not literal reading, across their grain, with precise attention to. . . . tropes, nuances, inflections, single instances, asides, trifles, silences, ambivalences, and discrepancies between author's

J. Philp (✉)
Macleay Museum, University of Sydney, NSW, Australia
e-mail: jude.philp@sydney.edu.au

S. Byrne et al. (eds.), *Unpacking the Collection*, One World Archaeology,
DOI 10.1007/978-1-4419-8222-3_12, © Springer Science+Business Media, LLC 2011

[or viewer's] expectations and perverse experience. Their [i.e. texts] representations of past indigenous worlds are always narrow and deformed, but in some cases . . . they are virtually all there is.' Douglas directs our enquiry towards the intersection between two distinctive historical paths: the Kanak people and the museum agent. This chapter is primarily concerned with understanding this intersection from the viewpoint of the Museum's agent. I conclude that further research is needed to understand how South Pacific islanders contributed to the networks that fed objects and specimens into nineteenth century museums.

In September/October of 1897, Charles Hedley, conchologist with the Australian Museum, took a holiday to New Caledonia. Much of the AM collection from New Caledonia results from this vacation. Few of the objects were physically collected by Hedley himself but rather came to the museum through a multitude of colonial relationships, both institutional and personal. One of the most interesting aspects of these social relationships, and a process through which the AM most effectively directed and extended its holdings, was exchange between museums (see also Wingfield Chapter 5). The exchange process is almost unmentioned in the histories of anthropology collections and museums, yet it was one of the principal mechanisms through which nineteenth century museums were able to meet their objective of representative selection and universal collection.

This process of exchange has its origins in the science of natural history for which the comparison of physical specimens is a key method of taxonomic research. Institutions and individuals were able to extend the range of material in their collections through capitalising on their networks and swapping or exchanging specimens within the network. In his article on exchange at Museum Victoria, Gareth Knapman (2009) emphasises the economic structure of exchange; my own focus has a greater emphasis on the social relations that made these exchange networks possible. This exchange mechanism, originally used for natural history specimens, was extended towards material culture in the nineteenth century when ethnography became a key discipline of the colonial and national museum.

This chapter deals largely with nineteenth century history, but its significance is entirely twenty-first century. The inner workings of museums, concentrating as they do on research, management and conservation of collections, are generally obscure to outsiders. Yet the questions of why an institution collected this or that, the relationships between collectors and the people from whom they collected, and the value of the information stored along with the objects themselves, are issues of interest and consequence to many people from producer communities as well as to social theorists.

The Exchange Industry

As a commonplace transaction between museums in the nineteenth century, exchanges were essential for the supply of adequate reference material for classification. Since the basic work of the institution was classification, cataloguing and display of collections along taxonomic lines, the exchange of 'duplicate' material was essential. For example, if a museum had 100 specimens of *Plebidonax deltoides* (pipi shells, a kind of bivalve) from a seashore location, five or ten could be maintained for the museum, and the other 95 used to exchange with museums that lacked the particular species or species variant. Having been brought back from far-flung places, the specimens were then sent out on other journeys. In this way, over the course of two centuries, birds, insects, mammals and marsupials sailed across the seas more than once.

From the 1800s museums had shifted away from the 'cabinet of curiosity' to systematic ordering and display. In France, the biologists Jean-Baptiste Lamarck (1744–1829) and Geoffrey Saint-Hilaire (1772–1844), among others, forged a plan for the comparative anthropology of people, customs and technologies (Stocking 1964: 135) by expanding the museum's classificatory role to human endeavours. Meanwhile in Britain during the 1850s, Augustus Lane-Fox (1827–1900) (later known as Pitt Rivers) amassed objects to depict his specific vision of human evolution through the objects people made and used (Haddon 1907: 220). This Pitt Rivers collection would become the most famous example of rampant collecting based on the comparative analysis of the technologies of the world's peoples. Few museums would achieve the global diversity of Pitt Rivers, but many anthropology museums aspired to obtain representative samples of objects from across the world, from particular regions or cultural groups. Added to the requirement for being comprehensive was a sense of urgency that collections had to be made before the changes brought by industrialisation and colonialism took full effect and the so-called 'primitive' societies ceased to exist (see Kuklick 1991). The twin efforts of taxonomy (which required diverse specimens for comparison) and cultural diversity drove the exchange industry in relation to the cultural or ethnographic objects of non-European cultures.

I use the term 'exchange industry' because in any given year in the nineteenth century the AM alone dealt with over thirty institutions and individuals; it acquired thousands of objects and specimens through exchange and sent out thousands in return. In years when specimens and objects were desired for exhibition at an International Exposition, most specimens thought suitable were 'written off' in the registers, as curators took the opportunity to see what was available to negotiate for exchange (Anthropology Registers, AM).

A summary of the incoming collections in Table 12.1, derived from the 1896 Curator's 'Report to the Trustees,' shows that around 20% of the ethnographic collections were acquired by exchange, much less for entomology, but rather more for molluscs, while in the bird department half of the year's collection was obtained in this way (AM Annual Report 1896–1897). There was no mineral curator at the time, so exchange was one of the few ways that this collection could be augmented. Increasing the size of the collection was only one benefit of the system; it could also be used to refine the collections by weeding out items thought to be overrepresented (called 'duplicates') or simply unwanted. The main challenge for curators was to keep a balance for the future between the desired objects and those that would need to be sent out. In any year it was important not to carry over too much exchange 'debt' while at the same time making sure that the collections exported

Table 12.1 The incoming and outgoing materials in the Australian Museum departments in 1896. The high collected total of ethnography is from Funafuti

Collection	Donated No	%	Purchase No	%	Exchange No	%	Collected No	%	Total No	%
Molluscs	396	62	9	1.5	195	31	35	5.5	634	4
Entomology	1381	10	5125	38	798	6	6326	46	13630	86
Birds	288	42	8	1	336	53	32	5	664	4
Minerals	165	41	6	1	176	44	55	13	402	3
Ethnography	151	28	49	9	116	21	233	46	549	3
Total	2380	15	5197	33	1621	10	6681	42	15879	100

Source: Australian Museum Cultural Collections documentation 1882–1920

were of sufficient quality to maintain a good exchange relationship with external organisations and individuals.

Exchanges were established principally with national and state institutions, occasionally with individuals, who were generally established and published collectors such as the Italian Enrico Giglioli, who exchanged on his own behalf and for his institution, Florence's Royal Zoological Museum. There were also the 'men on the ground' such as M.E. Thouveroy of Tahiti. In 1897, the AM received from him eleven South Seas butterfly specimens, representing six species valued at five shillings, and sent out ten Australian specimens representing seven species valued at five shillings (AM Archives 1897 Exchange letter book: 3/97). While the AM strove to obtain material to its advantage, on paper at least, and monetary values were accorded to each item in and out, each exchange was considered to be financially equal. In the best-case scenario, the exchange would be balanced, but if not, accounts were carried over. With some museums and individuals the AM carried debts and surpluses over decades until the desiderata could be located. In the 1897–1898 Annual Report to the Trustees, AM Curator Robert Etheridge (1846–1920) writes that 'A number of old exchanges were found to be unadjusted in favour of the Australian Museum – for instance, with the Tasmanian and British Museums and the Zoological Society of London. By your authority I took steps to reduce these, and am glad to say that the last-named body has responded with the most satisfactory results to us' (Etheridge 1897).

To manage the complexities of accounts, the AM maintained Exchange Letter Books that tracked the flow of specimens in and out among the large number of correspondents. Additional correspondence between the head curator and the scientific officers in charge of collections amply illustrates, in the AM case at least, the push and pull between the internal work of the museum in terms of maintaining collection material for research versus the need to have specimens of sufficient quality, or at the least quantity, for exchange.

To create equivalences in the exchanges of such a wide range of materials, a value had to be found for just about anything that could be considered of interest. In one particularly odd exchange Thomas Anderson-Stuart (1856–1920) of the University of Sydney wrote to the Trustees enquiring 'I understand that you have two hair balls that you do not care for. . .' The two balls (from a cow's stomach) and an Egyptian mummified hand were duly sent to Anderson-Stuart. An equivalent in value was found by Anderson-Stuart in a Solomon Islander ear ornament, castanets and tongs. The agreed value on both sides of the exchange was £1-1s (AM Archives 1898–1899 Exchange Letter Books: 1/98, 1/99).

As in this case, the specimens and objects usually went 'out' (as they termed it) with minimal information. For example, 'Australia' and 'Solomon' were the vague geographic references for either display or research. This is a curious inconsistency in museum processes. For while collectors were urged to maintain full and accurate records; and while collectors were urged to maintain full and accurate specimens compared along geographical lines, within their exchange actions they obscured such details. Consequently when dealing with exchanged material, museums today are left with a substantial number of items that lack an adequate provenance. Occasionally, however, one can follow the path of the exchange back to the original information, which at times can be quite detailed and even include names of producer, time of collection, village location or use (Philp 2004: 99). The pathway is usually quite explicit within each institution because the transactions were only possible through the maintenance of tight accounting systems, since exchanges could only work on a global scale through a coordinated network of trusted partners.

Making Relations

In this section I will provide a brief background to the partners involved in the exchange of Kanak cultural material: the Australian Museum and the Musée de Nouvelle Calédonie. In the eighteenth century specimens were exchanged, bought and sold by individuals who knew each other personally through their membership of specialist societies. These societies became adjuncts to the nineteenth century museum, which continued this tradition of trading with well-known associates (Naylor 2002: 496). In a broad way the practices of the Australian Museum can be understood as largely derived from the British world of the learned society, while the Noumea Museum in New Caledonia arose from the creation of the International Exposition (see below). Each institution is typical of a particular kind of trusted pathway through which objects and specimens were exchanged to their 'mother' countries. A subject for later study is the way that Britain and France relied on exchanges implemented though colonial museums and expositions to acquire material with minimal cost; here I will concentrate solely on the dealings between the AM and the Musée de Nouvelle Calédonie.

The AM was established in 1827 partly through the insistence of a man with superior links to most of London's natural history societies: Colonial Secretary to NSW Alexander Macleay. Macleay had been Secretary of the Linnean Society. He was a close friend and exchanged and purchased specimens with the most noted naturalists of his day (e.g., Stamford Raffles, Richard Owens, Nicholas Alyward Vigors, William Kirby). The AM was first known as the Sydney or Colonial

Museum, changing its name to the 'Australian Museum' in 1836. It was not until the collections moved to their permanent home in the new College Street building in the 1850s that it largely left behind its 'learned society' roots (see Strahan 1979: 2; Healy 1997: 81).

Just a few years later in the French penal colony of Nouvelle Calédonie, the French State established a small museum in Noumea (Musée de Nouvelle Calédonie 2010). Funds from France supported the acquisition of 'curiosités indigènes', along with natural history specimens, for the purpose of representing the colony in the World Fairs. In 1895, the collection was given a name – the Musée Colonial – public rooms were created and a specialist curator, Jules Bernier, was appointed (Musée de Nouvelle Calédonie 2010). Shortly afterwards, the AM and the Noumea Museum became exchange partners.

Each museum had its own 'set' of exchange partners, although it is unlikely that any museum could develop their collections purely through exchange. Apart from anything else, they needed to have sufficient material of quality to offer other partners. This was particularly the case for the AM following the catastrophic loss of almost all of its ethnographic collections on September 22, 1882, when the Sydney International Exposition building, where they were temporarily housed, burnt to the ground. The fire was of such intensity that the following day only ash remained (Proudfoot et al. 2000: xiv). To counter this devastating loss, large quantities of material were purchased to restock the collections. Consequently, the number of objects acquired would far exceed the modest 2000 lost. Fortunately, this was the heyday of the exploration of Papua New Guinea and of expanding trade empires, such as Burns, Philp & Co., when Sydney was seemingly awash with available materials (see Torrence and Clarke Chapter 2). Restocking appears to have been carried out opportunistically. From 1883 to the 1890s, the AM purchased around 3000 spears and arrows from Buka and Bougainville (many with over-weaving of orchid stem and other personal embellishments) in bulk lots of 100. Many of the objects acquired did not remain at the Museum but were used to fill up orders of exchange, some finding their way to the Noumea Museum (AM Anthropology Department Registers 1883–1920).

To properly understand how the exchange networks functioned, I will use two case studies: one concerning institutions with formal exchange relationships (the AM and the Noumea museum) and the other an individual (Charles Hedley). While institutions often established exchange relationships through correspondence, a greater focus on individual agents shows that profitable relationships were made when there was an intermediary known to both institutional parties. I will show how Hedley, as an agent in this movement of material culture, also shaped what was collected through his choices, previous experiences and friendships.

Charles Hedley (1862–1926)

Hedley's holiday to New Caledonia was important to the AM for it gave the institution the opportunity to expand its holdings from an underrepresented geographic area. In order to understand something of Hedley's methods of collecting and the ideas that informed his choices, it is necessary to understand something of his background. Charles Hedley was the son of Mary (née Bush) and Canon Thomas Hedley, a Fellow of Trinity College, Vicar of Masham and a man of independent means. Ill-health would determine Charles's professional life. After brief schooling in England (where he gained a prize for his shell collection), Hedley and family moved to the French Riviera, possibly as a seaside cure for his chronic asthma (Fairfax 1983). He migrated to the antipodes in 1881, first to New Zealand and then Queensland for '3 years daily toil ... with an American axe' (Hedley 1897a: 251). This work ended when he injured his arm to such an extent that farming was no longer possible. From farming he turned to conchology, first at Queensland Museum and then in 1891 at the AM where he would remain for the rest of his working life (Anderson 1936). Research in Queensland and British New Guinea established his reputation as a conchologist. At first his interest in the anatomy of molluscs revealed his French influences, but at the AM he soon became a rigorous taxonomist.

Throughout Hedley's professional life he seemingly never lost love of travel and exploration. The products of his fieldtrips show his interest in ethnography as well as that of natural history, topics normally combined in the meetings of the learned societies of Sydney to which he belonged, such as the Linnaean Society of NSW, the Ethnographic Society and Australasian Association for the Advancement of Science. At these meetings he would have heard about travel and cultural groups in the Pacific from a number of scientists and professional colleagues, as well as missionaries with an interest in ethnology, natural history and collecting, such as George Brown (whom he describes as 'his friend' (Hedley 1897a: 243)).

As well as learning from his society associates and AM colleagues, Hedley travelled and collected ethnographic objects from the Pacific area on several occasions. His trip to Funafuti as conchologist and ethnologist with the Royal Society expedition of 1896 is of greatest relevance here. Hedley spent over 2 months in the company of British and Australian scientists and crew in Funafuti. In his resulting publications one can glean some hints as to what would capture his interests in New Caledonia (Hedley 1896–1900). Hedley's published description of the ethnology of Funafuti owed a great deal to *Notes and Queries in Anthropology* (Read 1899: 178), the publication of the Royal Anthropological Institute that set out questions and instructions to collectors to ensure the 'right' information was recorded and the most desirable specimens for science were secured (see Urry 1972). From the 1874 edition he adopts appropriate forms of measuring people, uses the Royal Geographic Society orthography for language (vowels as in Italian, consonants as in English), and notes A.C. Haddon's concern with the 'dying out' of Oceanic peoples and the modifications of their customs (Hedley 1897a: 233). In short, he read carefully and thoroughly in order to equip himself with the tools of a nineteenth century ethnologist.

In his *General Account* for the Funafuti volumes, Hedley (1896) predominantly quotes verbatim slabs of other observers' texts along with third-party observations and information from 'natives'. One example is the quotation about the origins of a chiefly staff: 'A most decisive proof of their history [the people of the Ellice Group] was recently obtained by Dr G.A. Turner while visiting the missions of the group. He was shown, and he ultimately obtained, a spear or staff. . .' Hedley

(1896: 42) references the quotation to W. L. Ranken writing in the *Journal of the Anthropological Institute* in 1877. Turner's 'visit' was anytime between 1843, when he began as a missionary in Samoa, and 1862 when he retired (Tcherkézoff 2008: 11–2). 'Recently' is not relative to 1896, or to 1877, but some 30 or 40 years before.

A junior player in the ethnographic field, Hedley (1897a: 232) is both dismissive of European understanding as 'superficial' and accepting of European description. The *General Account* combines the words of 'natives' with those of armchair observers, missionaries, traders and sailors. Hedley establishes all information as 'fact' without much questioning of its validity. His greatest source of information, he writes, came from Mr James O'Brien, an Ellice Island resident of some 50 years, who acted for him as interpreter and ethnographer (Hedley 1896: 43, 46). O'Brien also had the questionable distinction of having destroyed the 'last temple of Funafuti' (Hedley 1896: 48). Another explanation for his dependence on prior accounts comes from a curiously off-hand comment. Hedley (1896: 42) writes that 'Funafuti is, however, a most unfavourable locality for studying the relations of the Ellice Islanders. About 30 years ago most of the adult population were kidnapped by a Peruvian slaver … The atoll has since received an immigrant population from various sources.' Hedley (1897a: 230) also draws parallels between Ellice Island customs and those from New Guinea and Aboriginal Queensland along with sweeps through various Polynesian islands. Nevertheless, he seems confident enough to author an ethnographic description, to collect the material culture of the islanders, and even to make some tentative analysis, in which he describes the peoples as Tokelau in type, bearing a general cultural similarity to Japan via Polynesia.

In contrast, in his descriptions of each kind of Funafuti object, Hedley is as rigorous and thorough as he is with his own specialist subject conchology. Every item is described, many are drawn, and there are minor observations about divergence (Fig. 12.1). Ever the naturalist, he also includes taxonomy of fishhooks, complete with genus and species (Hedley 1897a: 271). Having written up his description of Funafuti ethnology for publication, he leaves for holidays in September of 1897.

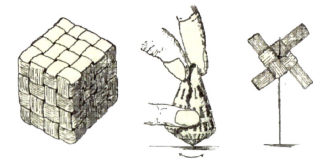

Fig. 12.1 One of Hedley's (1897: 304) typically fine drawings of Funafuti ethnologic objects. He collected similar toys in New Caledonia

La Grande Terre, Nouvelle Calédonie 1897

The place Hedley chose for his holiday was ideal for his work. It had the mystique of a country visited if only briefly by the British seaman James Cook. Since the environment and geography of the main island, La Grande Terre, was similar to the Queensland territory he knew well from Moreton Bay but had fauna and human culture that linked it to the islands of the Pacific, the island posed an interesting puzzle for ethnographers and natural historians, like himself, who were busily pursuing questions of origin. It was also a colony in a state of upheaval. In 1903, the missionary and ethnographer Maurice Leenhardt observed to his parents as he carefully noted the genealogy of one Kanak leader, Mindia of Néja of Houailou, 'We got down 7 or 8 generations, and you can clearly see all the descendants who perished when the whites arrived. It's so striking that it looks like a crime' (quoted in Clifford 1980: 521).

From the beginnings of European activity in the Pacific, Kanak people suffered through the onslaught of introduced diseases, desecration of land (for sandalwood) and labour kidnapping ('blackbirding') that was sadly typical of the first half of the nineteenth century (Shineberg 1967). But it was with the beginnings of the penal colony in New Caledonia from the 1850s and the gradual arrival of tens of thousands of French prisoners that the full impact of foreigners made severe and long-lasting impact on Kanak life. Kanak people resisted the arrival of the first French missionaries to Balade in 1843 as well as the activities of blackbirders and traders. In the same decade some took advantage of changing times to make new claims and alliances. Later in 1878 Kanak *tribu* fought the French colonists as a united force (Douglas 1990). Suppression of the insurrection, involving great loss of life, was followed by intensified European settlement and removal or dislocation of Kanak people from their ancestral lands, along with the destruction of whole villages and gardens. As had been witnessed in Australia, the removal of people from the land, which socially, philosophically and spiritually embodied them, resulted in a serious decline in the population. In innumerable ways Kanak *tribu* declined to be terrorised and adopted a variety of ways to actively maintain their world within the new regime. One of these strategies (Fig. 12.2) was to send messages through knotted cords or bouquets of plant material (Leenhardt 1930: 44, 51 quoted in Muckle 2002: 28).

Hedley arrived in New Caledonia in a particularly tense period for both settler and Kanak alike. Periodic battles were springing up across La Grande Terre, but the French were quick to suppress any activity that might lead to another uprising. As summarised by Adrian Muckle (2002: 28), action to suppress anticipated revolts occurred 'at Moindou in 1885, at Ponerihouen and Kone in 1884–1885 and 1888, at Canala and La Foa in 1890, at Kone and Touho in 1893, in the Wagap region in 1895–1896, at Hienghene in 1897. . . . Nearly all of these instances involved the mobilisation of troops or Kanak auxiliaries, arrests, the internment of individual Kanak and, at Hienghene and Poyes, the loss of life and the destruction of villages.' Adding to the unsettling times was the discovery and mining of nickel in 1864 and subsequent mining together with the importation of labourers from Japan, Indonesia

Fig. 12.2 This photograph titled 'Kanak police' c.1890s was sold through the Sydney studio, Charles Kerry, although probably not taken by them. It is typical of the kind of visual information about New Caledonia available to Hedley (Courtesy Macleay Museum, University of Sydney HPC-ACP.1475)

and Indochina. The administration's cessation of convict transportation in 1897 led to increasing numbers of freed convict settlers on land occupied by Kanak *tribu*. It is into this world that Hedley headed for his holidays.

Kanak Collections

As noted previously, Charles Hedley had just finished his Funafuti work when he went to New Caledonia. As I will show, he used quite similar methods for collecting Kanak objects as he had used to collect information in Funafuti. Hedley was able to shortcut the time it would take to establish reasonable social and trade relationships to acquire objects directly from Kanak people by going through intermediaries who were locally residing European-origin collectors.

There is no real narrative of Hedley's trip once he arrived in New Caledonia. Only a few letters to the AM curator Etheridge and a sketchbook of drawings (Hedley 1897b) chart his time away from the AM. These show that Hedley left Sydney in the company of a junior and temporary AM employee, John Jennings, and that he went first to Noumea to work on the exchanges before moving on. No diary or letters depict his time and experiences. It is possible to reconstruct his trip, I argue, through the AM Anthropology Department registers, which detail four separate donations

(Dubois, Hadfield, Higginson, and Henry), in addition to those of Hedley. In the following section I will describe Hedley's holiday before turning to look at what kind of material the AM acquired through these various donations and exchanges. Each set of objects has a slightly different character: some are large scale and dramatic in nature, whereas others are more domestic. These variations suggest that Hedley did not purposely bring together this material, as he had with the Funafuti collections, but rather that he was a facilitator.

When he arrived in Noumea, Hedley presented himself to the Museum curator, Jules Bernier. He describes Bernier as a quiet and studious gentleman situated in a little corner of the museum and surrounded by papers and geological samples and specimens. He writes (Hedley 1897a: H27/1897) that Bernier has said 'he will give me all he can spare and is helping me with letters etc. I have made several drawings (from the Museum)' and 'I leave on the 29th for Oubatche ... I hear that the natives are numerous and least civilized'. Etheridge (AM 1897–1898 Outward Letter book: 762/97) sent an encouraging letter to Hedley in return: 'My dear Hedley, Your letter of Sept. 29th has duly come to hand. I sincerely hope the Auckland man will not forget the Maori weapons, we are much in wanting these. Do everything you can to cultivate Curator Bernier – ask if he will supply N.C. lizards etc. in spirit, good skins suitable for...dry mounting ...' Bernier must already have had an idea of what the AM wanted, having received a letter in September confirming the arrival at the AM of specimens on exchange and also stating that 'the curator asks me to remind you of a promise made some time ago that you would send a stone god. He would also be very pleased to receive a specimen anytime you have one to spare. And he would also like to have a New Caledonian bat and bat skins suitable for dry mounting' (AM 1897–1898 Outward Letter book: 721/97).

Hedley had been industrious in those first few days in Noumea. As well as convincing the New Zealander that he should collect a representative sample of Maori weaponry to donate to the AM, he had selected and organised 28 ethnographic Kanak things 'desirable by the Australian Museum' (Bernier 1897: 57). After Hedley set off for Oubatche in late September, the Museum got busy with calculations.

Prior to Hedley's visit the AM had an established exchange relationship with the Noumea Museum. The last consignment of minerals and insects to and from the Noumea Museum had left the AM owing £2 on this account. The receipt of the 28 Kanak objects took this total up to £15 (AM 1896–1899 Exchange schedule: 34/97). To balance the amount, 64 ethnographic objects, valued at £8-4s, and 144 molluscs, valued at £7-11s, including specimens collected by Hedley at Funafuti, were sent from Sydney. Table 12.2 shows the materials in these outwards and inwards transactions (AM 1896–1899 Exchange schedule: 34/1897, 57/1897). These exchanged items from the Noumea Museum include architectural elements, aspects of gardening culture and aspects of Kanak social structures such as shell currency. There are also items for example, the toys, that are typical of exchange 'duplicates'.

Hedley's small notebook with pencil drawings indicate other kinds of objects in the Noumea Museum at the time of his visit and include human sculptural forms

Table 12.2 The items received from the Noumea Museum compared with those sent in exchange by the Australian Museum. The total value on both sides was calculated as £15-15s

Australian	Museum	Noumea	Museum
Drum	New Guinea	Toy	Houailou
Club	New Britain	Top	Houailou
Ornament	New Hebrides	Pipe	Houailou
Club	New Britain	Whistle	Houailou
Arm ornament	New Guinea	Bailer	Nakety
Stone item	NSW	Bark cloth beater	Canala
Arm ornament	SE coast, Papua	Club head	Isle of Pines
Neck ornament	SE coast, Papua	Shell currency	New Hebrides
Club	New Ireland	Toy	Houailou
Boomerang	NSW	Toy	Houailou
Boomerang	NSW	Circumcision tools	Houailou
Arm ornament	Bougainville	Circumcision tools	Houailou
Stone axe	Lachlan River NSW	Drill	New Caledonia
Neck ornament	Astrolabe Bay, Sepik	Stone object	La Foa
Neck ornament	Chads Bay, NE NG	Stone object	Isle of Pines
Neck ornament	Aroma, Papua	2 stone objects	Canala
Neck ornament	Kingsmill Islands	Stone object	St Vincent
Neck ornament	Marshall Islands	Digging stick	Canala
Belt	BNG	Bird body	New Caledonia
Club	Cloncurry, QLD	Finial	La Foa
Bag	Cairns	2 Incised poles	La Foa
Adze	Australia	3 Mineral species	
Belt	Port Essington	43 Palaeontology	
3 Stone artefacts	Hobart, TAS	145 Molluscs	
Hammerstone	NSW		
Stone axe	Kingswood, NSW		
Sword	Collingwood Bay, PNG		
Sword	Russell River, QLD;		
Boomerang	NSW		
Basket	Russell River QLD		
Palaeontology – 7 species (49 specimens)			
4 mammals			

Source: Australian Museum Cultural Collections documentation 1882–1920

and different kinds of clubs (Hedley 1897b). This notebook, which also includes drawings of the Marist Brothers collection and views from some of the places he visited, is almost the only personal documentation of the holiday. 'Paine, Thio, Kanala, Houilou, Koumac, Nakety are localities (towns) in New Caledonia' is also written on one page but may be a passing geographical note. The main information as to where Hedley went on his holidays other than Oubatche comes from the collections and a mention in his Funafuti paper on molluscs about collecting shells at Hienghène (Hedley 1899: 499).

In a period of just seven days in which he moved across many areas with distinct languages, Hedley collected (and later donated to the AM under his own name) over a hundred objects from three east coast locations (Paine, Mount Paine and Oubatche), mostly with local names attached (Table 12.3). How was this possible? It is unlikely that he was able to establish good relationships with Kanak people in such a short period of time, not least because of the language barriers and the state of conflict in the country. The detail of the objects for such a short trip, during which he was also collecting and looking for shells, leads me to propose that Hedley did not personally collect these things from individual producers but rather relied on the people with whom he found accommodation or others who spoke French and/or English.

It is of course possible that the language names shown in Table 12.3 were supplied by Bernier in Noumea. This is unlikely, however, because Hedley's drawings of objects in Noumea Museum have no information of this kind, nor do the objects received through exchange. More probably Hedley repeated the methods he had used in Funafuti: he asked a colonial resident to supply 'local' information. As well as collecting from intermediaries, Hedley probably appropriated some material. Since on other fieldtrips Hedley looted objects from sites (see e.g., Florek 2005: 47), it is reasonable to suppose that the objects connected to graves, including the human skull, were collected in this manner. It is indeed possible that the drawing of the two skulls at Paine includes the skull then taken to the AM (Fig. 12.3).

As mentioned, along with the exchange overseen by Hedley and the material donated in his own name, the AM received further material from four donors presumably living in New Caledonia. The AM also purchased a collection from Hedley's colleague John Jennings. It is to this collection I will now turn, as the collection of objects purchased from Jennings are different in nature from those of Hedley's and, by their difference, serve to highlight Hedley's influence on the material deposited by him.

The AM's acquisition of John Jennings's collection is the largest group of objects received from New Caledonia at this time. Exchange Schedules for April and May 1897 (AM 1896–1899 Exchange schedule: 41/97) indicate that Jennings already had an interest in collecting and had exchanged an adze from Mortlock Island for a club from New Britain in the AM. Jennings and Hedley both signed out preserving spirits and collecting equipment on exchange before their departure to New Caledonia. Collectors could acquire specialist materials from the museum stores 'on exchange' for a portion of the collection they would make (AM 1896–1899 Exchange schedule: 20/98). Only one piece of further information is recorded by the AM about Jennings. In late 1898, 96 objects, largely from Thio on the southern end of the east coast of New Caledonia, came into the AM from Mr Atkinson of Thio with a letter from MacDonnell & Atkinson of Sydney declaring that Jennings 'of the Australian Museum' was in New Caledonia in September/October 1897 and had organised for the objects to be sent to the Museum C.O.D. (AM 1898 Inwards Letter book: M16/1898). In the museum records these objects are described as a purchase from MacDonnell. The purchase included shell currency, two man-sized feathered masks adorned with high hair-wigs and greenstone valuables.

The donation through Hedley of Kanak objects from Paine, Mount Paine and Oubatche is domestic in nature, with local names supplied. The collection from

Table 12.3 The material Hedley donated to the Australian Museum under his own name

Oubatche	Language name	Mount Paine	Language name	Paine	Language name
1 anklet	oon	1 arm ornament	gougout	5 shell knives	Bakaiyan & batungan
1 skirt	poura	2 armlets		1 tattoo equipment	balitche
1 vine skirt	'batche' vine	1 shell belt	Bwiri of 'wongi'	3 combs	manda
1 feather ornament		1 leaf toy	baignalum	2 skirts	
1 axe	Gui paik	1 leaf whistle	ngor	1 skirt basket	
1 child's hair sample	dingat	2 leg ornaments		1 flying fox wool belt	dongan
1 tabu knot (taken from grave)	torp	1 jade necklace	meillewe	1 toy ball	Bout
1 fern offering (taken from grave)	wailip	1 chief's spear		1 fan	Hango
3 arrows (fishing)	Nain, dunuk & yap	1 carved spear	toowanda	2 flutes	N da
1 bailer	dahri	1 tapa for mourning	ha	2 chief's dance spear	toowanda
1 basket		2 fish line and hook	maiawe	2 spear	gahaindi
1 clay pot		3 lancet models	hambui	Chief's head ornament	
1 bow				1 spear	hooeng
1 yam tool				3 spear-throwers	Ginhaik with paik
1 fire-making kit				4 bags with slingstones	wendat
1 fish trap				1 sling	boit
				2 club	bwegegap
				2 swagstraps	
				1 skull taken from grave	
				1 prawn net	choua
				3 baskets	
				1 clay pot	jilech
				4 plates	gatch
				1 palm plate	hoi
				1 bow	mornginget
				1 pump drill	arigaiya

Source: Australian Museum Cultural Collections documentation 1882–1920

Fig. 12.3 A drawing simply titled 'Paine' from Charles Hedley's notebook (1897b) (Courtesy of the Australian Museum AMS272, Papers of Charles Hedley)

Jennings includes large and ceremonial material. What about the nature of the four donations that Hedley presumably organised? Fifty objects from New Caledonia were registered from the four donors and they, like the material donated by Hedley, include good provenance and local names supplied, but there are no inward or outward letters or notes relating to their consignment. These donations were received from Madame Dubois (25 largely domestic items from Touho), Reverend Hadfield (13 objects showing technology of the Loyalty Islanders), Mr Higginson and A.O. and J. Henry (10 currency items from Oubatche). The collections had presumably been arranged between Hedley and Higginson, Dubois and the others either in Noumea or in the villages. Hedley was evidently so inspiring in his conversations that these five individuals sent their material to the AM presumably at their own expense.

The collections acquired through exchange and from Jennings have a different 'character' to those donated through Hedley and the others. This probably reflects the circumstances of their acquisition. Along with the higher-status items from the Noumea Museum, which had the time and money to collect, the objects delivered C.O.D. from Jennings are the most prestigious in nature. Unlike Hedley, Jennings was without independent means and without a job. Most likely he looked to purchase objects with a view to making money from their sale. If this is true, there would be less interest on his part about how Kanak people lived their lives and more interest in those things that looked most prestigious (like the masks), or carried the greatest indigenous value (such as the shell currency). Why he did not return to collect them is a mystery.

The material Hedley acquired under his own name is quite the opposite, possibly because he paid for it himself and arranged its transport. The items are of a personal nature, or relate to senior leaders (*grande chef* in New Caledonian parlance), such as the flying fox wool belt and spears, perhaps because Hedley acquired the objects from local European residents of Paine and Oubatche. Unlike Hedley, these unknown people would have had to establish some form of continued, if tense, relationship with the landholders, or took advantage of police arresting Kanak leaders to procure interesting 'chiefly' items from the police. James Clifford (1980: 521) writing of Christian and Kanak belief systems noted that 'in local tradition the chief was a sacred personage, 'older brother' and mediator with the ancestors. His 'word' (*parole*) was the unity of the clan, and thus the state of his 'soul' was of far-reaching importance; it expressed the power of the group.' Such things probably entered the collecting market as Kanak people were forced from their villages, or when messages and other symbols that may be interpreted by the French as threatening were intercepted.

The material was derived from different relationships, networks and forms of exchange: interpersonal (between Dubois and the other 'local' donors), institutional (between the AM and Noumea Museum) and colonial (objects acquired through circumstances of the state). But Hedley's short three-week holiday increased the Museum's collection of material culture originating in New Caledonia from under 50 to over 300. Objects included greenstone adzes, basketry, skirts, slings and sling stones, house finials, door jambs, small currency and fishing equipment. The greatest expense for the AM was the cost of freight and accounting with the Noumea Museum and MacDonnell; all other Kanak objects were donated. Without Charles Hedley's intervention, it is likely that the AM would have solely relied on the institutional exchange relationship and consequently only acquired a small collection: possibly twenty or so objects over a period of ten or 20 years.

The Other Side

So far this chapter has only followed Hedley's part in this series of acquisitions made in New Caledonia. Of those objects that were sent to Noumea on exchange (Table 12.2), each had come into the AM from a previous series of networks. One of these items is an arm ornament from 'New Guinea' that was the product of an exchange with an unknown exhibitor in the Colonial and Indian Exhibition of 1886. There is also a group of material derived from the Bismarck Archipelago. These detail a profitable relationship that lasted over 20 years between the AM and the Samoan-American trader Emma Coe ('Queen Emma') and her husband Thomas Farrell, sister Phoebe and Phoebe's husband Richard Parkinson. These collections, when fully 'unpacked', have the power to illuminate the networks of Pacific peoples during this period, to show the complexities of life for Kanak and New Britain people alike as Europeans and others arrived on their islands to collect examples of the diverse practices of humankind.

Europeans sought objects to enrich their understanding of the world's peoples by systematically ordering kinds of things (such as fishhooks) and exhibiting them to the public. In turn, Kanak people and other indigenous groups used the objects they acquired from Europeans within their own worldviews. On some of the green-stone axes, for example, bindings of flying fox wool are replaced with blue and red cloth. The following quote indicates the quite different cultural purposes of local and foreign 'exchange goods' today in greeting and through ceremony.

> When we meet with people we always exchange small gifts. The importance of the gift is not its value, you can exchange things which are very low in value. The important thing is just to exchange and to talk to the people. And by doing it whenever you arrive in a new house you give this small thing and you talk on it. This is directed to the living people but also to the invisible world you don't see (Emmauel Kasarhérou, curator of Noumea's Musée Tjibaou, 2000).

At the start of this chapter I drew attention to Douglas' statement that the histories of peoples can be seen through looking closely at the objects and the ways that they came to be acquired. Amongst the objects sent to the AM from the Noumea Museum were three 'stone objects'. These long yam-shaped stones are most probably the 'stone gods' Etheridge sought for the collections in 1897. Such objects have value for Kanak people in the making and protection of garden places. Yet the exchange process has almost entirely obscured their identity, and with it an understanding of their use. It is not, however, obliterated. With persistent enquiry, language skills and much assistance and support from Kanak knowledge holders, it should be possible to 'return' to these objects the meanings that have been masked through the industry of exchange.

Unpacking Hedley's Collections

The exchange industry was a product of the professionalization of the nineteenth-century museum. In combining the objectives of science and public education, museums were driven to collect and display a great variety of material culture and specimens to explain complex ideas such as evolution. The establishment of the learned society went hand in hand with the developments in museums. Both assisted in promoting the collecting endeavour and establishing 'gaps' where more information and research were needed. These practices meant that tens of thousands of cultural objects were sent around the world, sometimes as 'fillers' for exchange accounts dealing mainly with natural history and other times as the primary object or purpose of the exchange. This predominantly nineteenth century phenomenon has meant that museums around the world currently have collections of things that are dislocated from their original contexts and meanings. These exchanges in turn relied on single museums acquiring large collections from which they could dispense items.

At first glance, the New Caledonian collections of the AM are unconnected artefacts of nineteenth century Kanak culture. One can look closely at what kinds of objects were included in Hedley's exchanges and donations to bring to light connections within the material and to people on New Caledonia. Those objects exchanged with the Noumea Museum, as well as those acquired by Jennings, were from areas of La Grande Terre where by the 1890s French incursions into Kanak life were strong. Objects from Hedley's associates were from areas where Kanak still had a foothold on their lands, but where relations with the French colonials were fragile at best.

Through understanding the role that Charles Hedley played in the acquisition of the AM collection of Kanak objects, some attempts at unpacking these collections can be made. By concentrating on Hedley, one can follow a common thread in the making of these collections: a series of relationships between people and institutions built on a shared belief in the worth (financial or ideal) of these objects for scientific study. This common principle was also promoted through the mechanism of exchange where objects were further abstracted from their cultural origins to be swapped and shared internationally as single examples of a particular cultural type.

References

Anderson, Charles
    1936 Charles Hedley. *Proceedings of the Linnean Society of New South Wales,* 61:209–214.

Australian Museum
    1896–1897 Annual Report.
    1897–1898 Annual Report.

Australian Museum Archives (AM)
    1896–1899 Exchange Schedules.
    1897–1898 Outward Letter Books.
    1897–1898 Inward Letter Books.

Australian Museum Cultural Collections Documentation
    1882–1920 Anthropology Department Registers labelled A, B and E.

Bernier, Jules
    1897 Letter to Robert Etheridge. *AM Letter Books*, 57:97.

Clifford, James
    1980 Fieldwork, Reciprocity, and the Making of Ethnographic Texts: The Example of Maurice Leenhardt. *Man,* 15:518–532.

Douglas, Bronwen
    1990 'Almost Constantly at War'? An Ethnographic Perspective on Fighting in New Caledonia. *Journal of Pacific History,* 25:22–46.
    1998 *Across the Great Divide: Journeys in History and Anthropology.* Overseas Publishers Association, Amsterdam.

Etheridge, Robert (Jnr)
    1897–1898 Annual Report to the Trustees.

Fairfax, Denis
    1983 Hedley, Charles (1862–1926). In *Australian Dictionary of Biography,* edited by Bede Nairn and Geoffrey Serle, Vol. 9, pp. 252–253. Melbourne University Press, Melbourne.

Florek, Stan

2005 *The Torres Strait Islands Collection at the Australian Museum*. Technical Reports of the Australian Museum Sydney No. 19. The Australian Museum, Sydney.

Geismar, Haidy and Anita Herle

2010 *Moving Images. John Layard, Fieldwork and Photography on Malakula Since 1914*. Crawford House, Adelaide.

Haddon, Alfred C.

1907 The Method of Pitt-Rivers. *Folklore,* 18:217–220.

Healy, Chris

1997 *From the Ruins of Colonialism: History as Social Memory*. Cambridge University Press, Cambridge.

Hedley, Charles

1896–1900 *The Atoll of Funafuti, Ellice Group: Its Zoology, Botany, Ethnology, and General Structure Based on Collections Made by Charles Hedley, of the Australian Museum, Sydney, N. S. W.* Australian Museum Memoir III. Australian Museum Trust, Sydney.

1896 *General Account of the Atoll of Funafuti*. Australian Museum Memoir III, Pt. 1. Australian Museum, Sydney.

1897a *The Ethnology of Funafuti*. Australian Museum Memoir III, Pt. 4. Australian Museum, Sydney.

1897b 'Sketchbook' Australian Museum AMS72, box 3.

1899 *The Mollusca of Funafuti, Part I*, Australian Museum Memoir III, Pt. 7. Australian Museum, Sydney.

Kasarhérou, Emmanuel

2000 *Earth beat*. ABC Radio National. http://www.abc.net.au/ra/carvingout/issues/tjibaou.htm accessed 2/2/2010.

Kirshenblatt-Gimblett, Barbara

1998 *Destination Culture: Tourism, Museums, and Heritage*. University of California Press, Berkeley.

Knapman, Gareth

2009 Exchanges and the Historical Construction of Collections In *Inspiring Action, Museums and Social Change: a Collection of Essays,* no editor, pp 59–75. Museums etc, Edinburgh.

Kuklick, Henrika

1991 *The Savage Within: The Social History of British Anthropology, 1885–1945*. Cambridge University Press, Cambridge.

Muckle, Adrian

2002 Killing the 'Fantome Canaque': Evoking and Invoking the Possibility of Revolt in New Caledonia (1853–1915). *Journal of Pacific History,* 37:25–44.

Musée de Nouvelle Calédonie

2010 Historique du musée. http://www.museenouvellecaledonie.nc/portal/page/portal/smp/musee/historique, accessed 1 February 2010.

Naylor, Simon

2002 The Field, the Museum and the Lecture Hall: The Spaces of Natural History in Victorian Cornwall. *Transactions of the Institute of British Geographers*. New Series 27:494–513. London.

Philp, Jude
  2004 Embryonic Science: The 1888 Torres Strait Photographic Collection of A.C. Haddon. In
      Woven Histories, Dancing Lives: Torres Strait Islander Identity, Culture and History, edited
      by Richard Davis, pp. 90–106. Aboriginal Studies Press, Canberra.

Proudfoot, Peter, Rosylyn Maguire, and Robert Freestone (editors)
  2000 *Colonial City Global City: Sydney's International Exhibition 1879.* Crossing Press,
      Sydney.

Read, Charles
  1899 The Ethnology of Funafuti [Ellice Group] by Charles Hedley. *Journal of the
      Anthropological Institute of Great Britain and Ireland*, 28:177–178.

Shineberg, Dorothy
  1967 *They Came for Sandalwood: A Study of the Sandalwood Trade in the South-West Pacific,
      1830–1865.* Melbourne University Press, Melbourne.

Stocking, George W.
  1964 French Anthropology in 1800. *Isis,* 55:134–150.

Strahan, Ronald (editor)
  1979 *Rare and Curious Specimens: An Illustrated History of the Australian Museum 1827–
      1979.* The Australian Museum, Sydney.

Tcherkézoff, Serge
  2008 *'First Contacts' in Polynesia, The Samoan Case (1722–1848): Western
      Misunderstandings about Sexuality and Divinity.* ANU E-Press. Australian National
      University, Canberra.

Urry, James
  1972 Notes & Queries on Anthropology and the Development of Field Methods in British
      Anthropology, 1870–1920. *Proceedings of the Royal Anthropological Institute*, 1972:45–57.

Chapter 13
Death, Memory and Collecting: Creating the Conditions for Ancestralisation in South London Households

Fiona Parrott

Abstract This chapter presents case studies of the collections that played a part in peoples' understanding and experience of death and bereavement, from an ethnographic study of households, loss and material culture in South London. The focus on death, memory and collecting serves to highlight the way events and relationships shape and rework collections in domestic settings. It parallels the study of museum collections in this volume by unpacking the shifting relationships between objects, individuals and families. Specifically, observations on the display of collections belonging to the dead, commemorative acquisitions for collections, and intergenerational collecting illustrate how transformations in the agency of individual collectors, and the agency of objects in the lives of those anticipating death or dealing with bereavement, unfold. Personhood, in these examples of collecting, is shaped by mnemonic connections between people and things, but these are shaped by ideas and institutions linking the individual, the family and nation, the house and the museum. Cultural practices of collecting involve many ways of locating the self in the collective and the collective in the self, indeed domestic collectors viewed the museum as a transcendent place for the immortalisation of collections and selves. The case studies deal in different ways with the potential contradictions of securing future remembrance but equally they reveal aspects of the complexity of small-scale, 'private' collecting, that bring the material and social life of museum collections conceptually 'closer to home'.

Introduction

Collecting incorporates a variety of practices, which are entangled with the museum, other spaces, practices and epistemologies (Macdonald 2006; Harrison Chapter 3). This chapter, in contrast to others in this volume, presents an ethnographic study of

F. Parrott (✉)
Department of Sociology and Anthropology, Faculty of Social and Behavioural Sciences, University of Amsterdam, Amsterdam, The Netherlands
e-mail: f.r.parrott@uva.nl

S. Byrne et al. (eds.), *Unpacking the Collection*, One World Archaeology,
DOI 10.1007/978-1-4419-8222-3_13, © Springer Science+Business Media, LLC 2011

collections that exist largely outside of the museum in contemporary London house-holds. The research was undertaken as part of a larger study of the material culture of loss and separation conducted in collaboration with Daniel Miller, which involved a sample of eighty households from a lengthy South London street. While the larger study on loss and material culture included a range of households of diverse cultural backgrounds (see Miller and Parrott 2007, 2009), the self-described collectors were predominantly those of English origin, including homeowners, private and council tenants. This chapter offers a series of vignettes of contemporary English cultural practices of collecting from this group of colocated households. Returning to these homes multiple times over the course of 18 months, the research involved informally meeting participants and formally photographing and narrating these interiors in an ethnographic dialogue that focused upon bereavement, death and its anticipation, and individual and familial intentions to remember and memorialise themselves and others (Parrott 2007, 2010).

Individuals' and families' collections encountered on this street often assembled diverse connections over time and space, rather than attachments to the locality in which they were placed. The focus on death and remembrance highlights the dynamics of household collecting, the creation, movement and disassembly of these collections connected with the movement and absence of people and the forma-tion and dissolution of households. This grants a particular view on collections as networks of social and material agency that parallels the museological concept of collections as dynamic assemblages explored in this volume. The way collec-tions are treated in homes has been informed by museological discourse, just as practices of popular collecting have contributed to changing ideas about museums and exhibitions in Britain. This chapter sheds light on some of the relationships between objects and collectors, which might otherwise be inaccessible in the colo-nial contexts that dominate the other case studies presented in the book. In this sense, this chapter is intended to complement and broaden the theoretical focus on ethnographic collections in other chapters by posing a series of questions that arise from a more anthropological and biographically oriented study of collecting in a contemporary context.

Death, Collecting and Consumption

Some authors have suggested that all collecting behaviour is aimed at resolving the uncertainty posed by the lack of control we have over the arbitrariness of death. Baudrillard (1994), in *The System of Collecting*, focuses on the principles of order created in the act of collection, which underpin the possession of the object, the inte-gration of object with person and ultimately, 'the exercise of control over the world' and the self that the collection represents. The mastery implied by the ordered sys-tematised relationship to objects is a broad theme invoked by collecting, from the study of colonial collecting as a project of recontextualisation and knowledge cre-ation about 'the Other' (Macdonald 2006), to popular collecting as a counter to modern forms of insecurity (Belk 1995; Martin 1998). Baudrillard suggests that anxieties about death are resolved through the establishment of a cyclical temporal order through the collection: 'Collecting simply abolishes time. Or rather: by establishing a fixed repertory of temporal references that can be replayed at will...collecting represents the perpetual fresh beginning of a controlled cycle...of birth and death' (1994: 16). Death is absorbed into the series and cycle of the collection itself.

By Baudrillard's account, mourning is continually enacted through collecting, though in a regressive manner. The weakness of Baudrillard's and other more psychological and symbolic approaches to death and collecting is a tendency to absolve collecting of its social and historic context. By contrast, other contributions have offered a more socially and historically located consideration of the role of collecting in coming to terms with death. For example, Stewart's (1994) analysis of the collecting activities of Charles Willson Peale focuses on child mortality at the end of the eighteenth century and unpacks the relationship between the arrested life of the display, Peale's loss of his own children and certain referential paintings within his collection. This more biographical and historically located approach to the study of collecting is emphasised in this chapter.

Several aspects of collecting as a cultural practice are suggestive of the relationship between collecting and death in the English home. From its early modern European origins, collecting practices realised particular cultural forms that were directed towards the creation of a durable legacy beyond the self as well as a form of knowledge of the world (Pearce 1995; Auslander 1996; Macdonald 2006). The metaphors of the museum and the mausoleum have also been applied to 'dusty' collections of objects in the home. While negative in their assessment of the 'life' and sensibility of objects in these contexts that have been removed from use, they also reference the lasting significance given to objects through the museum and the practice of collecting (Macdonald 2006).

Collection involves setting objects apart from other objects through particular levels of attention, namely particular technologies of storage, cataloguing and display (Belk 1995; Macdonald 2006). These allow for the controlled structuring of memory and time within the collection itself, and in this ethnography their curation may be seen to lend itself to an expression of the care of the self and ones' relationships through commemorative practice. This aspect was highlighted by Walter Benjamin who described collecting as 'the art of living intimately allied with memory' where each acquisition becomes a point of reference in an individual's life (Benjamin 1969: 215). However, problems with the profusion of objects and size of collections, ambiguity over their utility or availability for touch and play, are equally implicated in the remembrance, acceptance and continuation of collections after the death of a loved one.

The home in Britain is the place in which evidence of peoples' pasts are amassed, and increasingly where memorials or 'souvenirs' to the dead are created and displayed as part of materialisations of identity and belonging (e.g. Hallam and Hockey 2001; Layne 2000; Miller and Parrott 2007). In contrast to other chapters in the book, the case studies in this chapter specifically highlight peoples' concern with mass-produced goods. In the museum and through museum-like collections in the home, the setting apart and display of these objects, as Macdonald (2002) argues, is both intimately connected to the world of commodities and transformative: 'however mundane they were before, they are now to some extent sacred' (2002: 92). In this way, collecting may be seen as a form of consumption and the role of a museal consciousness is part of an attempt to establish different kinds of relationships to ephemeral objects (Belk 1995), which take on a particular resonance in the context of death.

By focusing on death and collecting in domestic settings, this ethnographic account helps to theorise collecting as cultural tradition and a relational, spatial and temporal organising practice located in everyday lives (Pearce 1995; Macdonald 2006). In some respects, this approach parallels other chapters in this volume that analyse national and colonial collections as the product of networks of relationships between people, things and institutions (Wingfield Chapter 5; see also Thomas 1991; Gosden and Knowles 2001). The relationships in which objects in collections are 'entangled', as gifts, acquisitions and souvenirs, are implicated in the continuing biography of collections in relation to death and dying. However, the fine-grained approach to objects, stories and histories taken in this contemporary ethnography helps trace the sensory, linguistic and material registers through which different individuals and identities are given agency, immortalised and remembered through collections. In particular, the nature of the collection as a composite and partible 'object' is explored as a material and social assemblage that supports both the expression and subsumption of individual subjectivities or interests within a central or collective material narrative, and which may be passed on, disassembled and distributed.

Memories of a Collection

Collections that belonged to the dead typically exert a weighty and emotional presence, not least because they represent the labour of their maker over time. This can lend the collection a monumental quality as a personal memorial, but frequently relatives were at a loss to know what to do with collections in which no one else seemed to express an interest or which were of little market value to other collectors. When finding a more intimate home for collections, smaller collections were often passed on to someone immediately connected with the relationships and spaces that constituted the collection in the first instance. This was the case for Rachel, a local charity worker who received a collection of miniature vehicles that belonged to her father.

Popular collections, such as this one, often establish and conform to gendered images through what is collected (Pearce 1995; Belk 1995; Martin 1998). This collection of cars, specifically work-related vehicles, shaped the gendered character of the memorial. Indeed, men were often remembered through 'masculine' goods, related to work, hobbies or sports in the home (Miller and Parrott 2007).

Rachel became the recipient because she had given her father some of the cars as gifts, 'I bought him the steam roller because he used to drive one and some of the others'. Gift giving and shopping has been shown more widely to be an important mediator of kin relationships in Britain, and collections often become a convenient focus for gift giving (Pearce 1995; Miller 1998). Commonly, the presence of gifts in the collection from a specific donor precipitated the return or gift of the collection to that friend or family member if they were still living.

Rachel displayed the cars arranged in rows in the upstairs hallway of the home she shared with her husband (Fig. 13.1). She described the display: 'They are a bittersweet thing, but they are all sitting nicely on a bookshelf there'. Her memories of the collection involve some of the tensions that arose when children wanted to handle the cars, 'he would say "you can't touch that because it's special to me". Originally he put them on little shelves and because the kids like them he actually ended up putting them in the attic and I was so angry, and I thought 'you mean sod'. He did love us all, but we all have a dark side'.

Fig. 13.1   Rachel's display of her father's miniature vehicle collection (Photo by Fiona Parrott)

Through the display of his collection Rachel exhibited her continued care towards and remembrance of her father. She did not continue the collection but it did not prevent them from being actively involved in memory work. For example, around the anniversary of her father's death she brought the steamroller downstairs to her study desk and placed it alongside an assemblage of a framed poem and photographs created for the event (Fig. 13.2). The return of the steamroller to the collection, the part to the whole, helped signal the end of her mourning period.

A single item may have specific resonance. However, it was with some reluctance that relatives broke up collections and distributed their constituent objects. Alternatively, a selection of items may metonymically reference the whole in practices of display that retain but also control the monumentality of the collections of the dead. For example, in a different home, one interviewee who received his father's art collection chose to display one picture at a time, cycling through the whole collection over time.

Fig. 13.2 Rachel's display of the miniature steamroller in front of poems and photographs on the anniversary of her father's death (Photo by Fiona Parrott)

Collecting to Remember

As Pearce (1995) notes, 'one may inherit a complete collection, and it will have a sincere place in one's own life. But unless it is added to, it remains essentially the collection of the dead person' (1995: 235). The activity of collecting shapes or transforms these identifications.

Collecting in response to loss may only indirectly implicate the deceased. For example, it is often noted that Freud began his collection of antiquities following his father's death (Forrester 1994). The collecting habit provides a framework for activity, an aspect which has been thought to help people through periods of instability and transition (Pearce 1995). The development of this potential into a dedicated collection was illustrated by a middle-aged interviewee, June, in her family household, where each new acquisition was made to remember her mother. Collecting was appropriated as a practice of commemoration and routine of remembrance.

June's collection provided a way of incorporating a relationship to the deceased within an active form of self-creation and family practice. The living room of June's large council flat was lined with shelves, most of which were filled with a display of toy clowns. There were more boxes stored in her and her husband's bedroom. After her mother died June wanted the ornamental clowns that belonged to her mother, 'she didn't have very many, she just had a few'. About three days after her mother died, June's husband bought her a clock with a clown on the face intending to recall her mother and to show his care for his wife at this difficult time: 'I thought "oh that's so nice" and I thought that's it, I'm going to buy clowns'. The incorporation of the deceased into a gift-giving ritual prompted the continuation of the collection as a larger context for future gifts and acquisitions. Gift giving and consumption rituals allow for the remembrance and recognition of the deceased through acquisition (Layne 2000).

The special quality of the collection is that the clowns condense a new history at the same time as they consolidate a relationship to the past. Whenever June and her family went on holiday, they looked out for clowns, 'the big clowns we used to see them everywhere but we haven't seen them for ages those ones'. Each find serves to bring her mother into the moment, 'I think "oh my mum would have liked this one". And the children say "Nanny would have liked that clown" so they know as well'. While it is June's collection, the activity of collecting involves the whole family, from her husband's first gift of the clown clock to the children. In this way they all become involved in the activity of remembrance.

Each successive acquisition refers back to the original object and tastes of her mother. The original clowns belonging to her mother are absorbed into a larger whole. Each new clown serves as a memory of the intention to remember in each new context and the collection establishes the commitment to continue remembering in the future. Just as photographs are a cultural technology of remembrance in that they manifest the intention to remember in the future, so this collection grows as a cumulative monument to memory. The memory of her mother perpetually finds new places in the dynamic life of the family, of holidays, trips out and through gifting.

June's practice represents one of the most prominent examples of how a collection may honour the memory of the deceased by turning each acquisition into a ritual of remembrance. By far the most common form of recontextualisation of the presence of the deceased in collections was the incorporation of an individual memento into a larger biographical collection, most commonly a music or book collection but also a wardrobe of clothing or collection of cooking utensils (Miller and Parrott 2007; Parrott 2007). In this manner a large proportion of the eighty households found a meaningful place for memories of the deceased, as one memory of a relationship among many.

Alternatively, the variety of possible material responses to loss allows people to engage in different types of memorial practice, from a highly visible way of honouring the deceased in the living room, prompting shared exchanges about the collection between viewers, to a 'private' digitised collection of images on a personal computer. Digital images of people and objects were increasingly shaped into 'collections' in the home and online archives of images of objects were also accessed from the home providing new resources for individual and collective remembering. One middle-aged man searched through images stored on eBay, the online marketplace, after his father's death, collecting images of old objects listed for sale that dated to the time of his father's youth. The nostalgia for old objects, the reference point of his father's youth and his access to these collections of images, provided a way for this man to think about and remember his father. These examples show more precisely how collecting in response to loss is not only part of muse-ological and archival discourse but also a personal motivation (Macdonald 2006; Edwards 2006).

Collecting to Secure Memory in the Future

Collections whose continued significance were assured even after the death of their founders, placed individual interests within the wider project of family and generational remembering. When seeking to extend one's agency through one's children and grandchildren, one must deal effectively with the issue of transmis-sion (Marcoux 2001). What I show is that embedding memories in the lives of others relies on the sensory or memorable character of the collected objects, the composite and partible nature of these collections, and the extension of these col-lections through other media including digital archives and photographs, to mediate relationships between individuals.

A Template for Memory

An object as mundane or kitsch as a charm bracelet may become a complex means of securing and controlling future remembrance. This involves both narrative develop-ment and material transformation (Bal 1994). Charm bracelets have been established as a readymade focus for a set of small collected objects – the charms. These are often selected as souvenirs. For example, Marjorie's first husband was an ambas-sador. The children had grown up in many different places around the world. When they were first married he gave her a charm bracelet with a globe charm to signify that he was 'giving her the world'. Marjorie and her first husband proceeded to col-lect charms everywhere they lived and travelled, and this first composite object is a well-known story piece in the family.

After Marjorie was widowed she began a long-term relationship with Gregory, a divorcee. Marjorie had a large family of children and grandchildren who knew Gregory well. What was notable was the way the charm bracelet was turned into a generative practice or template. Successive younger generations were incorporated into a centralised narrative founded on Marjorie's original collection of charms and their significance. Gregory was also involved. He collected many things digitally, including maps, so he catalogued all the charms and recorded their associations with

Marjorie on his computer. This allowed Marjorie to hand the original bracelet on to her daughter-in-law, who cried profusely on its reception. Recording these stories and images of each charm facilitated Marjorie's ability to give away the original bracelet and ensured they created permanent records of the oral narrative for the future.

Marjorie and Gregory bought charm bracelets for every grandchild and, as a couple, continued to collect charms on the many cruises they took together, giving them as gifts every Christmas. Gregory also catalogued every grandchild's additional charm and the meaning and reason for its selection electronically. Charms of the world, collected and recorded, provided a technology of remembrance that incorporated the founding relationship to a deceased husband within a set of objects and stories in which her second husband and younger generations became involved. Far from being an isolated example, there were many examples of collecting practices which progressively and retrospectively established the unity of the self or the couple through the family through particular media.

A Time for Memory

Mr and Mrs Davis were the second generation to hold and sustain their family collection of Christmas decorations and lights. It included glass decorations from the 1930s to Bakelite lights from the 1950s to decorations collected yearly in the UK and abroad. Christmas was a religious festival for this Catholic family and the highlight of their social year when they entertained a stream of family and friends. It was also the time when they would display parts of the collection. Only a small part of the collection could be displayed each year so they took care to make each display different. Figure 13.3 shows the display on a visit in December 2007. Within the family, photographs taken each year helped to record the distinctions between years, generating a sense of linear historicity in a cyclical event.

The care of the larger collection involved repair, packing and ordering of the decorations and lights in their individual boxes over many weeks of the year. Like many domestic collections it combined decorative display or utilitarian function, blurring the boundaries between homemaking, collecting and heirlooms. However, as a collection it was subject to characteristic forms of acquisition, storage, cataloguing and care.

The Christmas collection established a ritualised container for family memory work. Interest in the collection and thus family unity was, it seems, evidenced from birth. In-laws were also able to participate as Mr Davis often commented on how the 'outlaws', as he jokingly called them, demonstrated a similar 'love for Christmas'. When every child and every grandchild moved out to form their own independent household, they received a box of Christmas decorations that formed a microcosm of the whole, including some of the oldest decorations and the new. Multiple family boxes continued to grow in tandem with the others as every Christmas became a time for gifting new additions to all the respective collections as well as through

Fig. 13.3 Christmas decorations and lights on display in Mr and Mrs Davis's home in December 2007 (Photo by Fiona Parrott)

individual acquisitions. One year, Mr and Mrs Davis distributed large hand-painted baubles of village snow scenes collected on a holiday to the Philippines. This practice of distributing representative parts of the collection allowed the Davis's to consolidate collecting through the extended family in each independent household.

Mr and Mrs Davis were secure in the knowledge that they would be subsumed as ancestors within the continuing life of the collection and family, just as Mr Davis's parents had become a revered remembered presence. Maurice Bloch (1998) describes for the sacred ancestral houses of the Zafimaniry of Madagascar how the house of the 'founding couple' becomes a ritual focus for descendants. They are present, not as two individuals but as a conjoined couple in the body of the house, much as in this case, the couple are conjoined in the body of the collection. The collection testifies to the process of marriage and the enlarging of the family by its material growth and through the stories woven around the decorations, narrated year on year. The stories relating to the founding couple are more formal and reverent than those involving younger generations, which were more humorous and informal.

However, unlike a sacred house that establishes a link to place and land, these collections are notable for being subject to practices which help make them portable and reproducible. Like the charm bracelets, the partible and generative dimensions of these Christmas collections immortalise the kin group in a highly mobile London or UK population.

Photographs enhance the distributive power of the collection. Taking photographs allowed the Davis family to create portraits of themselves, family, friends and visitors against the stage of the decorated tree and room. Having a portrait painted with one's collection is not a new activity (Stewart 1994). However, photographic portraits with the Christmas collection were reproduced and distributed on a greater scale, extending its remembrance in the homes of friends and visitors as well as family. But a hierarchy of access pertained to the objects of the collection, for example, the son who expressed the most interest in the collection had begun to take more responsibility for its curatorship and care in his parents' house.

Narratives of Memory

To collect is 'to consolidate identity through a retrospective articulation of fragments' and 'the discursive articulation of those fragments as part of personal narrative' (Bann 1994: 78). To paraphrase Bloch, collecting objects or souvenirs is not a substitute for the internalisation of memory but a device that facilitates the internalisation or the moulding of the recipient (Bloch 1998). Nowhere was this more evident than with the collection of McDonald's Happy Meal toys made by Anna and her children. These mass-produced toys are provided with children's meals at McDonald's and are designed to be collected, with series and sets on specific themes.

Anna was an engineer with three children aged between eight and twelve, one of many to have collected these toys. They were collected over a period of six years. Anna explains, 'They were close together so it was quite hard work so we had to figure out a way of making it fun. Because I love the children and children's toys and they liked McDonald's we just got into collecting McDonald's Happy Meal toys. I just think they are so incredibly well made, such beautiful things and they're free, you get them with the meal…we used to sit in for an extra half hour playing with the toys and doing all the stickers and it was fantastic because they were happy and I was happy…They weren't allowed to open them till after they'd finished eating. So there was a little bit of a ritual…I actually had another child to keep playing with them!'

For Anna, the specificity of the memories relating to each collected toy is not comparable to the memories of toys the children played with over longer periods. The weekly acquisition and series of characters and themes, often relating to films on release at the same time, gives the collection a temporal structure that makes it, as she says, 'rooted in time'. Anna explains, 'You could only get a collection like this by having three children and building it up.'

Building it up includes further 'rituals' of consolidation beyond those of acquisition: 'Every summer we get them out like this on the floor here and they play with them again. So they can tell me which toy it was when the fight happened at McDonald's or when we went on holiday in Devon and had to drive from our cottage that was miles away to Plymouth because we would have missed a week. They would remember and then I would have a stronger memory and then I'd remember the toy.' The narration of memories associated with the collection takes place as staged events. Brought out in plastic boxes, the children and sometimes Anna as well play with the mixed-up series and often sort them into runs. At the end of a few days of play, Anna checks that they are all returned to the box. Anna explicitly relates these activities of recollection to the anticipation of her own death and the way she imagines the children will relate to these toys in the future. She compares her family memory practices with those of her sister who keeps things enshrined and 'out of the sticky hands' of her children, saying 'when her children find these things [after her death] they'll mean nothing to them'.

However, to resolve the tension between the significance of the rituals of play and the need to set a collection of special objects apart, the toy collection actually exists in two forms. A second set is sealed in their plastic bags in the attic, retained for the future in pristine condition. This collection also becomes a focus for value construction. While Anna suggests that this collection could be sold as 'their inheritance', the children say they 'will never sell it'. Thus the potential for divestment and proposed financial worth works to secure emotional worth. There is completeness to this dual collection, as Anna calls it, 'it's the past, the present and the future'. Producing children, producing the collection and producing memory to paraphrase Bloch are part of the maintenance of what has been and will not decay (Bloch 1998: 73).

Anna explains the sensory significance of plastic, 'there's something about plastic, I think in the end it does rot but it doesn't really deteriorate. Because it's not expensive it's not seen as having any value but I see it as actually this fabulous material. It is brilliant for toys, brilliant to make things. I also have this big collection of Tupperware'. Here the durability of the plastic and the value she gives to the mass-produced material also makes it appropriate to the work of memory.

Anna is unperturbed by their lack of uniqueness as collected objects, but she does see them as specific to a particular generation of children: 'They are part of everyone's childhoods in this generation'. This generational distinction is important. Anna contrasts the brightly coloured plastic toys with her parents' aesthetic regime, 'They would like them to have these antique wooden toys, I mean someone will bring out some disgusting thing made of tin from Victorian times and wax lyric about it and it just doesn't appeal to me…The fact we live in a modern house was a real insult to my mother'. Anna forges a distinctive, nuclear family through the politics of sensory signification and mass consumption. These Happy Meal Toys are 'moral emblems' as well as 'mnemonic devices' in which sensory phenomena function as social symbols in association with individual and collective memories (Howes 2003: 44). Anna may be remembered as an ancestor while her parents may not.

These toys are the subject of specialist collectors' books replete with colour images that testify to their popularity and mass distribution. The youngest son enjoys looking at such a book. These toys, or as Anna calls them, 'moments of happiness', consolidate a project of collective family memory harnessed to both the collection and the global fame of McDonald's. This 'memory' is embodied in things, holds interests in a network of consumers, and is sedimented in the bodies of a mother and her children. The collection and the work of acquisition, remembering and play, create the conditions for their reconnection.

Marcoux (2001), in his work with elderly residents in Montreal, described how securing remembrance of the self in the lives and homes of others through passing on personal objects is an attempt to invent oneself as an ancestor. These examples of family collecting are in accord with this perspective. Martin (1998) has also described how adult collectors may be influenced by the collecting activity of previous generations, more loosely calling this the acceptance of a 'sacred trust' (Martin 1998: 58). In all three examples, people engaged in innovative ways with the problem of securing memory through the process of collecting, within or across multiple independent nuclear households.

Museums, Memory and Identity

When participants in this study talked of finding a museum for a collection, as members of the Davis family did of their father's multiple collections, they spoke of it with the hope of finding a suitable home after his death for a collection that had grown beyond the remit of the family. Museums commonly represent the ultimate legitimisation of the intention to give objects in a collection, and thus the totality of the self, a more lasting life and significance (Macdonald 2006). This process is also reflected in the origins of the sorts of colonial collections discussed in other chapters in the book. Yet by ensuring a rational precept for their collection to be held in perpetuity, the collector or collectors and collection must serve a larger purpose. These practices are historically gendered: creating the self through the unity of the family and the home may be seen as feminine; creating the self through absorbing the individual into the imagined body of the nation may be seen as more masculine. Baekeland (1981), for example, has described how men have aspired to create collections with public functions.

The specificity of the person may be erased in the process of transforming them into another type of ancestral presence in the house of the museum. This loss of the personal or the authority of the collector is not taken lightly, particularly if it means dismantling the collection, as demands placed upon museums to ensure the retention of the collection as a unified whole in these situations have testified (Shelton 2001; Elsner and Cardinal 1994). Museum collections are grown in part, through such practices that deserve further consideration. However, family and community museums and attentiveness to the demands of source communities mean that museums must allow for the type of multiple and multilayered identifications described in this chapter to take place. Increasingly, colonial objects located in museums are simultaneously family or ancestral objects for indigenous groups, and museums must understand how the death rituals and traditions of remembrance of specific cultural groups bear upon display and access to these artefacts (Allen and Hamby Chapter 9). If 'culture' acts upon museum practice, this chapter recalls that museum and household collecting practices are similarly based on cultural traditions, including those responding to the events of death.

Certain exhibitions, such as the Peoples' Shows, have put the types of household collections discussed here on public display, and in Lovatt's (1997) account the delight that accompanies this is discernable in the labelling of a collection belonging to a deceased daughter, 'Angie's collection meant everything to her. . . . She would love to know it is now being exhibited!' (Walsall Museum and Art Gallery: label)' (1997: 200). Domestic collectors in London, however, more commonly engage in a process of negotiation with the interests of their own relatives to secure the remembrance and continued care of their collections. The agency of the museum was greatest in their imagination of the museum, playing a key role in the sacralisation of objects in collections in everyday life.

Conclusion

This chapter sought to unpack the relationship between death, memory and collecting by examining collecting practices in contemporary London households, connected with episodes of loss and bereavement. The intention was to illustrate how collecting acts as a spatial and temporal organising practice stretching across domestic and museum settings and how the agency of the idea of the museum and collecting as an identity practice is located in everyday lives. This contrasts with perspectives on collecting behaviour as an exercise of individual control over the world and of death or as a practice that makes up for a broader sense of loss in modernity. As a cultural tradition however, the notion of the collection as a durable legacy and structuring habit established the significance of the collection to the anticipation of death and as a response to bereavement.

First, I considered how collecting created monumental mementos passed on after death, sometimes with difficulty, often to those who have formerly gifted some of its parts. Collections which were created and passed on give form and presence to the identity of the deceased. This may make inheritors ambivalent about their display, and parts may be hidden away or individual items recontextualised through other activities. Second, collecting offered a response to loss as commemorative practice. As Macdonald (2006) has commented, collecting in response to loss is not only part of museological and archival discourse but also a personal motivation infused by the same discourses of loss and the preservation of identities through their material traces (Macdonald 2006). Collecting as commemoration builds a memorial to the scale of this ritual activity performed by the bereaved. We saw how an individual might involve others in this performance. Third, intergenerational collecting was observed as most successful at securing future remembrance, ensuring the remembrance of individuals, couples and families, within and through collections. What was particularly striking was the investment put into replicating, reproducing, growing and embedding the memories of these collected objects in the bodies of kin recipients.

Ordinary and ephemeral consumer objects such as charms, Christmas decorations and McDonald's Happy Meal toys became the unlikely means for one generation to create the conditions for their own ancestralisation among the next. The material qualities of the objects at hand, from indestructible plastic to bright decorative glass, were used to create a material politics of memory among parents and children, incorporating in the case of the Christmas collection, more than three generations, drawing a distinction in the case of the Happy Meal toys. Both the affordance of the objects and the structure of the collections as wholes were productive in socially specific ways.

The museum was viewed as the final and transcendent place for the immortalisation of collections. The role of the museum was considered not only as a model or idea, giving lasting significance and sacralisation to ordinary objects, but also as a specific practice of self-immortalisation, whereby a person is more or less absorbed into the body of the museum through their collection.

What this chapter has sought to show is that collecting is a complex practice, taking place at multiple scales from the individual to the family to the nation, from the house to the museum and from the sensory body of commodities to the order of the whole collection, to the narrative memories inscribed in bodies. Most pertinent to the discussion of agency and identity, collections involve many ways of locating the self in the collective and the collective in the self that deal in different ways with the potential contradictions of securing future remembrance. Collecting is much more than an 'identity parade' (Winsor 1994); it is a complex, emotive and sensuous relational practice wherein objects are capable of condensing and holding many layers of contradictory meanings (Tilley 1999). Domestic collecting in this chapter has been shown to be a generative practice that not only stabilises identities but one that also incorporates potential for the reconstruction and renegotiation of collective and individual identifications, particularly when they act as a focus for community sociality and remembrance.

References

Auslander, Leora
  1996 *Taste and Power: Furnishing Modern France*. University of California Press, Berkeley, CA.

Baekeland, Frederick
  1981 Psychological Aspects of Art Collecting. *Psychiatry* 44: 45–59.

Bal, Mieke
  1994 Telling Objects: A Narrative Perspective on Collecting. In *The Cultures of Collecting*, edited by John Elsner and Roger Cardinal, pp. 97–115. Reaktion Books, London.

Bann, Stephen
  1994 *Under the Sign: John Bargrave as Collector, Traveller, and Witness.* University of
    Michigan Press, Ann Arbor, MI.

Baudrillard, Jean
  1994 The System of Collecting. In *The Cultures of Collecting*, edited by John Elsner and Roger
    Cardinal, pp. 7–24. Reaktion Books, London.

Belk, Russell W.
  1995 *Collecting in a Consumer Society.* Routledge, London.

Benjamin, Walter
  1969 *Illuminations.* Schoeken, New York, NY.

Bloch, Maurice
  1998 *How We Think They Think: Anthropological Approaches to Cognition, Memory and
    Literacy.* Westview Press, Oxford.

Forrester, John
  1994 'Mille e tre': Freud and Collecting. In *The Cultures of Collecting,* edited by John Elsner
    and Roger Cardinal, pp. 224–252. Reaktion Books, London.

Gosden, Chris, and Chantal Knowles
  2001 *Collecting Colonialism: Material Culture and Social Change.* Berg, Oxford.

Hallam, Elizabeth, and Jennifer L. Hockey
  2001 *Death, Memory and Material Culture.* Berg, Oxford.

Howes, David
  2003 *Sensual Relations: Engaging the Senses in Culture & Social Theory.* University of
    Michigan Press, Ann Arbor, MI.

Layne, Linda
  2000 He Was a Real Baby with Baby Things. *Journal of Material Culture* 5: 321–345.

Macdonald, Sharon
  2002 On 'Old Things': The Fetishization of Past Everyday Life. In *British Subjects: An
    Anthropology of Britain*, edited by Nigel Rapport, pp. 89–106. Berg, Oxford.
  2006 Collecting Practices. In *A Companion to Museum Studies*, edited by Sharon Macdonald,
    pp. 81–97. Blackwell, Malden, MA.

Marcoux, Jean-Sebastian
  2001 The 'Casser-Maison' Ritual: Creating the Self by Emptying the Home. *Journal of
    Material Culture* 7: 213–234.

Martin, Paul
  1998 *Popular Collecting and the Everyday Self: The Reinvention of Museums?* Leicester
    University Press, London.

Miller, Daniel
  1998. *A theory of Shopping.* Polity, Cambridge.

Miller, Daniel, and Fiona R. Parrott
  2007 Death, Ritual and Material Culture in South London. In *Death Rites and Rights*, edited by
    Belinda Brooks-Gordon, Fatemeh Ebtehaj, Jonathan Herring, Martin Johnson, and Martin
    Richards, pp. 147–62. Hart Publishing/Cambridge Socio-Legal Group, Oxford.
  2009 Loss and Material Culture in South London. *Journal of the Royal Anthropological
    Institute* 15: 502–519.

Parrott, Fiona R.
  2007 Mais où a-t-on donc rangé ces souvenirs? *Ethnologie française* XXXVII: 305–312.
  2010 Bringing Home the Dead: Photographs, Family Imaginaries and Moral Remains. In *An Anthropology of Absence: Materializations of Transcendence and Loss*, edited by Mikkel Bille, Tim F. Sorensen, and Frida Hastrup, pp. 131–138. Springer Press, New York, NY.

Pearce, Susan
  1995 *On Collecting: An Investigation into Collecting in the European Tradition*. Routledge, London.

Shelton, Anthony
  2001 Introduction: The Return of the Subject. In *Collectors: Expressions of Self and Other*, edited by Anthony Shelton, pp. 9–12. Horniman Museum/Museu and Antropologico da Universidade de Coimbra, London.

Stewart, Susan
  1994 Death and Life, in that Order, in the Works of Charles Willson Peale. In *The Cultures of Collecting*, edited by John Elsner and Roger Cardinal, pp. 204–223. Reaktion Books, London.

Thomas, Nicholas
  1991 *Entangled Objects: Exchange, Material Culture, and Colonialism in the Pacific*. Harvard University Press, Cambridge, MA.

Tilley, Christopher
  1999 *Metaphor and Material Culture*. Blackwell, Oxford.

Winsor, John
  1994 Identity Parades. In *The Cultures of Collecting,* edited by John Elsner and Roger Cardinal, pp. 49–67. Reaktion Books, London.

Chapter 14
Trials and Traces: A. C. Haddon's Agency as Museum Curator

Sarah Byrne

Abstract Alfred Cort Haddon (1855–1940) is most well known for organising The Cambridge Anthropological Expedition to the Torres Strait and New Guinea (1898–1899). What is less commonly known is that Haddon also spent 13 years acting as an advisory curator at the Horniman Museum in London (1902–1915). There, he exerted considerable influence on the running of the Museum, from its day-to-day management to its acquisition policies. This chapter explores Haddon's personality as museum curator, paying particular attention to the way in which his relationship with source communities, professional colleagues, auction houses, dealers and missionaries influenced which artefacts he acquired for the Museum and which he rejected. The study provides fresh insights into the professional life of a man who played a central role in the establishment of institutional anthropology in Britain.

Introduction

Ethnographic collections manifest a complex array of social relationships, negotiations and processes. While much attention has been paid to the motivation of field collectors, the role of museum curators in the formation of the collections has largely been overlooked. Since museum curators are the pivotal agents around which museum collections are built, the factors motivating their intentions, desires and opinions warrant further academic attention. This chapter explores Alfred Cort Haddon's role as advisory curator with the Horniman Museum, London, between 1902 and 1915 by examining the British New Guinea and Torres Strait objects he acquired. Drawing on some aspects of Bruno Latour's (1997, 2005) actor-network theory, I will explore the various relationships or *trials* Haddon had with source communities, professional colleagues, auction houses, dealers and missionaries, unpacking what evidence or *traces* these left behind in the collections he amassed. Haddon's prominent role within a newly emergent anthropological discourse and his extensive field experience meant that he was one of the earliest expert curators collecting within a museum setting.

S. Byrne (✉)
Centre for Museums, Heritage and Material Culture Studies, Institute of Archaeology, University College, London, London, UK
e-mail: s.byrne@ucl.ac.uk

S. Byrne et al. (eds.), *Unpacking the Collection*, One World Archaeology,
DOI 10.1007/978-1-4419-8222-3_14, © Springer Science+Business Media, LLC 2011

Collections and Agency

The position of ethnographic objects has largely waxed and waned throughout the history of anthropology. During the heyday of evolutionary anthropology in the late nineteenth century and early twentieth century in Britain, field, theoretical and museum anthropologists were largely operating under an unifying doctrine whereby 'facts and artefacts were thus considered to share a similar status' (Shelton 2000: 180). The move towards functionalism in the first decade of the twentieth century undermined the role of ethnographic collections. Indeed, Bronislaw Malinowski's disregard for ethnographic collections is well known. One of his contemporaries at the British Museum once remarked how 'the intractability of hard dead things, divorced from their true setting seemed at times to daunt and even repel him' (Braunholtz 1943: 15). Ethnographic collections largely remained unfashionable until a renewed interest in the 1980s when academics called for a 'process of *recontextualization* or redefinition,' which 'should be of interest to anthropology, for it not only informs us about ourselves but also recurring features of culture contact, culture domination and culture change' (Ames 1986: 34, Italics original). It has really only been with increasing involvement of source communities in the last decade or so that a more intimate understanding of the historical and contemporary meaning of ethnographic collections has begun to be achieved. This process is challenging museums to devise new ways that shared histories and agency can be researched and presented. Of particular importance is the 'recognition of the very personal connections that can be made between families, communities, images and artefacts' (Peers and Brown 2003: 7). Focusing on these more personal elements is important, not only because it forefronts local agency but also because it encourages a deeper consideration of the face-to-face interactions between different people and between people and things. By following the experiences of the different actors involved, this essentially 'bottom-up' approach is helping unpack the different relationships inherent within collections.

Approaching agency in this way allies itself with Latour's actor-network theory and particularly his suggestion that you need 'to follow the actors themselves' (Latour 2005: 12) so as to understand the *social*. His suggestion that 'if you mention an agency, you have to provide an account of its action, and to do so you need to make more or less explicit which trials have produced which observable traces (Latour 2005: 53)' is directly relevant for collections research. Conceptualising ethnographic objects as 'traces' through which agency can be revealed is useful and identifies them as conduits for revealing social interaction. A 'trace', in this context is best conceived as any evidence found within the collection that reflects human agency. These 'traces' are naturally present at different levels; they are evident within the object itself, reflecting the decisions involved in its making and any subsequent modifications thereafter. Equally the 'trace' can be the actual object, its very presence at a specific place and time reflects the agency of those involved in moving the collections from source to museum

Fig. 14.1 Alfred Cort Haddon, resident curator at the Horniman Museum from 1902 to 1915 (Courtesy of The Horniman Public Museum & Public Park Trust)

site. Latour's actor-network theory sees all actors as a 'full blown mediators' (Latour 2005: 128), facilitating a view that all 'trials' or relationships and experiences involved in creating and assembling museum collections are worthy of investigation.

This chapter examines one type of actor in the formation of museum collections: the curator. Alfred Cort Haddon was advisory curator with the Horniman Museum, London, between 1902 and 1915 (Figs. 14.1 and 14.2a, b), during which he accumulated artefacts from all over the world from auction houses and dealers. There is a clear bias in his acquisition policy in favour of objects from British New Guinea and Torres Strait, undoubtedly linked to his specialised knowledge of these regions' material culture. Haddon's many professional contacts within Pacific anthropology and the networks in which he circulated also influenced the type and quality of objects purchased by him and presented to the Museum. The importance of museum curators in assembling collections is often downplayed in favour of field collectors. Yet it is museum curators who are pivotal agents, arguably because they are involved in interacting with the largest number of external agents in shaping a group of objects into a coherent collection (see also Philp Chapter 12 and Wingfield Chapter 5).

By focusing on the agency of a museum curator, I am also deliberately drawing attention to the fact that the more personal and idiosyncratic aspects of agency are not just relevant when considering the relationship source communities have with collections but are also pertinent in relation to collectors. The agency of collectors and curators has too often been eclipsed by a focus on the governing ideologies or system in which they operated. This ultimately creates a forced

Fig. 14.2 (*left*) The Horniman Museum in 1901, the year it was donated to the London County Council (Courtesy of The Horniman Public Museum & Public Park Trust) and (*right*) the Museum today (Courtesy of Sarah Carpenter)

tension between the individual and their relationships with external agencies. I argue that Haddon's agency as curator was as much influenced by his personal relationships as by the evolutionary theory he embraced. In the same way Latour (2005: 22) points out how 'in each course of action a great variety of agents seem to barge in and displace the original goals' and that action by its very nature is 'borrowed, distributed, suggested, influenced, dominated, betrayed, translated' (Latour 2005: 46). The various decisions Haddon made whilst collecting objects for the Museum were not as systematic as they might first appear. It would be misleading here to think of Latour's 'network' as any kind of concept replacement for 'system'. Indeed, Latour has tried endlessly to detach the two, 'a network is a concept. It is a tool to help describe something, not what is being described' (Latour 2005: 131). It is this more methodological idea of a network that is applied here. It is a conceptual entry point into the idiosyncrasies of Haddon's acquisition policy, revealing what 'trials' produced the specific 'traces' still evident in the Horniman collection today. By situating Haddon's agency as museum curator in relation to his encounters with source communities, professional colleagues, auction houses, dealers and missionaries, I aim to provide a more intimate understanding of the collections he amassed and, in doing so, reassemble Haddon's agency as curator.

Encountering Communities

When Haddon assumed his role as Advisory Curator in 1902, following his 1888 and 1898 expeditions, his knowledge of British New Guinea and Torres Strait material culture was well established. To fully understand Haddon's agency as museum curator, it is essential to consider his fieldwork experiences and interactions with source communities. The maiden voyage of 1888 was the turning point of Haddon's career. Four months into the expedition, he sums up activities.

> I fancy a fair verdict would be (1) coral reef investigator – much less done than I should of liked, but I am making a start – (2) General marine zoology about as much as I could reasonably expect to do. (3) Anthropology much more than I anticipated (Haddon 1888–1889: 52).

Haddon's historic metamorphosis from marine biologist to anthropologist was not overnight. Quiggin (1942: 82) points out that 'he had always intended to make the most of his opportunities of seeing and learning what he could of his first "savages"' and 'he also had a secondary motive for getting in touch with them as he hoped to recoup himself for some of the expenses of the journey by collecting "curios" for museums'. After he made his first acquisitions of a drum and a mask on Murray Island 'belonging to one of the old boy's son who was away working in the mainland but whose father took it on himself to trade for his absent son' (Haddon 1888–1889: 6), artefact collecting became daily practice. Within a few weeks, it became 'usual to make enquiries for ethnological specimens' (Haddon 1888–1889: 8). Collecting was no passing fancy. His diary entries became dominated by detailed accounts and sketches of the function, technology and design of the various artefacts he encountered and collected. During this 1888 expedition he collected around 250 artefacts, including tobacco pipes, masks, personal ornaments, clubs, bows and arrows, masks, dance paraphernalia and clothing (see Moore 1982: 38). The majority of these objects were offered to the British Museum with a few duplicates being sold or donated to some smaller institutions, including the Horniman Museum. These objects became central to Haddon's anthropological writings (e.g., Haddon 1894, 1946; Haddon and Hornell 1936–1938) and were used to expound his theories on art, anthropology and the role of museums. Haddon's field experiences and interactions with source communities not only instilled in him an understanding of the use and meaning of various objects within their local context but helped form his ideas on museums and material culture. 'It is the non-understanding of objects that makes visits to museums frequently dull or uninteresting. As a matter of fact, objects are really interesting in themselves' (Haddon 1904: 4).

The 1888 expedition ignited in Haddon a passion for preserving knowledge of traditional culture that became the driving force behind his career as an anthropologist and influenced his choice of objects for the Horniman Museum. He once remarked how 'posterity will have plenty time in which to generalise and theorize but it will have scarcely any opportunity for recording new facts. The apathy of our predecessors has lost to us an immense amount of information' (Haddon 1894: 270). In protest to such apathy, Haddon's career was characterised by an overwhelming and voracious energy and urgency. His fears that the knowledge of customs would be lost convinced him that urgent fieldwork and collecting was the only way to save such vanishing data. He invested a huge amount of energy into collecting and documenting artefacts through writing and photography. He attempted to reawaken traditional customs, for instance, by commissioning specific items (Herle 1998: 96–96). He was especially preoccupied with traditional costume, once declaring how 'our first business was to get the women to appear in their native dress – after much time they did so and retired to their houses with much laughing and giggling' (Haddon 1888–1889: 15). On another occasion, however, when he 'could not get the women to wear grass petticoats,' he was not dissuaded once he 'proved that they were used' (Haddon 1888–1889: 20). This highlights an important point: Haddon's priority rested with preserving knowledge rather than the culture practice itself. Once the knowledge was not lost, then there was less pressing need to preserve the practice.

Haddon's (1897: 305–306) urgency for more fieldwork to save the 'vanishing knowledge' of the region resulted in the organisation of the 1898 Cambridge Anthropological Expedition to Torres Strait (see Herle and Rouse 1998). Haddon organised and planned the expedition in line with his concept of anthropology as an all-encompassing discipline by incorporating expertise from a wide range of scientific pursuits such as zoology, psychology, physiology and biology. He therefore sought 'the co-operation of a staff of colleagues, each of whom have some special qualification' (Haddon 1901: viii). As Herle and Rouse (1998: 1) acknowledge, this approach was not without its problems: 'on the eve of the 1898 Expedition to the Torres Strait, British anthropology was in search of self-definition. Situated precariously between the arts and the natural sciences, it was struggling for legitimacy in the academy while lacking both recognisable boundaries and unifying paradigm'. One area that benefited from this decisively broad stance was Haddon's collecting strategies. As Strathern (1999: 7) points out, 'one of the rubrics which Haddon and his colleagues worked in the Torres Strait was to gather as much material as possible', resulting in the diverse and well-documented ethnographic collections we have today.

During the 1898 expedition, Haddon amassed a broader range of material than on his previous expedition. This included both everyday items such as grass skirts, food bowls, shell hoes and fire sticks as well as ritualistic objects such as masks, ancestor posts and bullroarers. Unlike the previous expedition, Haddon was now collecting artefacts with established anthropological agendas. The amateur's passion so vivid in his 1888 journals was overtaken by a more academically informed method of collecting. The 10 years since the first expedition had seen Haddon's full conversion to anthropology. A simple child's toy was now interpreted as a possible 'link in a chain of evidence of race migration' (Haddon 1898: 92). Objects were also collected with his professional reputation in mind. For instance, he delighted in the acquisition of a musical instrument at Kerepenu (10th June 1898) because 'H. Balfour of the Pitt Rivers Museum at Oxford has written a paper recently on precisely the same "horn"' (Haddon 1898: 118). He also became more wary of taking objects at face value and not 'to assume an object is native to the district because it is found there but always make enquiries' (Haddon 1898: 118). The 1,300 objects (some 40 boxes) collected during the 1898 expedition were very well documented and the majority even had their local names attached. All artefacts (bar a few duplicates) were presented to the Cambridge University Museum in recognition of their financial support of the expedition (see Herle 1998: 79). Today the Museum boasts 3,670 objects in the Haddon Collection, including some 1245 artefacts from the Torres Strait, and 1227 from New Guinea.

The relationship between Haddon's field experiences and his identity as museum curator is important to unpack because it is these field experiences that ultimately underpinned his ideas about the function and nature of anthropology. As museum curator, he was not acquiring objects directly from community members, but rather through the filter of auction houses and dealers. Yet his field experiences and cross-cultural relationships were to prove central to his decision making. In this way, his decisions 'overflow' with elements that are already in the situation coming from some other time and some other 'place' and generated by some other 'agency' (Latour 2005: 166). His memories of field collecting and encounters and exchanges in British New Guinea and the Torres Strait impacted on his decisions and desires as museum curator. As Benjamin (1969 [1931]: 60) aptly points out, 'every passion borders on the chaotic, but the collector's passion borders on the chaos of memories' The specific 'traces' or impact these 'trials' had on formation of collections at the Museum will be more fully expounded below.

From the Field to the Museum: Interacting with Colleagues

On the 19th January, 1901 Frederick John Horniman donated his museum to the London County Council. The majority of objects had been accumulated during Horniman's travels as a tea merchant to Egypt, India, Ceylon, Japan, Canada and the USA. Others had been 'acquired in England' through auction houses because they 'either appealed to his fancy or which seemed likely to interest and inform those whom circumstances prevented from visiting distant lands' (Gomme 1902: 6). Collecting objects with such haphazard fancy was something Haddon vehemently disagreed with. Indeed, following his very first visit to the Horniman Museum in July 1901, he remarked how 'the day has passed when we can consider a collection of "curios" as a museum. If properly arranged, a museum is an educational institution of the greatest value, as information is conveyed visually with accuracy and great rapidity' (Gomme 1901: 1–2).

On December 7, 1901, G. L. Gomme, the clerk of the London City Council, recommended to the Museum's subcommittee that 'the best course to adopt with regard to the staff and the rearrangement and relabelling of the exhibits, would be to endeavour to obtain the services of a consulting curator, of some eminent authority upon museum work, such as Dr. Haddon at a nominal salary of say 50 guineas a year, to retain the present curator, Mr. R. Quick as resident curator and also to pertain the services of Mr. R. Slade, the naturalist' (Gomme 1901: 134). Haddon was the perfect choice not only because he was a renowned anthropologist, but given his zoological background, he could also advise on the natural history collections. When 'Dr. Haddon expressed his willingness to accept the post of advisory curator of the Museum', he put forward a proposal to rearrange the whole museum under the three chief categories of anthropology, art and history 'with the object of supplying the only place in London where education from the objective be obtained' (Gomme 1902: 151–152). The long-lasting impact of the 'Haddon Years' had begun.

Haddon took the lead in the 'scientific' rearrangement of the Museum with great fervour. Each year a different section of the ethnological collections was organised in line with an evolutionary schema. For instance, the 1904 Annual Report acknowledges how 'progress has been made in the arrangement of certain parts of the collection, chiefly in connection with art of existing primitive races' (Gomme 1905: 6) with a special case being erected on the 'Evolution of Art'. The meaning of these rearrangements in the context of the evolutionary and educational ideas of the day has already been subject to attention (see Levell 2001). Although ideas of social evolution undoubtedly governed many of Haddon's decisions as curator, overemphasis on these results in the neglect of the more intimate aspects of Haddon's influence. Shelton (2001: 12) recognises this preoccupation with systems of collecting as 'the museum's attempt to banish the personality of the passionate collector'. Haddon was not a slave to the evolutionary system and was aware of the multiple ways in which artefacts could be successfully displayed, as is clear from the following statement:

> The main object of collections of this nature is to illustrate the past and present culture of man, in other words to show that the things he makes or has made for utilitarian and non-utilitarian purposes. The objects themselves may be regarded from points of view of space and time. Specimens may be collected from all parts of the world and these may be arranged according to countries and peoples, as is the case with the collections in the Ethnographic Department of the British Museum, or they may be classified according to subject in order to illustrate the geographical distribution and local varieties of that class of object; or they may be arranged to demonstrate their evolution, as is well done in the Pitt Rivers Museum at Oxford (Haddon 1904: 10).

Haddon also assumed control over the acquisition budgets. At each subcommittee meeting objects were 'offered for presentation' and 'for sale' and the 'specimens purchased at auctions' were reported to the council. An analysis of hundreds of these meetings shows that without exception the council agreed with Haddon's recommendations. Being in financial control of acquisitions did not come easy to Haddon; he was well known for his philosophical attitude towards money (see Quiggin 1942: 113). When first appointed, he was given 'an expenditure of a sum of money not exceeding £10, between any two ordinary meetings of the committee, on the purchase of any articles which he may consider necessary for adding to the collection at the Museum, or if any illustrations and maps etc. which may be needed' (Gomme 1902 (14th Feb): 2). By the end of 1902, it was already obvious that Haddon was overenthusiastic with the committee's finances. By December of that same year the council called for the 'attention of Dr. Haddon. . .to the fact that he has again exceeded the amount of £10 which he was to spend on emergency' (Gomme 1902 (5th Dec): 128). This overspending did not cease, and eventually a motion was passed in the council on 22 January 1904 stating that 'the advisory curator be asked to indicate briefly in all further cases his reasons for suggesting the purchase of objects', a task he had to follow throughout his tenure at the Museum.

Haddon's influence and control over museum policies also extended into issues of staffing. A strained relationship developed between Haddon and resident curator Richard Quick, whom Haddon viewed as an 'old school' curator because he was primarily interested in the aesthetics of art and artefacts, whereas Haddon was 'scientifically' informed. On 18 December 1903, Gomme reported to the subcommittee that Haddon 'has been continually hampered by the incapability of Mr Quick to grasp the underlying plan of such arrangement' (Gomme 1903: 1). It was decided 'that the only possible course for the Committee to take is to make a change in the post of resident curator' (Gomme 1903: 1). In September 1904, Haddon recommended Herbert Spenser Harrison as the new resident curator, a post he was to occupy for no less than 37 years. Haddon and Harrison were associates, having first met at the University College of Cardiff where Harrison lectured in biology. Harrison had also converted from zoology to anthropology, shared an evolutionary outlook, and therefore ascribed to Haddon's vision and transformation of the Museum. Whilst Haddon's passion for acquiring artefacts may have burned holes in the council's pockets, the same passion dramatically transformed the Museum and improved the quality of collections housed there forever.

Equally important was Haddon's relationships with colleagues outside of the Museum. Between 1906 and 1915, there was a significant increase in donations of British New Guinea and Torres Strait material to the Museum. Haddon's reputation was so well established that he was frequently offered objects as loans/donations. For example, Ethel Simmons wrote to him on February 19, 1906, stating how 'having heard of your interest in ethnography, particularly in connection with the Pacific, I am writing to know if you would care to have the loan of some curios I have. These are 2 Dancing masks, fish rods, war drum, spears and bows all from the Elema Country in the Gulf of Papua'. Indeed, 30% of all acquisitions from British New Guinea and the Torres Strait during Haddon's tenure were presented to him, largely from his professional colleagues. James Edge-Partington gave a number of items from New Ireland and the Trobriand Islands to the Museum. Dr. Gunnar Landtman donated a group of material that included a panpipe, flute, stringed instrument and two wooden initiation figures from Kiwai in Papua New Guinea. In 1906, following the Cooke-Daniels expedition, C.G. Seligman presented a lot of 54 objects from different areas throughout the Papuan Gulf to Haddon for inclusion in the Horniman displays.

Focusing on the nature of Haddon's relationships and interactions with his colleagues provides an appreciation of the parameters in which he was working and the relationships that enabled or restricted acquisitions. Whilst slightly restricted by finances, Haddon had significant authority over what objects were acquired and what objects were rejected by the Museum. Haddon's relationships with professional colleagues left as many 'traces' in the shaping of the collections at the Horniman as any other interactions during the process of objects moving from the field to the Museum.

Acquiring at the Auction Houses

Frederick Horniman's original collection of 217 New Guinean objects that Haddon inherited were *all* purchased from auction houses, the majority originating from Stevens Auction Rooms (Covent Garden, London). Between 1902 and 1915, Haddon acquired 504 objects from British New Guinea and the Torres Strait. My analysis found that only 116 objects were acquired from auction houses, representing a 75% drop in reliance on these sources since Horniman's time. This can be explained by the lack of detailed information normally associated with objects from auction houses and dealers.

Haddon was very ethical and precise about the provenance of the artefacts he collected during fieldwork. His concept of local 'intensive study' and analysis of local styles and art forms convinced him that accurate provenances were essential (Haddon 1894, 1895). He once remarked how 'I value the information I have gathered concerning the things as being of more value. There is no merit in mere collecting' (Haddon 1888–1889: 24). The three lots of his own material that he sold and donated to the Horniman Museum in 1906, 1912 and 1915 were extremely well documented. The first lot that he donated in 1906 (6.300–6.317) were mostly duplicates from the 1898 expedition. Given the fact that he had to hand over the majority of this collection to the Cambridge museum where he had no control over its fate at this time, these duplicate items must have been precious to him. In 1912, when he sold 50 artefacts to the Museum, the majority of which were from Murray Island, he made a comprehensive list of each artefact and handwrote labels detailing object function and local names. The final lot of artefacts that Haddon donated to the Museum in 1915 (15.129–130, 15.174–15.182) derived from the Percy Sladen Expedition of 1914, his final expedition to New Guinea and the Torres Strait.

Whilst it was easier to control documentation of his own collections, maintaining such high standards in his role as museum curator must have come as a challenge. Museums depended so much on secondary (other collectors) and tertiary sources (auction houses/dealers) for their acquisitions that accurate provenances were not always easily deduced. Out of the total 116 objects purchased by Haddon at auction houses, 97 of these were purchased between 1904 and 1905. This period of bulk buying was very deliberate since it was the period when the Museum was undergoing 'very considerable re-arrangements' (Gomme 1905: 6), being transformed from a cabinet of curiosities to a museum that would 'illustrate the evolution of culture' and 'help to supply one of the educational needs of London' (Gomme 1904: 10). In 1904, Haddon purchased 64 objects from the W. D. Webster collection at Stevens' Auction Rooms. In 1905, he also acquired lots from William Oldman, (5.2–5.11) 'whose collection of Oceanic and especially Polynesian art was rivalled only by size and quality by the British Museum' (Anon 1949: 1) and from F. Smith, a dealer in ethnographic objects in London.

An analysis of artefacts purchased by Haddon in 1904 and 1905 reveals some interesting patterns (see Fig. 14.3). The significant amount of weaponry purchased was evidently acquired for the new 'Stone Implements' section and the section on 'War and Chase' set up in 1905, where weapons were displayed 'as far as possible,

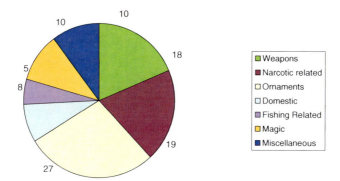

Fig. 14.3 Number of British New Guinea and Torres Strait objects acquired by Haddon from auction houses and dealers, 1904–1905 (data obtained with kind permission of The Horniman Public Museum & Public Park Trust)

in the order in which it is probable that they were first invented or employed' (Gomme 1906: 7). The narcotic items were purchased to be displayed in the 'Evolution of Art' case set up by Haddon in 1904, which included a large number of bamboo smoking pipes from British New Guinea. There were 20 bamboo smoking pipes from 'New Guinea' in Horniman's original collection, and Haddon continued to add to this. It is interesting to note that 4 out of the 5 Kiwai pipes he purchased in 1904 from the Webster collection (4.169–4.173; Fig. 14.4) were described as being 'unused, with no bowl' but as having 'burnt decoration'. Although Haddon usually preferred used items, these particular artefacts were purchased specifically to illustrate their geometric design rather than their function. Haddon, like Henry Balfour (Pitt Rivers Museum, Oxford; see Wingfield Chapter 5), rejected aesthetics as a

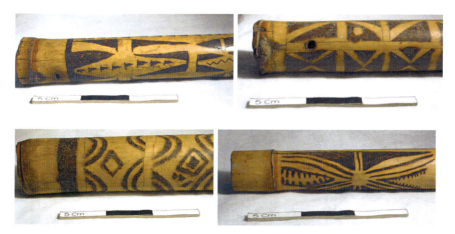

Fig. 14.4 Selection of Kiwai tobacco pipes purchased by Haddon in 1904 from the Webster collection at Steven's Auction Rooms, showing a variety of geometric designs (Courtesy of The Horniman Public Museum & Public Park Trust)

reason for acquiring objects. Instead his 'purpose' was to study art from a biological point of view, by comparing the 'lifelines' of different designs and 'the linear development of ornament from naturalistic to geometric and abstract' (Coombes 1994: 49; see Levell 2001). Another lot of artefacts bought for their design qualities were bark belts from British New Guinea (4.148–4.152), about which Haddon (1895: 32) notes that 'there is a wonderful diversity of pattern in these belts, yet, at the same time, there is a fundamental similarity in the style of the designs which clearly indicates a community of origin.' The pipes and bark belts served to highlight geometric patterns or what Haddon interpreted as the 'middle phase' in the evolution of design.

While 'discriminate acquisition by purchase or gift' (Gomme 1914: 6) continued throughout Haddon's time at the Museum, it is the early period of 1904–1905 that such discriminative acquisition is most obvious. Haddon usurped the auction house as an easy way to acquire objects to 'fill the gaps' in his transformation of the Museum (see Fig. 14.5). It is important to stress that Haddon was visiting the auction house as an expert; he had held, bought, analysed and wrote about the vast majority of British New Guinea and Torres Strait material under the hammer. Just as Stocking (1983: 75) pointed out how Haddon, 'as an academic man with field experience in ethnography was a rarity in British anthropology', it can be equally acknowledged that a man of Haddon's standing was even more of rarity in the London auction houses of the day. Although his acquisition policies were largely being governed by the system he was enforcing, his personal idiosyncrasies and ideas about material culture and memories of time spent in the Torres Strait and British New Guinea

Fig. 14.5 View of the Horniman Galleries during Haddon's tenure (Courtesy of The Horniman Public Museum & Public Park Trust)

influenced his choice of objects. Buying from auction houses is likely to have compromised many of Haddon's collecting ideals and concerns over the authenticity of objects. But as his 'leading motive [was] to convert a somewhat heterogeneous collection into one which will be of service to students of all ages' (Haddon, Harrison and Gomme 1912: 11), it meant that he had to acquire artefacts quickly from these less 'reputable' sources. Juxtaposing Haddon's ideals as collector and his practical duties as museum curator allows us to uncover some of the inherent tensions he may have experienced in these different roles. It also reveals that Haddon's relationships with the objects themselves were flexible and depended on the social circumstances in which he found himself. Latour's actor-network theory also recognises this inherent fluidity in the relationship between people and things. He writes that 'continuity of any course of action will rarely consist of human-human connections' or of 'object-object connections, but will probably zigzag form one to the other' (Latour 2005: 75). This is particularly true in relation to a curator, who needs to strike a delicate balance between his/her various curatorial needs whilst all the time making sure to uphold the relationships that facilitated them.

Relationship with Missionaries

Haddon displayed a mixed attitude towards missionaries. On the one hand, he was critical of their impact on local custom and culture. For example, in 1888 on a visit to Saibai island, Haddon (1888–1889: 84) lamented how 'civilisation has taken away their manly enterprises- *viz.* fighting- the missionaries have abolished their dances and their feasts.' Yet, during both expeditions Haddon relied heavily on missionaries as 'provisioners, brokers, translators and important sources of local knowledge' (Herle and Rouse 1998: 13). In particular he formed close relationships with Rev. James Chalmers (*Tamate*) in New Guinea and Rev. S. McFarlane in the Torres Strait. It is alleged that he was even converted to anthropology by a missionary, one Rev. W. W. Gill. The *General Ethnography* section of his expedition reports demonstrates his dependency on missionaries. It is largely a compendium of local knowledge, folklore and information derived from his contact with missionaries, who like him conversed with the locals in broken pidgin.

Haddon's twofold attitude to missionaries influenced his acquisition policy at the Horniman Museum. In June 1902, Rev. Wilfred H. Abbott wrote to Haddon introducing himself as 'the first white settler in the Collingwood Bay District, North East Coast,' where 'my people are still cannibals and are still in the Stone Age using flint and bone implements' (Abbott 1902a: 1). Abbott sent some specimens for Haddon's review, which he then recommended the council to purchase. Analysis of this group of material and its associated documentation reveals some important insights into Haddon's personality as museum curator and relationship with missionaries. The group of objects included a collection of 'primitive' tools in the form of four greenstone adzes (3.63–3.66), three kangaroo jaws used as chisels (3.58), a wooden gardening hoe (3.59), a wooden rasp wrapped in fish skin (3.57), a stone axe

(3.51), a piece of worked obsidian that was used for shaving and cutting hair and two obsidian flakes (3.69 & 3.55). There was a small collection of fishing equipment, which included two netting needles (3.68 & 3.61) and a few pieces of turtle shell also used in netting (3.67), as well as a number of domestic items such as a sago spoon and pounder (3.52 & 3.53). Other items included shell money (3.54), a women's mourning necklace (3.56), two boar's tusks (3.60) and four shells (3.62).

The acquisition of the Abbott collection took over six months to finalise because of Haddon's suspicions of certain artefacts.

(a) Is this really shell money? I meant cowries worn on the forearm, this specimen has been newly mounted, have you got an original mounting?
(b) The handle, at all events, if it is a sago beater looks quite new, has it ever been used?
(c) Have any of the white cowries ever been used? Or are they merely examples?

The large axe-blade which is separate looks as if it had been recently rubbed at its edge – the string looks very suspicious. The shell necklaces being un-mounted are useless museum specimens (Haddon 1902:1).

Throughout Haddon's expeditions he became very familiar with local materials and frequently lamented the introduction of European ones. Once during a visit to Warrior Island in 1888, he wrote how he regarded the '"decently clothed" – the women with long calico gowns' as 'a most disappointing sight' (Haddon 1888–1889: 13). During dugong fishing on Thursday Island local fishermen informed him that 'homemade rope is preferred to commercial rope as it is light and floats on the surface of the water whereas hempen or manila rope sinks' (Haddon 1888–1889: 53). Therefore, it is not surprising that Haddon is suspicious of the newly mounted shell money. Despite Abbott's repeated assurance that 'the shells, the necklace I sent you was not remade up for me. I don't know the string used, further it has undoubtedly been worn' (Abbott 1902b: 1), and his observation that the locals 'are continually making and remaking their ornament' and that 'they like the new fibre as much as I do' (1902b: 1), Haddon remained unconvinced and requested specimens be 'made up with old string.'

It is not clear when the distaste for collecting hybrid objects was first articulated in anthropology, but Haddon may well be one of the earliest collectors to be so vocal about it. Other collectors such as Rev. George Brown, a Methodist minister based in New Britain from 1860 to 1917, were also conscious of attaining 'untainted' specimens (see Gardner 2001: 48). Rejection of hybrid artefacts became an important collecting criterion in the Pacific for many decades to come. Some thirty years later Beatrice Blackwood (1935: 1) was to reject a model boat offered to her on Buka Island because 'it had European paint on it.'

Haddon was also suspicious that certain objects from the Abbott collection had been specifically manufactured for sale, but he was duly rebuked by him.

The large axe blade has not been recently rubbed at the edges as far as I know. I am rather amused at this. My natives only saw a white man for about three months in a year. I have never known them to sell a stone axe to anyone except me. I don't think it would be worth their while to fake up a stone axe, they get the stone from the Hill Tribes, they don't make them themselves. However I will send another axe blade instead, that I see has been broken with use. I mean the edge (Abbot 1902b: 2).

Given that Haddon prided himself in his reputation as a scientific collector, it is not surprising that the possibility of acquiring forgeries worried him; indeed, he was not alone. Between 1880 and 1900 the Australian Museum specifically set aside a special category for 'fakes' from Oceania (Philp 2003). An equally concerned colleague, James Edge-Partington (1901: 69) noted that 'at a recent sale the most obvious forgeries from New Guinea were offered and eagerly bought'.

> I use the term 'forgery' for want of a better; the specimens are of genuine native manufacture, and display in details of art and manufacture, the characteristics of the locality whence they come. At the same time they are of no practical use in themselves; their existence, which they owe ultimately to the development of civilised trades, is in fact illogical, except as a means to obtain for their makers certain coveted articles of European manufacture. In a word they are not what they pretend to be' (Edge-Partington 1905: 72).

That Haddon's concept of 'forgeries' was very much in line with Edge-Partington probably relates directly to his own prior experiences of locals trying to sell him 'fake' artefacts. One such incident happened on Kiwai Island on the 4 June, 1898.

> The Motu people especially the women are such keen traders that they condescend to forge 'curios'. Some of the coral they brought had never been used – as there were no signs of friction on the surface – this I pointed out to them, later and then the next morning the same pieces of coral were again to appear for sale but in the meantime they had rubbed on something or other, but it was easy to detect this and they only smiled when I told them what they had done. They will often pick up casual stones and try and pass them off as objects in use and as something 'very good' (Haddon 1898: 156).

What is important here is that Haddon's concept of 'authentic' objects, his rejection of hybrid artefacts and his awareness of the deliberate manufacture of objects for sale, all influenced not only his field collecting but also the type and 'quality' of artefact he acquired for the Horniman Museum. It was in Haddon's relationship with missionaries, in particular, that such concerns were played out. The agency of the missionaries, mediated by Haddon, also left specific traces behind that impacted on the formation of the collections.

Another characteristic of Haddon's collecting policies, which is linked both to his relationship with missionaries and source communities, was his desire to obtain what he deemed as the most 'primitive' artefacts. Haddon's definition of a 'primitive' object centred either on the technology involved in producing the artefact or the material used in its manufacture. These objects were useful to him, given that they could be slotted into the earlier phases of the Museum's evolutionary displays. Haddon was also committed to collecting these kinds of objects before they fell out of use. The correlation of 'primitive' material with 'primitive' artefact also influenced how the displays were arranged. For example, in describing 'spoons from all countries,' Haddon (1904: 21) insinuates that the most primitive ones were from Oceania because they were made from coconut and scallop shells. He accumulated a large number of these 'primitive' vessels: some 30 odd spoons; gourds; vessels and food bowls made from coconut and a number made from shell. He also acquired a large number of stone artefacts such as stone clubs, daggers, boring drills, axes, adzes, etc., as well as some wooden implements including bark beaters, arrows, flat clubs, pounders, etc. Objects made from even less 'civilised' materials were also accumulated: for example, kangaroo jaw chisels (3.58); bat bone needles (3.61); rasps with shark skin (5.10, 8.307, 8.308, 9.173); shell and coral-bladed hoes; axes; adzes; clubs; knives and spoons (6.138, 6.405, 6.417, 12.130–12.133, 12.172). The commitment Haddon had towards retrieving and salvaging such artefacts is nicely demonstrated by an incident that occurred on Kiwai Island (September 15, 1898).

> Then by dumb show and broken English I asked for a shell-hoe. I feared these were out of use but was overjoyed when one was brought to me for which I gave a fish hook. In a very short time I had half a dozen on the same terms. Hardly anything else during the whole trip pleased me more than to secure some specimens of this very rare and primitive agricultural implement especially as I had give up hope of obtaining it (Haddon 1898: 225).

The fact that such an incident pleased him more than 'hardly anything else during the whole trip' indicates how his passion for collecting endangered artefacts took precedence over everything else. This urgent 'salvage' paradigm was a central concern within nineteenth century anthropology more broadly. As Gruber (1970: 1294) points out, 'the vanishing savage was a constant theme. And out of an amalgam of moral and scientific concerns, an emergent anthropology- whether its focus was on the group or on the species – found a method and a role.'

Conclusion

By considering a number of *trials* that influenced Alfred Cort Haddon's tenure as museum curator with the Horniman Museum and the *traces* these experiences and relationships left behind, I have traced his agency from the field to the museum. Haddon's experiences in the field were particularly formative and greatly influenced his views on material culture and authenticity, which subsequently propelled his desire to collect objects of high quality for the displays at the Horniman Museum. His field experiences also instilled in him certain ferocity of commitment towards the preservation of traditional culture, which meant his relationships with colleagues who did not share his vision were oftentimes strained. Yet Haddon was highly respected, and many colleagues regularly donated objects to him for exhibits at the Museum. His relationship with auction houses was essentially uneasy, but he seemed to take a pragmatic stance, recognising the importance of these places as important sources of objects needed for the creation of his vision. Haddon largely lamented the impact of missionaries, building close relationships with some whilst being distrustful of others. The many influences that impacted on Haddon's day-to-day decision making whilst at the Museum epitomises Latour's (2005: 46) notion of agent as not necessarily the source of action 'but the moving target of a vast array of entities swarming toward it'. Yet it is these subtle and somewhat fleeting interactions that have lasted, permanently materialised in the collections we see today.

Susan Pearce's (1995: 1) point that 'objects embody human purposes and experiences, and they invite us to act towards them' invites us to find methodologies in which such purpose can be unpacked. Following Haddon's agency in relation to the Torres Strait and British New Guinea collections at the Horniman Museum is but one actor-network; an understanding of this collection can be built upon further by following other trajectories and other actors to see where they might lead us.

Acknowledgements I thank the Horniman Museum and in particular Dr. Fiona Kerlouge for providing me with access to the collections and giving me permission me to use both historic and object photographs in this chapter. I would also like to thank Dr. Bill Sillar and Dr. Nick Merriman who read an earlier version of this chapter and provided useful comments and feedback. I would also like to thank Annie Clarke, Robin Torrence and Rodney Harrison and other WAC participants for their helpful comments on this draft.

References

Abbott, Wilfred H.
  1902a Letter to A. C. Haddon explaining his specimens. Horniman Historical Archive (O- Oceania).
  1902b Letter to A. C. Haddon defending his specimens. Horniman Historical Archive (O- Oceania).

Ames, Michael
  1986 *Museums, The Public and Anthropology: A Study in the Anthropology of Anthropology.* University of British Columbia, Vancouver.

Anon.
  1949 Obituary of W. Oldman. Horniman Historical Archive (O- Oceania).

Benjamin, Walter
  1969 Unpacking My Library. In *Illuminations*, translated by Harry Zohn.Originally published 1931. Schocken Books, New York, NY.

Blackwood, Beatrice
  1935 *Both Sides of Buka Passage.* Clarendon Press, Oxford.

Braunholtz, H. J.
  1943 Address. In *Professor Bronislaw Malinowski: An Account of the Memorial Meeting held at the Royal Institution in London on July 13th 1942*. Oxford University Press, London.

Coombes, Annie E.
  1994 *Reinventing Africa: Museums, Material Culture and the Popular Imagination.* Yale University Press, London.

Edge-Partington, James
  1901 Note on Forged Ethnographical Specimens from the Pacific Islands. *Man* 1: 68–69.
  1905 Note on a Forged Ethnographical Specimen from the New Hebrides. *Man* 5: 71–72.

Gardner, Helen
  2001 Gathering for God: George Brown and the Christian Economy in the Collection of Artefacts. In *Hunting the Gatherers: Ethnographic Collectors, Agents and Agency in Melanesia, 1870s–1930s*, edited by Michael O'Hanlon and Robert L. Welsch, pp. 35–54. Berghahn Books, Oxford and New York.

Gomme, George L.
   1901 Report 7th December 1901. London County Council Historical Records and Buildings
      Committee (March–December 1901), London Metropolitan Archives (LCC records).
   1902 Report 17th January 1902. London County Council Historical Records and Buildings
      Committee (March–December 1901), London Metropolitan Archives (LCC records).
   1903 Report to the Horniman Museum Sub-Committee (18th December). *Committee Minutes*,
      London Metropolitan Archives (LCC records).
   1904 *Second Annual Report of the Horniman Museum and Library 1903*. London Metropolitan
      Archives, (LCC records).
   1905 *Third Annual Report of the Horniman Museum and Library 1904*. London Metropolitan
      Archives, (LCC records).
   1906 *Fourth Annual Report of the Horniman Museum and Library 1905*. London Metropolitan
      Archives, (LCC records).
   1914 *Eleventh Annual Report of the Horniman Museum and Library 1913*. London
      Metropolitan Archives, (LCC records).

Gruber, Jacob W.
   1970 Ethnographic Salvage and the Shaping of Anthropology. *American Anthropologist* 72(6):
      1289–1299.

Haddon, Alfred Cort
   1888–1889 *Journal of Haddon's First Expedition to the Torres Strait and New Guinea*.
      Cambridge University Library, Cambridge.
   1894 *The Decorative Art of British New Guinea: A Study in Papuan Ethnography*. Academy
      House, Dublin.
   1895 *Evolution in Art*. W. Scott, London.
   1897 The Saving of Vanishing Knowledge. *Nature* 55(1422): 305–306.
   1898 *Journal of Haddon's Cambridge Anthropological Expedition to Torres Strait*. Cambridge
      University Library, Cambridge.
   1901 *Head-Hunters, Black, White and Brown*. Methuen, London.
   1902 18th July Letter to W.H. Abbott highlighting his suspicions about his specimens.
      Horniman Historical Documents, (Oceania–A).
   1904 *Report on Some of the Educational Advantages and Deficiencies of London Museums*.
      Presented to the Museums Association. London Metropolitan Archives, London.
   1946 *Smoking and Tobacco Pipes in New Guinea*. Cambridge University Press, Cambridge.

Haddon, Alfred Cort, Herbert S. Harrison, and George L. Gomme (editors)
   1912 *Guide for the Use of Visitors to the Horniman Museum and Library* (2nd edition). London
      County Council, London.

Haddon, Alfred Cort, and James Hornell
   1936–1938 *Canoes of Oceania*. Bishops Museum Special Publications 27–29. Bernice P.
      Bishop Museum, Honolulu.

Herle, Anita
   1998 The Life-Histories of Objects: Collections of the Cambridge Anthropological Expedition
      to the Torres Strait. In *Cambridge and the Torres Strait, Centenary Essays on the
      1898 Anthropological Expedition*, edited by Anita Herle and Sandra Rouse, pp. 77–106.
      Cambridge University Press, Cambridge.

Herle, Anita, and Sandra Rouse (editors)
   1998 *Cambridge and the Torres Strait. Centenary Essays on the 1898 Anthropological
      Expedition*, pp. 1–23. Cambridge University Press, Cambridge.

Latour, Bruno
   1997 *On Actor-Network Theory: A Few Clarifications*. Centre for Social Theory and
      Technology, Keele University, Staffordshire.

2005 *Reassembling the Social: An Introduction to Actor-Network Theory*. Oxford University Press, Oxford.

Levell, Nicky
    2001 Illustrating Evolution: Alfred Cort Haddon and the Horniman Museum, 1901–1915. In *Collectors, Individuals and Institutions*, edited by Anthony Shelton, pp. 253–279. Horniman Press, London.

Moore, David R.
    1982 *The Torres Strait Collection of A. C. Haddon: A Descriptive Catalogue*. British Museum Publication, London.

Pearce, Susan M.
    1995 *On Collecting: An Investigation into Collecting in the European Tradition*. Routledge, London.

Peers, Laura, and Alison Brown
    2003 *Museums and Source Communities: A Routledge Reader*. Routledge, London.

Philp, Jude
    2003 Email in regards to forgeries, 15th August 2003.

Quiggin, Alison H.
    1942 *Haddon the Head Hunter – A Short Sketch of the Life of A. C Haddon*. Cambridge University Press, Cambridge.

Shelton, Anthony
    2000 Museum Ethnography. In *Cultural Encounters-Representing "Otherness"*, edited by Elizabeth Hallam and Brian Street, pp. 153–193. Routledge, London.

Shelton, Anthony (editor)
    2001 Introduction: The Return of the Subject. In *Collectors, Expression of Self and Other*, edited by Anthony Shelton, pp. 11–22. Horniman Press, London.

Stocking, George W.
    1983 The Ethnographer's Magic, Fieldwork in British Anthropology from Tylor to Malinowski. In *Observers Observed: Essays on Ethnographic Fieldwork*, edited by George W. Stocking, pp. 70–120. University of Wisconsin Press, Madison, WI.

Strathern, Marilyn
    1999 *Property Substance and Effect – Anthropological Essays on People and Things*. Athlone Press, London.

Simmons, Ethel
    1906 Letter to A.C. Haddon at the Horniman Museum, dated February 19. Horniman Historical Archive (O- Oceania).

Index

Printed by Books on Demand, Germany